Intimate States

Intimate States

GENDER, SEXUALITY, AND GOVERNANCE IN MODERN US HISTORY

Edited by
Margot Canaday, Nancy F. Cott,
and Robert O. Self

THE UNIVERSITY OF CHICAGO PRESS
CHICAGO AND LONDON

The University of Chicago Press, Chicago 60637
The University of Chicago Press, Ltd., London
© 2021 by The University of Chicago
All rights reserved. No part of this book may be used or reproduced in any
manner whatsoever without written permission, except in the case of brief
quotations in critical articles and reviews. For more information, contact
the University of Chicago Press, 1427 E. 60th St., Chicago, IL 60637.
Published 2021
Printed in the United States of America

30 29 28 27 26 25 24 23 22 21   1 2 3 4 5

ISBN-13: 978-0-226-79461-7 (cloth)
ISBN-13: 978-0-226-79475-4 (paper)
ISBN-13: 978-0-226-79489-1 (e-book)
DOI: https://doi.org/10.7208/chicago/9780226794891.001.0001

Library of Congress Cataloging-in-Publication Data

Names: Canaday, Margot, author. | Cott, Nancy F., author. | Self, Robert O.,
    1968– author.
Title: Intimate states : gender, sexuality, and governance in modern US history /
    edited by Margot Canaday, Nancy F. Cott, and Robert O. Self.
Description: Chicago : University of Chicago Press, 2021. | Includes bibliographical
    references and index.
Identifiers: LCCN 2020053633 | ISBN 9780226794617 (cloth) | ISBN 9780226794754
    (paperback) | ISBN 9780226794891 (ebook)
Subjects: LCSH: Marriage—Political aspects—United States. | Sex—Political
    aspects—United States. | Reproduction—Political aspects—United States. |
    Families—Political aspects—United States.
Classification: LCC HQ535 .I585 2021 | DDC 306.810973—dc23
LC record available at https://lccn.loc.gov/2020053633

♾ This paper meets the requirements of ANSI/NISO Z39.48-1992
(Permanence of Paper).

Contents

Introduction

MARGOT CANADAY, NANCY F. COTT,
AND ROBERT O. SELF

Intimacy and state power may appear to be far apart. The close ties and living arrangements of intimate life seem to inhabit a realm of their own, and the laws, treaties, and bureaucracies of the state another. This book works against the grain of such assumptions, beginning instead with the proposition that state practices inhere in life events that we think of as very personal. We aim to show that what we call *intimate governance* is central to the social and political history of the modern United States. The new essays in this volume bring questions about statecraft into explorations of the history of intimate life, urging readers to see with fresh eyes and sharper focus something they may have missed: that the realm of the intimate is ideal terrain for historians of the state.

Once we bring governance and intimacy together analytically, we can see this. We can see that household economic and sexual relations have been scripted by laws structuring what is public and private. It follows that state operations from the past into the present cannot be fully understood without looking into conduct as intimate as sex. Sexuality, marriage, and reproduction—our most private expressions of self—are bound up in a vast legal architecture meant to support what is seen as public order and the public good. Viewed from this perspective, both intimacy and state power acquire a fresh look. Our intimacies emerge as ordered and obligated as well as personal and willful. State power becomes intelligible as diffuse and social, as much as hierarchical and bureaucratic. Its effects, as they are absorbed into ordinary lives, become at times indistinguishable from society itself.

Precedents for this book's endeavor date from the late 1970s, when new scholarly attention to women put pressure on the presumed boundary between public and private, exploding the notion that intimate life was divorced from the market or from politics.[1] The insight that what transpired in households could not be cleanly separated from the institutions and workings of the economy, the public sphere, and political life opened new analytical vistas for historians of gender, race, and sexuality. The decades of scholarship that followed transformed US history.[2] Yet the subsequent historiography of American statecraft has seldom incorporated this scholarship, positioning it as part of the history of women and gender rather than the history of the state, even when the findings explicitly addressed policymaking (as, for instance, in feminist scholarship on the origins of the welfare state). Instead, historians of the state have credited their subfield's recent resurgence to borrowings from political science.[3]

This neglect of gender and sexuality by historians of the state—despite the way that those fields of social life are organically dense with state-society connections—may reflect in part a problem of scale. Historians thinking about statecraft have generally turned away from the scale of the intimate even as they have abandoned models of the state that stress its centralized power. "'The bigger, the better,'" Suleiman Osman writes drily of this tendency, noting that for many such historians, "larger scales appear[ed] . . . more real . . . as well as more powerful and just."[4] The opposite might be said of most recent historians of gender and sexuality, who have not displayed much direct interest in how state power is constituted and changes over time, even in work suffused with references to state practices.[5]

If life at an intimate scale were in the foreground of historical thinking about state power in the United States, what would be the result? The analysis would query less what the state *is* than what it *does*, by examining diverse state operations and effects. It would thereby resist disputes that have preoccupied generations of historians and political scientists, about the American state being weak or strong, big or small, exceptional or not among Western nations. The emerging picture would complement historians' recent theorizing that has sidelined the typological question—how to characterize exactly what "the state" is.[6] Rather than assessing weakness or strength, emphasis on intimate life would lead to highlighting the ways that state power has been shared and divided among the national government and the states and localities. Federalism, in other words, would appear front and center, as historians of intimate governance in the United States pursue the changing dispersion of power among local, state, and federal levels of authority over time, and chart the ways federalism itself was reconstituted in creating modes of reaching into intimate life.

One dimension of federalism in particular would become far more visible to historians if intimate governance were foregrounded: what is called the "police power," a power over social life both immense and diffuse. The meaning of "police" in that phrase is easy to mistake now; it is an archaic usage, closer to today's word "policy" than to a synonym for "cop." The police power is the authority to create and maintain a harmonious public order, intended to benefit community welfare without trampling unduly on individual freedoms (though necessarily restricting them somewhat). And it lies in the hands of local and state authorities, not the federal government. Since the US Constitution never mentioned the police power, by means of the Tenth Amendment it rested with the several states.[7]

Too often neglected in comparison with state power to construct markets and regulate the economy, conduct foreign affairs, or make war, the police power is the foundation of intimate governance. It covers a vast array of human activity, from land use to sexual regulation, enabling state actions to press into the intimate scale to construct a public order linking the maintenance and health of the polity to the intimacies of marriage, family, and sexuality. Constitutionally licensed to do so, states or their chartered county and city subordinates regulated those intimate domains through much of the nineteenth century, while also administering schools, poor laws, public roads, and myriad other components of social and economic activity.[8] The scale of the intimate allows us to see all this better, much like examining something under a microscope.

With that lens focused, the household formed by marriage comes into view as the central pivot of intimate governance—indispensable to understanding the modern history of the state. A major state institution of both privilege and regulation, the household is one of the most obvious instances of state power enacted through social life—by ordinary people simply living their lives. Its reach and influence are horizontal, exercised not through a single act but through being deeply embedded in the legal substructure of the social and economic order.

The very boundary between public and private, the single most important boundary produced through state action over many centuries, posited the household to be separate from the state. A major dimension of state power lies in articulating boundaries where state control begins or ends, as some historians have recently emphasized. This insight echoes the political scientist Timothy Mitchell, who contended twenty years ago that "the boundary of the state . . . never marks a real exterior. The line between state and society is not the perimeter of an intrinsic entity that can be thought of as a freestanding object or actor. It is a line drawn internally, within the network of institutional mechanisms through which a certain social and political order is maintained." Mitchell further observed that "producing and maintaining the distinction between state and society is itself a mechanism that generates resources of power."[9]

A corollary observation can be made about the concepts public and private. Their production as distinct and coherent domains, in both law and ideology, "generates resources of power" from which state practices gain authority in social life.[10] Longstanding Anglo-American legal tradition has made suitably formed households into linchpins of the social order, undergirding authorities' ability to maintain public harmony, governability, and safety. Marriage between a man and a woman founded a household; he became its head and its political representative, responsible for the economic support of his wife and all his dependents (including children, servants, apprentices, slaves, and even sundry relatives)—all of whose labor he could command. This traditional household design was economic at its core. Putting the work of dwellers in the household together for collective sustenance, it was meant to assure provision for all of them and place no burden on state expense. If their combined efforts resulted in wealth, it belonged to the head of the household as inheritable private property.

Households were to be central governing sites, establishing sexual predictability, economic obligation, and (until women could vote) political representation.[11] Each household also embodied ancient hierarchical relations of domination and submission: the relation of sovereign to people, parent to child, man to woman, and master to servant and slave. These asymmetries of gender, age, and servitude—and where racial slavery existed, of race—were assumed to be natural, and from repetition in households came to pervade society. Yet hierarchical household relations did not simply occur naturally. They required the force of law. State actions—laws and their enforcement—established and defined not only the roles and rules of labor and property but also individuals' very identities, in their social and legal statuses: one was formally, legally, a "wife," "husband," "minor," "apprentice," "slave." Lives and behaviors falling outside the household framework—such as prostitution, out-of-wedlock pregnancy, homosexuality, marital infidelity or desertion, vagrancy, and juvenile delinquency, to name a few—were considered disorderly, and because they deviated they required discipline, repair, or punishment. In Anglo-American law, the enactment of such remedies fell to local authorities under their longstanding police power.

The household became a container, so to speak, in both the neutral and the restrictive sense of that word. It also held back the potentially disruptive and obstreperous forces of sex, want, and delinquency. In the best cases, it held its members inside comfortably, having bread and shelter and a place to be secure from unruly others. In worse cases, where domestic violence or abuse took place, the state looked aside—on the premise that conduct inside the household was private. Sex between a husband and wife accorded with public order, while sex outside the marital household risked unsupported progeny and might unleash wanton antics with dangerous social effects. Children born to married parents (that is, into a proper household) were "legitimate" because their birth accorded with state rules and expectations. Others were "illegitimate."

Race entered this legal edifice powerfully. The Chesapeake colonies, where inheritable racial slavery prevailed, had set the rule in the 1660s that an enslaved woman's child was also a lifelong slave (whoever the father)— thus offering slave masters an economic incentive to rape their female slaves. Prohibitions of slave marriages and punishments for marrying across the color line also originated there. Eventually the great majority of states prohibited, nullified, and/or criminalized marriage of whites to African Americans; many states extended the ban to Asians and Native Americans. Couples joined across the color line could never have "legitimate" children in most American states. These laws did not prevent interracial sex—much of it white men's crude exploitation of women of color—but marked such sexual relationships as always illicit, even if intentional and loving. These laws persisted in thirty states until the US Supreme Court called them evidence of white supremacy and declared them unconstitutional in 1967.[12]

Centuries long and arcing across the Atlantic and into colonial and eventually US state law, the entwining of the patriarchal household and local police power in the eighteenth and nineteenth centuries provided the template for intimate governance. The years between the Civil War and the Great Depression then brought a period of unprecedented destabilization of the household as it had been conceived in the prior two centuries. Emancipation, the rapid spread of wage labor, urbanization, mass immigration, and colonialism propelled social transformations that weakened the patriarchal household, which proved unable to constrain the forces unleashed by a modern industrial society.

Our volume begins with the turning point of the Civil War and Reconstruction, not because intimate governance lacks early antecedents but rather to highlight the importance of the modern period in opening a new era for household-focused statecraft. In order both to bolster the male-headed household and to compensate for its failings, intimate governance in the United States underwent a remarkable period of expansion and innovation. State and federal officials pursued innovations in the governance of intimate life on a new scale, unlike anything contemplated in antebellum America. Statecraft's focus on the household, having guarded the dominion of the patriarch over his family for centuries, turned toward repair of social ruptures when that dominion weakened. The resulting iteration of state actions, practices, and effects modernized intimate governance and deepened its social power.

Marshaling their police power, states led this expansion and modernization. New initiatives and forays were launched at a rapid pace between the 1870s and 1930s, pushed by a revolving cast of reformers, public officials, journalists, religious leaders, academics, demagogues, and a not infrequently panicked public. Emerging social science methods—from crime statistics and family budget studies to the social survey, Deweyian empiricism, and Freudian psychology—often backed the expansion of intimate governance, but just as frequently it was Christian morality, white supremacy, or, from a different ideological direction, progressive reform aims. New marital, age of consent, child custody, reproductive, and public health and hygiene laws filled state law codes. Entirely new state structures emerged, from family and juvenile courts to youth reformatories and state eugenic departments, as did novel legal instruments, such as anti-prostitution abatement orders and protective labor laws.

States led the way in deploying the police power to serve intimate governance, but evolving federal encroachments placed a new rival in the field. Through creative reinterpretation of federal powers over commerce, immigration, and citizenship, the Congress and presidents and the US Supreme Court found one way after another to overcome the incapacities of the federal government. To accomplish on-the-ground aims such as sexual policing, the federal government at important points accomplished goals through public-private partnerships, licensing nongovernmental entities such as religious and secular voluntary associations to do its work. (State and local governments developed similar arrangements.) The results can be seen from federal use of moralistic vigilance societies to capture pornographers during Ulysses S. Grant's presidency to federal use of church-run agencies to encourage marriage during George W. Bush's. Today, even though the separate states retain primary jurisdiction over intimate domains, a proliferating array of federal laws, codes, and court decisions blanket the same area, exercising what seems to amount to police power, although rarely under that name.[13]

In part, the new era of federal intimate governance emerged from the Civil War and Reconstruction, when military exigencies compelled the US government to assume powers it had not had before. In one important episode, while the Union Army was occupying the defeated Confederate South (before the Southern states were reconstituted and accepted back into the Union), the federal government exercised the police power there in the absence of legitimate state and local authorities. The US Freedmen's Bureau enforced the victorious Union's understanding of public order, which included encouraging and performing marriages among the newly emancipated, who as slaves had been prohibited from marrying formally.[14]

The federal government exercised the police power constitutionally in the occupied South because no state governments existed there, and similarly, as the United States expanded its empire, all the land acquired through wars and treaties became federal territory. That meant Congress could make laws there at the most intimate level. Armed with that authority, the president and the Congress battled against polygamy practiced by the Church of Jesus Christ of Latter-Day Saints in the Utah territory. Far more often the federal government exercised intensive intimate governance over indigenous peoples. From the founding of the Bureau of Indian Affairs, federal authorities managed schooling and marriages and other intimate matters in native families, often with coercive means, such as the infamous practice of rending families apart by forcing boarding-school attendance on native youth. In a similar fashion, the federal government intruded into intimate life in Cuba, Puerto Rico, and the Philippines after conquering and occupying these overseas islands. Across its colonial possessions, federal officials deployed intimate governance as a tool of dominion.[15]

In its energetic diversity and institutional density, intimate governance never spoke with a single voice, either of liberation or oppression. State power is most usefully understood as a cumulative construct. This volume's explorations reveal that intimate governance varied (and varies) across levels and uses several modalities—in turn vigorous or anemic, protective or repressive, coercive or nurturant, plainly visible or altogether hidden. It helped and harmed, freed and confined, in countless different ways. Despite this variability, the underlying logic of intimate governance remained remarkably consistent in being directed against household destabilizations. State operations stepped in when the social tremors and dislocations produced by industrial society compromised the household's efficacy as the buttress of public order. Faced with an increasingly racially and sexually diverse society dependent on wage labor and lashed to the boom-bust cycles of market capitalism, advocates of intimate statecraft, from across the political spectrum, launched counterrevolutions intended to shore up or substitute for the threatened household.

By focusing on intimate realms, this volume captures the reality of state actions as emanating not from a stable entity—"the state"—but from a shifting pattern of governing powers working through society, economy,

and culture.[16] Our approach is to center the problems intimate-state builders identified and to trace the social effects produced by their remedies.
The problems they saw and tried to solve in the decades after Reconstruction and into the twentieth century were predominantly of two kinds: the
growing inability of the household to contain sexuality, and its failure to
contain economic dependency and vulnerability. Intimate statecraft conceived these problems as threats to social hierarchies and corrosive of
public order. Attempts to resolve them produced two distinct, sometimes
intersecting, trajectories of state innovation.

The household never contained sexuality completely, but the transformations of the late nineteenth century accelerated the release of sexual
behavior into the public sphere in unprecedented ways. Much of the impetus was economic—work left the home as the nation industrialized, and
sexuality followed it. The spread of wage labor gave single men and single
women more opportunities to live apart from families, and a market in
commercial sex arose to meet their new circumstances. Cheap pornography abounded, along with multiple venues for prostitution, an increasing availability of contraception, and a burgeoning leisure culture with
movie parlors and dance halls and the "cheap amusements" they offered.
The concentration of vice in certain segments of the city only made its
emergence more obvious to moral and social reformers who expressed—
and soon acted upon—their disapproval, eventually bringing agents of
the state into their campaigns of repression.[17] The initial focus of their
policing was heterosexual rather than homosexual deviance (although the
emphasis would shift over the first half of the twentieth century), but the
more important binaristic boundary was always the one that existed between the household and its deviant perimeter. Outside the household, the
sexuality that state officials sought to restrict or redirect could be hetero-
erotic or homoerotic, while queerness *inside* the household, too, might be
seen as needing to be policed, as the suspicions aroused by non-family
households in Stephen Vider's consideration of zoning cases in this volume demonstrate. More often, though, across the period under consideration, the state let all sorts of queerness alone if it was safely ensconced
inside the household, but scrutinized those who were seen as unattached
from the household (such as transients) as potential sexual deviants.[18]

As sexuality escaped the household, reformers of various stripes
adapted state powers at local, state, and federal levels to repair the social
fabric. The ways they did so reflected the alternating confluence of state
knowledge, state tools, and state interest, and the variation can make
the state seem chaotic rather than consistent. We can see examples in
this volume in Susan Pearson's discussion of changes in the use of birth

certificates to register or resist the early twentieth-century stigma on "illegitimate" births, or in the federal use of immigration laws to address the "white slave" panic in Grace Peña Delgado's analysis, or in the use of injunctions directed against perceived moral disorder, described here by William Novak.

How far agents of the state used the police power to manage these new "social problems" depended in part on the extent of public notice, which could sometimes escalate into full-blown "sex panics."[19] Vigorous eruptions of state and even federal effort in certain times and places both stimulated and responded to public outcries. Two such seeming spikes appear in the federal- and state-level engagement with reformer Anthony Comstock's crusade against obscenity, discussed by Jeffrey Escoffier, Whitney Strub, and Jeffrey Colgan, and, much later, the homosexual purges and sexual psychopath laws of the Cold War era that provide the context for Timothy Stewart-Winter's and Regina Kunzel's essays.[20]

States' attempts to regulate sexuality outside the married household sometimes had unintended consequences, creating additional problems to be solved by state actions. The closing down of urban red-light districts, for example, did not suppress prostitution as much as shift control of the industry from madams to pimps. State-created same-sex environments in prisons and the military tended to foster queer intimacies—a fact about which bureaucrats fretted considerably.[21] African American girls sent to Progressive Era state institutions for alleged delinquency distressed their keepers by engaging in lesbian relationships with white inmates, Tera Agyepong shows in her essay. The "true" target of state sexual intervention can be hard to pinpoint because the reason for enforcing a particular regulation could easily be about something else—often, maintaining race and class hierarchies as well as gender conformity and household integrity. For example, African American families in the South subjected to discrimination for bearing children out of wedlock were treated that way sometimes in response to civil rights activism, Serena Mayeri's essay shows. Anne Gray Fischer's examination of policing prostitution in the 1960s likewise shows racial motives in what purported to be sexual control. Paisley Currah's contribution reveals that state rules about sex classification that historically have impeded the full selfhood of trans people were often not created with them in mind; rather, those laws originated in intents "to limit the rights and resources available to women."

Alongside the failures of households to contain sexuality, which generated one historical trajectory of state innovation, were their failures in the economic realm. Even more prolific in invention, a second historical trajectory of state innovation aimed to redress the inabilities of households to contain and support the array of needy individuals spawned by industrial society. Intimate governance should not be understood as simply punitive; from Reconstruction on, statecraft invented new approaches to aiding vulnerable populations. Humanitarian concerns about the health and well-being of the poor and disadvantaged—who lacked inclusion in proper households—vied with public anxiety about their potential "dependency" on the government purse. Molly Ladd-Taylor's essay in this volume, examining sterilization as a "welfare" policy, illuminates an intrusively misguided expression of such mixed motives.

In this second major trajectory of state innovation, public provisioning included an expanding array of laws and programs aimed at materially sustaining people who were economically adrift from household support, or those vulnerable to such a fate. Never narrowly limited to what Americans came to call "welfare" (government payments to low-income mothers), the broad public welfare system devised at state and federal levels superseded the previous poor law tradition inherited from Elizabethan England.[22]

The conjoining of intimate and economic domains has been central to the building of state capacity. Disdain for public dependency has been a powerful force in American life, but a progressive impulse to protect the welfare of the population through public action grew across the early decades of the twentieth century into a broad social, legal, and intellectual movement that cast federal and state authorities as legitimate distributors of benefits. Federal entry had begun during Reconstruction, with the provision of a Civil War veterans' pension system that benefited veterans' widows as well as veterans themselves. The pension system brought monetary support and, along with it, novel forms of surveillance to assure widows' deservingness. The practice of intrusive checking into widows' suitability for pensions projected federal authority into intimate life in a way unimagined in the Constitution.[23]

To impose regulation and legitimacy upon the distribution of benefits, post–Civil War state health and welfare systems embedded the marriage-based family in their structural architecture. The moral credibility of the married household and the desire to promote that household thenceforward shaped the routes of state power. Few dimensions of governance in modern America better illustrate the social character of state power than its making marriage a boundary between "private" and "public" dependency. To assure that demarcation while constructing a new regulatory racial order, for example, many reorganized Southern states after the Civil War, as Stephanie McCurry's essay relates, declared free African American couples married to each other by law—whether the couple consented or not.

In time, marital status took up residence in virtually every nook and cranny of law and public policy. While both old-age benefits and assistance to families with dependent children under the Social Security Act of 1935, with its dense thicket of marital rules, comprise the best-studied example, over the course of the twentieth century governments channeled an increasing range of benefits through marital relationships. Marriage became the "gateway to public and private benefits," in Mayeri's words. Despite the fact that the separate states and not the federal government have the power to validate marriage and design its rules (within constitutional limits), by 1996 a Government Accountability Office study (prompted by the federal Defense of Marriage Act) could identify 1,049 separate places in the corpus of federal law in which marital status stipulated relationships, rights, benefits, or obligations. The individual states had their own lengthy and intricate lists.[24]

Family law, child protection, and direct aid became interlinked sites through which innovations in state powers grew during the twentieth century. Though marriage laws required husbands to support their wives, the extent of husbands' desertion led every state between 1890 and 1915 to enact new laws making a husband's failure to support his dependents a crime—and to create specialized family courts to enforce the mandate and adjudicate disputes. The individual states, with occasional federal assistance, took up a watch over children—validating parentage, providing for education, shepherding children through family dissolution, punishing and/or rehabilitating those thought to need it, intending to protect children from abuse and serving as their custodian of last resort—with the double aim to guide in moral development and to ensure that children matured into contributing members of self-supporting households.[25] Protecting children as a route to securing the health of the social body led states to develop novel forms of knowledge as well as new ameliorative programs, including another new judicial realm: the juvenile court. Additionally, following the model of federal pensions for Civil War widows, the federal government and individual states provided direct income payments to classes of "deserving" women: largely military widows, low-income women with young children, and those eligible for Social Security survivor benefits.

State protection and access to public provision nonetheless came with surveillance and the potential for coercion. Citizens gaining benefits found their intimate lives constrained by law and subject to the discretionary judgment of state actors such as judges and administrative clerks and officials. Here the policing of sexual deviance and the provisioning of welfare intersected. State agents providing support were substituting (in effect) for the lacking household head, and likewise stepped in to govern nonnormative households toward respectability. A historical pattern prevailed: for women, sexual respectability was a condition of state aid. In corollary, class advantage allowed greater freedom. After *Roe v. Wade*, Johanna Schoen shows, poor women were "among the first to lose access" to legal abortion because they could not afford it without state aid. Denial of Medicaid funding for abortion impacted poor women of color most severely.[26]

Modern health and welfare provisioning supplanted the poor laws but preserved the traditional moral distinction between the "deserving" and "undeserving" poor—a distinction sharply drawn around sexual respectability. For example, agents routinely investigated the intimate lives of women receiving aid under the Social Security Act, until organized protests by the welfare rights movement sparked a series of Supreme Court rulings that quashed the practice. These investigations intended to deny benefits where they found a "man in the house," or to force the man in question to provide child support, or both. This reinforcement of the masculine requirement to provide support, bringing surveillance along with it, puts a spotlight on the state aim to minimize dependency on the public purse.[27]

Because ideas about marriage, health and welfare, dependency, and deservingness have joined intimate and economic life together in countless laws and rules, there is no single approach or attitude, from repressive to protective to liberatory, that characterizes state power in these domains. But an enduring governing principle in the United States has been to minimize any drain on public coffers by assigning economic support to the private household. To "follow the money" in this light is to see dependency not solely as an economic category but also as a moral one, closely attached to normative ideas about the proper intimacies of sexuality, marriage, and households. As a result, state practices relied on and fostered a gender and racial division of economic citizenship and moral economy that conferred privilege and distributed social disadvantage in highly unequal ways.[28]

In constituting the household and responding to the household's failures to contain sexuality and dependency, intimate governance has endured through American history. Its expansion and adaptation since the Civil War have rendered it an inescapable force in the making of the modern United States. As we have sketched this pattern, we are not claiming to have summary answers to questions we have raised, or to present this as a definitive volume. The essays in the volume reflect preoccupations (and perhaps biases) of current scholarship, of course. Repressive state actions show up here more than instances of protection or care, and many sites and policies worth examining are neglected, including the armed forces, carceral and religious institutions, and imperial locations. We are conscious of lacking attention to intimate lives among many racial and ethnic groups, and in relation to HIV/AIDS or disability. We hope that our beginning in this volume will spark a great many more investigations. Having brought intimacy and state power into closer proximity, we would like to see that conjunction become more frequent in historical study.

In pointing out the prevalence of the household model of intimate sexual and economic order, we intend to emphasize continuity, yet not at the expense of change over time. Apparent and indeed real continuity has overlaid many changes in the last century and a half. Seen from close up, changes such as the birth of Social Security, the decriminalization of abortion, and the legalization of gay marriage can appear to be decisive departures. But seen from a longer vantage, the continuities are strikingly visible, especially the resiliency of the household as the crux of intimate governance. Across the whole of the period covered in this volume, two major forces pushed adaptations in state practices: the economic pressures of capitalism and the legal expansion of individual rights. Together, those two forces gradually but decisively disaggregated the nineteenth-century household and its ordering of sexuality and labor. Intimate governance had helped make that household what it was, just as it has been central to overseeing its transformation.

Indeed, the post-1960s expansion of individual rights, particularly among women and LGBT people, has raised the possibility that intimate governance might secure sexual freedom and reproductive autonomy—rather than, as earlier, contain and limit them. The extent and durability of such guarantees ought not be overstated, and rights gained in those domains continue to be politically contested and constitutionally incomplete. Individual rights claims are made all along the political spectrum, in opposition to these gains as well as in support. Yet it is difficult to regard the recognition of reproductive rights, sexual autonomy, and marriage equality under the Fourteenth Amendment, and the advent of new state-level prohibitions of marital rape, sexual harassment, and anti-LGBT discrimination, as anything other than a new direction for intimate governance. As we write this introduction, whether momentum in these areas will solidify into a lasting order is not at all clear.

A striking feature of this long view, in which continuities prevail even as changes accumulate, is that adaptations in intimate governance lend themselves to no clear periodization over time. Nor do they suggest an overall move from strong regulation to liberality. Definitions have evolved, to be sure. What made up household "order" changed with wives' emergence into legal and economic individuality, and again with state acceptance of unmarried couples as responsible co-heads, and again with same-sex couples' eligibility to marriage, for example. Likewise, what constituted "deviance" has changed: as heterosexual sex outside marriage became widely acceptable in the later part of the twentieth century, for example, or yet again when homosexual sex was decriminalized in this century. State techniques, too, have emerged and evolved: from family and juvenile law to municipal abatement ordinances, from the Comstock Law to sexual harassment jurisprudence or the criminalization of HIV exposure.[29]

Nor is it clear, when the state is examined from the angle of the intimate, that the resulting historical record aligns with turning points usually emphasized. Reconstruction, the Progressive Era, the New Deal, Great Society, the rights revolution, and the Reagan Revolution and subsequent turn to free-market ethics and deregulation all played *some* role in shaping intimate governance, but none seems to have been as decisive as the broader, and ongoing, destabilization of the household that characterized the long sweep from Reconstruction to the present. And this suggests that much may be gained by loosening the tie of our political histories to well-known temporal anchors, which have certainly illuminated but also may have constrained our collective historical vision.

Conceiving of governance in the broadly social way we have here side-steps a common fallacy regarding intimate domains: that the presence of state power signals repression and its absence liberty. Intimate governance can be harshly repressive, and many of this volume's essays illustrate that it is those on the social margins, more than those whose behavior follows social norms, who most often see and feel the state intruding into their "innermost private lives."[30] Not to recognize that would represent a willful misreading of the historical record. Yet state *inaction*, or absence, can equally engender repression, or inequity, in intimate settings. Rather than envisioning intimate governance solely along a spectrum from repression to liberty, it is more useful to regard it as productive of social relations and identities, and thus helping to bring social life itself into being. To remake social life, Americans participated in a vast and concerted state-building project—intimate governance—across the last third of the nineteenth and throughout the twentieth centuries. Our hope is that this volume helps make that project, and its legacies, more visible.

Notes

1. For example, M. Z. Rosaldo, "The Use and Abuse of Anthropology: Reflections on Feminism and Cross-Cultural Understanding," *Signs: A Journal of Culture*

and Society 5 (Spring 1980): 389–417; Carole Pateman, "Feminist Critiques of the Public/Private Dichotomy," in S. I. Benn and G. F. Gaus, *Public and Private in Social Life* (London: Croom & Helm, 1983); and Frances E. Olson, "The Family and the Market: A Study of Ideology and Legal Reform," *Harvard Law Review* 96 (1983): 1497–1578. Our historiographical footnotes throughout will be illustrative rather than comprehensive.

2. For example, Sonya Michel and Seth Koven, "Womanly Duties: Maternalist Politics and the Origin of Welfare States in France, Germany, Great Britain and the U.S. 1880–1930," *American Historical Review* 95, no. 4 (October 1990): 1076–1108; Stephanie McCurry, "The Two Faces of Republicanism: Gender and Proslavery Politics in Antebellum South Carolina," *Journal of American History* 78, no. 4 (March 1992): 1245–64; Evelyn Higginbotham, *Righteous Discontent: The Women's Movement in the Baptist Church* (Cambridge, MA: Harvard University Press, 1993); Linda Gordon, *Pitied But Not Entitled: Single Mothers and the History of Welfare* (Cambridge, MA: Harvard University Press, 1994); Elsa Barkley Brown, "Negotiating and Transforming the Public Sphere: African American Political Life in the Transition from Slavery to Freedom," *Public Culture* 7, no. 1 (Fall 1994): 107–46; and Linda K. Kerber et al., eds., *U.S. History as Women's History* (Chapel Hill: University of North Carolina Press, 1995).

3. Karen M. Tani has stressed the (gendered) ways that histories of the welfare state are understood as separate from the history of statecraft in "From the Well-Regulated Society to the Modern American State," *American Journal of Legal History* 57 (2017): 245. See Julian Zelizer's introduction to his *Governing America: The Revival of American History* (Princeton, NJ: Princeton University Press, 2012) for an example centering American Political Development in the reemergence of interest in statecraft within history.

4. Suleiman Osman, "Glocal America: The Politics of Scale in the 1970s," in *Shaped by the State: Toward a New Political History of the 20th Century*, ed. Brent Cebul, Lily Geismer, and Mason Williams (Princeton, NJ: Princeton University Press, 2019), 249–50.

5. We offer this observation not as a critique of the history of sexuality but as a recognition that its intellectual priorities have been elsewhere.

6. For example, William J. Novak, "The Myth of the 'Weak' American State," *American Historical Review* 113 (June 2008): 752–72; and Gary Gerstle, *Liberty and Coercion: The Paradox of American Government from the Founding to the Present* (Princeton, NJ: Princeton University Press, 2015).

7. During the Constitutional Convention, James Madison insisted that freedom went hand in hand with well-regulated "police" (or policy). It was the several states' role, not that of the federal government, he said, to establish and keep the two in balance: "The *freedom of the people* and their *internal good police* depends" on maintaining the state governments "in full vigor." See William Novak, *The People's Welfare* (Chapel Hill: University of North Carolina Press, 1996), 9–17, quoting Madison on 11, and 255–56nn44, 46, 48.

8. Novak, *The People's Welfare*; and see Gerstle, *Liberty and Coercion*, esp. 55–68. Cities, chartered as municipal corporations by the states, exercised police power of their own in the early republic, but whenever conflict occurred antebellum

courts sent that power into the hands of the states. See Jon Teaford, "City versus State: The Struggle for Legal Ascendancy," *American Journal of Legal History* 17 (1973): 51–65.

9. Timothy Mitchell, "Society, Economy, and the State Effect," in *State/Culture: State Formation after the Cultural Turn*, ed. George Steinmetz (Ithaca, NY: Cornell University Press, 1999), quotation on 83. Cf. *Boundaries of the State in U.S. History*, ed. James T. Sparrow, William J. Novak, and Stephen W. Sawyer (Chicago and London: University of Chicago Press, 2015).

10. This conceptualization harked back to the ancient Greek city-states, in which the *oikos* (household) and the *polis* (polity) represented a primordial division. The *oikos* (root of the English word *economy*) represented labor for sustenance as well as the intimate arena of sex and family, while the polity was the arena of free men (only) who engaged in creating the republic. See Hannah Arendt, *The Human Condition* (New York, 1958), 22–78; Morton Horwitz, "The History of the Public/Private Distinction," *University of Pennsylvania Law Review* 130, no. 6 (June 1982); and, for a stimulating more recent analysis, Susan Gal, "A Semiotics of the Public/Private Distinction," *differences: A Journal of Feminist Cultural Studies* 13, no. 1 (2002): 77–95.

11. On the historical centrality of the marital household to the governing public order, see Sarah Hanley, "Engendering the State: Family Formation and State Building in Early Modern France," *French Historical Studies* 16, no. 1 (1989): 4–27; Mary L. Shanley, "Marriage Contract and Social Contract in Seventeenth-Century English Political Thought," in Jean Bethke Elshtain, ed., *The Family in Political Thought* (Amherst: University of Massachusetts Press, 1982), 80–95; Michael Grossberg, *Governing the Hearth: Law and the Family in Nineteenth-Century America* (Chapel Hill: University of North Carolina Press, 1985); Nancy F. Cott, *Public Vows: A History of Marriage and the Nation* (Cambridge, MA: Harvard University Press, 2000); and Carole Shammas, *A History of Household Government in America* (Charlottesville: University of Virginia Press, 2002).

12. See Tera Hunter, *Bound in Wedlock: Slave and Free Black Marriage in the Nineteenth Century* (Cambridge, MA: Harvard University Press, 2017); and Peggy Pascoe, *What Comes Naturally: Miscegenation Law and the Making of Race in America* (New York: Oxford, 2009).

13. For a summary of methods of federal aggrandizement, see Gerstle, *Liberty and Coercion,* 5–9; cf. Karen Tani, Brent Cebul, and Mason B. Williams, maintaining the importance of the "middle tier"—political scientist Martha Derthick's terminology for the states—in "Clio and the Compound Republic," *Publius: The Journal of Federalism* 47 (2017): 243–47.

14. See Laura F. Edwards, "'The Marriage Covenant Is at the Foundation of All Our Rights,'" *Law and History Review* 14 (1996); Amy Dru Stanley, *From Bondage to Contract* (New York and Cambridge: Cambridge University Press, 1998); and Cott, *Public Vows,* 80–95.

15. See Brenda J. Child, *Boarding School Seasons: American Indian Families, 1900–1940* (Lincoln: University of Nebraska Press, 1989); cf. Ann Laura Stoler's conception of European empires governing through intimate life in *Carnal Knowledge*

and Imperial Power: Race and the Intimate in Colonial Rule (Berkeley: University of California Press, 2002) and her edited collection, *Haunted by Empire: Geographies of the Intimate in North American History* (Durham, NC: Duke University Press, 2006), extending similar analysis into North America.

16. The volume's essays, each of which we will mention briefly in what follows but will not summarize, offer illustrations from many directions.

17. See John D'Emilio and Estelle Freedman, *Intimate Matters: A History of Sexuality in America,* 3rd ed. (Chicago: University of Chicago Press, 2012 [orig. 1988]); Kathy Peiss, *Cheap Amusements: Working Women and Leisure in Turn-of-the-Century New York* (Philadelphia: Temple University Press, 1986); Elizabeth Alice Clement, *Love for Sale: Courting, Treating, and Prostitution in New York City, 1900–1945* (Chapel Hill: University of North Carolina Press, 2006); and Cynthia Blair, *I've Got to Make My Livin': Black Women's Sex Work in Turn-of-the Century Chicago* (Chicago: University of Chicago Press, 2010).

18. On queer domesticities, see Lauren Jae Gutterman, *Her Neighbor's Wife: A History of Lesbian Desire Within Marriage* (Philadelphia: University of Pennsylvania Press, 2019); and Stephen Vider, *The Queerness of Home: Gender, Sexuality, and the Politics of Domesticity* (Chicago: University of Chicago Press, 2021). On sexual suspicion of transients, see Margot Canaday, *The Straight State: Sexuality and Citizenship in Twentieth-Century America* (Princeton, NJ: Princeton University Press, 2009), 96–131.

19. Gayle Rubin first labeled such outbreaks "sex panics" in "Thinking Sex: Notes for a Radical Theory of the Politics of Sexuality," in Carole Vance, ed., *Pleasure and Danger: Exploring Female Sexuality* (Boston: Routledge and Kegan Paul, 1984), 267–31.

20. For an example of state-level "Lavender Scare" purges, see Stacy Braukman, *Communists and Perverts under the Palms: The Johns Committee in Florida, 1956–1964* (Gainesville: University Press of Florida, 2012).

21. See, for example, Ruth Rosen, *The Lost Sisterhood: Prostitution in America, 1900–1918* (Baltimore: Johns Hopkins University Press, 1982), 30–33; Allan Berube, *Coming Out Under Fire: The History of Gay Men and Women in World War II* (New York: Plume, 1991); and Regina Kunzel, *Criminal Intimacy: Prison and the Uneven History of Modern Sexuality* (Chicago: University of Chicago Press, 2008).

22. See Michael B. Katz, *In the Shadow of the Poorhouse: A Social History of Welfare in America* (New York: Basic Books, 1986); and Donna Cooper Hamilton and Charles V. Hamilton, *The Dual Agenda: Race and Social Welfare Policies of Civil Rights Organizations* (New York: Columbia University Press, 1997).

23. Amy E. Holmes, "'Such is the Price We Pay': American Widows and the Civil War Pension System," in Maris A. Vinovskis, ed., *Toward a Social History of the American Civil War* (Cambridge: Cambridge University Press, 1990); Theda Skocpol, *Protecting Soldiers and Mothers: The Political Origins of Social Policy in the United States* (Cambridge, MA: Harvard University Press, 1992); and Megan J. McClintock, "Civil War Pensions and the Reconstruction of Union Families," *Journal of American History* 83, no. 2 (September 1996): 456–80.

24. US General Accountability Office, *Defense of Marriage Act*, GAO/OGC-97–16

(Washington, DC: January 31, 1997); and Anna Marie Smith, "The Sexual Regulation Dimension of Contemporary Welfare Law: A Fifty State Overview," *Michigan Journal of Gender and Law* 8, no. 2 (2002): 121–218.

25. See Michael Willrich, "Home Slackers: Men, the State, and Welfare in Modern America," *Journal of American History* 87 (September 2000): 460–89; and Eve P. Smith and Lisa A. Mewkel-Holguin, eds., *A History of Child Welfare* (New York: Routledge, 2018).

26. See Gordon, *Pitied But Not Entitled*; and Jennifer Nelson, *Women of Color and the Reproductive Rights Movement* (New York: NYU Press, 2003).

27. Alison Lefkovitz, "Men in the House: Race, Welfare, and the Regulation of Men's Sexuality in the United States, 1961–1972," *Journal of the History of Sexuality* 20, no. 3 (September 2011): 594–614; Premilla Nadasen, *Rethinking the Welfare Rights Movement* (New York: Routledge, 2012); and Andrew Pope, "Making Motherhood a Felony: African American Women's Welfare Rights Activism in New Orleans & the End of Suitable Home Laws, 1959–1962," *Journal of American History* 105, no. 2 (September 2018): 291–310.

28. Cf. Nancy Fraser and Linda Gordon, "A Genealogy of Dependency: Tracing a Keyword of the U.S. Welfare State," *Signs: A Journal of Culture and Society* 19, no. 2 (1994): 302–36; and Alice Kessler-Harris, *In Pursuit of Equity: Women, Men, and the Quest for Economic Citizenship in 20th Century America* (Oxford: Oxford University Press, 2001).

29. On HIV-specific criminal laws (on the books in twenty-six states in 2018), see https://www.cdc.gov/hiv/policies/law/states/exposure.html; and Trevor Hoppe, *Punishing Disease: HIV and the Criminalization of Sickness* (Berkeley: University of California Press, 2017).

30. The phrase comes from Evelyn Brooks Higginbotham, "African-American Women's History and the Metalanguage of Race," *Signs: A Journal of Culture and Society* 117, no. 2 (1991), in which she writes (265): "The categorization of class and racial groups according to culturally constituted sexual identities facilitated blacks' subordination and rendered them powerless against the intrusion of the state into their innermost private lives."

1

Reconstructing Belonging

The Thirteenth Amendment at Work in the World

STEPHANIE MCCURRY

INTRODUCTION

This chapter grapples with the implications of an act of state authority arguably unparalleled in US history: slave emancipation. The temporary war powers claimed by the US government created a state big enough to destroy a category of private property—property in persons—worth $4 billion in 1860. That big state lasted long enough to enact and enforce the Thirteenth Amendment, which permanently emancipated four million people. We know this, of course, but without sufficiently appreciating the intimate matters involved in that state decision which destroyed slavery and the world built on its foundation. In the postwar American South, emancipation involved a revolution in every household. Political and domestic affairs could not be separated. It is a perspective abundantly evident in the sources, although one usually overlooked by political historians and those interested in state power and state formation.[1]

With emancipation, the US government destroyed the antebellum form of the Southern household, liberated enslaved people to form free families, and forced the reconstruction of every household and family in the former slave states. This long, excruciating, and violent process was evident in the policies and actions of the federal government and its agencies, including the US Army and the Bureau of Freedmen, Refugees, and Abandoned Lands; Southern state governments scrambling to write new constitutions and frame laws; the courts enforcing the laws and adjudicating disputes; and, above all, in the actions of newly liberated African Americans attempting to destroy previous owners' possessive claims over their bodies and family members. The destruction of slavery meant the remaking even of notions of love and family, and of race—or white supremacy—and all that it involved. Emancipation was a process that reconfigured subjectivity itself.

The implementation of the Thirteenth Amendment showed the deep reach of the state into private life. Of all the civil rights emancipation implied, none was more readily acknowledged than the right of free people to marry and claim their children as their own. The definition, recognition, and enforcement of freedpeople's marital and parental rights was key in the construction of a new post-emancipation legal order. Most enforcement of the amendment happened at the level of state constitutions and laws; and its full scope can only be assessed with due attention to the "domestic relations" of marital and parental rights, fought over by newly freedpeople, former slaveholders, and legislators within the ex-Confederate states.

That history is a reminder that the family itself is a realm of governance, a polity, and one of great significance to states.[2] There was nothing new about that. But in 1865, both institutions were in a state of flux and the former Confederacy was occupied territory, creating a new scope of action. In that highly contingent postwar context, the US government exerted its power not just to police or constrain, but to assist and protect African Americans in their intimate lives. In this, as we will see, Freedmen's Bureau agents responded to demands that issued from the citizens themselves, prominent among them freedwomen who, in the South as in other post-emancipation societies, played a key role in asserting new rights for themselves, their children, and their families. The slew of bastardy or paternity cases Black women filed against former owners in 1865 and 1866 represents one sharp and understudied element of that historical process.

The extent to which the Thirteenth Amendment set the state to meddling in private family affairs has not much been appreciated by legal scholars, even those who leave little doubt about the "constitutional revolution" it initiated.[3] Much can be gained by connecting state power to intimate matters with respect to the amendment; such an approach brings into conversation the literatures on the law, the state, and women, gender, and the family, which are too often separated. Even as scholars tear down the myth of the weak American state and advocate a "state in society" approach, they exhibit a striking lack of interest in the key matter of slavery and emancipation (and the period of the Civil War and Reconstruction at the center of political histories of the US state). Moreover, notwithstanding a call for a broader approach to "the political," these new histories of the state take little notice of the distinguished body of feminist scholarship on gender and politics, which over the last twenty-five years has redefined the boundaries of "the political" to include precisely the kinds of personal or domestic relations on which enforcement of the Thirteenth Amendment turned.[4]

Emancipation was an excruciatingly intimate event for all parties to the process. Disentangling families formed under slavery was no easy task— all the more so because slaveholders did not just let go of the people they had claimed as theirs. The dynamics of the process require us to contend with the emotional and psychological elements (what Judith Surkis calls the "affective supplement") of the legal history.[5] One key goal of this essay is to show how centuries of sexual violence against slave women, and the children born as a result, set a deep explosive charge under every negotiation over the terms of freedom in the postwar South.

THE THIRTEENTH AMENDMENT: PASSAGE AND RATIFICATION

Passage of the Thirteenth Amendment was a crucial achievement of the Lincoln administration and a measure of state authority so untrammeled that it can be said to have remade the United States.[6] The total, immediate, and uncompensated abolition of slavery was codified in the amendment and imposed on the rebel states as a condition of readmission to the Union. It was "one of the largest liquidations of private property in world history," fully two-thirds of the capital wealth of the Southern states.[7] A measure entirely unthinkable in 1860, it was achieved (in part) in 1863 only as an executive order issued as a war measure.[8] Revising the US Constitution by amendment thus was essential. The amendment and its implementation stand at the very center of arguments about the Civil War as the "birth of the modern American state."[9] Enforcement in the defeated Confederate states represented an assertion of central state authority in the affairs of the separate states inconceivable in the first republic.

Even in the Republican-controlled 38th Congress, passage of the amendment was not an easy proposition. It passed in the House of Representatives on January 31, 1865, on an almost party-line vote of 119 to 56, a stripped-down but revolutionary measure ending the national government's recognition of legitimate property in human beings.[10] The amendment was quickly ratified by numerous Northern states and small Unionist governments of occupied Confederate states, but Union border states remained opposed. The Kentucky legislature declined to ratify even on condition of compensation and a strictly limited set of civil rights for newly freed slaves; tellingly, the one new right the state was willing to grant was recognition of marriages and parental relationships.[11] In mid-April 1865 when Grant accepted Lee's surrender, the amendment remained short of the votes needed for ratification. Its fate thus fell into the hands of the defeated Confederate states, and their defiant posture did not bode well. President Johnson urged provisional governors to ratify as the basis of a lenient reconstruction and readmission.[12] But when constitutional conventions convened in the fall of 1865, every ex-Confederate state balked.

What ensued in the state of Georgia was indicative of the South as a whole. Tasked with writing a new state constitution, convention delegates begrudgingly declared all slaves in the state "emancipated from slavery" by virtue of the "war measure" the United States had imposed, but denied the Emancipation Proclamation's constitutionality and refused to ratify the Thirteenth Amendment, deferring that decision to the legislature. Not one Southern state convention ratified.[13] Like border-state Democrats, delegates feared particularly the enforcement clause contained in Article 2: "Congress shall have power to enforce this article by appropriate legislation." Benjamin Perry, the provisional governor of South Carolina, told President Johnson that his state would never consent to a clause which "may be construed to give Congress power of local legislation over the negroes and white men."[14] In Perry's view, the state should control what emancipation meant and what civil rights it conferred.

By December 1865, Southern legislatures' debates about ratifying the Thirteenth Amendment were conducted side by side with those on what would be known as the "Black Codes." By writing separate codes of law for "free persons of color"—codes that harshly criminalized the exercise of basic civil rights, including freedom of assembly, mobility, and employment—Southern states sought to constrain the meaning of freedom for African Americans and remand the class back to plantation labor.[15] President Johnson kept up pressure for ratification, issuing assurances about the limits of the amendment. By December 1865, enough Southern states had ratified to secure adoption. What the amendment required by way of individual rights was left purposely vague. South Carolina ratified while attaching a declaration prohibiting Congress from "legislating upon the political status of former slaves, or their civil relations."[16]

Georgia was the last state to ratify. The Georgia constitutional convention made a down payment on the legal work of reconstruction by abolishing slavery and calling elections for December 1865 (with only "free white male citizens of this state" as voters). It acknowledged the legal mess emancipation created, specifying the hierarchy of law that would now pertain in the state: the US Constitution, Georgia Constitution, and then state laws, *excepting* those "as refer to persons held in slavery," declared "inoperative and void." Delegates left it to future legislators to write the laws that would recognize and govern the newly freed population, but they made

one exception: Section 9, which prohibited "forever . . . the marriage relation between white persons and persons of African descent," and ordered
the General Assembly to enact laws to punish any officer or minister who
knowingly "marries such persons together."[17] That proactive move showed
the immediate recourse to marriage laws to mark racial difference. The article was written before the state passed any law recognizing former slaves
as free people of color with a right to enter the contract of marriage.

On December 18, 1865, the Thirteenth Amendment to the US Constitution was officially adopted. The arduous political course of the amendment
initiated a far longer legal history. Defining and enforcing the terms of
the Thirteenth Amendment involved the government—federal, state, and
local—in the most intimate aspects of Southerners' lives, since even the
narrowest interpretation of the amendment included the right to personal
liberty and property, to marry, and to make parental claims to children.

STATE LEGISLATION AND THE LEGAL HISTORY
OF MARITAL AND PARENTAL RIGHTS

To implement the Thirteenth Amendment required nothing short of a new
legal order to recognize former slaves as free people *and* members of free
families. Marriage law was an indispensable instrument in the construction of a new postwar juridical order. Like lawmakers across the colonial
world, those in the US South relied on the regulation of marriage (and sex)
as the weight-bearing foundation of racial difference.[18] At the very least, as
Alexander Tsesis notes, the amendment had to proscribe the kind of "arbitrary interference with family life" that prevailed under the law of slavery.[19]

Defining marital and parental rights was a foundational part of the reconstruction project. The process started during the war. Enslaved couples
had been denied the right to legal marriage; their families were constituted
on a different basis since the passage of maternal descent laws in the
1660s.[20] By 1860, enslaved couples, families, and kinship groups adopted
multiple and flexible forms. Under the circumstances of slavery, in Tera
Hunter's words, marriage had evolved to "encompass committed conjugal
relationships, whether legal or not, monogamous, bigamous, polygamous,
or serial," and heterosexual intimacy included a range of domestic arrangements, not all of which were thought of as marriages.[21]

If the customary and breakable forms of enslaved families served masters' interests under slavery, they constituted the makings of a social crisis
in the post-emancipation world. Universal emancipation was unthinkable
without the prior disciplinary structure of the patriarchal family. That was
certainly the view of Union policymakers who moved during the war to

impose monogamy and the forms of the patriarchal family on slaves as terms of emancipation.[22] The scale of the wartime task was dwarfed by the one that awaited upon passage of the Thirteenth Amendment. Enforcement involved the massive agenda of liberating African American people from the families or households in which they had been held as slaves—and establishing them at law and custom as free, self-owning persons with paramount claims to their spouses and children. The making of free families and free homes was a deeply contested process, both within the Black community and in brutal negotiations with ex-slaveholders.[23] It was, among other things, a massive legal undertaking that involved the federal government, state constitutional conventions and legislatures, the US Army, the Freedmen's Bureau, and (where they operated) local civil courts, state appeal courts, and federal district courts and newly expanded courts of appeal.

The first order of business was to build the edifice of state law required to enact the Thirteenth Amendment. In December 1865, Georgia legislators turned to the task. By early 1866 they had the scaffolding of a new legal order that recognized free families of "persons of color." In a series of acts, numbered consecutively 250–54, they created a new class of "free people of color," defined as those "having one eighth negro or African blood, in their veins," and specified their civil rights. They validated the marriages of former slaves that had been illegal under slavery; legitimized the children born of those relationships; and wrote the constitutional prohibition on interracial marriage into statute law. They also rewrote the apprenticeship law to allow the binding out of free Black children by the courts, while requiring the consent of parents—not a small concession.[24]

By early 1866 the legal framework of free families had been erected in Georgia. Against claims of love and possession by old owners, freedpeople had meaningful new legal rights: to make binding claims on each other as husband and wife, and on their children as parents. They also had a federal agency, the US Freedmen's Bureau, and an army of occupation, to back up those rights with force if need be. Freedpeople lost little time in putting their new powers to work.

The recognition of freedpeople's marriage and parental rights was fundamental to the new legal order in the Southern states, not least because of the obligations they incurred. Southern states attempted to construct a new social and racial order by defining legally which "family" relationships were natural and legitimate and which unnatural and illicit.[25] The "Act to Prescribe and Regulate the Relation of Husband and Wife Between Persons of Color" not only recognized couples as legally married; it coerced monogamy and heterosexual marriage *without the consent of the couples themselves*. Like most Southern states, Georgia passed a blanket law that declared all "persons of color" "now living together as husband and wife" to be legally married. Freedpeople were thus married without their consent or benefit of a license or ceremony, a provision that caused a cascade of legal problems in the courts for the remainder of the century.[26] Another provision ordered those with more than one spouse to select one of their "reputed wives [or] husbands" and submit to a ceremony of marriage. That provision meant that "persons of color" could find themselves divorced without their consent as well. Those who persisted in acknowledging more than one spouse would be "prosecuted for the offence of fornication, or fornication and adultery, and punished accordingly." The suspicion of illegitimacy and disrepute hanging over enslaved people's marriages in Union eyes throughout the war was thus reproduced in state law afterward.

The law that finally recognized freedpeople's marriages as legitimate was thus simultaneously an act of affirmation and of cultural violence against the pluralist normative forms long adopted by African Americans.[27] In that sense it has to be understood as part of a much larger reconstruction of race and white supremacy itself on new terms, which was also the intent of the law criminalizing marriage across the color line. Written into the constitution a few months before, it was made part of statute law for purposes of enforcement.[28]

The laws recognizing African Americans' parental rights were no less critical to the new racial architecture of the state of Georgia. They baldly reflected determination to impose the burden of dependent African American children on individual parents. In this ambition, the state government was no different from the federal one, although there was considerable conflict between them over what the law required. The Georgia law specified that "among persons of color, the parent shall be required to maintain his, or her children, *whether legitimate or illegitimate*." It was carefully written to bypass any prior condition of marriage to establish the obligation of support. It further specified that every "colored child born" was to be declared the legitimate child not just of his mother but of "his colored father," if acknowledged by that father. The matter of white men's obligation of support of their "colored" children was carefully circumvented.[29]

The moment of reconstruction was a pivotal one in the history of race in the United States. The raft of legislation constructing new families for "free persons of color" was fundamental to the production of claims about racial difference (read inferiority) designed to legitimize practices of domination—"racecraft," as Karen and Barbara Fields have termed it. "Racist concepts do considerable work in political and economic life," they point out, "but, if they were . . . without intimate roots in other phases of life, their persuasiveness would accordingly diminish." As the process of implementing the Thirteenth Amendment in Georgia shows, Southern states' paths to a new kind of white supremacy were driven by concerns that were nothing if not intimate.[30]

The federal government was deeply invested, too, both in imposing the legal order of the heterosexual patriarchal family on freedpeople *and* in protecting their rights as husbands, wives, and parents within it. In the immediate postwar period, 1865–1867, the US Army and the Freedmen's Bureau were the main representatives of federal power in the occupied South.[31] Bureau agents had no power to write, but only to enforce, the laws of the Southern states where they operated, producing a complex dynamic. In that moment of legal uncertainty, the conflict between military and civilian law and authority became an element of the political struggle. In April 1866, mere weeks after the Georgia legislature adjourned, Brigadier General Davis Tillson, the assistant commissioner of the Freedmen's Bureau in Georgia, issued Circular No. 5, which bundled all the new laws "relative to marriage and divorce" and published them for the guidance of "Officers and Agents of the Bureau and the freedpeople of this State." That pairing of federal agents and freedpeople signaled a new political order. For the first time in US history, African Americans possessed rights the federal government was pledged to protect.[32] As punitive as the state laws could be, federal agents' enforcement represented a frontal challenge to the power of the South's ruling class, men who were now "masters without slaves," living under federal authority.[33]

The struggle between individual state and federal authorities is a key part of Reconstruction history, initially manifest in the battle over the rights conferred by the Thirteenth Amendment.[34] In that moment of legal uncertainty and conflict between military and civilian law and authority, what emerged was a plural legal system.[35] Even after enactment of the Civil Rights Act (1866), congressional passage of the Fourteenth Amendment's guarantee of national citizenship and protection of civil rights (1866), and the Military Reconstruction Act(s) putting the states back under military occupation (1867), the issue of when, and under what circumstances, federal authorities superseded local and state ones was highly contested. In 1866 and 1867, the Bureau generally held that federal authorities deferred to local courts for the enforcement of freedpeople's new civil rights. That expectation held *where* the civil courts were in operation (a highly variable matter), where Blacks had the right to testify against white people, and *until* Bureau agents discerned, and formally alleged, violation of freedpeople's constitutional rights. At that final point cases could move to Bureau courts, military tribunals, or federal courts.[36] Under the Johnson administration the Freedmen's Bureau courts and military courts took up the burden.[37] If local civil authorities failed to respond, field officers had discretionary authority to arrest those who violated freedpersons' rights and hold them for trial. "Family law" was at the heart of the jurisdictional battle.

MAKING FREE FAMILIES: THE DESTRUCTION

OF SLAVEHOLDERS' POSSESSIVE CLAIM

The sexual violence of slavery charged every negotiation about the terms of freedom in the postwar South and pulled the federal government deep into the intimate affairs of families Black and white. The destruction of plantation households and creation of new free families was a difficult process, not least because of the deeply fraught forms of belonging that had to be undone. Slave-owning men and women accustomed to mastery did not simply surrender possession of "their" people. The nature of the possessive claim engendered by generations of ownership is difficult to discuss, but it was a key element of the affective politics of the period, critical to understanding what freedpeople were up against.[38]

The most acute issues involved claims to children illegally held by former masters or bound out to them, in court-approved apprenticeships. Freedpeople fought to reverse all these effects of slavery on their families and to assert their equal legal rights. Thousands filed suits to cancel apprenticeship contracts and reclaim their children. Some freedwomen moved to hold former owners accountable for the support of children fathered by them under slavery. Forced to adjudicate matters of paternity, federal officials found no place to hide from the ugly reality of slaveholders' power. The nature of the "familial" ties, shaped by centuries of sexual violence against African American women, was exposed and contested with emancipation.

Planters' refusal to surrender people formerly held as slaves was a massive issue of governance in the early postwar years. The Freedmen's Bureau, whatever its limitations, represented freedpeople's best hope of countering planter power. Many Bureau officials, detailed directly from the army, did not understand the nature of the ties they were called on to adjudicate. Gertrude Thomas's family is a case in point. Like so many slaveholders who gave their name to the people they owned, Thomas, a planter woman from Augusta, Georgia, regarded her "servants" as part of her family.[39] Her claim was deeply embedded in the material relations of slavery, including the sexual violence that undergirded them in her own family. Slaveholders had long cast their ownership of human beings in

familial terms—historians have referred to it as "paternalism"—and planters continued to appeal to it when they became "masters without slaves."[40]
Needless to say, this was not a view of family to which enslaved people or
their descendants ever subscribed. Slavery had set the terms of family life,
love, and belonging in the plantation household. With defeat and emancipation, all the terms had to be reset.

Gertrude Thomas's life (and forty-year record of it) leave little doubt
that emancipation required the reconstruction not only of her household
but of subjectivity itself. Like newly freedpeople all over the South, those
at Thomas's plantation left to form their own free families out of the reach
of former owners. As her large household shrank, Thomas's claim to "her
people" also died. She experienced it all as a personal loss and repudiation
of her possessive claim, and she expressed it in many ways, including by
trying to hold on to a child called "Betsy" against the wishes of the girl's
mother, Sarah. Sarah, owned by Thomas previously, was forcibly separated
from her daughter for more than a year and made an elaborate plan to
reclaim her when Betsy was sent to town on an errand. Sarah was forced
to steal her daughter back because Thomas believed Betsy belonged to her
family rather than to Sarah's. "I felt interested in Betsy," she wrote the day
her mother took her. "She was a bright quick child and raised in our family
would have become a good servant. As it is she will be under her mother's
influence and run wild in the streets." Gertrude Thomas could not bear
the claims of family made by servants upon "her negroes." Slaveholding,
the owning of persons over lifetimes and generations, had real subjective effect. "I never liked extorted love or labour," Thomas said. But she
did like both. Slavery—and its expropriated emotional labor—was hard
to replace.[41]

All over the South, African American parents had to fight their old owners and go to court to reclaim their children. Bureau agents in Augusta,
Georgia, were overwhelmed with demands for help. As early as June 1865,
Captain John Emory Bryant issued a public warning about "complaints . . .
that certain parties refuse to allow wives to leave their premises with their
husbands, or parents to take charge of their children." Such people were
put on notice that "freedmen in this regard have the same right that white
citizens have" and interference would be met with "severe punishment."[42]
The most common cases involved children bound out to planters by the
county courts in violation of the state's apprenticeship law, which required
the consent of parents. This widespread practice was designed to thwart
the workings of the Thirteenth Amendment. Barbara Fields described how
on "the very day of emancipation . . . [former slaveholders] began seizing
freedmen's children and whisking them off to the county seats, some-

times in wagonloads, to be bound as apprentices by the county orphans' courts."[43] Many of the children were not orphans at all.

In October 1865, the assistant commissioner in Georgia issued a circular laying out guidelines for binding children out, insisting on the rights of parents, and mandating Bureau oversight, especially in cases involving former owners.[44] Though the Georgia apprenticeship law required parental consent, it left plenty of room for abuse. County courts had great latitude in apprenticing not only orphans but minors whose parents "reside out of the county" or who "are unable to support them." Single mothers were especially vulnerable in this regard. Outraged by the willingness of local authorities to disregard the law and oblige their friends with cheap labor, the Bureau swung into action, investigating parents' complaints and voiding contracts using their own military courts or bringing cases in county courts, appealing to higher state courts, and filing affidavits before US commissioners to transfer cases to federal court. After 1866 they brought apprenticeship cases on the basis of the Civil Rights Act. Even conservatives like General Tillson in Georgia regarded the separation of families as the worst feature of slavery and fought hard to enforce parental rights.[45]

It took the federal government to enforce freedpeople's basic Thirteenth Amendment rights against individuals and state authorities intent on denying them. In Burke County where Gertrude Thomas lived, parents filed so many complaints against their former owners and the apprenticeship practices of the local courts that the assistant commissioner ordered an investigation. The subsequent report identified the "growing evil in this county of the total disregard of its inhabitants to the laws established for indenturing children," and raised fears of a system that encouraged treatment "as severe as they received under the bondage of slavery." In the aftermath, the sub-assistant commissioner ordered the cancellation of a whole slew of apprenticeships, including some "done without the mother's consent."[46] For generations, in many different places of emancipation, mothers had served as the first line of defense of their children's fragile claim to freedom.[47] In the United States in the first years of freedom, it was no different.

Freedpeople's pursuit of their rights to their children dragged Bureau officials into the most private affairs of Southern citizens. Troubling, even traumatic, complications leap off the page in any reading of apprenticeship cases. Many of the mothers and children carried the same surname as the employers they sued, men who were also their former owners. The full nature of the "familial" ties was often unclear, including to federal officials; old owners who staked possessive claims were not uncommonly *themselves fathers* of the children in question. The explosiveness of the postwar process was inseparable from the long history of rape, sexual violence, and coerced intimacy under slavery—and the presence of children born as a result.

The Thomas family's history is again a case in point. Gertrude Thomas spent much of her adulthood fending off the fear that her father and husband shared the general depravity of the sex. Observing that the enslaved woman Lurany, her father's slave, had a daughter Lulah who was "as white as any white child," Thomas's thoughts went immediately to her father. There was "some great mystery about Lurany's case," she acknowledged, since Lurany's children clearly had white fathers—but who? A few years later Thomas got her answer at the reading of her father's will. The knowledge nearly killed her. She never said exactly what, and the "secret" has fascinated many historians.[48] But her father's will, on file in Richmond County, Georgia, leaves little mystery about the paternity of Lurany's children, because it made special arrangements for Lurany and her living children and grandchildren, willing them to his neighbors, two men he obviously trusted. Out of all of Turner Clanton's many slaves, only Lurany's family (and one enslaved man) were mentioned by name or covered by the arrangement in his will.[49] Although neither Gertrude Thomas nor her biographer ever acknowledged it, all doubt about the paternity of Lurany's children was laid to rest in August 1865, when Lurany, now identifying herself as "Mrs. Clanton," walked into the newly opened Freedmen's Bureau Court in Augusta, Georgia, and brought a case against the estate of her former owner, Turner Clanton. The agent and judge, John Emory Bryant, recorded her testimony: that "Mr Clanton was [the] father of children of Mrs Clanton (colored)," that at his death he "gave all their freedom and willed a part of the property to the family," that the executors had withheld the property from them and continued to hold some of the children "as slaves." Lurania Clanton had come to claim her children, their freedom, their property, and the family name.[50] Gertrude Thomas's father was also the father of Lurany's children; Lulah and Amanda were her half-siblings.

The challenge presented by "white slave children" was hardly peculiar to the Thomas family. There were 588,000 mixed-blood people in the United States in 1860, W. E. B. Du Bois pointedly noted. "Sexual chaos was always the possibility of slavery," he wrote.[51] Men like Turner Clanton wreaked havoc on their families, creating such chaos in Southern society that matters of lineage could never be sorted out fully or the fear of incest allayed.[52]

ADJUDICATING PATERNITY

Starting in the summer of 1865, numbers of African American women did something previously unthinkable: They moved, as Lurania Clanton did, to hold their former owners legally accountable for children fathered by them under slavery, filing complaints to force them to acknowledge paternity and pay support. Under slavery, Black women had no legal recourse against sexual predations by any white man. Rape of enslaved women was not a crime; states did not recognize informal marriages of white men with free Black or enslaved women; free Black women could not testify against white men in bastardy proceedings. Seizing the levers of state power newly available to them, formerly enslaved women claimed the civil rights secured by the Thirteenth Amendment and Civil Rights Act.[53] Their fights belonged to a larger struggle to rebuild families and communities in the aftermath of slavery, but also to Black women's pursuit of sexual justice.[54] Initiating complaints at Freedmen's Bureau offices across the South, the women forced agents to confront the horrifying details of the sexual violence routinely perpetrated by masters and to act on what they learned. The testimony the women gave, like that many others would later give about the Ku Klux Klan, was a radical act in itself, a way of "resisting violence discursively," as Kidada Williams put it.[55] They did it to "compel" the men to support their children and enable the mothers to put their new households on a viable footing. But they also did it, as one said, "to obtain justice for myself and my children."[56]

Freedmen's Bureau agents were the front line of the national state, and they pursued the women's charges, often doggedly. In forcing local white men to support their illegitimate children, Bureau men's moral sense aligned with their desire to get freedwomen and children off the welfare roll. But their reports make it clear that what they learned often outraged their sense of justice. Agents initially inclined to give the benefit of the doubt to accused white men (some of them powerful in the community) often reversed course once they heard the women's testimony. She "has made the matter appear in a very different light from what you did," one agent wrote Dr. James Cook after he took Eliza Cook's deposition.[57]

Even a small sample of cases conveys the enormity of what the women exposed about slavery.[58] Nine of ten freedwomen identified their *former owner* as the father of the children in question, establishing beyond a shadow of a doubt the sexual violence at the core of their experience as enslaved women. A disturbing number of the women (seven of ten) carried their masters' family name, as Eliza Cook did, confirming that slaveholders' paternalist pretensions had violent, substantive sexual meaning— even as the men tried to deny biological paternity. Numbers of the women and children were described as "white," or almost white, evidence of an intergenerational pattern of sexual violence such as had been suffered by Lurania Clanton. Lucy Ann Bibb was "as white as white people," and two sisters who were described as "mixed-race" women together had eight children, "all of which," the agent reported in shock, "are white." Taken together, the cases present a horrifying portrait of what women suffered under slavery and of the redress they sought as free persons.[59]

One devastating detail that emerges from the women's testimony is how many of those seeking justice had been themselves bought as children or born into the families of the men who raped them. Mary Flower testified under oath that she had been bought by Jesse Flower when she was about eleven years old; Isabella Holley said she came into her master's "possession" when she was twelve and remained with him until she was "emancipated by the National Government." Flower testified that Jesse Flower would not let her marry anyone else, and that he had five children with her. Flora Murphy was born and raised in the house of the master who fathered her children.[60]

In depositions in offices from Virginia to Texas, the women offered narratives of abuse that range from outright rape to the claim, made by more than one woman, that her former owner and the father of her children had "lived with her as a wife" or "had always promised to be a husband to me." Whatever the details, the cases overlap in essentials—ownership—rendering any question of consent irrelevant. Isabella Holley swore under oath that William Holley was the father of nine children with her, four of whom were still living. "These children were all his, he being their father," the agent noted emphatically in his report. Selma Brown said simply that eight years previously her owner "forced her to submit to his desires." Many of the women ended those long relationships themselves the moment they were free to do so. But a number testified that they had been "driven out" by the former master or mistress at precisely the moment slavery ended. "Since I have been made free he neglects and refuses to render me any assistance to support myself or my children," Flora Murphy testified. Freedom changed her master's calculations—and hers too. He threatened to kill her if she went to the Bureau. She went nonetheless, to "obtain justice for myself and children." John Holbeck, she told the agent, must "be compelled to contribute something toward the support of *his* and my children."[61]

Paternity cases filed with the Freedmen's Bureau leave little doubt about the reach of the central state into the most intimate realms of Southern families and households, white and Black, as part of the enforcement of basic Thirteenth Amendment rights. They show African American women, emancipated not six months before, using the federal government to redress the sexual injuries of slavery, force accountability for past harms, assemble the resources by which they could establish themselves and their children as free families in free homes, and force the recognition of their civil rights as free people. Publicly identifying the white fathers of their children, these cases forced agents to adjudicate paternity claims that pitted the word of a freedwoman against that of her former master and to act on the results. The facts that emerged upon investigation confirmed the truthfulness of the women's accounts and in some cases were so shocking that federal officials felt compelled to act in the public interest.

That was the judgment arrived at by the provost marshal of Gallatin, Tennessee, in the case of the sisters Mary and Rachel Malone. Their mother, Rebecca Malone, initiated the case in July 1865, at the Freedmen's Bureau office about twelve miles from the plantation on which she and her daughters still lived, as when enslaved. Rebecca Malone reported their former owner, David Chenault, to the local Freedmen's Bureau, after he ordered her daughters off his plantation. Upon sworn testimony of Rachel and Rebecca Malone, the agent learned that Chenault was the father of Mary Malone's six children, four of whom were still living, and "all of which," he said, "are white." Chenault had a longstanding relationship with Mary. He had assured her mother that he intended to "buy [Mary] as his wife . . . and that neither herself nor her children should ever be slaves." He did buy Mary, and he bought Rebecca's other two children. But Chenault also forced a sexual relationship on the younger daughter, Rachel, and had two children with her. He tried to hide his paternity by making Rachel give away the first child, which she refused to do. Both sisters, Rachel and Mary, swore under oath that they had never had sexual intercourse with any other man. Chenault had three additional children with "his white wife," as Rebecca Malone called her.

Chenault had taken such sexual license as a white man and master that he had a Black wife, a white wife, and another Black woman, all mothers of his children, some born within two months of each other. When Rebecca reviled Chenault "about such conduct, having two sisters and wife in the same yard, he said, well Aunt 'Becca' I can't help it" and begged "me to keep the matter secret, which promise I kept until his abusive treatment, I could not withhold it longer." When the provost marshal received the case record, he sent it up the chain of command to Major General Clinton B. Fisk, the head of the Freedmen's Bureau in Tennessee, recommending it as "one wanting special attention." The "citizens want some example" to be made in such cases, he insisted, invoking the public interest in holding Chenault accountable. "The cause of this colored family is worthy of vindication." Chenault was subsequently instructed to make three cash payments to the women "by order of Genl. Fisk."[62] The involvement of a high official in securing some measure of justice for a "colored family" is one striking example of what had changed with freedwomen's new access to the levers of federal government in their campaign for sexual justice and civil rights.

The freedwomen who brought these suits knew the law and pushed the federal government to enforce their rights against the white supremacist regime of Southern legislators and courts.[63] Eliza Cook began her effort to make her master pay to support his children when the ink on the Civil Rights Act was barely dry. She informed a Bureau agent in July 1866 that since the bastardy laws of North Carolina discriminated against Black women, she was entitled to relief "by and under the Civil Rights Bill passed by the Congress of the United States in its last session."[64] The Act had been passed in April. She refused to settle her case against James Cook, the son of her former owner, and when she insisted on pursuing it in US District Court, the federal government backed her up. Drawn into the awful details of the paternity of her nine children, the local agent turned to the head of the Bureau in Raleigh. They sought legal advice about whether they could, in fact, bring the case in federal district court under the civil rights bill as Eliza Cook wanted to do, *because* she "is not embraced in the bastardy acts of North Carolina as white women are." By that point, he and all the other Bureau men fully accepted the truth of Cook's bastardy suit and supported her right to redress. "All the children begotten on her body by said Cook were born while she was a slave," the case stated plainly, and now she must find relief through "the interposition of military authority." Her case was put before the US District Court as a test case for the enforcement of the civil rights of free people as conferred by the Thirteenth Amendment and defined by the Civil Rights Act. Judge George Washington Brooks refused to hear it on the grounds that the Civil Rights Act was not intended to create new laws to remedy injustices for slavery. It is not clear what happened to Eliza Cook's case. When her file closed, the acting sub-assistant commissioner in North Carolina had just sought instructions from General O. O. Howard, the head of the Freedmen's Bureau, since all "resources through the Civil Law seems to be exhausted."[65]

CONCLUSION

Freedpeople were determined to make the promise of the Thirteenth Amendment real in relation to their marital and parental rights. But implementing even those basic civil rights required destroying the edifice of slavery in law and social life in the post-emancipation South. That meant forcing revision of every Southern state constitution and body of laws, and the robust intervention of the federal government in every locality in the former Confederate states. To trace that process is to see the reach of the state into the intimate affairs of Southerners, white and Black, touching on the most personal matters of marriage and the family, love and belonging, sex, race, and power in what was a formative historical moment for the nation.

This *is* the history of the state, even if political historians and those interested in state formation continue to ignore it. In his recent book *The Second Founding*, Eric Foner leaves no doubt about the enormity of the task the destruction of slavery posed for the federal government. "Plantation slavery was a total institution," he writes, "the foundation of comprehensive systems of labor, politics, and race relations."[66] But, as we have just seen, it was more than that. Slavery was also, even more fundamentally, the foundation of a system of family relations and law, without which no state can function. Any new political history of Reconstruction will have to account for that. Only then can we take the proper measure of what emancipation required by way of political transformation and central state power in the period of the Civil War and Reconstruction.

We do need a new history of the "state in society." And William Novak and others are right in insisting that we should not construct a history of state formation defined exclusively by the size of the federal government. But surely any such history of the US state would have to account for temporal change in the division of power, authority, and jurisdiction between the separate states and the federal government that came with the second founding. It would also have to embrace a more expansive definition of "the political." Given what we have learned here about the centrality of "domestic relations" to reconstructing the constitutional and political order, it is abundantly clear that any "new" history of the state will have to abandon the intellectual sexism that continues to plague the field and build on insights about the boundaries of the personal and the political, public and private, and the intertwining of marriage, family, sexuality, and the state, built up over twenty-five years of feminist scholarship.

NOTES

1. For two classic statements, see Eric Foner, *Reconstruction: America's Unfinished Revolution, 1863–1877* (New York: Harper and Row, 1988); and Richard Bensel, *Yankee Leviathan: The Origins of Central State Authority in America, 1859–1877* (New York: Cambridge University Press, 1990).

2. Camille Robcis, *The Law of Kinship: Anthropology, Psychoanalysis, and the Family in Twentieth Century France* (Ithaca, NY: Cornell University Press, 2013), 4; and Stephanie McCurry, *Women's War: Fighting and Surviving the Civil War* (Cambridge, MA: Belknap Press of Harvard University Press, 2019).

3. Akhil Reed Amar, *America's Constitution: A Biography* (New York: Random House, 2005), 349–402, quotations 351, 380, 360; Bruce Ackerman, *We the People: Transformations* (Cambridge, MA: Belknap Press of Harvard University Press, 1998); and Alexander Tsesis, *The Thirteenth Amendment and American Freedom: A Legal History* (New York: New York University Press, 2004).

4. William Novak, "The Myth of the Weak American State," *American Historical Review* 113 (June 2008): 752–72; and Novak, "The Concept of the State in American History," in *Boundaries of the State in U.S. History*, ed. James T. Sparrow, William J. Novak, and Stephen W. Sawyer (Chicago and London: University of Chicago Press, 2015), 325–49, quotation 341. For the larger agenda, see the introduction to *Boundaries of the State in U.S. History*, 1–15; and Brian Balogh, *A Government Out of Sight: The Mystery of National Authority in Nineteenth Century America* (New York: Cambridge University Press, 2009). For feminist scholarship, see Nancy F. Cott, *Public Vows: A History of Marriage and the Nation* (Cambridge, MA: Harvard University Press, 2000); and Amy Dru Stanley, *From Bondage to Contract: Wage Labor, Marriage, and the Market in the Age of Slave Emancipation* (New York: Cambridge University Press, 1999). My views are laid out in Stephanie McCurry, *Masters of Small Worlds: Yeoman Farmers, Gender Relations, and the Political Culture of the Antebellum South Carolina Low Country* (New York: Oxford University Press, 1995); and *Confederate Reckoning: Power and Politics in the Civil War South* (Cambridge, MA: Harvard University Press, 2010).

5. Judith Surkis, *Sex, Law, and Sovereignty in French Algeria, 1830–1930* (Ithaca, NY, and London: Cornell University Press, 2019), 137.

6. Michael Vorenberg, *Final Freedom: The Civil War, the Abolition of Slavery and the Thirteenth Amendment* (Cambridge: Cambridge University Press, 2001); and Amy Stanley, "Instead of Waiting for the Thirteenth Amendment: The War Power, Slave Marriage, and Inviolate Human Rights," *American Historical Review* 115, no. 3 (June 2010): 732–65.

7. Steven Hahn et al., eds., *Freedom: A Documentary History of Emancipation, 1861–1867,* ser. 3, vol. 1, *Land and Labor, 1865* (Chapel Hill: University of North Carolina Press, 2008), 392. Chris Hayes calculates its contemporary value as a share of household wealth (16 percent in 1860) at $10 trillion; Hayes, "The New Abolitionism," *The Nation*, April 22, 2014. Johnson, "Amnesty Proclamation" (May 29), in *The Papers of Andrew Johnson*, vol. 8, ed. Leroy P. Graf and Ralph W. Haskins (Knoxville: University of Tennessee Press, 1989), 128–31.

8. *Emancipation Proclamation*, January 1, 1863, https://www.ourdocuments.gov/doc.php?flash=false&doc=34. The Proclamation freed only those enslaved in Confederate states and parts of states still in rebellion.

9. Foner, *Reconstruction*, 23.

10. More expansive versions were defeated. See Cott, *Public Vows*, 79–81.

11. Vorenberg, *Final Freedom*, 252, 216–32.

12. *Amnesty Proclamation*, May 29, 1865.

13. *Journal of the Proceedings of the Convention of the People of Georgia, Held in Milledgeville in October and November 1865, Together with the Ordinances and Resolutions Adopted* (R. M. Orme & Sons, 1865), Art, 1, Sec. 20, see pp. 38, 139; and Dan T. Carter, *When the War Was Over: The Failure of Self-Reconstruction in the*

South, 1865–1867 (Baton Rouge: Louisiana State University Press, 1985). Michael Perman, *Reunion Without Compromise: The South and Reconstruction, 1865–1868* (Cambridge and New York: Cambridge University Press, 1973).

14. Vorenberg, *Final Freedom*, 219, 229.

15. Black Codes are reprinted in *Laws in Relation to Freedmen*, 35th Cong., Sen. Exec. Doc., No. 6.

16. Vorenberg, *Final Freedom*, 230.

17. *Journal of the Proceedings of the Convention of the People of Georgia . . . 1865*, Article V, Sec. 5, Sec 9.

18. Surkis, *Sex, Law, and Sovereignty*; and Emmanuelle Saada, *Empire's Children: Race, Filiation, and Citizenship in the French Colonies* (Chicago and London: University of Chicago Press, 2012).

19. Tsesis, *The Thirteenth Amendment*, 21; and Thomas Morris, *Southern Slavery and the Law* (Chapel Hill: University of North Carolina Press, 1996).

20. *Partus sequitur ventrem* held the status of children born in the colonies to be bond or free according to the status of the mother. Law of Virginia, passed 1662.

21. Tera W. Hunter, *Bound in Wedlock: Slave and Free Black Marriage in the Nineteenth Century* (Cambridge, MA: Belknap Press of Harvard University Press, 2017), 85.

22. Cott, *Public Vows*; and McCurry, *Women's War*, 63–123.

23. The concept of free homes is from Thavolia Glymph, *Out of the House of Bondage: The Transformation of the Plantation Household* (New York and Cambridge: Cambridge University Press, 2008).

24. "An Act to Define the Term 'Persons of Color'" [No. 250]; "An Act to Prescribe and Regulate the Relation of Husband and Wife Between Persons of Color" [No. 252]; "An Act to Prescribe and Regulate the Relation of Parent and Child Among Persons of Color, in this State and for other Purposes" [No. 253]; "An Act to Alter and Amend the Laws of this State in Relation to Apprentices," *Acts of the General Assembly of the State of Georgia* (Milledgeville, GA, 1866), pp. 239, 240, 6–8.

25. For a complete list of marriage laws passed by Southern states, see Freedmen's Affairs: Laws Relating to Freedmen, 39th Congress, 2nd Sess., 1866–1867, S. Ex doc. 6.

26. Hunter, *Bound in Wedlock*.

27. Act No. 252, *Acts of the General Assembly*; and Peggy Pascoe, *What Comes Naturally: Miscegenation Law and the Making of Race in America* (Oxford: Oxford University Press, 200), 17–74.

28. Act No. 254, *Acts of the General Assembly*.

29. Act No. 253, *Acts of the General Assembly*.

30. Karen E. Fields and Barbara J. Fields, *Racecraft: The Soul of Inequality in American Life* (London and New York: Verso, 2012), 11; and Hannah Rosen, *Terror in the Heart of Freedom: Citizenship, Sexual Violence, and the Meaning of Race in the Postemancipation South* (Chapel Hill: University of North Carolina Press, 2009). Laws against interracial marriage were often struck down by Reconstruction courts; Pascoe, *What Comes Naturally*.

31. Donald G. Nieman, *To Set the Law in Motion: The Freedmen's Bureau and the Legal Rights of Blacks, 1865–1868* (Millwood, NY: KTO Press, 1979).

32. Brig. Gen. Davis Tillson, Augusta, GA, April 7, 1866, General Orders, Special Orders and Circulars Issued, vol. 26, pp. 338–42, Georgia assistant commissioner (hereafter GAC), RG 105 (Records of the US Bureau of Refugees, Freedmen, and Abandoned Lands), National Archives, [FSSP A-10919]. Subsequent notes will cite RG 105 sources more briefly by using only the file numbers indicating where copies of the originals reside in the files of the Freedmen and Southern Society Project, University of Maryland, College Park. On "moments of legal uncertainty," see Surkis, *Sex, Law, and Sovereignty*, 9.

33. James L. Roark, *Masters Without Slaves: Southern Planters in the Civil War and Reconstruction* (New York: W. W. Norton, 1977).

34. Foner, *Reconstruction;* Robert J. Kaczorowksi, *The Politics of Judicial Interpretation: The Federal Courts, Department of Justice, and Civil Rights, 1866–1876* (New York: Fordham University Press, 2005; orig. pub. 1985); and Nieman, *To Set the Law in Motion.* The MRAs worked to protect African Americans' civil rights in face of white supremacist violence. Alan Trelease, *White Terror: The Ku Klux Klan Conspiracy and Southern Reconstruction* (New York: Harper and Row, 1971).

35. On plural legal systems and jurisdictional fights in occupation governments, see R. W. Kostal, "The Alchemy of Occupation: Karl Loewenstein and the Legal Reconstruction of Germany, 1945–1946," *Law and History Review* 29, no. 1 (2011): 1–52; and Surkis, *Sex, Law, and Sovereignty.* Lauren Benton and Richard J. Ross, eds., *Legal Pluralism and Empires, 1500–1850* (New York: New York University Press, 2013).

36. Nieman, *To Set the Law in Motion*, 4; Kaczorowski, *Politics of Judicial Interpretation*, 24, 57; and Paul Cimbala, *Under the Guardianship of the Nation: The Freedmen's Bureau and the Reconstruction of Georgia, 1865–1870* (Athens and London: University of Georgia Press, 1997). Federal courts included longstanding US District Courts, and US Circuit Courts newly expanded in 1869.

37. Department of Justice involvement and use of federal courts picked up in 1870 under the Grant administration and was most notable in the Klan trials (1871–1872). Kaczorowski, *Politics of Judicial Interpretation*, chapter 3.

38. On the affective politics of slavery, see especially Annette Gordon-Reed, *The Hemingses of Monticello: An American Family* (New York: W. W. Norton and Co., 2008).

39. Diary, Ella Gertrude Clanton Thomas Papers (hereafter cited as EGCT Papers), David M. Rubenstein Rare Book & Manuscript Library, Duke University. The published version is Virginia Ingraham Burr, ed., *The Secret Eye: The Journal of Ella Gertrude Clanton Thomas, 1848–1889* (Chapel Hill: University of North Carolina Press, 1990).

40. Roark, *Masters Without Slaves*; Eugene D. Genovese, *Roll, Jordan, Roll: The World the Slaves Made* (New York: Pantheon, 1974); and Stephanie McCurry, "The Two Faces of Republicanism: Gender and Proslavery Politics in Antebellum South Carolina," *Journal of American History* 78, no. 4 (March 1992): 1245–62.

41. Burr, *Secret Eye*, 267–68, 370; and McCurry, *Women's War*, 124–202.

42. Captain John Emory Bryant's Labor Regulations, June 12, 1865, reprinted in Cimbala, *The Freedmen's Bureau: Reconstructing the American South After the Civil War* (Malabar, FL: Krieger, 2005), 149–52.

43. Barbara Jeanne Fields, *Slavery and Freedom on the Middle Ground: Maryland in the Nineteenth Century* (New Haven, CT, and London: Yale University Press, 1985), 138; and Karen L. Zipf, "Reconstructing 'Free Woman': African-American Women, Apprenticeship and Custody Rights During Reconstruction," *Journal of Women's History* 12, no. 1 (Spring 2000): 8–31.

44. Circular No. 3, Brig. Gen. Tillson, Oct. 14, 1865, ser. 636, vol. 26, GAC [FSSP A-10916].

45. On Bureau use of federal courts to enforce the Civil Rights Act, see Nieman, *To Set the Law in Motion*, chapter 3; and Cimbala, *Under the Guardianship of the Nation,* 194–203.

46. Capt. Geo. R. Walbridge to Col. C. C. Sibley, Savannah, GA, Feb. 19, 1867, T. R. Littlefield to Lt. W. F. Martins, Jan. 23, 1867, all filed with M-16 1866, Letters Received, ser, 631, GAC [FSSP A-289].

47. Elizabeth Colwill, "Freedwomen's Familial Politics: Marriage, War, and Rites of Registry in Post-Emancipation Saint-Domingue," in *Gender, War and Politics: The Wars of Revolution and Liberation—Transatlantic Comparisons, 1775–1820*, ed. Karen Hagemann, Gisele Mettele, and Jane Randall (Basingstoke: Palgrave Macmillan, 2010), 10–24.

48. Diary, Apr. 15, 1864, July 4, 1864, and Aug. 27, 1864, EGCT Papers, Duke University, ed. Burr, *Secret Eye*, Aug. 27, 1864, 231–32.

49. Will of Turner Clanton, Probate Records, Richmond County, Georgia, Family Search.Org, accessed July 20, 2016. The will also stated that heirs who challenged the provision would be disinherited.

50. Court Docket Augusta 1865, J. E. Bryant, [Entry No. 5], Records of the Field Offices for the State of Georgia, Bureau of Refugees Freedmen and Abandoned Lands 1865–1872, M1903, Reel 48, archive.org.

51. W. E. B. Du Bois, *Black Reconstruction in America, 1860–1880* (New York: Free Press, 1998), 35–36.

52. Alexis Broderick Neumann, "American Incest: Kinship, Sex and Commerce in Slavery and Reconstruction," PhD diss., University of Pennsylvania, 2018.

53. The Civil Rights Act was written to define and enforce the rights the Thirteenth Amendment secured. The amendment provided congressional authority to do so.

54. Crystal N. Feimster, "'What If I Am a Woman': Black Women's Campaigns for Sexual Justice and Citizenship," in *World the Civil War Made*, ed. Gregory Downs and Kate Masur (Chapel Hill: University of North Carolina Press, 2015), 249–68.

55. Kidada Williams, *They Left Great Marks on Me: African American Testimonies of Racial Violence from Emancipation to World War 1* (New York: NYU Press, 2013), 6.

56. Flora Murphy to D. T. Corbin, May 23, 1866, Letters Received, ser. 3201, Charleston Dist. SC, RG 105 [FSSP A-7174].

57. A. G. Brady to Dr. James Cook, July 12, 1866, BB-094 1866, Letters Received, ser. 15, box 25, RG 105 [FSSP A-2946].

58. Based on ten cases identified in a selective search of the files of the Freedmen and Southern Society Project. See also Alexis Broderick, "'If I Had My Justice': Freedwomen, The Freedmen's Bureau, and Paternity in the Post-Emancipation

South," in *Expanding the Boundaries of Black Intellectual History*, ed. Leslie Alexander et al. (Evanston, IL: Northwestern University Press, 2021).

59. Lucy Ann Bibb to OB, Louis CH, Gordonvil, VA, June 29, 1867 [FSSP A-8177]; Deposition of Rebecca Malone, Gallatin, TN, July 15, 1865 [FSSP A-6169].

60. Deposition of Mary Flower, Macon, GA, April 4, 1866 [FSSP A-5092]; Isabella Holley to Maj. A. W. Bolenius, June 28, 1867, [FSSP A-2997]; Deposition of Flora Murphy.

61. Deposition of Mary Flower; Lucy Ann Bibb to OB; Isabel Holley to Bolenius; Deposition of Selma Brown, Wharton County, Texas, May 1867 [FSSP A-3167]; Deposition of Flora Murphy.

62. Deposition of Rachel Malone, July 15, 1865, Deposition of Rebecca Malone, July 18, 1865, Deposition of Mary Malone, July 18, 1865 and letter of Lt. Robert McMillan (provost marshal) to Major General Fisk, Gallatin, TN, July 18, 1865, Order of Genl Fisk, July 26, 1865 [FSSP A-6169].

63. Laura Edwards has recently criticized the overemphasis on rights claims in the Reconstruction literature, but the paternity cases evidence the new language and redress available by civil rights laws. Edwards, "Reconstruction and the History of Governance," in Downs and Masur, *The World the Civil War Made*, 22–45.

64. Deposition of Eliza Cook, July 12, 1866, Letter of Lieut. McAlpine, Assistant Commissioner to Col. F. Wells, July 13 or 15, 1866 [FSSP A-2946].

65. North Carolina Assist. Commissioner J. Bomford to General O. O. Howard, December 13, 1866 [FSSP A-2946]; Zipf, "Reconstructing 'Free Woman.'" Eric Foner discusses Supreme Court jurisprudence on the Thirteenth Amendment and Civil Rights Act which began in 1872, but clearly the adjudication (and narrowing) of federal government authority started earlier in the lower courts in cases like these. Foner, *The Second Founding: How the Civil War and Reconstruction Remade the Constitution* (New York: W. W. Norton, 2019), 128–32.

66. Foner, *The Second Founding*, 40.

2

The Comstock Apparatus

JEFFREY ESCOFFIER, WHITNEY STRUB,
AND JEFFREY PATRICK COLGAN

Between 1873 and 1957, sexual discourse and behavior in the United States
was regulated by the political and legal framework established by the federal "Comstock Act" of 1873. This law, entitled the "Act for the Suppression
of Trade in and Circulation of Obscene Literature and Articles of Immoral
Use," was passed primarily at the instigation of moral reformer Anthony
Comstock. The law stated that

> No obscene, lewd, or lascivious book, pamphlet, picture, paper, print
> or other publications of an indecent character, or any article or thing
> designed or intended for the prevention of conception or procuring of
> abortion, nor any article or thing intended or adapted for indecent or
> immoral use or nature, nor any written or printed card, circular, book,
> pamphlet, advertisement or notice of any kind giving information, di-
> rectly or indirectly, where, or how, or of whom, or by what means either
> of the things before mentioned may be obtained or made, nor any let-
> ter upon the envelope of which, or postal-card upon which indecent or
> scurrilous epithets may be written or printed, shall be carried in the
> mail. . . .[1]

Prior to the passage of the Comstock Act, the Customs Act of 1842 (enforced only by US customs inspectors) had prohibited the importation
of obscene literature into the United States. Before then, the regulation
of sexual morality, including obscenity, was typically the responsibility
of local governments. Beginning in the 1850s, publishers of pornography
sought to avoid local prosecution by distributing pornography through the
mail. During the Civil War, Union soldiers routinely sought and received

"fancy" (i.e., erotic) novels and pornographic images through the mail—something that horrified Anthony Comstock when he served in the army during the war. In 1865, in an effort to restrict the "obscene books and pictures" circulating among the Union soldiers, the Post Office asked Congress for the power to ban all obscene materials from the mail by making it a crime to mail such material.[2] The resulting Postal Act of 1865 was the first example of legislation at the federal level to regulate the domestic distribution of obscenity. The act failed to have visible impact on the regulation of obscene materials, however, because the Post Office was prohibited from opening sealed envelopes, and had no way of identifying obscene materials while they were in the mail. The law depended on recipients complaining to local authorities.

This was the state of affairs when Anthony Comstock, the twenty-eight-year-old leader of the nascent New York Society for the Suppression of Vice, went to Washington in 1872–1873, with support from the YMCA as well as his own organization to lobby for the passage of what eventually became the Comstock Act.[3] The law passed Congress without any significant debate. President Grant was apparently unwilling to sign the bill unless he was assured that Comstock himself would be enforcing it.[4] While Congress made Comstock an *unpaid* postal inspector, he was, nevertheless, considered an official of the Post Office and his appointment gave him *authority* and *the capacity to make arrests*. The law in general was breathtakingly broad, not just in its elevation of private citizen Anthony Comstock, but in the way it enabled the regulation of sexual morality to move from local communities to the national level. It did so through the Post Office, the nation's major communication medium and at that time the most important and largest branch of the federal government. The Post Office was the one federal agency present in every county in every state.[5]

In addition to utilizing the wide geographic reach of the Post Office itself, the new law appointed Comstock as a postal inspector and applied a vague and much broader definition of "obscenity" that included sexually explicit materials, nudity and "racy" writing, photographs, and drawings; descriptions of sexual physiology, contraception, and/or the termination of pregnancy; as well as political or polemical discussions of free love, the legal status of marriage, and psychological or spiritual advice relating to marital sexuality. The law also banned any indecent, scurrilous, or salacious public statements more generally. In addition to the restrictions on public speech, the 1873 law sought to prohibit many forms of sexual behavior indirectly through the regulation and restriction of economic activities that provided materials and/or services that might be construed as the promotion of "lust" or "vice," to use Comstock's own terms. Items used to prevent pregnancy (condoms) or to facilitate sexual pleasure (dildos) were considered obscene under the law. It offered no specific enforcement mechanisms beyond judges issuing warrants to seize material in response to written complaints; it was precisely this hazy terrain that Comstock would concretize then dramatically expand.

The 1873 Comstock Act was thus the first step in the creation of a federal regulatory framework to enforce Christian sexual morality, as it was understood at the time, in the United States. This framework, much of which consisted of regulation at the state and local level, eventually covered a broad range of moral offenses, prohibiting drinking and public amusements on the Sabbath, ending gambling, pornography, and prostitution, and achieving temperance, and sought to use the state to institute a Christian society.[6] While decidedly novel in its scope and ambition, the application of this framework depended upon existing nineteenth-century tools of statecraft.[7] The nineteenth-century American system of government bifurcated political sovereignty into two separate structures: (1) a diffuse federal structure that covered external and interstate transactions; and (2) highly concentrated instruments of power at state and local levels.[8] The concentration of power to affect individuals at state and local levels, and the absence of any constitutional authority for the federal government to regulate sexual conduct, as well as the law's omission of enforcement mechanisms or financial compensation for Comstock, should have presented serious obstacles to the law's efficacy.[9]

Yet the opposite was true, and this presents a serious puzzle for historians. Comstock himself bragged that over the course of his career as a "vice crusader," he had arrested 4,000 people, driven fifteen people to suicide, destroyed more than four million pictures, and seized fifteen tons of books and 142 tons of printing-press plates.[10] Comstock had prosecuted publishers, booksellers, health activists, proponents of birth control, feminists, free love advocates, religious freethinkers, sexual reformers, and abortionists. Comstock routinely sacrificed numerous other laws in order to enforce the 1873 Act. He had no compunctions about soliciting materials to entrap his targets or purchasing obscene publications or banned services (abortions, contraceptives) under false names.[11] Though previous scholarship has acknowledged and studied the outsized character of Anthony Comstock, and dealt with the civil libertarian movements that would lead to the Act's ultimate loss of authority, the drama and zealotry of Comstock's methods have often distracted scholars from conducting a rigorous and systematic analysis of Comstock's regulatory apparatus and the structural bases that ensured its prolonged success.

A focus on statecraft (rather than Comstock's indomitable, relentless, and unscrupulous character) serves to emphasize Comstock's success as a result, in part, of broader strategies developed by the federal government during these years in order to expand into arenas of governance constitutionally left to state or local governments.[12] One of these strategies was *surrogacy*—which involved the federal government, as the historian Gary Gerstle has argued, "using a power explicitly granted by the Constitution to expand its authority into forbidden legislative terrain." Surrogacy works by employing an existing federal structure to extend federal power into an area and to meet policy aims not designated or sanctioned in the Constitution; federal authority acts through a pre-existing arm of the government in ways beyond its primary and customary functions.[13]

The Comstock Act was, for example, focused on stopping the promotion, sale, and distribution of the proscribed items through the US mail. It rested on the federal government's power to supervise the mail and regulate interstate commerce—this was the power explicitly granted by the Constitution. Surrogacy came into play when that power was expanded to proscribe the advertising, distribution, and sale of "obscene" literature and materials through the mail. The law also specified criminal penalties for violating the law:

> That whoever . . . shall be deemed guilty of a misdemeanor, and on conviction thereof in any court of the United States . . . he shall be imprisoned at hard labor in the penitentiary for not less than six months nor more than five years for each offense, or fined not less than one hundred dollars nor more than two thousand dollars, with costs of court.[14]

A further strategy utilized by the federal government to get around constitutional limitations was *privatization*, which entailed letting private groups assume work that the federal government could not.[15] In such cases, these private bodies ostensibly covered the cost of those services. Thus, Anthony Comstock and the New York Society for the Suppression of Vice were given responsibility to provide an officially sanctioned public service ("the suppression of vice") to the American public at no direct cost to the federal government. The Society, an offshoot of the YMCA in its mission to provide Christian support and reinforce "social purity" among young men, was founded in the philanthropic vein—and in this vein, the Society paid Comstock an annual salary and covered his expenses. The formation of cooperative local societies for the suppression of vice in many of the nation's largest cities during these years further spread Comstock's power through privatization.

The use of the tools of *surrogacy* and *privatization* thus allowed the Comstock apparatus to bypass constitutionally imposed limits and construct a regulatory structure that significantly altered American sexual conduct and discourse for more than eighty years. Related structural elements that enabled the incredible success of Comstockery included the vague yet broadly inclusive definition of obscenity; the passing of the "little Comstock laws" in the states that synchronized the enforcement of federal law with the states' police powers; the establishment of local vice societies to aid the law's enforcement; and the publicity given to Comstock's dramatic arrests and trials to intimidate his opponents.

These interlocking structural features, along with the absence of an organized civil libertarian movement until World War I, are what made Comstockery so effective and long-lived. Comstock not only deeply influenced the way sexuality was regulated during his long reign; he also affected the state. While Anthony Comstock effectively dictated the terms of his own historical narrativization, he missed one—and perhaps only one—opportunity at self-promotion, namely emphasizing his central role in Reconstruction-era state building.[16] While recent scholarly work has helped dispel what William Novak calls "the myth of the weak American state" in the nineteenth century, Comstock's role in reconfiguring the state is still more obscured than clarified by historians' reliance on moralism and censorship as analytical lenses.[17] Comstock built on a foundation that preceded the "salary revolution," in which prosecutors, tax collectors, naval officers, and even diplomats carried out the work of the state for direct personal compensation from "clients," and his efforts paralleled those of contemporaneous blurrings of public/private interests in the American Humane Society and temperance movement.[18] Moreover, Comstock alone harnessed the ascending power of the mass media. He weaponized celebrity and in many ways enforced his authority through it, shaping intimate governance from the center of a limelight that nonetheless kept the structural operations of his project shrouded in darkness, and capitalizing on the vagueness of his anomalous, liminal position between official government agent and concerned citizen to render even more opaque the nature of his power. This chapter considers the whole apparatus that Comstock constructed as one window into the burgeoning of federal power over intimate life during the late nineteenth and early twentieth centuries.

THE COMSTOCK APPARATUS

While sex was not a "polite" topic in American society before the Civil War, it was not an altogether forbidden topic. Sexual discourse was a multivocal network of normalized and heterodox expressions that consisted of several

distinct frameworks, among them a pre-colonial vernacular and folk discourse that had been reinvigorated by the Great Awakening of evangelical
Christianity in the 1820s and 1830s; a free-thinking discourse that stressed
reproduction, contraception, health, and the physiology of sex that had
emerged among labor activists, feminists, and social reformers and then
was later picked up by the advocates of free love, participants in sexual uto-
pian communities, and anarchists; and finally, that of a freewheeling and
outspoken male subculture that emerged in the largest cities in the 1840s
which was organized around prostitution, theater, boxing, and drinking,
and became known as the "sporting" life.[19]

The Comstock Act did not *directly* regulate or proscribe specific forms
of sexual behavior, nor was it an example of "classical" censorship—that
is, either prohibiting the production of obscene materials at their source
or directly excising obscene passages from various publications.[20] Rather,
the Comstock regime focused on *regulating the markets* in which specific
products that elicited "proscribed" behavior were sold. The framework of
law and discourse created by Comstock's implementation of the 1873 law
consisted of a definition of obscenity, federal and state laws, judicial strategies, voluntary organizations, and sensationalist journalism, which added
together made it a powerful means of influencing sexual attitudes and
conduct. The framework reshaped sexual discourse in the United States
and drove sexual speech into the private realm, excluding from public discourse explicit discussion of the physiology of reproduction and the physical and social consequences of sexual behavior both inside and outside
marriage. It did not distinguish educational, informational, and scientific
representations of sex from prurient ones. It implicitly condemned sex
outside marriage, homosexuality, and other nonnormative sexualities.[21]
And it fostered the development of black markets for contraception, abortion, and pornography.[22]

The Comstock apparatus (as a whole) included the 1873 Act, "Little
Comstock" laws adopted by individual states criminalizing the advertisement and sale of obscene items, local vice societies that supported
Comstock's endeavors (through surveillance and reportage), journalistic
and public discourse such as the press hailing or condemning Comstock,
and the courts (to establish the legal definition of "obscenity"). The apparatus indirectly targeted particular types of sexual activity (and in corollary the individuals who practiced them): *masturbation* (and the arousal
through *sexual fantasies*) was the behavior encouraged by pornography
and other sexual aids (dildos, etc.); *nonreproductive heterosexual intercourse*
was enabled by the availability of contraception and abortion; and *non-*

marital sexuality by the doctrines of "free love." Within this framework, three key categories of targeted persons emerged: (1) the sexually obsessed young man masturbating and engaging in illicit sex; (2) the contracepting woman; and (3) the free-lover male or female who sought to justify sexual intercourse outside marriage. The focus on such categories of persons not only allowed for new concepts with which to parse the social milieu, but they could also lead individuals to see themselves anew and self-identify in relation to forms of illegal and socially condemned sexual behavior.[23] For example, the specter of the sex-obsessed young man could serve as a cautionary tale for the onanist, a worry for the conservative parent, and a perceived menace against which religious groups could rally. Only heterosexual reproductive sexuality within marriage—what Freud ironically called "civilized sexual morality"—was an acceptable form of sexuality.[24]

While Comstock was undoubtedly sincere in his belief that these "dangerous" forms of sexual behavior undermined Christian morality, they also played to a number of social fears felt by middle-class and ruling elites during the late nineteenth century: (1) that excessive masturbation drained energies that could otherwise be put to use in economic activities; (2) that uncontrolled working-class and immigrant sexual behavior would demographically and politically overwhelm the sexual morality of the Protestant family; and (3) that free love, promoted as it was purportedly by anarchists, would (along with other "unchristian" forms of marriage such as Mormon polygamy and Native American and African American common-law marriages) undermine the sanctity of the marriage contract and disrupt the standard American family structure.[25] Thus, the Comstock apparatus successfully combined efforts to regulate sexual behavior and to exercise some governance over (immigrant and working-class) populations.

The productive effects of the Comstock apparatus that delineated new categories of people—or gave a unique American twist to inherited categories—crucially aided the Comstock apparatus to overcome the limitations of a weak federal government; hybridize state and local, public and private, and legal and journalistic processes and precedents; and use the resulting apparatus to act effectively. The power of these productive effects resulted from the conflation of perceived moral threats, such as nonreproductive and nonmarital sexuality, with economic practices and saleable goods. Once the abstract fears were given concrete targets, moral crusaders could more effectively direct their efforts and rally public support. Through such means and the regulation of the markets, the Comstock apparatus managed to perform inchoate biopolitical functions in the late nineteenth century.[26]

BUILDING THE COMSTOCK APPARATUS:
THE LITTLE COMSTOCK LAWS AND VICE SOCIETIES

Following the federal law's passage, more than thirty states passed or revised "little Comstock laws" modeled on the federal legislation by 1900. Nine states already had similar laws on the books before 1873 (see table 2.1). The passage of "little Comstock laws" at the state level was by far the most effective means to enhance the repressive potential of the federal law. The states were not constrained by whether or not the mail was used. They had the power to ban and criminalize the advertisement, distribution, sale, and display of the proscribed items.[27] The state laws legitimated and facilitated enforcement of the federal proscriptions, and it was actually the state laws in many cases that allowed Comstock to stage arrests and put the offenders on trial. Using Comstock's own reports, we estimate that state laws accounted for 76.5 percent of the arrests made over approximately forty years. The federal law of 1873 was powerful not so much in and of itself, but because of the hybrid state that it licensed; that is, the federal law and the "little Comstock laws" in concert extended the reach and efficacy far beyond that which could be achieved by the state or federal laws alone.

Far more research stands to be done about the passage of the various little Comstock laws, but it is clear that the federal law stimulated state legislatures to act. This was predicted by one of the Comstock Law's leading sponsors in Congress, who in 1873 proclaimed that "calling the attention of the country to this monstrous crime, and the determination of . . . Congress to go to the furthest constitutional point, within their power of legislation for its annihilation will incite every State Legislature to enact similar laws for its final destruction."[28] Over the next twenty years, many states, abetted by local vice societies and their allies, did indeed pass such laws (or updated earlier laws) (see table 2.1).

New York State, for example, had passed a comparable law (originally sponsored by the YMCA) in 1868. Since that one was rarely enforced, Comstock promoted a strengthened and sweeping obscenity bill (based on the federal act) in 1873. Comstock and the New York Society for the Suppression of Vice (NYSSV) were instrumental in its passage by the State Assembly.[29] In 1879, the New England Society for the Suppression of Vice (later known as the New England Watch and Ward Society), which Comstock had helped found, introduced a bill modeled on the federal act to the Massachusetts state legislature. The "Act Concerning Offenses Against Chastity, Morality and Decency" passed virtually without discussion or dissent.[30] Shortly after it passed, Ezra Heywood, a free love advocate based in Boston, protested the bill to little effect. A similar bill was passed in Connecticut

TABLE 2.1. State anti-obscenity laws and prohibited activities (1845–1899)

Date law enacted	State	Pornography	Contraception	Abortion	Sexual aids
1845*	IL	X	X	X	X
1847*	MA	X	X	X	
1849*	WI	X	—	X	—
1857*	ME	X	X	—	
1864*	OR	X	—	—	—
1868*	FL	X	—	—	X
1868*	NY	X	X	X	
1870*	AZ	X	X	—	—
1870*	PA	X	X	X	—
1873	CA	X	X	X	
1874	VA	X	—	—	X
1877	NV	X	X	—	—
1878	GA	X	—	—	X
1879	CT	X	X	X	
1879	MO	X	X	—	—
1880	VT	X	—	—	X
1884	AL	X	—	—	—
1884	LA	X	X	X	
1884	NM	X	—	—	—
1884	TN	X	—	—	—
1885	CO	X	X	—	
1885	NE	X	X	X	—
1885	NC	X	—	X	—
1885	OH	X	X	—	X
1887	ID	X	X		—
1888	MD	X	—		X
1890	WY	X	X	X	X

(continued)

TABLE 2.1. continued

Date law enacted	State	Pornography	Contraception	Abortion	Sexual aids
1891	NH	X	—	X	—
1891	OK	X	—	—	—
1892	MI	X	X	X	—
1894	KY	X	—	—	X
1894	MN	X	X	—	—
1894	SC	X	—	—	X
1895	ND	X	—	X	X
1896	IN	X	X	X	—
1896	RI	X	—	—	X
1897	IA	X	—	X	X
1897	MI	X	X	—	X
1897	TX	X	—	—	—
1898	NJ	X	X	—	—
1898	UT	X	—	—	X
1899	WV	X	—	—	X

* Passed before the Comstock Act of 1873.

Blank cells in the table represent items with inconclusive evidence.

Sources: Martha Bailey, "Momma's Got the Pill: How Anthony Comstock and *Griswold v. Connecticut* Shaped U.S. Childbearing," *American Economic Review* 100, no. 1 (March 2010): 98–129.

On the coding of the Comstock statutes from 1873 to 1973, see Martha Bailey and Allison Davido, "Legal Appendix to "Momma's Got the Pill," https://www.researchgate.net/publication/242455567_Legal_Appendix_to_Momma's_Got_the_Pill.

An updated version appears in Martha Bailey, Melanie Guldi, Allison Davido, and Erin Buzuvis, "Early Legal Access: Laws and Policies Governing Contraceptive Access, 1960–1980," Working Paper, University of Michigan, http://www-personal.umich.edu/~baileymj/ELA_laws.pdf; Mary Ware Dennett, *Birth Control Laws* (New York: Frederick H. Hitchcock, 1925); C. Thomas Dienes, *Law, Politics and Birth Control* (Urbana: University of Illinois Press, 1972).

Note: Martha Bailey and her colleagues have systematically reviewed the state Comstock laws in order to assess their impact on the availability of contraception. We have extended that information on the little Comstock laws to other issues (pornography, abortion, and sexual devices) covered by the law in each state.

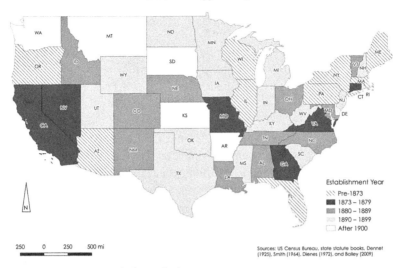

FIGURE 2.1. State anti-obscenity laws.

at the same time—although with slightly more discussion than had taken place in other cases.[31] By 1893, similar laws had passed in New Hampshire, Maine, and Vermont.[32]

A benefit of supplementing the federal act with the little Comstock laws was that the state and local governments handled the logistics and costs of enforcement. The New York Society's Act of Incorporation (by the New York state legislature) states that

> The police force of the city of New York, as well as all other places where police organizations exist, shall, as occasion may require, aid this orga-
> nization, its members or agents, in the enforcement of all laws which now exist or which may hereafter be enacted for the suppression of the acts and offenses, the enforcement of the laws for the suppression of the trade in and circulation of obscene literature and illustrations, ad-
> vertisement and articles of indecent and immoral use, as it is or may be forbidden by the laws of the State of New York or of the United States.[33]

Ironically, the police were instructed to aid the Society; the Society was not instructed to aid the police. This makes clear the centrality of private actors in enforcing the law as well as the way that enforcement costs were borne by local governments. New York State's Comstock law was amended two years later, to proclaim that "Any agent of the New York Society for the Suppression of Vice upon being designated thereto by the sheriff of any county in the State, may within such county make arrests and bring before any court or magistrate thereof having jurisdiction, offenders found violating the provisions of any law for the suppression of the trade in and circulation of obscene literature and illustrations, advertisements and articles of indecent or immoral use, as it is or may be forbidden by the laws of this State or of the United States."[34] Comstock estimated, while proclaiming that the New York Vice Society's activities cost taxpayers nothing, that the *total cost* (to the taxpayer) of policing the "vicious classes" in New York City was $3.4 million—a sum that included police officers, judges, district attorneys, and assistants, plus clerks and stenographers, all of whose services Comstock and his associates drew upon repeatedly to prosecute their cases.[35]

Despite their widespread adoption, the Comstock laws by themselves were not sufficient to regulate and limit the circulation of obscene materials effectively. Neither the federal nor the state Comstock laws could be enforced without information on the marketing, sale, or distribution of the materials banned by the laws, or without some organization or agency to collect that information.

For the federal Comstock Act to be effective, it was necessary to collect information about obscene materials before they were delivered. The Post Office could not do that, and local police departments would have had to establish something like "vice squads" in order to do that locally.[36] The New York Society for the Suppression of Vice and the other local societies performed this task. They served as the surveillance arm of the Post Office and local police (see table 2.2).

Comstock and the New York Society encouraged establishing local societies or "branches" for the suppression of vice that spread well beyond New York. In 1878 the New England Society for the Suppression of Vice was founded; in 1879 the Western Society for the Suppression of Vice, which had offices in Cincinnati, Chicago, and St. Louis, was founded; in 1888 the Society for the Suppression of Vice in Baltimore City was created; and in 1893 in San Francisco the Pacific Society for the Suppression of Vice and the Prevention of Cruelty to Animals and Children was formed.[37] By the 1890s, societies for the suppression of vice operated in eight of the ten largest American cities—Philadelphia and New Orleans being the exceptions.[38]

These societies for the suppression of vice were a critical component of the Comstock apparatus. Not only did they function as intermediaries with law enforcement agencies, but they also gathered information and provided surveillance. The New York Society identified the offending individuals as well as businesses that violated the Comstock laws. Comstock was sometimes considered, depending on whether one was a supporter or an opponent, as either a "detective" or an "informer." His methods were

TABLE 2.2. Societies for the suppression of vice (1873–1893)

Year founded	Society	Location(s)	Rank pop. (1880)
1873	New York Society for the Suppression of Vice	New York City, Brooklyn	1, 3
1878	New England Society for the Suppression of Vice	Boston	5
1879	Western Society for the Suppression of Vice	Chicago, St. Louis, Cincinnati	4, 6, 8
1888	Society for the Suppression of Vice in Baltimore City	Baltimore	7
1893	Pacific Society for the Suppression of Vice and the Prevention of Cruelty to Children and Animals	San Francisco	9

Source: US Census, "Population of the 100 Largest Cities and Other Urban Places in the United States, 1790–1990."

usually quite direct. His most commonly used methods of collecting information were (1) reading the advertisements in the sensationalist press (such as *Leslie's Illustrated Weekly*) in order to identify the vendors offering "obscene" publications, devices, and advice that were liable to prosecution under the Comstock laws; and (2) sending a "decoy letter" asking for a vendor to send the materials that Comstock thought might be obscene.

Illinois provides a vivid example of Comstock's interactions with both state-level regulation and also the regional vice societies. While an 1873 state statute placed "obscene or immoral publications," along with bawdy houses, under the purview of local ordinances, in May of that year obscenity was added to the state criminal code, with penalties of up to six months' imprisonment and a $1,000 fine for each offense.[39] An 1894 tract, *A Victim of Comstockism* by R. Frankenstein, covers the 1891 prosecution of Chicago bookseller George Wilson and captures the interplay of state and federal authority. It begins with the rhetorical move to conflate Robert McAfee, the head of the Western Society and a federally appointed postal inspector in his own right, and Comstock (who was not an active force in Wilson's case).[40] Using his established tactic of decoy letters, McAfee solicited Wilson's list of "publications suitable for private reading." Upon receiving it, he placed an order for four books, then ordered Wilson's arrest. While all of the mail had been sent and delivered within Illinois, the charges were federal, based on using the mails to advertise information about obscene materials. In fact, all four books, including such titles as *Mysteries of the Court of London* and *Stolen Sweets*, had been reviewed in mainstream publications and were widely available in Chicago newsstands and libraries. Local obscenity charges thus seemed unlikely and unreasonable. But shifting the terrain to a federal court, and the charge to the *advertising* of the books, helped obscure their prevalence. Wilson was found guilty and sentenced to two years' imprisonment.[41]

Frankenstein delivered an astute structural analysis of the system Comstock and McAfee had built, which was based on pushing for the broadest possible legal scope, to serve "the necessity for the continuance of a society which pays them salary and *expenses of investigation*." The duo worked in tandem, as when McAfee secured an easy and undisputed legal finding against Boccaccio's *Decameron* in Indiana, and Comstock then immediately informed dealers on a national level that the book had been declared unmailable. To keep the apparatus running, "If no one voluntarily violated the awful majesty of the Federal Postal Laws, somebody must be driven or trapped to do it."[42] Hence the decoy letters. Comstock himself would return to Chicago later that decade to serve moral and legal judgment on marital sex-manual author Ida Craddock, whom he would eventually drive to suicide in 1902. Frankenstein's account and analysis of Comstock's prosecution of Wilson detailed how the synchronization of the state and federal laws was exploited to ensure convictions. The interplay between the state and federal laws—including the application of state legal precedents in order to reinforce the federal law—provided a wide range of legal options. This fluid legal framework and the support of the vice societies were essential structural features of the Comstock apparatus.

DEFINING OBSCENITY: POLITICS, LAW, AND RESISTANCE

The success of the enforcement of the little Comstock laws and the broad public support for the local vice societies depended upon (1) a broad legal definition of obscenity; and (2) the role of the press in making public the debates surrounding obscenity. Battles over the definition of obscenity (and the freedom of sexual speech) took place in the courts, with the press and public opinion operating as a secondary site of struggle. In court, the battle against obscenity was repeatedly characterized by Comstock and his allies as a moral battle, disconnecting it from constitutional challenges (such as lodged by free love advocate/anarchist Ezra Heywood and his distributor D. M. Bennett) and questions of governmental regulation more broadly conceived. The trials provided platforms that enabled Comstock to stigmatize and criminalize his opponents and publicize his agenda. They also served as a way for Comstock's opponents to test the public support and legal foundations for opposition to Comstock's regulatory order.[43] The trials served as "didactic, clarifying, compelling and ritualistic" public narratives par excellence.[44]

Comstock had learned the value of publicity early in his career as a moral crusader. Before the Comstock Act was passed, his previous arrests in New York were widely covered in the press. Throughout his career he frequently alerted reporters to upcoming arrests and brought them along as witnesses.[45] In 1872, obscenity emerged as a significant component in one of the most famous scandals in late nineteenth-century America. In 1872, Victoria Woodhull published an exposé of the adulterous affair between Henry Ward Beecher, one of the most prominent preachers in the United States, and Elizabeth Tilton. She was the wife of Theodore Tilton, Beecher's protégé and the ghostwriter of many of his articles.[46] The scandal that ensued resulted in a series of trials that were among the most widely reported of the time. In 1872 Woodhull was arrested, at Comstock's instigation, and charged (under the Postal Act of 1865) with sending obscene material through the mail—publication about an adulterous affair was considered "obscene."[47] Woodhull was tried and acquitted on the technicality that the 1865 Act did not cover newspapers. In 1873, Beecher's church (Plymouth Church in Brooklyn Heights) held a board of inquiry that exonerated Beecher and excommunicated Theodore Tilton. Tilton subsequently sued Beecher for adultery. Beecher's trial ran from January through June 1875 and resulted in a hung jury. Having observed the power of the media in the Beecher-Tilton affair, Comstock never ceased to use the press to cover trials, arrests, and convictions in order to stigmatize his opponents.

The unusually broad definition of obscenity set out in the 1873 law reflected Comstock's own belief that "Lust is the boon companion of all other crimes. There is no evil so extensive," he wrote, that does "more to destroy the institutions of free America. It sets aside the laws of God and morality; marriage bonds are broken, most sacred ties severed. State laws ignored, and dens of intamy plant themselves in almost every community, and then reaching out like immense cuttlefish, draw in, from all sides, our youth to destruction."[48] His expansive definition of obscenity also increased the social base of support for the Comstock Act. Pornography was a relatively narrow issue, seen as primarily relevant to young men or children. But contraception and abortion appealed to a broader audience concerned about sexual morality and the stable reproduction of the bourgeois family. It also reflected concern about the sexual norms of immigrants, working-class people, and the unrestrained male sexuality so prevalent during the nineteenth century.[49] According to Comstock's paradigm of moral regulation, obscenity and sex were inherently dangerous. He made no distinction between a pornographic novel and educational literature on birth control. In Comstock's terminology, "indecent rubber articles," for example, included both condoms and dildos.[50] He portrayed obscenity as diabolical: "designed and cunningly calculated to inflame the passions and lead victims from one step of vice to another, ending in utmost lust. And when the victims have been polluted in thought and imagination and thus prepared for the commission of lustful crime, the authors of their debasement present a variety of implements by the aid of which they promise them the practice of licentiousness without its direful consequences to them and their guilty partners."[51] Pornography, Comstock thus concluded, opened the road to every other form of "dangerous" sexuality. Comstock's crusade against obscenity was precipitated by his discovery that a personal friend had been "led astray," "corrupted and diseased" by reading a book of pornography, and had become sexually obsessed and visited a brothel, where he was infected with a sexually transmitted disease.[52]

The Comstock Law's broad definition of obscenity allowed him to attack free love advocates and anarchists who were the most outspoken advocates for sexual liaisons outside marriage, for birth control information, and for educational literature about sexuality.[53] Comstock devoted an entire chapter of his book, *Traps for the Young*, to what he called "Free Love Traps" in order to warn his followers against the movement of those who make the word "'love' . . . its watchword, [which] distorts and prostitutes its meaning, until it is the mantle for all kinds of license and uncleanness. It should be spelled l-u-s-t to be rightly understood, as it is interpreted by so-called liberals."

In 1882 Comstock arrested Ezra Heywood, along with his distributor D. M. Bennett, for sending *Cupid's Yoke*, a rambling and awkwardly written pamphlet by Heywood, through the mails. In *Cupid's Yoke,* Heywood had argued that marriage was a social contract that made a married woman into a "prostitute for life." Free love, he argued, would create more equality between men and women and thus make sexuality more amenable to reason. Both Heywood's and Bennett's trials were widely publicized, and both went to jail as a result of Comstock's efforts. And these early cases against the free love advocates were very influential—undercutting the First Amendment defense and upholding the constitutionality of the law.[54] Modern First Amendment doctrine didn't develop until the early twentieth century, after some of the most aggressive rights claims had been lodged by labor activists.[55]

The first really effective challenge to Comstock's hegemony came from birth control activist Margaret Sanger and her allies. First active on labor issues and left-wing and anarchist politics, Sanger became increasingly interested in women's sexuality and reproductive health during the 1910s. With anarchist backing, she launched *The Woman Rebel* in 1914, a magazine devoted to promoting contraception. Postal authorities banned five of its seven issues from the mail. At the same time, she published a short pamphlet called *Family Limitation*, which included detailed information and graphic descriptions of various contraceptive methods. Indicted for violation of the Comstock Law, she fled the country rather than stand trial. She returned soon after to continue the fight for many years—during which she was arrested at least eight more times. The court's opinion in an appeal of one of her convictions in 1918 exempted physicians from the Comstock Act's ban on contraception information furnished to women for health reasons, thus limiting the impact of the Comstock Law's contraceptive provision to some extent.[56]

During the 1920s the American Civil Liberties Union took up the issues raised by birth control activists. Rather than be publicly associated with birth control, the ACLU reframed the issue as one of "freedom of speech." Between 1925 and the 1950s, the ACLU emerged as the primary political antagonist of the Comstock Law's "definition" of obscenity and in the process developed the modern doctrine of First Amendment rights. Cases concerning obscenity and pornography would eventually test the limits of these rights.

Despite the social and cultural changes of the twentieth century, Comstock's ultimate, though somewhat pyrrhic, victory was secured by the Supreme Court in *Roth v. United States*. The First Amendment, Justice William Brennan declared, did not protect obscene material. As such, Comstock's spirit prevailed. However, Brennan's vision of sexual and literary legitimacy in 1957 looked vastly different from Comstock's more repressive one, and his liberalism helped unleash the so-called sexual revolution.[57] But in *Roth*'s fundamental holding that the Comstock Act was indeed constitutional, the Court limited its scope yet reaffirmed its legitimacy. Brennan's restriction of obscene material to that "utterly without redeeming social importance" specifically protected "unorthodox ideas, controversial ideas, even ideas hateful to the prevailing climate of opinion."[58] "Sex and obscenity," he bluntly added, "are not synonymous." But nothing in *Roth* touched on the structural questions of enforcement that Comstock had exploited so effectively, and indeed, a sustained and operationally nebulous public/private arena would continue to mark obscenity regulation as government agents worked in tandem with such groups as Citizens for Decent Literature in the 1960s, National Federation for Decency in the 1980s, and a proliferation of Comstock successors into the twenty-first century.[59] The sexual exceptionalism that had allowed Comstock to operate without accountability would be sutured into a regulatory apparatus that preferred not to acknowledge the social costs or look too closely at who benefited. By keeping the doctrinal discussion at the conveniently abstract level of free speech and the "marketplace of ideas," modern obscenity doctrine continued to avoid interrogating the anatomy of the Comstock apparatus.

The Comstock Act established a regulatory apparatus that combined discursive formations, the police, courts, and private moral entrepreneurs in order to enforce Christian sexual morality. It made no distinction between informational or euphemistic representations of sex from prurient or explicit ones. Sex outside marriage, homosexuality, and other nonnormative sexualities were implicitly condemned by the Act's prohibition of the distribution of any product (including books, pamphlets, and newspapers) that facilitated sexual behavior other than that of procreative heterosexual behavior within a monogamous marriage. Dependent, in part, on the zeal and character of Comstock himself, the wide impact of the Act on the American legal framework and American sexual discourse broadly can be attributed to four structural bases: the broad definition of obscenity, the creation of state obscenity laws, the establishment of local vice suppression societies, and the public attention given to Comstock's arrests and trials. Without these structural bases and the utilization of the constitutional workarounds such as *privatization* and *surrogacy*, Anthony Comstock's project would never have moved beyond that of a momentary moral panic, and American legal history and the history of American sexual discourse would have been markedly different.[60]

NOTES

1. The law—commonly called the Comstock Act—consists of five sections. US Code 17 Stat. 598 (1873), full text available at http://uscode.house.gov/statviewer .htm?volume=17&page=598#.

2. Judith Giesberg, *Sex and the Civil War: Soldiers: Pornography and the Making of American Morality* (Chapel Hill: University of North Carolina Press, 2017), 12–33.

3. Heywood Broun and Margaret Leech, *Anthony Comstock: The Roundsman of the Lord* (New York: Albert and Charles Boni, 1927), 75–144; and Helen Lefkowitz Horowitz, *Rereading Sex: Battles over Sexual Knowledge and Suppression in Nineteenth-Century America* (New York: Alfred A. Knopf, 2002), 299–385.

4. Daniel P. Carpenter, *The Forging of Bureaucratic Autonomy: Reputations, Networks and Policy Innovation in Executive Agencies, 1862–1928* (Princeton, NJ: Princeton University Press, 2001), 84.

5. Throughout the nineteenth century, the US Post Office was the largest branch of the federal government and the most visible. See Richard R. John, *Spreading the News: The American Postal System from Franklin to Morse* (Cambridge, MA: Harvard University Press, 1998); and Brian Balogh, *A Government Out of Sight: The Mystery of National Authority in Nineteenth-Century America* (Cambridge: Cambridge University Press, 2009), 219–76.

6. Gaines M. Foster, *Moral Reconstruction: Christian Lobbyists and the Federal Legislation of Morality, 1865–1920* (Chapel Hill: University of North Carolina Press, 2002); David J. Pivar, *Purity Crusade: Sexual Morality and Social Control, 1868–1900* (Westport, CT: Greenwood Press, 1973); and Nicola Beisel, *Imperiled Innocents: Anthony Comstock and Family Reproduction in Victorian America*, (Princeton, NJ: Princeton University Press, 1997), 25–103, 212–17.

7. William J. Novak, "The Concept of the State in American History," in *Boundaries of the State in U.S. History,* ed. James T. Sparrow, William J. Novak, and Stephen W. Sawyer (Chicago: University of Chicago Press, 2015), 325–49; see also Gary Gerstle, *Liberty and Coercion: The Paradox of American Government* (Princeton, NJ: Princeton University Press, 2015), 5–9, 17–54.

8. Gerstle, *Liberty and Coercion*, 54–86.

9. Geoffrey Stone, *Sex and the Constitution: Sex, Religion, and Law from America's Origins to the Twenty-First Century* (New York: Liveright, 2017), 90–107, 153–78; and Gerstle, *Liberty and Coercion*, 100–104.

10. Horowitz, *Rereading Sex*, 391–92; for one example of a life destroyed by Comstock, see Leigh Eric Schmidt, *Heaven's Bride: The Unprintable Life of Ida C.*

Craddock, American Mystic, Scholar, Sexologist, Martyr, and Madwoman (New York: Basic Books, 2010).

11. Walter Kendrick, *Secret Museum: Pornography in Modern Culture* (New York: Viking Penguin, 1987), 136; and Paul S. Boyer, *Purity in Print: Book Censorship in America from the Gilded Age to the Computer Age* (Madison: University of Wisconsin Press, 2002), 9–15.

12. Gerstle, *Liberty and Coercion,* 6–7, 100–106.

13. Gerstle identifies *privatization, surrogacy,* and *exemption* as three political methods to extend federal powers beyond those constitutionally allowed. States, on the other hand, had very extensive police powers. Gerstle, *Liberty and Coercion,* 5–9, 17–86, quotation on 6.

14. Comstock Act, US Code 17 Stat. 598 (1873).

15. Gerstle, *Liberty and Coercion,* 6, 118–23.

16. Gerstle. *Liberty and Coercion,* 100–104.

17. William Novak, "The Myth of the 'Weak' American State," *American Historical Review* 113, no. 3 (2008): 752–72.

18. Nicholas Parrillo, *Against the Profit Motive: The Salary Revolution in American Government, 1780–1940* (New Haven, CT: Yale, 2013); and Susan Pearson, *The Rights of the Defenseless: Protecting Animals and Children in Gilded Age America* (Chicago: University of Chicago Press, 2011).

19. See Horowitz, *Rereading Sex*; Timothy J. Gilfoyle, *City of Eros: New York City, Prostitution and the Commercialization of Sex, 1790–1920* (New York: W. W. Norton & Co., 1992); Patricia Cline Cohen, Timothy J. Gilfoyle, and Helen Lefkowitz Horowitz, *The Flash Press: Sporting Male Weeklies in 1840s New York* (Chicago: University of Chicago Press, 2008); and Donna Dennis, *Licentious Gotham: Erotic Publishing and Its Prosecution in Nineteenth-Century New York* (Cambridge, MA: Harvard University Press, 2009).

20. The Motion Picture Production Code of the 1930s and 1940s was an example of classic censorship, as described in Leonard J. Leff and Jerold L. Simmons, *The Dame in the Kimono: Hollywood, Censorship and the Production Code*, rev. ed. (Lexington: University Press of Kentucky, 2001). See also Robert Darnton, *Censors at Work: How States Shaped Literature* (New York: W. W. Norton, 2015), 13–20; and Darnton's *The Forbidden Best-Sellers of Pre-Revolutionary France* (New York: W. W. Norton, 1995). Werbel argues that censorship under the Comstock Law took three different forms: direct (when materials are seized and destroyed), social (when it influences public opinion), and regulatory (when it increases the cost of producing or consuming "obscene" materials). We are focusing on the regulatory aspect of censorship—though in our analysis "direct" censorship increases the cost of producing "obscene" materials; Amy Werbel, *Lust on Trial: Censorship and the Rise of American Obscenity in the Age of Anthony Comstock* (New York: Columbia University Press, 2018), 9–10.

21. Horowitz, *Rereading Sex,* maps the shifting discourses of sexuality in the nineteenth-century United States.

22. Dennis, *Licentious Gotham,* 275–304; Janet Brodie, *Abortion and Contraception in Nineteenth-Century America* (Ithaca, NY: Cornell University Press, 1994),

253–88; and Andrea Tone, *Devices and Desires: A History of Contraceptives in America* (New York: Hill and Wang, 2001), 67–87.

23. The Comstock apparatus is a good example of what Michel Foucault considered an "apparatus of sexuality"—that is, "a thoroughly heterogeneous ensemble consisting of discourses, institutions, architectural forms, regulatory decisions, laws, administrative measures, scientific statements, philosophical, moral and philanthropic propositions." See Foucault's discussion of an "apparatus of sexuality" in "The Confession of the Flesh," in *Power/Knowledge: Selected Interview and Other Writings, 1972–1977,* ed. Colin Gordon (New York: Pantheon Books, 1980), 194, 197. While conceived as primarily repressive, such regulatory apparatuses also have, Foucault argued, "productive" effects, in "producing" targeted individuals to see themselves as belonging to new categories of people. Michel Foucault, *The History of Sexuality, Volume 1, An Introduction* (New York: Pantheon Books, 1978), 15–49. See also Ian Hacking, "Making Up People," in *Historical Ontology* (Cambridge, MA: Harvard University Press, 2004), 103–5; and Kenneth Plummer, *Sexual Stigma: An Interactionist Account* (London: Routledge & Kegan Paul, 1975), 122–53.

24. Sigmund Freud, "Civilized Sexual Morality and Modern Nervousness," reprinted in *Sexual Revolution,* ed. Jeffrey Escoffier (New York: Thunder Mouth Press, 2003), 557–70.

25. G. J. Barker-Benfield, "The Spermatic Economy: A Nineteenth-Century View of Sexuality," in *The American Family in Social-Historical Perspective*, 2nd ed., ed. Michael Gordon (New York: St. Martin's Press, 1978), 374–402; and Nicola Beisel, *Imperiled Innocents*, 25–48; see Nancy Cott, *Public Vows: A History of Marriage and the Nation* (Cambridge, MA: Harvard University Press, 2001), 105–31, on the debates about marriage and various alternative arrangements after the Civil War.

26. See Michel Foucault's discussion of biopolitics in *Society Must Be Defended, Lectures at the College de France, 1975–1976* (New York: Picador, 2003), 244–54.

27. Mary Ware Dennett, *Birth Control Laws: Shall We Keep Them, Change them or Abolish Them* (New York: Frederick H. Hitchcock, 1926), 56–57.

28. *New York Times,* March 15, 1873, 3, col. 3; and Broun and Leech, *Anthony Comstock,* 130–44.

29. William J. McWilliams, "Laws of New York and Birth Control: A Survey," *Birth Control Review* 14 (February 1930): 46–47, 61–63.

30. Carol F. Brooks, "The Early History of the Anti-Contraception Laws in Massachusetts and Connecticut," *American Quarterly* 18 (Spring 1966).

31. NYSSV, *Annual Report 1880*, 6; Brooks, "Early History of Anti-Contraception"; and P. C. Kemeny, *The New England Watch and Ward Society* (New York: Oxford University Press, 2018), 77–79.

32. NYSSV, *Annual Report* 1896–1897, 10–12.

33. NYSSV, "Act of Incorporation," Section 3, in *Ninth Annual Report* (1883), 30–31.

34. New State Criminal Code, Section 1145, cited in Dennett, *Birth Control Laws,* 32.

35. NYSSV, *Seventh Annual Report* (1881), 13.

36. It appears that police department vice squads were first established in the

wake of the citizen-based vice commissions in the first decades of the twentieth century.

37. P. C. Kemeny, "'Banned in Boston': Moral Reform Politics and the New England Society for the Suppression of Vice," *Church History* 78, no. 4 (December 2009): 814–46; and Kemeny, *New England Watch and Ward Society*.

38. Beisel discusses the failure of the vice suppression movement in Philadelphia in *Imperiled Innocence*, 128–57.

39. Ch. 18, Art. 5, Sec. 1, pt. 45, Statutes of Illinois Construed, Containing the Following Acts of 1872, and Amendments Thereto, Made by the Acts of 1873, Also the Constitution of Illinois, vol. 1, ed. William Underwood (St. Louis, MO: W. J. Gilbert, 1873), 196; Crim. Code, Ch. 38, Sec. 223, Revised Statutes of the State of Illinois. A. D. 1874. Comprising the Revised Acts of 1871–2 and 1873–4, Together with All Other General Statutes of the State, in Force on the First Day of July 1874. Springfield, 1874, ed. Harvey Bostwick Hurd (Springfield: Illinois Journal Co., 1874), 386.

40. Wayne Fuller clarifies this point in *Morality and Mail in Nineteenth-Century America* (Urbana: University of Illinois Press, 2003), 251n43.

41. R. Frankenstein, *A Victim of Comstockism* (Chicago: Wilson, 1894), 22.

42. Frankenstein, *A Victim*, 14–16.

43. Otto Kirchheimer, *Political Justice: The Use of Legal Procedure for Political Ends* (Princeton, NJ: Princeton University Press, 1961), 422–23; and Ronald Christenson, "A Political Theory of Political Trials," *Journal of Criminal Law and Criminology* 74, no. 2 (Summer 1983): 547–77.

44. Awol K. Allo, "The 'Show' in the 'Show Trial': Contextualizing the Politicization of the Courtroom," *Barry Law Review* 15, no. 1 (Fall 2010): 48.

45. Werbel, *Lust on Trial*, 59–63.

46. Beecher was the brother of author Harriet Beecher Stowe, and a leading abolitionist before the Civil War; see Horowitz, *Rereading Sex*, 350–57.

47. Werbel, *Lust on Trial*, 63.

48. Robert Hamlett Bremner, *Traps for the Young* (Cambridge, MA: Belknap Press of Harvard University Press, 1967), 133.

49. The "sporting culture" that emerged in American cities in the antebellum period is symptomatic of a wider phenomenon that persisted up until the early twentieth century. See Horowitz, *Rereading Sex*, 123–24; male sexuality is a recurring topic in Paul Boyer, *Urban Masses and Moral Order in America, 1820–1920* (Cambridge, MA: Harvard University Press, 1978); and Mara L. Keire, *For Business and Pleasure: Red-Light Districts and the Relation of Vice in the United States, 1890–1933* (Baltimore: Johns Hopkins University Press, 2010).

50. Beisel, *Imperiled Innocence*, 40.

51. New York Society for the Suppression of Vice, *Second Annual Report*, 1876, 5; see also Beisel, *Imperiled Innocence*, 40.

52. Beisel, *Imperiled Innocence*, 37.

53. Martin Blatt, *Free Love and Anarchism: The Biography of Ezra Heywood* (Urbana: University of Illinois Press, 1990); Bonnie Haaland, *Emma Goldman: Sexuality and the Impurity of the State* (Montreal: Black Rose Books, 1993); and Terence

Kissack, *Free Comrades: Anarchism and Homosexuality in the United States, 1895, 1895–1917* (Oakland, CA: AK Press, 2008).

54. See Horowitz, *Rereading Sex*, 404–18.

55. *Gompers v. Buck's Range & Stove Co.*, 221 US 418 (1911). On the emergence of the modern First Amendment, see David Rabban, *Free Speech in Its Forgotten Years, 1870–1920* (Cambridge: Cambridge University Press, 1997).

56. Bailey, "Momma's Got the Pill," 98–129. On the 1918 legalization of condoms for prophylaxis against venereal disease, enabling their wide availability for contraception, see Andrea Tone, "Making Room for Rubbers: Gender, Technology and Birth Control before the Pill," *History and Technology* 18, no. 1 (2002): 51–76.

57. On the sexual revolution, see David Allyn, *Make Love, Not War: The Sexual Revolution, an Unfettered History* (Boston: Little, Brown, 2001); Jeffrey Escoffier, ed., *Sexual Revolution* (New York: Thunder Mouth Press, 2003); and Jeffrey Escoffier, "Pornography, Perversity and the Sexual Revolution," in *Sexual Revolutions,* ed. Gert Hekma and Alain Giami (Houndsmills, Basingstoke, Hampshire, UK: Macmillan Palgrave, 2014). For a challenge to the narrative of revolution, see Marc Stein, *Sexual Injustice: Supreme Court Opinions from Griswold to Roe* (Chapel Hill: University of North Carolina Press, 2011).

58. *Roth v. United States*, 354 US 476 (1957). See also Whitney Strub, *Obscenity Rules:* Roth v. United States *and the Long Struggle over Sexual Expression* (Lawrence: University Press of Kansas, 2013).

59. Whitney Strub, *Perversion for Profit: The Politics of Pornography and the Rise of the New Right* (New York: Columbia University Press, 2011).

60. For a discussion of the relationship of moral panics to state action in the late twentieth century, see Erich Goode and Ben-Yahuda Nachman, *Moral Panics: The Construction of Deviance*, 2nd ed. (Malden, MA: John Wiley, 2009), 21–33, and their discussion of the feminist anti-pornography crusade of the 1970s and 1980s, 218–44; also, Roger N. Lancaster's discussion of sex panics and the state in the twentieth-century United States in *Sex Panic and the Punitive State* (Berkeley: University of California, 2011).

3

Morals, Sex, Crime, and the Legal Origins of Modern American Social Police

WILLIAM J. NOVAK

INTRODUCTION

This volume on *Intimate States* is devoted to exploring the deep inter-connections between changing conceptions of gender and sexuality and changing technologies of governance and statecraft across modern American history. It emphasizes the ways in which American law changes, new forms of state power emerge, and socio-cultural relations are transformed at the busy intersection of law and society. Here, neither forms of state power nor socio-cultural understandings are taken as given; rather, emphasis is placed on the way both change over time through the collision of legal and state practices and changing socio-cultural exigencies. At the turn of the twentieth century, these reciprocal transformations combined to yield the genesis of modern American social police. The invention of social police was, in turn, an important incubator for the significant changes in criminal justice, policing, and carceral penalty that attended America's long twentieth-century war on crime.

Central to these developments was the initial effort of progressive reformers to reconstruct society, the social sphere, and social life as appropriate objects of legal and governmental supervision. Using modern "social science," new ideas of "social welfare" and "social control," and innovative techniques of social governance and social regulation, reformers pioneered new methods for policing "the social" in a modern age.[1] Many of those methods were simultaneously being applied to economic life in a parallel attempt at the "social control" of business, capitalism, and the market.[2] The end result was a multiplicity of new initiatives, programs, and powers that vastly expanded the reach of a modern American social state.

Modern social regulation involved a deep, thoroughgoing *socialization* that social theorist François Ewald described as a new way of conceiving of social obligations and legal-political relations, "where the link between one individual and another is always mediated through the society they form, with the latter playing a regulatory, mediatory, *and* redistributive role."[3]

This general process of "socialization" had significant implications for the interrelationship of law, gender, and sexuality. For here, Progressive Era legal and social reformers developed especially bold instrumentalities of state police power that allowed an unprecedented degree of state intervention to regulate prostitution, morality, sexuality, and what ultimately came to be known as "social hygiene." The injunction and abatement acts passed in thirty-eight states in the early twentieth century, highlighted below, exemplified this assertion of more generalized powers of state publicization, examination, medicalization, prohibition, internment, restriction, and control with regard to sexuality. In the modern social hygiene movement, the interpenetration of issues of morality, crime, and public health (all-too-frequently siloed in separate interpretive and historical frames) came together with special ferocity and intense social consequence. These were the beginnings of a new social police power crafted through the interplay of changing conceptions of gender and sexuality and changing techniques of law and regulation.

INVENTING A SOCIAL PROBLEM

The catalyst for this transformation of social law was a new conception of the "social" problem. Just as poverty and labor came into view in the Progressive Era as pressing "social questions" demanding new legislation, another range of "social problems" came similarly to the surface, with momentous policy consequences. New techniques of social provision ultimately created the foundation for an expansive modern social welfare state. But an equally expansive agenda of social policing, crime control, and penality simultaneously launched a new American police state.

A host of social tracts and treatises devoted to so-called "social problems," "social disorders," and even "social pathologies" proliferated, ranging from Samuel George Smith's *Social Pathology* (1911) to James Ford's *Social Problems and Social Policy* (1923) to Mabel E. Elliott and Francis E. Merrill's *Social Disorganization* (1934).[4] Here the general trend in thinking about "the social question" was clear, as author after author pivoted directly from discussions of poverty, economic inequality, and social provision to a different set of social concerns and social issues like immorality, defectiveness, and criminality. Stuart Alfred Queen and Delbert Martin

Mann's *Social Pathology* (1925) was exemplary of this tendency, transitioning from social reform concerns like child saving, child labor, and child support to the further underlying problems of the "unmarried mother," the "illegitimate child," "sex irregularity," "prostitution," and "syphilis and gonorrhea." Other social science treatises similarly moved from a concern with "pathologies of condition" like poverty to "pathologies of conduct," triggering not so much techniques of social welfare as a new criminology and social "therapeutics" implicating such things as social "sanitation," social statistics, inspection, public health, and even eugenics.[5]

Now, of course, the unequal and punitive treatment of the poor, the different, and the allegedly criminal had a legal history older than scripture, and had long been written into American law.[6] Something unique and significant was implicated, however, in the new socio-politico-scientific matrix of social problems and social pathologies. The modern socialization of dependency, disability, and delinquency transformed concerns that had once been thought of as occasional, exceptional, and anomalous into more of an ongoing, normalized, and everyday feature of modern social, legal, and political life. Here, the formal policing of the exception steadily gave way to a more generalized policing of the social norm, requiring the police power to become more continuous, efficacious, and expansive—capable of traversing the entire extent of the social body. As Michel Foucault once observed, here the power of social police no longer depended "on the innumerable, discontinuous, sometimes contradictory privileges of sovereignty, but on the continuously distributed effects of public power."[7]

The enlargement of problems, pathologies, and offenses deemed subject to modern social policing occurred in many arenas, but it was in the area of sex and sexuality that "social control," "social pathology," and "social morality" came together with spectacular force, insistently broadening the horizon of social police and expanding conceptions of "offense" and "criminality." Self-proclaimed "sex expert" and "international authority on sex control" Charles Margold's *Sex Freedom and Social Control* (1926) was emblematic of this trend toward viewing sex through the lens of a "social problem." Margold's text concluded that the invariably social and public nature of sex legitimated, indeed necessitated, greater social, legal, and public controls.[8] Margold was hardly alone.[9] Stuart Queen's *Social Pathology* relied on William Healy's famous *Individual Delinquent* and W. I. Thomas's equally influential *Unadjusted Girl* to expand the jurisdiction of the social control of sexual morality, noting that delinquency in girls was also bound up with "amusement, adventure, pretty clothes, favorable notice, distinction, freedom in the larger world," and the new mass entertainment venues of "unsupervised dance halls, amusement parks, low grade theaters, cabarets and excursion steamers."[10] Such texts routinely moved directly to the policing of "feeblemindedness," "nervous and mental diseases," "alcoholism and drug addiction," and the problems caused by sexually transmitted infections. In turn, each of those newly socialized categories of pathology, offense, or disability also expanded. In Elliot and Merrill's *Social Disorganization*, for example, the "crime" of prostitution was transformed from a relatively discrete and concrete offense into eleven ambiguous categories of various kinds of "loose women":

(1) "juvenile" prostitutes, girls from ten to fifteen who often appear in Juvenile Court on sex charges; (2) "potential" prostitutes, who are willing to accept money for sex relations which, however, may also be on a voluntarily free basis; (3) "amateur" prostitutes, who sell themselves occasionally but who continue to live at home; (4) "young professional" prostitutes, who have recently entered the regular life of a wanton; (5) "old professional" prostitutes, established residents of houses of prostitution; (6) "field workers," streetwalkers, who take men to their cheap rooms or to hotels; (7) "bats," superannuated prostitutes, rendered unattractive by drink and drugs to all but the least particular among the bums and homeless men; (8) "gold-diggers," called "boulevard" women, who may supplement their income from their regular patron by mercenary relations with other men; (10) "loose" married women, who deceive their husbands and receive pay; (11) "call girls," who receive remuneration from relations with men arranged by telephone calls from disorderly-hotel keepers and the like.

Elliot and Merrill also took notice of the roles of "ignorance," "feeblemindedness," "venereal disease," "organized vice," and "lonely and unattached young men living apart from their homes and families" in the etiology of prostitution, and expanded the sites for social surveillance from parlor houses, brothels, flats, disorderly hotels, and tenements to "soft-drink parlors, pool-rooms, lady-barber shops, manicure parlors catering to men, cabarets, night clubs, speakeasies, and the ubiquitous roadhouse."[11] These important changes in the nature, definition, and locus of morals and sex transgression were joined by a dramatic early twentieth-century expansion of American standards of criminal liability and public offense. This transformation in criminal justice has been the subject of much legal commentary over the last half century. Legal scholar Francis Allen, for example, originally dubbed it "nothing less than a revolution in public conceptions of the nature of crime and the criminal, and in public attitudes toward the proper treatment of the . . . offender."[12] At the core of this criminal justice revolution was a tremendous explosion of new penal regulations that vastly expanded the range of behaviors, identities, and activities subject to criminal or penal sanction. As Roscoe Pound—the American progenitor of "sociological jurisprudence"—captured the impact of this extraordinary development on the ground at the time, "Of the one hundred thousand persons arrested in Chicago in 1912, more than one half were held for violation of legal precepts which did not exist twenty-five years before."[13] Notably, morality and sexuality composed the key growth sector for this accelerated criminalization at the local, state, and federal levels. As Bill Stuntz observed with respect to federal developments, "Between the late 1870s and 1933, America's criminal justice system fought a series of cultural battles in which criminal law . . . was a key weapon: against polygamy, state lotteries, prostitution, various forms of opium, and, last but definitely not least, alcoholic drink. Taken together, these legal battles constituted a two-generation culture war [that] transformed both the law and politics of crime."[14]

Underwriting this revolution in conceptions of criminality and offense was the way in which new conceptions of "the social" and "social legislation" intersected with the heightened concern about immorality and crime. Again, Roscoe Pound most clearly articulated the basic move and its implications for modern criminal liability. For Pound, modern criminal law had "for its province the securing of [the whole scheme of] social interests regarded directly as such, that is, disassociated from any immediate individual interests with which they may be identified." In place of the primitive view of criminal law as retributive *ex post* punishment for past individual misdeeds and "vicious will," Pound endorsed a mobilization of legal institutions and police agencies protecting modern social interests via the establishment of a more *preventative* criminal administration: "What goes on *before* the commission of an offense, with the conditions that generate offenders . . . and leads up to the crime, often much more surely and inevitably than the committed crime leads to conviction and the appointed penal treatment."[15] As one legal historian put it, Pound's approach basically removed "the person" from criminal law, replacing it "with a new, amorphous victim, 'society,' whose 'social interests' are protected against 'anti-social conduct.'"[16]

Pound's interpretation of the implications of "the social"—social self, social interests, social legislation—for modern criminal administration mirrored the way his contemporary Ernst Freund saw modern law moving from an essentially common-law basis of "civil and criminal justice" in the "maintenance of right and the redress of wrong" to a modern police power concerned with "public welfare or internal public policy." In

Freund's view, the police power embraced "a variety of interests," most significantly "the primary social interests of safety, order, and morals." In modern states, police power in the pursuit of social welfare was not confined to the prohibition of individual harmful acts; rather, "The state . . . exercises its compulsory powers for the prevention and anticipation of wrong by narrowing common law rights through conventional restraints and positive regulations which are not confined to the prohibition of wrongful acts."[17] Twenty-five years after Freund, Francis Sayre's essay "Public Welfare Offenses" more fully elaborated this momentous shift in criminal law and morals policing away from the traditional preoccupation with individual responsibility, free will, concrete harm, *mens rea*, and retribution—from nineteenth-century protection of "individual interest" to a twentieth-century focus on "collective" and "social and public interests." In the twentieth century, according to Sayre, "correctional treatment [changed] from the barren aim of punishing human beings to the fruitful one of protecting social interests," that is, the public welfare.[18] The state's more general obligation to protect social interests and public welfare via the enforcement and administration of a modern regulatory regime replaced the more traditional schemas of the criminal law. Sayre's appendix detailed the ever-expanding genre of public welfare offenses (which did not require *mens rea*):

1. Illegal Sales of Intoxicating Liquor
    a. Sales of prohibited beverage
    b. Sales to minors
    c. Sales to habitual drunkards
    d. Sales to Indians
    e. Sales by methods prohibited by law

2. Sales of Impure or Adulterated Food
    a. Sales of adulterated or impure milk
    b. Sales of adulterated butter or oleomargarine

3. Sales of Misbranded Articles

4. Violations of Anti-Narcotic Acts

5. Criminal Nuisances
    a. Annoyances or injuries to the public health, repose, or comfort
    b. Obstructions to highways

6. Violation of Traffic Regulations

7. Violations of Motor-Vehicle Laws

8. Violations of General Police Regulations, Passed for the Safety, Health, or Well-Being of the Community[19]

Sayre's article was, according to one legal historian, a "blueprint for the twentieth century depersonalization of American criminal law and its transformation into a state regulatory scheme." This was nothing short of the beginnings of modern criminal administration and the twentieth-century American war on crime.[20]

Some of the controversial import of this dramatic social transformation in and expansion of modern American criminal, police, and regulatory law was suggested by legal realist Karl Llewellyn's quip that "when you take 'the legal' out, you also take out the 'crime.'" Llewellyn's point was that the shift away from traditional concepts of legal criminality to modern social and administrative policing involved an attenuation of the centrality of criminal acts per se and an increased focus on the policing of a broader array of social transgressions. Modern criminal law became increasingly "strategic," ceasing "to define the conduct and intent that prosecutors actually sought to punish, and instead treating crime definition as a means of facilitating arrests, prosecutions, and convictions."[21]

FROM SOCIAL HYGIENE TO THE INJUNCTION AND ABATEMENT ACTS

Though a great number of individual reforms and causes were embraced by this new criminal justice orientation toward social prophylaxis, prevention, deterrence, and treatment, the American Social Hygiene Association (ASHA) epitomized three especially important developments: (1) the broadening of the definition of crime or offense toward social infractions; (2) the development and transformation of specific legal and legislative techniques and practices; and (3) the increased medicalization of offense and crime through the deployment of the apparatus of public health. In the merging of new conceptions of "the social," "criminal administration," and "public health and hygiene," a new social police was born.

Officially established in 1913, the American Social Hygiene Association built upon a late nineteenth-century tradition that historians have traditionally discussed in terms of a "purity crusade."[22] But while moral reform had diverse roots in this period of American history from Comstockery and anti-pornography to temperance organizations and vice committees, what distinguished the social hygiene movement was its bold program of direct legal action. As early as 1905, for example, Prince Morrow's American Society for Sanitary and Moral Prophylaxis endorsed an extensive program of "sanitary, moral, and legislative" action against "the spread of diseases which ha[d] their origin in the Social Evil [i.e., prostitution]."[23] Harvard president emeritus Charles W. Eliot opened the first meeting of the ASHA with an ambitious call to social action and for legislation against "vice diseases" as grave dangers to family, society, and "civilization." Taking note of the "remarkable progress of medicine, and especially of preventative medicine," Eliot invoked the analogue of war in outlining the "new duties and responsibilities" imposed upon society: "In dealing with such portentous evils, society can no longer place first considerations concerning innocency, delicacy, and reticence, any more than in dealing with war. The attack on them must be public and frank."[24] Eliot's address—and indeed, the entire first volume of the Association's journal *Social Hygiene*—was nothing short of a detailed blueprint for the kind of expansive war on vice, crime, and immorality that transformed American criminal justice, promoting: (1) social surveys regarding sexual vice in American cities and towns; (2) legal studies of police and statutory action against vice; (3) legislation and improved police administration with regard to vice; (4) vice suppression and public health treatment of sexually transmitted diseases; (5) prosecution of those making a profit out of obscene publications, indecent shows, immoral plays, and prostitution; (6) regulation of "sexual perversions"; (7) temperance and tobacco regulation; (8) medical ethics; and (9) sex education.

What made the American social hygiene movement stand out in the crowded field of turn-of-the-century moral reform was the transformative nature of its approach to law reform. In a period already swelling state and federal criminal codes, social hygiene made additional inroads in the fields of morals policing, criminal administration, and sex regulation. Issues of *Social Hygiene* regularly concluded with a detailed "Resume of Legislation Upon Matters Relating to Social Hygiene," which canvassed proposed and enacted legislation state by state. In 1915, the Association reported the introduction of over eighty state bills (half of which became law) on sex and sexuality under the subject headings: (1) age of consent and fornication; (2) prostitution; (3) injunction and abatement laws; (4) state reformatories and industrial homes for girls; (5) perversion; (6) venereal diseases; (7) sterilization; (8) children; (9) amusements; and (10) amusements (with further numbered references to adultery, birth control, dance halls, employment agencies, hotels, indecent exposure, marriage, morals court, motion pictures, obscene literature, rape, saloons, and women police).[25] By 1917, forty-four state jurisdictions had introduced some 300 social hygiene measures, of which over 160 became law.[26]

Of special concern to the ASHA legal reform agenda was the crusade against prostitution.[27] Indeed, the Journal of the Association conveyed something of the fierce spirit of this Progressive Era cause when it reported (on the advice of fourteen vice commissions, seventy-two cities, and intellectuals like Abraham Flexner) that we "must throw down the gauntlet to the whole horrible thing."[28] Of particular concern to reformers was the seeming imperviousness to existing regulation of the "red-light" prostitution districts in most American cities, from New Orleans's notorious "Storyville" to the "Avenue for Ladies Only" in East Grand Forks, Minnesota, to Chicago's "Levee" district, composed of some 200 brothels, bucket shops, and gambling houses.[29]

In response, moral and hygiene reformers introduced one legal reform that epitomized the more general trend toward modern social police and criminal administration in this period. In the first issue of *Social Hygiene*, immediately after Eliot's introduction of the general legislative agenda, the next article took up "The Fight for a Red Light Abatement Law."[30] This might sound like a relatively specialized reform, but the deployment of injunction and abatement acts in a legal crusade against municipal "red light" districts displayed the intricate mechanics of legal and policy innovation very fully. Passing and enforcing injunction and abatement acts was one of the top priorities (indeed, near obsessions) of the social hygiene movement as well as of municipal vice committees, and they illuminated the innovative legal underpinnings of the new American war on vice and crime.

The injunction and abatement acts were new state police power statutes passed in at least thirty-eight states by 1920.[31] Universally regarded as an effective new weapon in the war on vice, the injunction and abatement acts ultimately succeeded in wiping out most municipal "red-light" districts within the next decade.[32] The acts were part of a much-commented-on revival of "government by injunction" in this period, of which the labor injunction is the best-known example. Like the labor injunction, the injunction and abatement acts introduced a new set of extraordinarily powerful law enforcement mechanisms and procedures. With roots in the late nineteenth-century fight against illegal saloons and liquor abatement, the injunction and abatement acts brought several efficacious innovations to the war on vice more generally.

First, the acts authorized legal proceedings against property owners rather than those found guilty of certain "immoral" acts or crimes. Indeed, the acts defined certain kinds of uses of property (e.g., upon which lewdness, assignation, or prostitution was conducted) as public nuisances per se, dispensing with elaborate findings of facts establishing nuisance-like conditions. Second, the acts authorized more summary proceedings before a judge in equity—dispensing with a defendant's right to a traditional criminal trial by jury. Third, the legislation vastly expanded the range of public and private persons who could initiate actions against such establishments (ultimately including virtually every citizen in certain counties, cities, or states), breaking with long-held common-law rules regarding the existence of special injury as a prerequisite. Fourth, temporary and permanent injunctive remedies made it possible to cease illicit activities at such properties immediately and perhaps permanently. Violations of such injunctions and restraining orders resulted in contempt of court. Finally, orders of abatement provided for buildings to be "closed" and for all property used in the conduct of the public nuisance to be sold. Additional taxes, fines, and jail time rounded out this vast list of new pains, penalties, and punishments.

But key to the success of the injunction and abatement laws was a more general legal transformation. Indeed, the injunction and abatement acts expanded the reach of state police power in the social and morals arenas, much as the idea of "public utility" (which deemed certain private economic activities "affected with a public interest") allowed expanding areas of business to be regulated.[33] The progressive public utility concept was the entering wedge of a larger reform agenda that expanded older forms of police power, generating a concept of economic regulation in the public interest that pushed well beyond earlier understandings of the common-law and constitutional limitations. Something akin to this same process underwrote the overall transformation of criminal justice and social policing in this period.

The doctrinal story of the road to injunction and abatement is relatively complex. But it built upon several developments already alluded to: the expansion of police power toward regulation of public morals; a new concern for the public welfare and society at large as objects of legal protection; and a shift from concern with remediation of crime after the fact to prevention of crime to assure future safety. Furthermore, the injunction incorporated techniques from equity law as a prelude to more robust and effective criminal administration

In the early nineteenth century, "disorderly houses" or "bawdy houses" had been suppressed primarily as common-law "nuisances." Nuisance law in that period distinguished sharply between a private nuisance and a public nuisance. A "private" nuisance referred to an offense at common law wherein a landowner was harmed in the enjoyment of private property. As such, it was remediable via an ordinary civil proceeding or lawsuit.[34] In contrast, a "public" (or common) nuisance (like a bawdy house), according to Blackstone, was an inconvenience or offense to the community and not merely to some particular person or property. It was criminally indictable—one of a class of minor crimes and misdemeanors such as keeping disorderly inns, bawdy houses, bothersome hogpens, malarial ponds, and the like. Upon criminal indictment, these nuisances could be suppressed.[35] Public nuisances were not generally subject to a civil suit without proof of some kind of "special," individualized injury or damage.

One important distinction between public and private nuisance concerned equitable remedies—that is, those devised by courts of equity—including the injunction. Equity (a supplement to common law and different from it) provided a more "administrative" way of doing justice without the aid of a jury. Its arsenal of extraordinary remedies made it potentially a formidable system of jurisprudence. But courts of equity were supposed to have given up criminal jurisdiction in the seventeenth century. If equity had no criminal jurisdiction, how could the injunction be deployed against the criminal offense of keeping a house of prostitution, a public nuisance?

Two important and somewhat esoteric nineteenth-century exceptions had created an entering wedge for legal and regulatory innovation. First, interference with public property rights—so-called purpresture—affected the "whole community in general" and was criminally indictable as a public nuisance at common law, yet nineteenth-century judges carved out room for an injunction to deal with such interferences and thereby protect public property.[36] So too in cases where a private individual experienced so-called "special damage" to private property from a public nuisance. From 1850 to 1900, American jurists expanded upon these exceptions, transforming equitable jurisdiction over nuisance into a powerful public policymaking instrument. What was originally a tool designed to mete out justice between particular private parties became a mechanism for regulating social and economic behavior deemed to be opposed to the public welfare. Though this juridical instrument might be applied to economic, health, and safety nuisances, its use grew especially robustly in the area of public morals. Throughout this period, the injunction was wielded against disorderly houses, illegal saloons, gambling houses, and even prize- and bullfights.[37] Much as the public utility concept pushed beyond common-law categories of common calling and common carrier regulation, these legal antecedents pushed policing of morals beyond early common-law limitations. The injunction was an important supplement

to indictment, deterring future conduct while also responding to past offense. Equity's summary procedures allowed a more proactive, comprehensive, and administrative approach to crime and police as opposed to
relying on case-by-case prosecution after the fact. Moreover, the injunction
took aim at property as well as person, and restricted the uses of property well into the future. By the late nineteenth century, nuisance law as a
regulatory tool was no longer impeded by elaborate requirements for the
factual establishment of some kind of special harm, and state attorneys
general found themselves increasingly utilizing the injunction and equity's
summary proceedings as a first-order crime-fighting tool.[38]

The injunction and abatement acts formally codified these developments and extended the regulatory and police project even further. Iowa
was among the first states to experiment with a statutory nuisance abatement scheme in its long fight against saloons and liquor. In 1884, after
increasing penalties and easing evidentiary requirements for proving the
existence of "houses of ill-fame," the state legislature turned immediately to the "sale of intoxicating liquor" and implemented a scheme that
would soon become a template for future injunction and abatement acts.
It featured, first, a general statement declaring as a matter of statutory
law that buildings, establishments, or "the ground itself" in or on which
the "unlawful manufacture or sale" of intoxicating liquor took place was
per se a public nuisance and thus abatable as such with additional fines
and prosecutions for the maintenance of said nuisance. Second, by abatement, the legislature meant the closing of the building for such purposes
as well as the removal, sale, and/or destruction of the "furniture, fixtures,
vessels, and contents" that also made up the public nuisance. Third, Iowa
declared that "any citizen" in the county could bring "an action in equity
to abate and perpetually enjoin" the nuisance, thus making the entire citizenry private attorneys general. And fourth, violation of such an injunction
subjected the offender to a "contempt" proceeding that brought further
fines and punishments.[39] Duplicated by other states in the alcohol context
in the late nineteenth and early twentieth centuries, these powerful and
expanding features became the weapon of choice of urban vice committees and the social hygiene movement in the early twentieth-century fight
against the "red-light."[40]

The injunction and abatement acts passed between 1910 and 1920 were
even more extensive and included harsher penalties than the predecessor
liquor acts of the 1880s. A 1914 Massachusetts anti-prostitution law, for example, kept open a large number of punitive options, including criminal
and civil forfeiture of the property. Upon a decree permanently enjoining
the establishment, the sheriff was directed to "sell all furniture, musical

instruments, and movable property used in conducting and maintaining the nuisance."[41] Courts were also given the discretion to keep the premises closed and prohibit any other use for considerable time spans. Most statutes included provisions further loosening evidentiary rules so as to expedite the removal of public nuisances.

Such extraordinary expansions in state policing authority were uniformly upheld by state courts. Indeed, from Boston to Sacramento, the enjoinment and elimination of brothels was legitimated with powerful defenses of the states' police power to regulate in the general interest of public health, safety, welfare, and morals. In *Chase v. Revere House* (1919), the Massachusetts Supreme Judicial Court upheld the state's 1914 statute by claiming that a legitimate exertion of the police power included "all necessary measures for the promotion of the good order of the community and the public morals."[42] There was no longer any discussion of the property basis of equitable jurisdiction or the limits of old common-law remedies. Instead, discussion turned exclusively to the reasonableness of direct legislative initiatives to secure public order and morals. As the Illinois Supreme Court declared in *People v. Smith* (1916), "Under the police power the State may interfere whenever the public interest demands it, and a large discretion is vested in the legislature to determine not only what the interests of the public require but what measures are necessary for the protection of such interest."[43] The Illinois court thus expressed a conception of general public regulatory power that was one of the primary outgrowths of the Progressive Era expansion of social police.

On the ground, the implications were all too clear as the injunction and abatement acts took center stage in the aggressive vice raids that ultimately sealed the fate of many American "red-light" districts. The *Chicago Tribune* regularly tracked Chicago's version of a "vice war" in terms that drove home the everyday effects of the Illinois Supreme Court's endorsement of broad regulatory powers of social police. On April 4, 1918, the *Tribune* noted, Chicago city officials (health commissioner, police chief and deputy, city prosecutors, state's attorneys, corporation counsel and, notably, Chief Justice Harry Olson of Chicago's Municipal Court) met in conference at the University Club to set in motion "all the city's judicial, police and prosecution powers" against prostitution. That evening, an extensive series of police raids on "cabarets, saloons, houses, and flats" led to the arrest of some 205 "immoral" women who would be subject to medical tests for communicable diseases and imprisoned at the isolation hospital or tried on state vagrancy charges. As the paper noted, "The health department can do this under its police powers." But another key part of this particular raid involved the exercise of the injunction and abatement act—as police and health officials posted signs warning property owners that "premises are being used for unlawful purposes" and would be subject to abatement. As Chief Justice Olson put it, "It makes no difference whether the cases are found in hotels, apartment buildings, or wherever, the signs will go up and persons found to be a menace will be handled by the health department." The *Tribune* concluded, "The police and other authorities expect to drive out some supposedly strongly entrenched vice spots by this method." Notably, this extraordinary exercise of local police power by municipal and state officials can be traced back to a "request from Washington" noting that the city had "ample power under its police and health department rules to rid the city of the element which is held to be a menace to men in uniform."[44]

CONCLUSION

In 1918, with American society on a war footing, Josephus Daniels, secretary of the navy and chair of the Interdepartmental Social Hygiene Board, charged the Law Enforcement Division of the War and Navy Departments' Commissions on Training Camp Activities to prepare "standard forms of laws" to be transmitted to all state legislatures concerning "the repression of prostitution, the control of venereal disease and for the rehabilitative and curative treatment of sex offenders." Daniels was joined on the Interdepartmental Social Hygiene Board by such important national officials as Secretary of the Treasury William McAdoo, Secretary of War Newton Baker, as well as representatives from the various military medical corps and the US Public Health Service.[45] The ensuing *Standard Forms of Laws* included model state laws for "the repression of prostitution," "fornication," "the control of venereal disease," "the establishment and management of reformatories for women and girls," and "the care of the feeble-minded" (which included provisions for "sterilization") and "defective delinquents"—the latter justified under the reasoning of the National Committee of Mental Hygiene that "large numbers of prostitutes are mentally abnormal" and that society needed to be protected "against the menace" of "unrestrained activity" by "sex offenders who are feeble-minded."

The centerpiece of this new military and civilian effort of social policing, however, was "the well-known Injunction and Abatement Act." The model act contained expansive applications to nuisances involving "lewdness, assignation, or prostitution," and targeted a range of potential persons involved. It charged state attorneys general as well as county attorneys or, indeed, "any person who is a citizen of the county" to bring an action in equity seeking a temporary injunction and restraining order. Trial proceedings allowed "general reputation" as well as other prima facie evidence of nuisance or knowledge thereof, as well as expansive provisions for the "order of abatement," the sale of property, "punishment for contempt," as well as a "tax against property."

The immediate reason for this unusual military interposition into state legislative and regulatory processes was the tremendous loss of fighting manpower because of venereal disease during the world war.[46] But the foundation for such an unprecedented and coordinated attack on sex offenders, prostitutes, the feeble-minded, and other "women and girls" had been built over the previous three decades as new conceptions of "social problems" intersected with potent new technologies of legal and social policing so as to create a fundamental realignment of "the intimate state." The repercussions of those changes regarding law, gender, and sexuality would have important ramifications from "the great war" to "the war on crime" and beyond.

NOTES

1. Of course, the historico-theoretical literature on modern social welfare and social policing is enormous. On social police, I have found most useful Michel Foucault, *Security, Territory, Population: Lectures at the College de France, 1977–1978*, ed. Michel Senellart (New York: Palgrave Macmillan, 2007); Jacques Donzelot, *The Policing of Families* (New York: Random House, 1979); François Ewald, "A Concept of Social Law," in *Dilemmas of Law in the Welfare State*, ed. Gunther Teubner (New York: Walter de Gruyter, 1988), 40–75; Nikolas Rose, *Powers of Freedom: Reframing Political Thought* (Cambridge: Cambridge University Press, 1999); David Garland, *The Culture of Control: Crime and Social Order in Contemporary Society* (Chicago: University of Chicago Press, 2001); and Dario Melossi, *The State of Social Control: A Sociological Study of Concepts of State and Social Control in the Making of Democracy* (New York: St. Martin's Press, 1990).

2. See for example John Maurice Clark, *The Social Control of Business* (Chicago: University of Chicago Press, 1926); American Economic Association, *Readings in the Social Control of Industry* (Philadelphia: Blakiston, 1942); and William J. Novak, "Law and the Social Control of American Capitalism," *Emory Law Journal* 60 (2010): 377–405.

3. Ewald, "Social Law," 41.

4. Samuel George Smith, *Social Pathology* (New York: Macmillan, 1911); James Ford, *Social Problems and Social Policy: Principles Underlying Treatment and Prevention of Poverty, Defectiveness and Criminality* (Boston: Ginn and Company, 1923); and Stuart Alfred Queen and Delbert Martin Mann, *Social Pathology* (New York: Thomas Y. Crowell Company, 1925).

5. Queen and Mann, *Social Pathology*. See especially the discussion on 153–94,

as Queen and Mann discuss "The Illegitimate Family" and "Prostitution"; and Smith, *Social Pathology*.

6. See for example Clark D. Knapp, *Treatise on the Laws of the State of New York in Relation to the Poor, Insane, Idiots, and Habitual Drunkards* (Rochester, NY: Williamson & Higbie, 1887); Florien Giauque, *A Manual for Guardians and Trustees of Minors, Insane Persons, Imbeciles, Idiots, Drunkards* (Cincinnati: Robert Clarke & Co., 1881); and Charles Richard Henderson, *Introduction to the Study of the Dependent, Defective, and Delinquent Classes and of their Social Treatment* (Boston: D. C. Heath & Co., 1893).

7. Michel Foucault, *Discipline and Punish: The Birth of the Prison*, trans. Alan Sheridan (New York: Vintage Books, 1977), 80–81.

8. Charles W. Margold, *Sex Freedom and Social Control* (Chicago: University of Chicago Press, 1926), vii, 4, 7–8, 16, 30.

9. Jane Addams, *A New Conscience and an Ancient Evil* (New York: Macmillan, 1912); Harry Elmer Barnes and Willoughby C. Waterman, "A Scientific View of Sex Problems," *Social Forces* 3 (1924): 149–54; Maurice A. Bigelow, *Sex Education: A Series of Lectures Concerning Knowledge of Sex in Its Relation to Human Life* (New York: Macmillan, 1916); and Havelock Ellis, *Sex in Relation to Society: Studies in the Psychology of Sex, Vol. VI* (London: Heinemann, 1946).

10. Queen and Mann, *Social Pathology*, 162–65; George B. Mangold, *Born Out of Wedlock: A Sociological Study of Illegitimacy* (Columbia: University of Missouri Press, 1921); Percy Kammerer, *The Unmarried Mother: A Study of Five Hundred Cases* (London: William Heinemann, 1918); William Healy, *The Individual Delinquent: A Text-Book or Diagnosis and Prognosis for All Concerned in Understanding Offenders* (Boston: Little, Brown, and Company, 1915); and W. I. Thomas, *The Unadjusted Girl: With Cases and Standpoint for Behavior Analysis* (Boston: Little, Brown, and Company, 1923).

11. Mabel E. Elliott and Francis E. Merrill, "Social Control of Prostitution," in *Social Disorganization* (New York: Harper & Bros., 1934), 181–183, 186, 190. For this list, the authors relied on Ben L. Reitman's *The Second Oldest Profession: A Study of the Prostitute's "Business Manager"* (New York: Vanguard, 1931), drawing attention to Reitman's "ingenious tabulation" of "extra-marital contacts" in Chicago, where "he estimates that there are fully 100,000 women who satisfy the illicit desires of 500,000 men outside the bounds of matrimony in that city alone." On sexuality, Elliot and Merrill further noted that prostitutes were "for the most part, women, although there is a group of men who sell themselves either to women or to their own sex. . . . Not only are there a considerable number of male prostitutes, but homosexuality is also common among female prostitutes."

12. Francis A. Allen, "Criminal Justice, Legal Values and the Rehabilitative Ideal," *Journal of Criminal Law, Criminology, and Police Science* 50 (1959): 226–32, 226. See also Allen, *The Borderland of Criminal Justice: Essays in Law and Criminology* (Chicago: University of Chicago Press, 1964); and Allen, *The Decline of the Rehabilitative Ideal: Penal Policy and Social Purpose* (New Haven, CT: Yale University Press, 1981).

13. Roscoe Pound, *Criminal Justice in America* (New York: Henry Holt and Company, 1930), 23; and Allen, *Borderland*, 3.

14. William J. Stuntz, *The Collapse of American Criminal Justice* (Cambridge, MA: Harvard University Press, 2011), 158–59.

15. Roscoe Pound, "Introduction," in Francis Bowes Sayre, *A Selection of Cases on Criminal Law: With an Introduction by Roscoe Pound*, abridged ed. (Rochester, NY: Lawyers Co-operative Publishing Company, 1930), xxvii–xxxvii, xxxiv–xxxv. For the best discussion of Pound's socialization of American law, see Michael Willrich, *City of Courts: Socializing Justice in Progressive Era Chicago* (New York: Cambridge University Press, 2003).

16. Markus Dirk Dubber, "Policing Possession: The War on Crime and the End of Criminal Law," *Journal of Criminal Law and Criminology* 91 (2001): 829–996, 850–51.

17. Ernst Freund, *The Police Power: Public Policy and Constitutional Rights* (Chicago: Callaghan & Company, 1904), 4–7. See also Aya Gruber, "Duncan Kennedy's Third Globalization, Criminal Law, and the Spectacle," *Comparative Law Review* 3 (2012): 1–26.

18. Francis Bowen Sayre, "Public Welfare Offenses," *Columbia Law Review* 33 (1933): 55–88, 68.

19. Sayre, "Public Welfare Offenses," 84–88 (citing some 400+ cases).

20. Dubber, "Policing Possession," 852–53.

21. Stuntz, *Collapse of American Criminal Justice*, 159.

22. David J. Pivar, *Purity Crusade: Sexual Morality and Social Control, 1868–1900* (Westport, CT: Greenwood Press, 1973); and Pivar, *Purity and Hygiene: Women, Prostitution, and the "American Plan," 1900–1930* (Westport, CT: Greenwood Press, 2002).

23. Prince A. Morrow, "Foreword: A Plea for the Organization of a 'Society of Sanitary and Moral Prophylaxis,'" *Transactions of the American Society of Sanitary and Moral Prophylaxis* 1 (1906): 17–25, 17. See also Morrow, *Social Diseases and Marriage: Social Prophylaxis* (New York: Lea Brothers & Co., 1904).

24. Charles W. Eliot, "The American Social Hygiene Association," *Social Hygiene* 1 (1914): 1–5, 2. The very first issue of *Social Hygiene* also included important articles on "California's Fight for a Red Light Abatement Law" by Franklin Hichborn, I: 6–14; Abraham Flexner on "The Regulation of Prostitution in Europe," I: 15–28; G. Stanley Hall on "Education and the Social Hygiene Movement," I: 29–35; Clark W. Hetherington on "Play Leadership in Sex Education," I: 36–43; and Vernon L. Kellogg on "The Bionomics of War: Race Modification by Military Selection," I: 44–52.

25. Included were thirty-eight measures for commercialized vice (pimping, pandering, white slavery, homes for girls and women); thirty-one bills regarding sex offenses (adultery, fornication, lasciviousness, age of consent, carnal knowledge, incest, rape, sodomy, and seduction); thirty-six bills on amusements, pictures, literature, and recreation; and sixty-six assorted medical measures (venereal diseases, fake-cure advertisements, venereal disease and marriage certificates, quarantine, midwives, unsanitary dwellings, and the sterilization of defectives. "Social Hygiene Legislation in 1915: A Summary of Bills Bearing upon Social Hygiene, Introduced in the Several State Legislatures Having Sessions in 1915," *Social Hygiene* 2 (1915): 245–56. See also Ronald Hamowy, "Medicine and the

Crimination of Sin: 'Self-Abuse' in 19th-Century America," *Journal of Libertarian Studies* 1 (1977): 229–70.

26. Joseph Mayer, "Social Hygiene Legislation in 1917," *Social Hygiene* 5 (1917): 67–82.

27. For classics in a voluminous historiography, see Mark Thomas Connelly, *The Response to Prostitution in the Progressive Era* (Chapel Hill: University of North Carolina Press, 1980); Ruth Rosen, *The Lost Sisterhood: Prostitution in America, 1900–1918* (Baltimore: Johns Hopkins University Press, 1982); Mara L. Keire, "The Vice Trust: A Reinterpretation of the White Slavery Scare in the United States, 1907–1917," *Journal of Social History* 35 (2001): 5–41; Allan M. Brandt, *No Magic Bullet: A Social History of Venereal Disease in the United States Since 1880* (New York: Oxford University Press, 1987); Daniel J. Kevles, *In the Name of Eugenics: Genetics and the Uses of Human Heredity* (Cambridge, MA: Harvard University Press, 1998): and David J. Langum, *Crossing over the Line: Legislating Morality and the Mann Act* (Chicago: University of Chicago Press, 1994).

28. Maude E. Miner, "Report of the Committee on Prostitution of the National Conference of Charities and Correction," *Social Hygiene* 1 (1915): 81–92, 81–82. As Miner summarized the failures of previous regulatory regimes: "As prostitution assumed alarming and threatening proportions and it was clearly seen that it was not possible to pursue a laissez faire policy, attempts were then made to regulate vice. Under this system, rules were laid down by the police with regard to maintaining outward order and conserving health. When rules have provided for concentrating resorts in one or more given districts of the city the special form of regulation has been termed segregation. As the systems of [past] regulation have proved ineffective, cities have been pushed, as the only hope, to a policy of suppression."

29. Connelly, *Response to Prostitution*, 93; Thomas C. Mackey, *Red Lights Out: A Legal History of Prostitution, Disorderly Houses, and Vice Districts, 1870–1917* (New York: Garland Publishing, 1987); Peter C. Hennigen, "Property War: Prostitution, Red-Light Districts, and the Transformation of Public Nuisance Law in the Progressive Era," *Yale Journal of Law and the Humanities* 16 (2004): 123–98; and Stephen G. Sylvester, "Avenue for Ladies Only: The Soiled Doves of East Grand Forks, 1887–1915," *Minnesota History* 51 (1989): 290–300.

30. Franklin Hichborn, "The Fight for a Red Light Abatement Law," *Social Hygiene* 1 (1915): 6–8; and Maude E. Miner, "Report of the Committee on Prostitution of the National Conference of Charities and Correction," *Social Hygiene* 1 (1915): 81–92.

31. Ala. Laws 1919 No. 53; Ariz. Rev. St. 1913 § 4340; Cal. Gen. Laws 1915 No. 2798; Colo. Laws 1915 c. 123; Conn. Gen. Stat. 1918 § 2705; D.C. (1913) 38 Stat. 280; Ga. Laws 1917 p. 177; Idaho Comp. Stat. 1919 § 7042; Ill. Laws 1915 p. 371; Ind. Ann. Stat. 1918 § 293a; Iowa Laws 1915 c. 71; Ky. Stat. 1918 § 3941m; La. Laws 1918 No. 47; Mass. Laws 1914 c. 624; Mich. Comp. Laws 1915 § 7781; Minn. Gen. Stat. 1913 § 8717; Miss. Laws 1918 c. 193; Mont. Laws 1917 c. 95; Neb. Rev. Laws 1913 § 8775; N.H. Laws 1919 c. 95; N.J. Laws 1916 p. 315; N.C. Laws 1913 c. 761; N.D. Comp. Laws 1913 § 9644; Ohio Laws 1917 p. 514; Ore. Laws 1913 c. 274; S.C. Laws 1918 p. 814; S.D. Rev. Code

1919 § 2078; Utah Comp. Laws 1917 § 4275; Va. Laws 1916 c. 463; Wash. Rem. 1915 Code § 946; Wis. Stat. 1917 § 3185b. See also Kans. Gen. Stat. 1915 § 3650; Maine Rev. Stat. 1916 c. 23; Md. Laws 1918 c. 84; N.Y. Laws 1914 c. 365; Pa. Laws 1913 No. 852; Tenn. Laws 1913, 2nd Sess. c. 2; Tex. Pen. Code 1916 Art. 501. Charles S. Ascher and James M. Wolf, "'Red Light' Injunction and Abatement Acts," *Columbia Law Review* 20 (1920): 605–8.

32. Galveston, Texas, was allegedly the only American city with a red-light district still standing in 1952. Bascom Johnson, "Good Laws . . . Good Tools: Injunctions and Abatements versus Houses of Prostitution," *Journal of Social Hygiene* 38 (1952): 204–11; and Robert McCurdy, "The Use of the Injunction to Destroy Commercialized Prostitution in Chicago," *Journal of Criminal Law* 19 (1929): 513–17.

33. William J. Novak, "The Public Utility Idea and the Origins of Modern Business Regulation," in *Corporations and American Democracy*, ed. Naomi Lamoreaux and Novak (Cambridge, MA: Harvard University Press, 2017).

34. *Eden on Injunctions* (New York, 3rd ed. 1852), Il: 259; Olin L. Browder, *Basic Property Law* (St. Paul: West Publishing, 1989), 116; James W. Eaton, *Handbook of Equity Jurisprudence* (St. Paul: West Publishing Co., 1901), 588.

35. William Blackstone, *Commentaries on the Laws of England* (Oxford, 1769), IV: 167.

36. *Attorney General v. Richard*, 2 Anstr. 603 (Eng., 1795); *Columbus v. Jaques*, 30 Ga. 506 (1860); *State v. Mayor of Mobile*, (Ala. 1838). John C. Bagwell, "The Criminal Jurisdiction of Equity—Purpresture and Other Public Nuisance Affecting Health and Safety," *Kentucky Law Journal* 20 (1932): 163–65.

37. *State v. Crawford*, 28 Dan. 726 (1882), 733–34; *State ex. rel. Crow v. Canty*, 207 Mo. 439 (1907). Here too the rhetoric and sense of moral crisis expanded. As the court in *Crawford* decried the social evil of illegal saloons: "It is a Pandora's box sending forth innumerable ills and woes, shame and disgrace, indigence, poverty, and want; social happiness destroyed; domestic broils and bickerings engendered; social ties sundered; homes made desolate; families scattered; heart-rendering partings; sin, crime, and untold sorrows; not even hope left, but everything lost; an everlasting farewell to all true happiness and to all the nobler aspirations rightfully belonging to every true and virtuous human being."

38. On direct injunctive action by state attorney general, see *Mugler v. Kansas*, 123 U.S. 623 (1887); *State of Texas v. Patterson*, 14 Tx. Civ. App. 456 (1896).

39. "An Act Relating to Sale of Intoxicating Liquors," *Acts and Resolutions of the General Assembly of the State of Iowa* (1884), Ch. 143, § 12, p. 149.

40. Peter C. Hennigan, "Property War: Prostitution, Red-Light Districts, and the Transformation of Nuisance Law in the Progressive Era," *Yale Journal of Law and Humanities* 16 (2004): 138–46.

41. *Massachusetts Acts and Resolves* 1914, 589.

42. *Chase v. Revere House*, 232 Mass. 88 (1918), 96.

43. *People v. Smith*, 275 Ill. 256 (1916), 259–60.

44. *Chicago Tribune*, "Vice Raids Aid U.S. and City in Health Drive," April 5, 1918: 15.

45. War and Navy Departments Commission on Training Camp Activities,

Standard Forms of Laws for the Repression of Prostitution, the Control of Venereal Diseases, the Establishment and Management of Reformatories for Women and Girls, and Suggestions for a Law Relating to Feeble-Minded Persons (Washington, DC, 1919).

46. For an excellent overview, see Kimberley A. Reilly, "'A Perilous Venture for Democracy': Soldiers, Sexual Purity, and American Citizenship in the First World War," *Journal of the Gilded Age and Progressive Era* 13 (2014): 223–55.

4

The Commerce (Clause) in Sex in the Life of Lucille de Saint-André

GRACE PEÑA DELGADO

By the time of her death in late 2013, few observers doubted that Lucille de Saint-André lived a full, if not remarkable life. As a journalist for two Canadian newspapers, Montreal's *Morning Star* and Toronto's *Star*, de Saint-André delighted her readership with myriad stories spanning nearly five decades of reporting on international events, among them the student massacre at the 1968 Olympic Games in Mexico City and the condition of Vietnamese refugees. Her reporting likewise delved into spiritual issues, considering at length the practice of Buddhism, to which she ultimately converted.[1] De Saint-André traveled internationally to write these stories, but officials barred her from entering the United States, though it had been the nation to which she and her family initially arrived after fleeing German fascism in 1940. The action that would separate de Saint- André from her family for three decades —crossing interstate lines against her will to practice prostitution in 1945 as an immigrant woman in violation of the 1917 Immigration Act—triggered her deportation from the United States for moral turpitude.

Over the next thirty years, as de Saint-André repeatedly attempted to cross into the United States to reunite with her family, she made legible a series of immigration statuses and crimes that, by the mid-twentieth century, bore the imprint of a mature global system of human migration and citizenship management: in 1940, as a German-Jewish refugee and internee in Vichy France's Camp de Gurs; in 1941, as a fugitive of the camp, a refugee from fascism, and a permanent resident of the United States; in 1945, as a prisoner in a Mobile, Alabama, jail cell; in 1947, as a deportee of the United States and a stateless person tentatively living in Canada; in 1948, as a deportee from Canada and a stateless person in France; in 1952, as a naturalized citizen of Canada; in 1971, as an inmate held in a New York City jail for immigration violations and as a volunteer deportee from the United States; in 1972, as a fifth-preference immigrant; and finally, in 1974, as the beneficiary of a presidential private bill that granted discretion in the enforcement of an otherwise unforgiving immigration law that, had it been enforced, would continue to separate de Saint-André from her New York City–based family.[2] In invoking the Commerce Clause in the 1910 white-slave traffic law (commonly known as the Mann Act) and coupling it with immigration law, Congress transformed de Saint-André, a dynamic and irrepressible woman, into a person incapable of volition, a criminal, and an immigrant suitable for deportation.

The story of de Saint-André is astounding. In disquieting fashion, it illustrates the grievous power of the postwar order of sovereign nation-states to decide political membership for immigrant women based on intimate conduct. From her 1945 arrest in Mobile, Alabama, to 1974, when de Saint-André entered the United States at the discretion of President Gerald Ford, the union of the Mann Act and immigration law constrained de Saint-André's movements in North America. For thirty years, de Saint-André carried the legal and personal burden of an immigrant woman deported for moral turpitude. But while the case of de Saint-André was unusually complex—and perhaps even singular among the thousands of immigrant women who were deported from the United States for practicing prostitution—her story was substantially more than this.

More fully, the case of Lucille de Saint-André directs us to consider the origins of American state power that brought together the Mann Act and the Immigration Act of 1907—and later the Immigration Act of 1917—to criminalize and deport immigrant women as immoral traffic. In tandem, the Mann Act and immigration law represented an arrangement of over-lapping legal provisions allowing Congress to punish immigrant women for the wrongs of sex—at national borders through the immigration power, and across interstate lines through federal power to control interstate commerce. When de Saint-André, a young immigrant woman, was taken across state lines and coerced into practicing prostitution, she became entangled in the sexual logic of the Mann Act and immigration law.

That is, de Saint-André became sexual commerce, a socially unclean commodity in the intercourse of cross-state traffic punishable by deportation. The Mann Act signaled a change in Commerce Clause jurisprudence by expanding congressional authority from regulating the transportation of goods across state and international lines to criminalizing people as commodities in the circulation of commerce. When the commerce power in the Mann Act interacted with deportation in immigration law, Congress achieved interior and national border control over immigrants' sexual morality.

The Mann Act thus raised several questions about what commerce entailed and whether people were commodities in the circulation of commerce. Until 1913, when the Supreme Court ruled in *Hoke and Economides v. United States* to uphold the Mann Act's broad definition of commerce to include "persons as well as property," these questions had been left unresolved.[3] In antebellum debates over slavery and immigration, legal efforts to define whether immigrants were persons exercising volition, or were trade goods circulating as commerce, became bound up in questions of federal authority to regulate slavery. If Congress regulated immigrants as commodities in interstate commerce, then it could likewise hold authority over the domestic slave trade. To settle whether people were commodities and thus subject to congressional regulation risked Southern states' control over their "peculiar institution." Correspondingly, immigrants-as-goods jeopardized state-level jurisdiction of immigration control. Once the abolition of slavery dispensed with that problem, Congress progressed cautiously to move immigration regulation from the states to the federal administration in the first three decades after the Civil War. By 1875, the Supreme Court had affirmed the federal government's jurisdiction over immigration as part of international commerce, but fifteen years later, the Court upheld *Chae Chan Ping v. United States* (1889), emphasizing instead the unilateral sovereignty of the nation-state as legitimizing federal control of human movement at national borders.[4]

Yet whether immigrants were commodities—and subject to regulation via the federal power over interstate and international commerce—remained an open question in the modern regime of national immigration control. Despite prior rulings confirming the nation's "inherent right [as] a sovereign power" to prohibit the entry of immigrants into its territory, a precise legal mechanism that constructed persons as immoral commerce was not yet instantiated in federal law until the ruling in *Hoke,* which upheld the Mann Act's capacious definition of "commerce" in the interstate Commerce Clause as "intercourse," implying people as goods. Through the Mann Act and immigration law, Congress crafted a sexual logic based on commerce as intercourse that worked to categorize and criminalize immigrant women such as Lucille de Saint-André as immoral traffic. Doing so further buttressed Congress's plenary power over immigration, specifically with the power to exclude foreign prostitutes at interstate and national borders and to deport them as it saw fit.

FIGURE 4.1. Congressman James R. Mann, sponsor of the White Slave Traffic Act. Courtesy of the Library of Congress.

To draw out why punishment for prostitution led to thirty years of separation between de Saint-André and her family, we need to reach backwards to key nineteenth-century judicial controversies over personhood, immigration, and the commerce power. How might we understand the way an otherwise minor and state-level crime for prostitution became tantamount to immoral traffic? Specifically, why did antebellum Supreme Court cases puzzle over whether slaves and immigrants crossing state lines were persons, or articles of commerce enter the early twentieth-century debate over white-slave traffic? Early to mid-nineteenth-century interpretations of the meaning and scope of the Commerce Clause help answer these questions. This clause in the US Constitution, which states that "Congress shall have power to . . . regulate commerce with Foreign Nations, and among the several states and with the Indian tribes . . . ," became a source of prolonged judicial debate because of its potential to wrest from states their regulation of the interstate slave trade and immigration as a function of their police powers.[5] In *Gibbons v. Ogden* (1824), US Supreme Court Chief Justice Marshall averred that "[commerce] is more than buying and selling . . . it is something more—it is intercourse. It describes the commercial intercourse between nations and parts of the nations. . . ."[6] Marshall's understanding of commerce as "intercourse" rested on social relationships among people involving conversations and meetings to transact traffic, meaning the purchase, sale, and exchange of commodities. Commerce resides in intercourse, including the transportation of persons and property on shipping lines, roads, and the telegraph or in person.[7] Yet Southern states' sensitivity about slavery made this definition threatening. If federal power over interstate commerce pertained to persons as well as goods crossing state lines, then Congress could regulate the interstate slave traffic. Pro-slavery advocates insisted that Congress had no such power, maintaining that Marshall's concept of commerce reserved to states' police powers a wide scope of legislative authority over domestic relations, including slavery.[8]

After Marshall's death in 1835, the commerce power remained a matter of considerable controversy under the pro-slavery chief justice Roger Taney.[9] *Mayor of New York v. Miln* (1837), the Court's first case on the constitutionality of states' immigration laws, addressed questions left open in *Gibbons*.[10] In *Miln*, the Court maintained that states had within their police powers the authority to collect information on all arriving passengers and to secure bonds against the future care of any person likely to become dependent on public support. Justice Philip Barbour, a states' rights Virginian who delivered the majority opinion, declared that the New York law in question did not infringe upon federal authority to regulate trade and commerce between foreign seaports and the port of New York. Barbour reasoned that foreign passengers, after they landed, transformed from commodities in international commerce under the control of the federal government to human beings regulated by the states' police powers.[11] Barbour's reconciliation in *Miln*—"that goods are the object of commerce . . . persons are not"—stood on a narrow application of the congressional commerce authority and a broad understanding of states' rights that accommodated an emergent view of federalism.

After the ruling in *Miln*, as the legal scholar Mary Sarah Bilder points out, the court tentatively agreed that white immigrants and indentured servants were persons under the regulation of the states, but future cases about the status of slaves as property triggered further debate over the commerce power.[12] The 1841 case *Groves v. Slaughter*, about the validity of the Mississippi state constitution barring slaves from the state for sale, at once raised the question of whether slaves were property or persons.[13] Despite this direct question about federal power over interstate slave trafficking, the Court once again deliberately and artfully avoided making any official determination upon the central issue—what or whom comprised commerce, and by extension, where was the proper domain to regulate commerce, the states or the federal government. To complicate matters, several justices in the *Passenger Cases* (1849) continued in their insistence that white immigrants stood apart from slaves, although decades later, lawmakers would make no such distinction in white-slave traffic law. Drawing on a racialized discourse of personhood and volition, Justice Peter Daniel strenuously argued:

> [Commerce is] applicable only to articles of trade proper . . . chattels, property, subjects in their nature passive and having no volition,—not to men whose immigration is the result of will, and could not be accomplished without their cooperation . . . The conclusion, then, is undeniable, that alien passengers . . . carrying into execution their deliberate intentions, never can, without a singular perversion, be classed with the subjects of sale, barter, or traffic; or . . . with imports.[14]

Daniel's view to assign volition to white immigrants also marked strict racial boundaries between Black chattels as commodities lacking personhood and white passengers as free individuals. By the mid-nineteenth century, Atlantic seaboard states could no longer request a bond against future incoming passengers, but local rights prevailed in important ways. States, insisted Chief Justice Taney, could continue to bar the entry of unwanted persons as an exercise of their police powers.

In that context, where local control permitted chattel slavery (persons as property), many abolitionists uncomfortably advocated for expanded federal power on the basis that bondspersons were inanimate goods in the exchange of commerce. Immigrant paupers were not defined as property. Their potential burden on community and state was regulated under traditional police powers. The opposing counsel in *Groves,* Robert J. Walker, reminded abolitionists of their "strangely inconsistent" if not disquieting position: "[It] is the abolitionists who must wholly deprive the slaves of the character of persons, and reduce them to the level of merchandise, before they can apply to them the power of [C]ongress to regulate commerce among the states."[15] Another variation of unfreedom abounded. Levi Woodbury, a justice from New Hampshire well known for his pro-slavery and nativist views, observed that white immigrants entering the country "as unwilling or passive" should likewise be considered objects of commerce like slaves.[16]

It would take the Union victory in the Civil War, and the transformation of the American polity into a more centralized state, to ground the belief in the inalienable rights of persons as human beings equal under the law.

Radical Republicans in Congress, through the Thirteenth Amendment, abolished slavery and indentured servitude and likewise condemned other types of private domination akin to slavery.[17] Yet when Reconstructors crafted the Fourteenth Amendment, they did not match in equal measure the clarity and force conveyed in the Thirteenth Amendment. In crafting the Fourteenth Amendment, Congress left out a phrase initially proposed, "all persons are equal before the law," a stipulation that could have constitutionally equalized men and women.[18] The distribution of rights under the amendment continued to disproportionately disadvantage women, even as its language affirmed equal protection under the law for "any person . . . within its jurisdiction," that is, the jurisdiction of any state.[19]

For two decades following Reconstruction, the commerce-power framework stood as the principal congressional tool in the control of immigration.[20] Lawmakers understood that immigrants, because they crossed international borders before they entered the United States, took part in international relations. By extension, the comity of nations through treaty agreements ensured the rights and privileges of immigrants. But in 1889, the postbellum regime of immigration control featuring the commerce power as its regulatory centerpiece gave way to the emphasis on the plenary power of the United States to restrict immigration as a matter of national sovereignty. The ruling in the 1889 Chinese exclusion case, *Chae Chan Ping*, described Congress's authority to regulate immigration as an inherent power of national sovereignty, consigning the commerce power to the margins of immigration matters until Congress revived it in the Mann Act—where it interacted with immigration statutes to deport women like Lucille de Saint-André.[21]

When Marshall first interpreted the Commerce Clause in 1824, he left Congress with a far-reaching scope of the commerce power that had the potential to regulate market relations regarded as socially unclean, including prostitution. Although American markets industrialized and expanded their global networks later, explains the legal scholar Jack Balkin, "the Court has never officially abandoned this . . . construction."[22] But before Congress summoned Marshall's definition into the arena of regulating prostitution in the early twentieth century, the federal regulation of lotteries, obscene literature, birth control devices, diseased livestock, and the impurity of food and drugs illustrated the elastic usefulness of the commerce power.[23]

The white slave, though, stood alone. Unlike lottery tickets, birth control devices, rabid cattle, or adulterated food, the female person—ostensibly a carrier and interstate object of unclean illicit intercourse—resurrected portions of the antebellum debate: were people articles of commerce and did Congress have the power to regulate them through the Commerce Clause? By deploying Marshall's concept of commerce as intercourse in passing the Mann Act, Congress answered these questions in the affirmative.[24] "Intercourse," in the vernacular of mid-twentieth-century America, typically referred to sexual relations, but in the parlance of the Mann Act and immigration law, intercourse corresponded to Congress's authority to negate sexual volition and expel foreign prostitutes as unclean traffic.

This construction of commercial intercourse as involving the movement of immigrant women across US interstate and national lines began in the European movement against white-slave traffic. Outcries to end the "procuration" of white slaves fueled a series of international conferences and draft conventions on "La traite des Blanches" in 1899, 1902, and 1904, attended by European states and kingdoms. No African, Asian, Middle Eastern, or Latin American nation took part in these draft conventions or the follow-up international conferences, nor did the concept of the white slave include women of color. In the 1904 Paris Treaty, representatives first defined "traffic" as a crime in the "trade of white women" and cast it as a lamentable outcome of international migration.[25] An ethos of strong centralized policing undergirded the recommendations in the 1904 Agreement encouraging states and kingdoms to set up their own reporting authority to gather information on foreign pimps and prostitutes and share it with other signatories.[26] To protect white women and girls against procurers, officials called for the exercise of surveillance at border entry points and for national police forces to supervise and, if need be, arrest individuals at railway stations or during conveyance.[27] As a result of the Paris Treaty, European borders became frontline spaces to fight the traffic in white slaves, while domestic transportation depots were perceived as points of interchange in the "criminal traffic" of white women and girls.[28]

The Paris Treaty influenced how American lawmakers initially conceptualized the trade in women and girls and its solutions. In the United States, as in Europe, the problem was cast as a racialized crime of immorality, and its remedies lay in the suppression of the traffic at international and interstate lines. The development of the early movement's language against the white-slave traffic is important to note. In the years following the Paris Treaty, lawmakers and moral reformers conflated the terms "immigration" and "importation" to cast the traffic in white women and girls to be as unjust as the interstate trade in Black slaves. Through this analogy, importation became a legal descriptor of harm understood as sexual commerce, a logic that the Mann Act and the Immigration Act of 1907 would later instantiate in law.

The discourse of white slavery disclosed a racial calculus consistent with the post-Reconstruction era of national reconciliation, which min-imized the brutality of chattel slavery. At times, though, the discursive power of white slavery went beyond false equivalency to the negationist pseudo-history of the Lost Cause, assigning greater importance to free-ing white slaves than to Black emancipation a half century earlier. The Chicago-based Reverend William Burgess, who was among Congressman James R. Mann's most ardent supporters, considered white slavery "far worse than negro slavery." Burgess maintained that "[m]any a negro had an honest home [and] was able by the provision of his employer to estab-lish a domestic circle. . . . Many an owner of black slaves conserved their purity and never thought of them for beastly purposes . . ." In Burgess's estimation, it was the white slave whose soul was "instantly blackened" by the "white slave system."[29] In holding to the view that slavery was a benign institution, white-slavery abolitionists like Burgess scrubbed away the ex-ploitation of the interstate slave trade as a system based on the control of persons as property. Nor did they trouble the dynamics assigning the right of ownership in Black persons to those who were politically free and racially white. The similarities of the two systems, as anti-white-slavery activists saw it, lay in their schemes as importation, a forced trade in hu-man bondage.

By 1907, the expansion of national immigration laws ostensibly equipped lawmakers and white-slavery abolitionists to stop the importa-tion of immoral traffic. With exclusion mechanisms established in the Im-migration Act of 1903, Congress expanded and defined criminal, intimate misconduct in broad terms as "immoral purpose" in the Immigration Act of 1907, specifically in Article 3. The new immoral purpose provision directly linked the sexual wrongs of white women and girls to their im-portation by procurers and procuresses. Crimes of immoral purpose and importation—and later, concubinage—were subject to federal regulation, with violations punishable by immediate deportation.[30] The Immigration Act of 1907, legislators believed, protected citizens from the importers of prostitutes and of foreign-born women or girls who would be forced into prostitution. More telling, the 1907 legislation extended the prosecutorial reach of Congress further than the Paris Treaty had recommended, by cre-ating nine classes of immigrants eligible for deportation for the wrongs of sex, emphasizing the language of immoral purpose, procurement, and im-portation.[31] They were: "prostitutes prior to or at the time of entry; women or girls coming for purposes of prostitution; women or girls coming for any other immoral purpose such as concubinage; persons who procure or import prostitutes; persons who procure or import women or girls for the purpose of prostitution; persons who procure or import women or girls

FIGURE 4.2. Procuress Fanny Loewy Kraft (Löwy). Immigration officials collected several photographs with reports of convicted madams and pimps in Europe, such as this one from the German national police. Courtesy of the National Archives.

for any other like immoral purpose; persons who attempt to import prostitutes; persons who attempt to import women or girls for the purpose of prostitution; and persons who attempt to import women or girls for any other like immoral purpose."[32]

To get to the root of the white-slave problem, the Immigration Act called for the establishment of a special commission to "make a full inquiry . . . into the subject of immigration" headed by Senator William P. Dillingham of Vermont. In the meantime, Bureau of Immigration officials took advantage of their role as US representatives under the Paris Treaty in 1908 to expand existing investigations into the sources of prostitution importation with the help of national police forces in signatory nations.[33] Such reports detailed ethnic and religious characteristics of previously jailed procurers and procuresses and women likely to emigrate and work as prostitutes in the United States. In return for their cooperation, European police officials in each country received from US Bureau of Immigration authorities information regarding women deported to their homeland as violators of white-slave and immigration laws.

The Bureau of Immigration reports confirmed earlier assumptions that white slaves were non-volitional migrants sourced from European traffickers, who imported them as sexual slaves into American cities. Frank Sargent, the commissioner-general of immigration, confirmed the early mind-set about the sources and circulation of the white-slave traffic whereby "Europe is a field in which 'white slaves' are recruited by human demons . . . [and] the United States is a field in which they are sold or farmed out."[34] Follow-up investigations by the Bureau of Immigration further established that the traffic in white slaves was "constantly being transacted in the importation and distribution of foreign women for purposes of prostitution."[35]

Since copious documentation confirmed the traffic in white slaves— documentation considered dubious by feminist activists such as Emma Goldman, and later, historians—lawmakers and their activist supporters believed that the Immigration Act of 1907 was inadequate to stop immoral persons from entering and moving around the United States. Late in 1909, upon receiving a report from the commissioner-general of immigration on the status of white-slave traffic and a preliminary draft report by the Immigration Commission, President William H. Taft urged more robust federal action to crush traffickers and to suppress local prostitution. One of the recommendations of the Immigration Commission, which described "the importation and harboring of alien women and girls for immoral purposes . . . as the most pitiful and most revolting phase of the immigration question," was to stop the interstate transportation of persons practicing prostitution.[36] Within eleven days, James R. Mann, an Illinois congressman and chairman of the House Committee on Interstate and Foreign Commerce, proposed a promising approach to, in his words, "put a stop to villainous interstate and international traffic in women and girls . . . and to prevent panderers and procurers from compelling thousands of women and girls [into] prostitution."[37] Throughout the congressional hearing, lawmakers connected Mann's legislation to the Immigration Act of 1907 as pursuing a common cause: to stamp out the importation and interstate traffic in white slaves. Mann borrowed the "immoral purpose" language from the 1907 Immigration Act, yet sought to distinguish his bill from an earlier piece of immigration legislation, cosponsored by William Bennet of New York and Benjamin Franklin Howell of New Jersey, seeking to remove the time limit on deportation of prostitutes, procurers, and madams. Mann, also encouraged by US attorney for Illinois Edwin W. Sims and the Immigration Commission, inserted the Commerce Clause as a regulatory centerpiece in his bill.[38]

The Mann Act implied Marshall's meaning for commerce as intercourse, including networks of transportation, navigation, communication, social activity in the exchange of people and goods, and international treaty agreements. The act made it a crime to transport women and girls—either immigrants or citizens—across interstate lines to prostitute them, to have sex with them outside the bonds of marriage, and to cohabitate with them. To criminalize traffickers, which was the Mann Act's ostensible intent, the commerce power analogized transporting women and young girls in interstate traffic to the conveyance of immoral commercial goods.[39] To prohibit interstate travel, Section 2, for example, barred transporting or assisting in their transport across state lines "any woman or girl for the purpose of prostitution or debauchery, or for any other immoral purpose."[40] This part of the white-slave traffic law imputed immorality to any person taking part in immoral commerce, that is, assisting a sex worker, concubine, or unmarried female companion across interstate lines.

As the Mann Act relied on the commerce power to ban immoral traffic over interstate borders, it likewise initiated new surveillance controls of known or suspected prostitutes crossing at US borders and ports of entry. Changes in the Immigration Act of 1907 proposed earlier by Bennet and Howell interacted with the Mann Act to expand its reach and power. On March 6, 1910, revisions to Sections 2 and 3 of the Immigration Act of 1907 extended the three-year period for excludable offenses to an unspecified length of time. The 1910 amendment to the Act of 1907 extended deportation from a tool of immigration control deployed at US national borders to one that sanctioned the removal of immigrant prostitutes from the interior of the country for post-entry immoral conduct without an explicit time limit.[41] "Thus," asserts the legal historian Daniel Kanstroom, "[the] 1910 refinement . . . created what amounted to the first true U.S. post-entry social control deportation law since the 1789 Alien Friends Act."[42]

With the federal government authorized by the Immigration Act of 1907 to deport immigrants in the interior of the United States, the Mann Act further refined policing of the wrongs of sex. Section 6, the longest portion of the act, authorized the commissioner-general of immigration to set up at border points of entry (as expected in the Paris Treaty) a system to "receive and centralize information on the procuring of alien women and girls with a view to their debauchery."[43] The ostensible immigrant-prostitute registry sought to codify the names, nationality, age, and parentage of confirmed prostitutes entering the United States, to determine, if possible, the identity of the person who induced them to leave their country, and establish a structure to "exercise supervision over such alien women and girls."[44] Although immigration officials at various border points of entry did take part in this collection of information, Section 6 did not intend the accumulated knowledge as evidence to deport or criminalize harborers of immigrant prostitutes. To better pursue charges against sex workers, Section 6 allowed "keepers" of houses of ill-fame to furnish information to the Bureau of Immigration in exchange for immunity from prosecution.[45]

Considering the chief purpose of the Mann Act—to punish traffickers plying immoral interstate and foreign commerce—this incongruous, if bewildering portion of the white-slave law seemed not to apprehend that brothel keepers and harborers of prostitutes were often also traffickers, and therefore would have no incentive to comply with the white-slave traffic law despite immunity from prosecution. This may explain the lackluster results of Section 6's prostitute registry. By 1915, only one brothel keeper complied with the Section 6 reporting mandate.[46] Yet this lack of cooperation did not discourage officials from gathering information on immigrant prostitutes outside Section 6 and beyond official border entry points.[47] Their swift and thorough investigations in the interior of the United States, which survived court challenges, led to a significant number of warrants for the "arrest and deportation of alien prostitutes."[48] In 1914, the commissioner-general of immigration reported the arrest and deportation of 392 immoral women, 154 procurers, and 155 persons supported by prostitution.[49] To bolster their cases for removal, officials drew on intelligence collected by Department of Justice officials, a relationship of cooperation sanctioned by both federal agencies to enforce the white-slave law.[50] Immigration agents likewise enjoyed leads by municipal police who had targeted foreign-born prostitutes as criminals violating local anti-vice laws.[51]

The regime of white-slave and immigration laws had its critics. Most who condemned this approach protested against Congress's constitutional right to regulate the interstate movements of prostitutes as human commodities, rather than the dubious mandate to compel private citizens and immigrants to report on foreign women who worked for them as prostitutes.[52] In 1913, three years after the Mann Act became law, the ruling in *Hoke v. United States* reaffirmed Congress's authority over both the interstate and cross-border movements of "persons as well as property" under the commerce power. In an insistent tone, Justice Joseph McKenna maintained that "Commerce among the states . . . consists of intercourse and traffic between their citizens, and includes the transportation of persons and property. There may be therefore a movement of persons and of property—that is, a person may move or be moved in interstate commerce."[53] To eliminate any further ambiguity, McKenna disavowed the opinion of Justice Philip Barbour nearly a century earlier in *Miln*: "the statement of Justice Barbour . . . that persons are 'not the subject of commerce,' has never received the sanction of the court, but has been expressly refuted."[54] Personhood, McKenna suggested, was immaterial

FIGURE 4.3. Mary Abastenia St. Leger Eberle's *White Slave*. Plaster cast. The statuette was featured at the 1913 Armory Show, a consequential year in the national crusade against white-slave traffic. Courtesy of Wikimedia Commons.

to white-slave traffic.[55] Still, McKenna did not deny the personhood of those who exchanged sex for money. "Of course, women are not articles of merchandise," he declared. But in the same breath McKenna accepted an interpretation of commerce as intercourse that analogized persons as property. Persons, he affirmed, were articles of commerce, as were property, livestock, and the mail.[56]

More explicitly, the movement of white slaves across international and interstate lines negated their consent. Without movement or without "intercourse" by use of the machinery of commerce (e.g., telephones, tunnels, train tickets, roads), traffickers could not carry out white slavery. In motion, and at the very moment of crossing from one state into another or from one country into another to sell sex, the female prostitute was transformed into a commodity-in-conveyance, a white slave. It was the act of traversing state or national borders via the machinery of commerce that nullified a woman's consent and made her a white slave. McKenna's decision that persons were commercial goods confirmed the logic held by the pro-slavery justice Levi Woodbury nearly seven decades earlier in the *Passenger Cases*: that unwilling immigrants should be considered objects of commerce like slaves. It is interesting to note that while the state distinguished between "aliens" and citizens in conferring rights claims in general (e.g., no judicial review for immigrant cases; deportation for immigrants), enforcing the white-slave traffic law made US-born prostitutes and traffickers legal analogues of "aliens" when they crossed interstate borders to ply their trade. All, irrespective of citizenship, were criminals under the Mann Act.

The interaction of the Mann Act with the Immigration Act of 1907 composed a far-reaching discourse, producing a broad corpus of the wrongs of sex. Extramarital relationships and male-female couples traveling together, as well as incidents of willing or unwilling prostitution, and other sexual associations such as concubinage and couplings that were noncommercial but includable within the wide definitional boundaries of "debauchery" and "immoral purpose," comprised a host of sexual wrongs. For example, Susan Ferrell, a twenty-four-year-old Cornwall, England, native, endured some of the harshest consequences of white-slave traffic and immigration laws. In 1915, Ferrell migrated to the United States to wed Joseph Griffiths, a naturalized American citizen and a longtime resident of Bisbee, Arizona. Ferrell "was in a family way before [she] left [Cornwall]" but somehow avoided inspection when she landed at Ellis Island. Ferrell met Griffiths in El Paso, Texas, where they lived as man and wife but did not marry despite Ferrell's pleas. In what amounted to an act of revenge against her lover's broken promise, Ferrell turned Griffiths in to El Paso police. Griffiths faced several charges under white-slave traffic and immigration laws that criminalized anyone who "persuaded, induced, enticed" a woman into international and/or interstate transportation for immoral purposes (including unlawful intimate cohabitation). Rather than treating the Ferrell-Griffiths relationship as consensual, albeit in Ferrell's estimation a personally unacceptable arrangement, the capacious language of "immoral purpose" comprehended their coupling as tantamount to sexual slavery.[37]

Under the Mann Act and the Immigration Law of 1907, the wrongs of sex infused the nonmarital relationship between Griffiths and Ferrell.

Griffiths's purchase of Ferrell's transportation fare and her later travel from England to Texas transformed her into a commodity-in-conveyance, as a person engaged in "foreign commerce, for immoral purposes . . . [and] without her consent."[58] The nonmarital cohabitation of the couple was construed as a deliberate act of "unlawful and felonious procurement of concubinage . . . [so] that Susan Ferrell should live with him . . . and have sexual intercourse with him." As an unmarried female immigrant, Ferrell faced deportation as an alien prostitute under the Immigration Law of 1907. If Griffiths had kept his original promise and married Ferrell, her alienage would have been transformed into derivative citizenship, a status that protected immigrant women from deportation. Ferrell's personal character would have also been elevated to a respectable, married woman whose unborn child would be bequeathed legitimacy and birthright citizenship. Matrimony would have transformed Griffiths from a deportable trafficker under the Mann Act into a reputable husband. For an immigrant woman, the punishment included removal from the country, even as Progressive Era moral reformers admitted that the "ruin" of immigrant girls was because of the lack of protection by government and private agencies. For her wrongs, immigrant officials deported Ferrell to Cornwall in late 1916.

Foes of white slavery constructed and relied upon a narrative of female victimization that assigned no blame—and no agency—to women and girls for their role in white slavery. A trope of victimization accompanied the white slave, a discourse that simultaneously softened her ruin and initiated her resurrection. Despite the trope of victimization, immigrant women had no recourse and experienced deportation as alien prostitutes. The wastefulness of this treatment did not escape the criticism of American feminists, including Jane Addams. "Certainly," asserted Addams, "the immigration laws might do better than to send a girl back to her parents, diseased and disgraced, because America had failed to safeguard her virtue from machinations of well-known but unrestrained criminals."[59] Though Addams's critique pointed to the harshness of deportation, the trope of victimization was an entrenched moral discourse that not only negated volition for prostitutes, free-union partnerships, and concubines, but likewise worked to legitimize and steady the protean assault on immigrant women accused of sexual immorality.

The sexual logic of the Mann Act and immigration law cast a wide net over intimate relationships, one that made a vengeful lover, a concubine, and even an erstwhile immigrant sex worker, such as Lucille de Saint-André, into a deportable white slave. By the mid-twentieth century, the convergence of immigration law and the Mann Act worked in tandem with the international system of nation-states through the refugee crisis of World War II, and endured in the life of de Saint-André until the mid-1970s. Still, as staggeringly as banishment from her homeland had seized upon de Saint-André earlier, it was her 1945 arrest in Mobile, Alabama, as an immigrant woman who followed her husband across state lines and was forced to support him through prostitution (four years after entering the United States) that actuated some of the severest dimensions of the international system of nation-states in which she lived.

She naturalized as a Canadian citizen in 1952 under that nation's "rehabilitated cases law" for immigrants who had engaged in crimes of moral turpitude, and lived practically free from any direct entanglements with the state until the early 1970s.[60] Between the early 1950s and late 1960s, de Saint-André's approaches to enter the United States were more conventional than they had been in the past: her brother successfully petitioned her entry as a fifth-preference immigrant; and on another occasion de Saint-André applied for and received a thirty-day visitor's visa to enter. The need to care for her bedridden mother in New York City suddenly interrupted that smooth current. These terms of entry proved inadequate for the long-term care needed by de Saint-André's mother. In a quandary, de Saint-André overstayed her visitor's visa and the New York City police soon apprehended her for violating immigration laws. After two weeks of imprisonment and the start of deportation proceedings, de Saint-André voluntarily removed herself to Canada before the court hearing.

This legal and personal crossroads for de Saint-André prompted her New York City–based family to call on their congressional representative, Bella Abzug, to take extraordinary action. In 1972, Abzug introduced House Report 6477, seeking a special benefit from the government to grant de Saint-André a visa and permanent residence, though that required waiving a provision in the Immigration and Nationality Law (1952) allowing the president to suspend or restrict the entry of immigrants who had engaged in prostitution or commercialized vice.[61] Abzug's private bill, entitled "A Bill for the Relief of Lucille de Saint-André," gradually worked its way through several immigration subcommittee hearings, Department of Justice meetings, and the floors of both the House of Representatives and the Senate. Finally, in late 1974—and on the very last day possible to sign H.R. 6477 into law—President Gerald Ford endorsed the private bill. This final action in 1974 effectively, and paradoxically, conferred on de Saint-André a visa and permanent residence—the same immigration status she held after entering the United States as a refugee from fascism in 1941.[62]

Lucille de Saint-André and many thousands of female immigrants and prostitutes lived through the interaction of white-slave law and immigration law, a legal union that rendered women as "white slave" commodities suitable for deportation, despite their willingness or unwillingness to engage in sexual commerce. When Marshall's early nineteenth-century interpretation of the Commerce Clause resurfaced in the global campaign against the traffic of so-called white slaves, it interacted with existing immigration law to become a far-reaching and durable force to suppress women's sexual behavior as immoral traffic. Progressive Era abolitionists, by identifying, classifying, and excluding the traffic in white slaves, accomplished what Black-slavery abolitionists never could until the Thirteenth Amendment. That is, Progressive Era abolitionists constructed a regime of federal power over the trafficking of persons, within national borders. By bringing sex into closer conversation with the decades-long debate over the Commerce Clause, we see more clearly that the Progressive Era controversy over sexual commerce reanimated antebellum disputes about states' control over chattel slaves and the regulation of immigration. Such a lens is significant. It links antebellum controversies over personhood and the movement of people to the twentieth-century deployment of the Commerce Clause to suppress immoral sexual traffic, which subjected female immigrants to the power and reach of America's activist intimate state.

NOTES

The author wishes to thank Mark Bradley, Bristol Cave-LaCoste, Anna Mae Duane, Walter Johnson, Ron Mize, and Jessica Pliley for reading and commenting on early drafts of the chapter. She wishes to extend a very special thanks to Maud Sandbo, the stepdaughter of Lucille de Saint-André and daughter of Robert Sandbo, Lucille's husband.

1. Lucille de Saint-André (née Blum) was born in Karlsruhe, Germany, on August 20, 1921. She not only wrote for the *Toronto Star* and the Montreal *Morning Star*, de Saint-André also covered the Toronto Film Festival and other cultural events for *Echo Germanica*, a German diasporic newspaper in Canada, until her death. For two obituaries, see the *Toronto Star* (http://www.legacy.com/obituaries/thestar/obituary.aspx?pid=168898728).

2. De Saint-André's several statuses were culled from documents from the House of Representatives and Department of Immigration and Naturalization Service in "1974/10/17 HR6477 For the Relief of Lucille de Saint-André," White House Records Office, Legislative Case Files, box 9, Gerald R. Ford Presidential Library, Ann Arbor, MI, from here on referred to as RLDSA. For her status as a Gurs internee, refugee, and permanent alien resident, and her naturalization as a Canadian citizen, see "Letter from Ira Gollobin with Enclosure from Alma Alwina Blum to Congressman Peter Rodino, Jr.," May 10, 1972, RLDSA; for her arrest in Mobile, Alabama, her deportation to Canada, and her subsequent deportation to France, see "Memorandum for the President," October 10, 1974, in RLDSA; for her

Canadian naturalization, see "Memorandum of Immunization for Immigration and Naturalization Service File RE H.R. 14572," June 7, 1973, RLDSA; as a fifth-preference immigrant, see "Letter from James F. Greene, Acting Commissioner, to Honorary, Peter W. Rodino, Jr., Chairman, Committee on the Judiciary," n.d., RLDSA. As a recipient of a private bill, H.R. 6477, see "Office to the White House Press Secretary, Notice to the Press, September 26, 1974 to October 18, 1974," October 7, 1974, in Gerald R. Ford Administration White House Press Releases, p. 12, RLDSA.

3. *Hoke and Economides v. United States*, 227 U.S. 308 (1913), p. 314.

4. *Chae Chan Ping v. United States* (The Chinese Exclusion Case), 130 U.S. 581, 609 (1889), 585. In the 1889 decision, the Court acknowledged the nation's "inherent right [as] a sovereign power" to prohibit the entry of aliens into its territory—an authority derived from Congress's foreign commerce power. The other Chinese exclusion cases that evoked national sovereignty were *Nishimura Ekiu v. United States*, 142 U.S. 651 (1892), and *Fong Yue Ting v. United States*, 149 U.S. 698 (1893).

5. Commerce Clause, Article 1, Section 1.

6. *Gibbons v. Ogden*, 22 U.S. (9 Wheat.) 1 (1824), 189–90.

7. In emphasizing traffic and intercourse in the definition of commerce, I am following the interpretation of commerce by the legal scholar Frederick Hale Cooke as "consisting in intercourse and traffic," including "purchase, sale, and exchange." Cooke, *The Commerce Clause of the Federal Constitution* (New York: Baker, Voorhies & Company, 1908), preface, iv.

8. The police powers in the American context were defined by Ernst Freund, the intellectual founder of the American administrative state. See Freund, *The Police Powers: Public Policy and Constitutional Rights* (Chicago: Callaghan & Company, 1904), 2–3. See the definition of William Novak, *The People's Welfare: Law and Regulation in Nineteenth-Century America* (Chapel Hill: University of North Carolina Press, 1996), 3, 44–47; and Markus Dirk Dubber, *The Police Powers: Patriarchy and the Foundations of American Government* (New York: Columbia University Press, 2005).

9. My highlighting of the question of articles of commerce follows from the scholarship of Bilder in "The Struggle over Immigration: Indentured Servants, Slaves, and the Articles of Commerce," *Missouri Law Review* 61, no. 4 (Fall 1996): 793–807.

10. *Mayor of New York v. Miln*, 36 U.S. (11 Pet.) 102 (1837).

11. *Miln*, 142.

12. See Bilder, "Struggle Over Immigration," 799–809, for a discussion of the unresolved nature of *Miln* vis-à-vis commerce and immigrant personhood.

13. For a full and satisfactory discussion of *Groves*, see David Lightner, "The Supreme Court and the Interstate Slave Trade: A Study in Evasion, Anarchy, and Extremism," *Journal of Supreme Court History* 29, no. 3 (2004): 229–53.

14. *The Passenger Cases: Smith v. Turner and Norris v. City of Boston*, 48 U.S. 283 (1849), 504–5.

15. *Groves v. Slaughter*, 40 U.S. (1841), 449, 649, 653.

16. *The Passenger Cases*, 48 U.S. (1849), 534–35. For a similar discussion, see Bilder, "Struggle Over Immigration," 816–18; Gerald Neuman, "The Lost Century

of American Immigration Law (1776–1875)," *Columbia Law Review* 93, no. 8 (December 1993): 1833–1901; and Matthew Lindsay, "Immigration as Invasion: Sovereignty, Security, and the Origins of the Federal Immigration Power," *Harvard Civil Rights- Civil Liberties Law Review* (CR-CL) 45, no. 1 (Winter 2010): 18–21. Woodbury's argument for concurrent powers was accepted in *Cooley v. Board of Wardens*, 53 U.S. (12 How.) (1851), 299.

17. Akhil Reed Amar, *America's Constitution: A Biography* (New York: Random House, 2005), 360.

18. For a further discussion of the Fourteenth Amendment and marriage, see Nancy Cott, *Public Vows: A History of Marriage and the Nation* (Cambridge, MA: Harvard University Press, 2000), 80. For an extended discussion of the "marriage cure" and sexual illicitness, see Ariela R. Dubler, "Immoral Purposes: Marriage and the Genus of Illicit Sex," *Yale Law Journal* 115, no. 4 (January 2006): 756–812.

19. U.S. Constitution, Amend. XIV, art. 1, sec. 1.

20. A few years after Reconstruction, the federal government gradually began to place immigration under its control. Two cases mark this gradual transformation: *Henderson v. Mayor of New York* City and *Chy Lung v. Freeman*. See *Henderson v. Mayor of the City of New York*, 92 U.S. 259 (1875) and *Chy Lung v. Freeman*, 2 U.S. 275, 280 (1875). For an excellent treatment of the case of the twenty-two women held in charge in *Chy Lung*, see Kerry Abrams, "Polygamy, Prostitution, and the Federalization of Immigration Law," *Columbia Law Review* 105, no. 3 (2005): 641–716.

21. *Chae Chan Ping v. United States*, 585.

22. Jack M. Balkin, "Commerce," *Michigan Law Review* 109, no. 1 (October 2010): 1–51, 21; Balkin, "Framework Originalism and the Living Constitution," 103 *NW. U. L Rev.* 459, 459–60 (2009), 575–85. For an example of the White Slave Traffic Law and human rights advocacy, see Amy Dru Stanley, "The Sovereign Markets and Sex Difference: Human Rights in America," in *American Capitalism: New Histories*, ed. Sven Beckert and Christine Desan (New York: Columbia University Press, 2018), 140–69.

23. *Swift & Co. v. United States*, 196 U.S. 375 (1905), established the notion of the "stream of commerce" or "current of commerce" to "include all initiatory and intervening acts, instrumentalities and exchanges that bring about the sale or exchange." States (1911) 220 U.S. 45, 31 Sup. Ct. 364; June 30, 1906, 34 Stat. 674; February 2, 1903, 32 Stat. 791; March 3, 1905, 33 Stat. 1264.

24. *Hoke and Economides v. United States* (1913). The case refuting Barbour's statement in *Miln* were the *Passenger Cases*, 7 How. 282, 429; *Henderson v. New York*, 92 U. S. 259; *Mobile v. Kimball*, 102 U.S. 691; *Gloucester Ferry Co. v. Pennsylvania*, 114 U.S. 196; *Pickard v. Pullman Car Co.*, 117 U.S. 34; *McCall v. California*, 136 U.S. 104; *Covington Bridge Co. v. Kentucky*, 154 U. S. 204.

25. International Agreement for the Suppression of the White Slave Traffic, May 18, 1904, 35 Stat. 1979, art. 1., 83.

26. League of Nations, *Protection of Women and Children, White Slave Traffic*, Library and Archives of Canada, Ottawa, Canada, Record Group 25, Box, 1403, file no. 1925–82, 35.

27. Letter from Robert Bacon, Acting Secretary of State to Kate Waller Barrett, National Superintendent, National Florence Crittenton Mission, Records of the

Immigration and Naturalization Service, Record 85, Series A: Subject Correspondence Files, Part 5: Prostitution and White Slavery, 1902–1933, Folder 2, 52483/1, January 16, 1906, p. 1.

28. For early interactions between vigilance groups and the Bureau of Immigration, see Oscar Straus to O. Edward Janney, December 27, 1900, pp. 1–5, folder 51777/30, White Slave Traffic, Texas and "First Annual Report, The National Vigilance Committee for the Self-Guarding of Unprotected Girls and Women and the Suppression of the White Slave Traffic," October 1, 1907, pp. 1–7.

29. William Burgess, *White Slavery and Its Remedies* (n.p., n.d. [probably 1911]), as cited in Jessica Pliley's "The Young and the Innocent: Age and Consent in the Enforcement of the White Slave Traffic Act," in *Child Slavery before and after Emancipation*, ed. Anna Mae Duane (Cambridge: Cambridge University Press, 2017), 159.

30. *Regulating the Immigration of Aliens into the United States*, 59th Cong., 2nd Sess., H. R. Rep. No. 7607 (1907). In 1908, addressing the "immoral purpose" of the 1907 Immigration Act, the Court ruled in *Bitty* that prostitution and concubinage were analogous and illicit acts of sexual relations. See *United States v. Bitty,* 208 US 393 (1908), pp. 401–3.

31. The Paris Treaty was entered into by the United States on June 6, 1908. International Agreement and . . . *Message from the President of the United States, with Accompanying Letters, In Response to Senate Resolution No. 86, of December 7, 1909. . . .* , S. Doc No. 214, pt. 2 (1906), 1. Also see "Proclamation of President Theodore Roosevelt," in House Report No. 61–47, 61st Cong., 2nd Sess. (1909), p. 15.

32. To Charles Nagel, Secretary of State, from Daniel Keefe, Commissioner-General of Immigration, "Suppression of the White-Slave Traffic," January 12, 1910, S. Doc. 214, pt. 2, 61st Cong., 2nd Sess. (1910), p. 3.

33. William Paul Dillingham, "Brief Statement of Conclusions and Recommendations of Immigration Commission, with Views of Minority," S. Doc. 783, 61st Cong., 2nd Sess. (1910–1911), p. 5.

34. *Annual Report of the Commissioner-General of Immigration*, 1908.

35. *Annual Report of the Commissioner-General of Immigration*, 1909, 116–17.

36. United States and William Paul Dillingham, *Importing Women for Immoral Purposes: A Partial Report from the Immigration Commission on the Importation and Harboring of Women for Immoral Purposes* (Washington, DC: Government Printing Office, 1909), 37.

37. Congress, H.R. Report no. 47, 61st Cong., 2nd Sess. (1909), p. 9–10.

38. The Mann Act, 36, Stat. 825 (1910). The Mann Act is often referred to as such, named for its main advocate, James R. Mann. The Act was officially called "The White Slave Traffic Act: An Act to Further Regulate Interstate and Foreign Interstate and Foreign Commerce by Prohibiting the Transportation Therein for Immoral Purposes of Women and Girls, and for Other Purposes." For House and Senate debates, see *Congressional Record,* vol. 45, part 1, 61st Congress, 2nd Session, January 19, 1910, pp. 804–23; and *Congressional Record,* vol. 45, part 8, 61st Congress, 2nd Session, June 25, 1910, p. 904.

39. *White Slave Traffic Law, Illegal Importation or Interstate Transportation of Alien Women or Girls for Prostitution*, 61st Cong., 2nd Sess., S. Rep. No. 886 (1910); U.S. Congress, H.R. Report. No. 47, 61st Cong., 2nd Sess. (1909), pp. 3–4.

40. *White Slave Traffic Law,* Section 2.

41. Immigration Act of February 20, 1907, chap. 1134, section 3, 34 Stat, 898, as amended in Act of March 26, 1910, chap. 128, 36 Stat. 265. The 1910 amendment changed Sections 20 and 21 of the 1907 Immigration Act. See *Bugajewitz v. Adams,* 228 U.S., at 592 (1913), and appeal submitted April 21, 1913.

42. Daniel Kanstroom, *Deportation Nation: Outsiders in American History* (Cambridge, MA: Harvard University Press, 2007), 126.

43. *Suppression of the White-Slave Traffic,* Senate Document No. 61–214, pt. 2, 61st Cong., 2nd Sess. (1910), p. 4; and *White Slave Traffic,* Senate Report No. 61–886, 61st Cong., 2nd Sess. (1910), p. 11.

44. *White Slave Traffic Law,* Section 6.

45. Letter to the Attorney General from Benjamin Cable, Acting Secretary of the Department of Commerce and Labor, December 10, 1910, folder 52809/7, p. 1, WSTF-NARA.

46. Memorandum for the Commissioner-General of Immigration from S. Warren Parker, Chief, Law Section of the Bureau of Immigration, March 7, 1915, folder 52809/7F, p. 4, WSTF-NARA.

47. Letter from the Office of the Solicitor, Department of Commerce and Labor to the Secretary of Commerce and Labor, no. 4167–3, November 29, 1910, folder 52809/7-B, WSTF-NARA.

48. Letter to All Commissioners of Immigration and Inspectors in Charge of Districts from the Commission-General of Immigration, October 15, 1913, folder 52809/7, WSTF-NARA.

49. *Annual Report of the Commissioner-General of Immigration*, 1914, pp. 7–8.

50. Letter to Commissioner-General of Immigration from F. W. Berkshire, Supervising Inspector, "Justice Department Circular, No. 174 Relating to the Enforcement of the White Slave Traffic Law," no. 2471, December 10, 1910; and November 23, 1910, folder 52909/7-C, WSTF-NARA.

51. Letter from Acting Commissioner of Immigration to Major Richard Sylvester, Superintendent of the Metropolitan Police, Washington, D.C., December 17, 1910, folder 52909/7-B, p. 2, WSTF-NARA.

52. For criticisms of the Mann Act, see White Slave Traffic Report, "Views of the Minority," 61st Cong. Sess. 2, report no. 886, pp. 29–32.

53. *Hoke and Economides v. United States,* 227 U.S. 308 (1913), 227.

54. *Hoke,* 314. The cases refuting Barbour's statement in *Miln* as by the argument for the government were the *Passenger Cases,* 7 How. 282, 429; *Henderson v. New York,* 92 U. S. 259; *Mobile v. Kimball,* 102 U.S. 691; *Gloucester Ferry Co. v. Pennsylvania,* 114 U.S. 196; *Pickard v. Pullman Car Co.,* 117 U.S. 34; *McCall v. California,* 136 U.S. 104; *Covington Bridge Co. v. Kentucky,* 154 U. S. 204.

55. *Hoke,* 227.

56. *Hoke,* 227.

57. *United States v. Joseph Griffiths*, Mittimus, February 9, 1916. "Cross Examination of Susan Ferrell by S. K. Williams on February 8, 1916," Jared Taylor Papers, MS 0178, folder 157, Arizona Historical Society.

58. *United States v. Joseph Griffiths,* p. 3.

59. Jane Addams, *A New Conscience and an Ancient Evil* (New York, 1912), 34–35.

60. To Chief, Operations Division from Chief, Admissions Division, "Section 5 (d), The Act, 1952—Rehabilitated Cases," June 15, 1953, Moral Turpitude, General File, 540–14, Library and Archives of Canada, Ottawa, Canada. Received by author as a successful petition of Canada's Freedom of Information and Protection of Privacy Act, September 4, 2016.

61. United States: Immigration and Nationality Act (last amended March 2004) [United States of America], June 27, 1952, Section 212f.

62. House of Representative and Department of Immigration and Naturalization Service in HR6477, "Private Law 93–97, For the Relief of Lucille de Saint-André," October 17, 1974.

5

"Facts Which Might Be Embarrassing"

Illegitimacy, Vital Registration, and State Knowledge

SUSAN J. PEARSON

In April 1915, J. A. Duclos, a doctor and the local registrar of vital statistics for Henderson, Minnesota, wrote to the State Board of Health about what he feared was a case of both an illegitimate and an unreported birth. A girl who worked in a store near his office had been visibly pregnant. After staying away from the store for a few weeks, the girl returned to work, but was no longer pregnant. The girl's mother, meanwhile, "was seen taking the train at 6 am, with a baby in her arms. . . . Now the birth of this child has not been reported." When Duclos wrote to the State Board of Health, the baby's whereabouts were not known, and as he complained, "That baby may have been dead for all I know." The State Board of Health wrote the girl's father admonishing him to report the birth since it had taken place in his house. But the board also offered that he could file the certificate directly with the state rather than with the local registrar to avoid "publicity."

Some months later, the board received an anonymously filed certificate with information about the child's legitimacy left blank.[1] Thus, although the girl in Henderson had been obviously pregnant, the girl's parents attempted to conceal the baby's birth: no doctor attended the birth, the baby was quickly taken out of town, and the birth was not initially reported. The certificate that was ultimately filed allowed the state to fulfill only one of its two goals in the case: it recorded the fact of the birth, but did not settle the matter of the child's birth status, legitimate or illegitimate.

As this case demonstrates, the state's interest in registering births intersected with its desire to know which children were the fruits of nonmarital sexual relations. But the state's investment in regulating nonmarital sex—and in marking the offspring of such as "illegitimate"—was not stable over time. Though recording bastardy was a centuries-old practice, in the

Progressive Era United States, it received renewed attention as part of a campaign that used birth registration to combat infant mortality. As the nineteenth turned into the twentieth century, states began to regard the registration of births—and of illegitimate births in particular—not only as an instrument to allocate property rights but also as an instrument to aid public health and child protection. State health and child welfare officials hoped to use birth registration as a trigger to intervention—by identifying all children registered as "illegitimate," the state could target those children and their mothers to promote breastfeeding, proper infant care, social services, and marriage.

By the middle of the twentieth century, the same desire to protect children through registration led to a movement to *remove* birth status from birth certificates. This spawned a debate between advocates of privacy and advocates of knowledge as a form of protection. Reformers argued that exposing children as illegitimate punished them for the sins of their parents and prejudiced their chances in life. Such exposure was predicated on a world in which birth certificates had become routine forms of identification for access to schooling, work, marriage, military service, and state and federal entitlements. In order to protect illegitimate children, states wanted to identify and count them, but in so doing it also stigmatized them. On the other side, state health and child welfare officials argued that states needed to know who among their population was illegitimate in order to offer the interventions that would protect illegitimate children from decreased life chances.

As legislators, child welfare advocates, and state registrars sought to protect illegitimate children from the revelations contained on their birth certificates, they developed procedures that sought to balance different categories of fact and different forms of state knowledge. This debate over whether to reveal or conceal illegitimacy on birth certificates sits at the intersection of two different trajectories of the "intimate" state. One is a story of increasing regulation, in which the Progressive Era is depicted as an era of growing state presence in people's lives across a variety of domains. The second story is one in which "privacy" is on the rise and, particularly in the second half of the twentieth century, the state retreats from the intimate lives of at least some people: birth control, abortion, and interracial marriage all become legal, for example.[2] On one hand, the Progressive Era campaign to promote birth registration, and to use birth certificates as a trigger for state intervention, conforms to a story of how the state increases its presence in people's lives. On the other hand, the decision by states and the federal government to conceal birth status in the mid-twentieth century fits with a story of the rising value of "privacy," the right not to be known or monitored by the state. Here the state seems to abdicate its interest in regulating nonmarital sexuality and in punishing out-of-wedlock childbirth. But what the removal of birth status reveals is that privacy should be understood not as the absence of an intimate state—rather, the state's power resides as much in the power to hide as to seek information. In the case of tracking illegitimacy, concealing birth status was every bit as tied to governance as was revealing it; indeed, both were undertaken in the name of a politics of state protection of vulnerable children. The state removed birth status from the face of birth certificates not because it lost interest in illegitimacy, but because its own technology of identification—the birth certificate—forced governmental actors to rethink whether protecting illegitimate children required revealing or concealing their status.

J. A. Duclos's efforts to track down and register a single illegitimate birth in Henderson, Minnesota, took place in the midst of a transformation in the role of birth certificates as technologies of identification. Although it was the first nation in the world to establish a regular population count, in the form of the decennial census, the United States lagged far behind other Western nations in recording "vital" events—birth, death, and marriage. Unlike the census, vital registration was left under state and local control, making its execution highly decentralized and scattershot at best. Among all the vital events, birth in particular escaped routine recording because it was less institutionalized than either marriage or death (most births occurred at home until the 1930s). In the late nineteenth and early twentieth centuries, states still failed to register between one-half and three-quarters of all births in the United States; registration was particularly tenuous among poor, immigrant, illiterate, and nonwhite populations. Indeed, it was not until the middle of the twentieth century that birth registration rates averaged over 97 percent for the nation as a whole and over 93 percent for nonwhites.[3]

Universal birth registration in the United States was achieved largely through two waves of reform effort. In the first wave, beginning in the 1840s, public health reformers interested in using vital statistics to improve the nation's health set out to remedy this situation. Led by men such as Lemuel Shattuck of Boston, Massachusetts, reformers lobbied for new legislation to centralize recordkeeping and increase enforcement of registration requirements. Shattuck and his allies appreciated that registering births could serve the legal purpose of establishing the facts of identity, but for them the object of reform was not so much to document individual identity as it was to provide a more efficient means for a state to know, understand, and govern its population as a whole. From the 1840s through the turn of the century, these public-health-minded reformers convinced a handful of states to modernize or create systems of vital registration that would both record individual births and deaths in the places where they occurred and centralize the records so they could be aggregated into a statistical portrait of the population.[4]

The desire for accurate population statistics and improved governance also motivated the second wave of reform, which began in the early twentieth century. In 1914, shortly after its creation, the US Children's Bureau launched a campaign to promote birth registration in the states. But this new generation of reformers also added an intensive focus on documenting individual identity through the birth certificate. To achieve the goal of full registration, federal agencies such as the Census and Children's Bureaus coordinated, with state governments, national organizations— from the American Medical Association to the General Federation of Women's Clubs—and state and local voluntary committees.[5] The Progressive Era campaign succeeded in transforming the birth certificate into a foundational and privileged token of identity. As child labor and compulsory schooling laws took effect across the nation, municipalities and states asked parents to provide proof of age for their children to enter and leave school. Reformers seeking to end child marriage and raise the age of consent likewise hoped to make birth certificates into tools of law enforcement. "In a multitude of ways," wrote the US Census Bureau's Cressy Wilbur in 1916, "the state is entering into the daily life of the people and requiring records of births and marriages and deaths for the interest of the individual."[6] Though Wilbur identified birth registration as in the interests of individuals, it was clearly also an instrument of "state simplification," a way for local, state, and national governments to both know citizens and radically reduce individual lives into a series of categories to make the administration of laws and bureaucracies more efficient.[7]

As soon as the US Children's Bureau launched its campaign for full birth registration in 1914, it began to pay special attention to the problems surrounding the registration of illegitimate births. The Bureau's attention to illegitimacy was part of a sea change in the state's framing of the problem of nonmarital births. Under British common law, bastards were considered *filius nullius*—the children of no one—and had no rights to parental care or inheritance. By discriminating against children born outside marriage, this system was designed to protect marriage as the only institution for the expression of sexuality and for the transmission of property and rights across generations. Promoting marital reproduction also protected the public from the obligation to care for children born without the right to support or inheritance. But this schema began to change in the nineteenth century as American judges developed a "best interests of the child" standard in family law. Gradually judges and legislators came to see the legal treatment of illegitimacy as not only a matter of protecting marriage, property, and the public coffers, but also a means of promoting the welfare of bastard children. Rather than using the legal status of illegitimate children to punish the illicit sex of their parents, new legal standards presumed the innocence of children and the injustice of punishing them for the sins of their parents. Reformed laws gave bastards the right to their mother's care, some inheritance rights, and allowed legitimation of offspring by subsequent marriage of their parents.[8] Such changes lessened but did not eliminate the state's distinctions between legitimate and illegitimate children and reflected, alongside the growth of instruments such as vital registration, a biopolitical investment in reproduction as a tool of public health rather than simply moral or economic order.

For the US Children's Bureau and other child welfare reformers in the early twentieth century, illegitimacy was a public health problem that demanded state intervention, and birth registration was the entering wedge. While all births in the United States were vastly underreported, child welfare reformers and vital statisticians believed that out-of-wedlock births were especially likely to escape notice. Underreporting of illegitimate births was a statistical problem insofar as it meant that communities could never know how many births really occurred, illegitimate or otherwise. In 1915, only sixteen states and twenty cities recorded the number of illegitimate births that occurred therein, and these statistics were considered largely unreliable. But, as John Anderson, the health officer of Spokane, Washington, wrote, "an illegitimate child is the same as a legitimate child so far as the value of vital statistics is concerned."[9]

The registration of illegitimate births would provide more than just good statistics, however. Child welfare reformers and vital statisticians alike linked the special vulnerability of illegitimate children to their lack of birth registration. "It is really more important that the birth of an illegitimate child should be recorded than of a legitimate child," explained H. M. Bracken of the Minnesota Department of Health, "for its birth certificate is, in a certain sense, a protection of the life of the child." Illegitimate children were as much as three times as likely to die in infancy and, even if they lived, they were often abandoned or placed out by their mothers. According to studies that Chicago's Juvenile Protective Association (JPA) undertook in 1914, unregistered children "are often treated as chattels instead of as human beings, and . . . they are frequently lost, sold, or abandoned." Of the 3,000 illegitimate children born in Chicago's hospitals in

1914, for example, the JPA found that one-third "were lost so absolutely that it was impossible to find any trace of them—even whether they were living or dead." And such numbers did not begin to account for the illegitimate children born to unattended mothers or in the city's unlicensed maternity homes.[10] Like the baby whose disappearance came to the attention of the registrar J. A. Duclos, many other illegitimate children were unregistered, untracked, and disposed of in an unregulated manner. An illegitimate child might be abandoned in a city's foundling home, sold for adoption in the thriving black market for white babies, or privately placed in a home by a pregnant woman's doctor or by her caseworker at a maternity home. The precarious early lives of illegitimate children were a product of the stigma attached to being born out of wedlock. This led women to hide their babies' births, to seek to rid themselves of the evidence of their criminal sexual activity, to assume false names when they delivered babies in maternity homes and hospitals, and to refuse to register the babies.[11]

Part of protecting illegitimate children was therefore to see that their births were registered. This would not only establish their personhood but also bring them to the attention of social service agencies that could provide them and their mothers with support. For child welfare reformers, the registration of a birth as illegitimate would ideally serve as a trigger for state and charitable intervention in the lives of unwed mothers and their babies. Knowledge, surveillance, and protection went hand in hand. Hastings Hart, the director of the Child-Helping Department of the Russell Sage Foundation, laid out his vision for linking registration to intervention in speeches before the American Association for the Study and Prevention of Infant Mortality and the American Public Health Association during the 1910s. Hart's plan imagined that anyone who knew of an illegitimate birth would be required to report it to a local board of health. The mother of such child would then be placed on "probation" for a year, during which time she would be under the guidance of either an institution or a visiting nurse, who would serve as her "probation officer." Such officers would encourage the mother to marry the child's father "if there appears to be a genuine affection between them," to nurse her child "on the breast" for at least six months unless physically unable, and to otherwise care for the child. And, of course, if the mother was unwilling to care for her child, the officer could "bring the case before the court . . . [and] punish the mother for contempt in case such order is not obeyed."[12]

While most child welfare reformers shied away from the harshest aspects of Hart's plan, in the 1910s several states, including Maryland, North Carolina, and South Carolina, forbade the separation of mother and baby until the latter reached six months of age. The goal was to keep the two together during the "nursing period." In Minnesota, hospitals and maternity homes were directed to "require their patients to nurse infants at the breast so long as they remain under the care of the institution."[13] Many other states and social service workers agreed that reporting of illegitimate births should be used to bring mothers and children into the ambit of the state. In 1920, the Children's Bureau organized regional conferences on illegitimacy in New York and Chicago, both of which issued recommendations for the reform of state laws regarding children born out of wedlock. Among these, the New York conference urged that "the bureau of vital statistics should report all births which are not clearly legitimate to the state department having the responsibility for child welfare" and either this agency or a court should determine the paternity of the child through "case work" or "legal proceedings." If a state had no agency dedicated to overseeing child welfare, it should create one with duties that included "assisting unmarried mothers and children born out of wedlock."[14] Without thorough birth registration, however, such plans would fail.

Child welfare reformers wanted to do more, however, than simply ensure that all illegitimate births were recorded. They also wanted to change the *way* that out-of-wedlock births were recorded, and here their public health goals were at odds with their social goals. From a public health point of view, it was essential that all births be recorded. State and social service agencies wanted both information about aggregate numbers of illegitimate births and knowledge of which particular children in a community were born to unmarried parents. But from a social point of view, reformers wanted to reduce the stigma attached to illegitimate children both to lessen their early vulnerability and also because they believed that it was unjust to make children suffer for the sins of their parents. The leading legal expert on bastardy laws, Ernst Freund, expressed this point of view when he argued, in a 1920 speech, that "the abstract desirability of complete data for registration or statistical purposes" should take a backseat to "the interest of the child" to be relieved of "stigma."[15] In adopting this attitude, American child welfare reformers were inspired by legal reforms pioneered in Norway that sought to assist illegitimate children by removing the legal distinction between children born in and out of wedlock. The so-called Castberg law held that all children were the legitimate offspring of their parents and were entitled to support and inheritance rights. The state would initiate paternity proceedings so that fathers could be held to account for maintenance until their offspring reached majority.[16]

Most American reformers interested in protecting illegitimate children found the Castberg laws too radical, but they did support legal reforms that would both materially support illegitimate children and reduce their social shame. When it came to the latter, reformers sought to change how birth status was recorded on birth certificates. At the regional conferences on illegitimacy that the Children's Bureau organized in 1920, discussion of how and what to record in cases of illegitimacy took center stage. "There is much controversy as to the method by which these births shall be so recorded as best to safeguard the child's legal status and property rights and at the same time protect him against any stigma," wrote the Children's Bureau's Emma Lundberg and Katharine Lenroot. In almost every state, a child's birth certificate would indicate whether she was legitimate or illegitimate. In most states, the certificate also recorded the name of both parents. In a handful of others, however, state law actually prohibited the birth record from including the name of the father of a child born out of wedlock. In either case, a child who had to use her birth certificate to prove her name, age, or citizenship would have to advertise her illegitimacy. "How should the child be protected," asked the Children's Bureau, "in the case of transcripts of his birth record for school enrollment, working papers, and similar purposes?"[17]

Most of the registrars, lawyers, social workers, and medical professionals who attended the conferences agreed that records of illegitimate births should be confidential, "open to inspection only upon order of court." Transcripts of birth records used "for school and work purposes should omit the names of parents."[18] In other words, many child welfare advocates agreed both that birth records should be closed to public inspection and that information about a child's birth status should be scrubbed from the public face of the birth certificate. In public at least, reformers wanted the state's legal distinction between illegitimate and legitimate children to be erased.[19]

Between the 1910s and the 1940s, the standard certificate of birth issued by the US Census Bureau continued to include a statement of legitimacy (see fig. 5.1). During the 1920s, however, several states adopted laws that treated birth records as confidential and that eliminated information about birth status from copies of birth records used for proof of age and other routine verifications. In these states, the full birth record was available only to the child, his or her parents, or by court order. In a handful of other states, state health officers used their discretionary power to adopt office procedures that ensured that birth certificates of illegitimate children were only issued "once careful inquiry has been made as to the use to which they are to be put." But in still other states, vital records were considered, by statute, as public records that should be available to any person who paid the required fee for their inspection and reproduction.[20] What was the

THE STANDARD CERTIFICATE OF BIRTH.

(Marginal text, left side, vertical): (Instructions on certain points may be printed on the back. Size of certificate, 6¼ x 7¼ inches.) MARGIN RESERVED FOR BINDING. WRITE PLAINLY, WITH UNFADING INK.—THIS IS A PERMANENT RECORD. N. B.—In case of more than one child at a birth, a SEPARATE RETURN must be made for each, and the number of each, in order of birth, stated. 8—854 G. V. S. No. 109

PLACE OF BIRTH	DEPARTMENT OF COMMERCE BUREAU OF THE CENSUS
County of	STANDARD CERTIFICATE OF BIRTH
Township of .... or	
Village of .... or	Registered No. ....
City of .... (No. ......)	.... St.; .... Ward)
FULL NAME OF CHILD	{If child is not yet named, make, supplemental report, as directed

Sex of Child	Twin, triplet, or other ? (To be answered only in event of plural births)	Number in order of birth	Legit- imate ?	Date of birth ....(Month).......(Day)....19...... (Year)

FATHER		MOTHER	
FULL NAME		FULL MAIDEN NAME	
RESIDENCE		RESIDENCE	
COLOR	AGE AT LAST BIRTHDAY .... (Years)	COLOR	AGE AT LAST BIRTHDAY .... (Years)
BIRTHPLACE		BIRTHPLACE	
OCCUPATION		OCCUPATION	

Number of children born to this mother, including present birth .... Number of children of this mother now living ....

CERTIFICATE OF ATTENDING PHYSICIAN OR MIDWIFE*

I hereby certify that I attended the birth of this child, who was .... (Born alive or Stillborn) at .... M., on the date above stated.

*When there was no attending physician or midwife, then the father, householder, etc., should make this return. A stillborn child is one that neither breathes nor shows other evidence of life after birth.

(Signature) ....
.... (Physician or Midwife)

Given name added from a supplemental report ...., 19

Address..

Filed ...., 19 .... REGISTRAR

11—355

REGISTRAR

FIGURE 5.1. The Standard Certificate of Birth, issued by the US Census Bureau and used by most states, included information about legitimacy on its face, indicated with a "yes" or "no" in the box just to the left of the date of birth. Source: Cressy L. Wilbur, *The Federal Registration Service* (Washington, DC: GPO, 1916).

virtue of the birth certificate was also its vice. Child welfare reformers were sure that the "public birth record" afforded children the best protection against premature labor, marriage, and other violations of childhood, but the fact that the information contained therein was "public" also hurt the most vulnerable among them: those children born to unmarried mothers.

Adopting a shortened form of the birth certificate for purposes of identification balanced the public health and social goals of child welfare reformers. By making birth certificates confidential, public health officials could continue to collect information about aggregate numbers of illegitimate children without exposing particular children to the "most distressing revelations."[21] Though this compromise was met with near-unanimous approval among social workers and child welfare advocates, some registrars of vital statistics worried that it changed the nature of the birth certificate. Where it had once been regarded as a particularly trustworthy document because it was a literal transcript of the facts of birth as they were recorded at the time of birth, now it was a partial transcript, so

altered to accommodate the intersection between the state's need for identification and the child's need for protection. In his correspondence with
Gerda Pierson, Minnesota's head of vital statistics, Stewart Thompson,
Florida's chief vital statistician, expressed such concerns. He told Pierson
that he found Minnesota's partial transcript "not proper" because "when
a certified copy is desired, the State Registrar is supposed to certify that it
is a true and correct copy of the original." But if registrars left off information such as legitimacy, then the record they issued "is not a true certifica-
tion."[22] In amending certificates through omission, Thompson believed
that registrars risked sacrificing both the credibility and the probative
value of birth certificates on the altar of the social good.

But partial transcripts were only one kind of solution (or problem). In
addition to making birth status confidential, during the 1920s and 1930s
some states also began to allow changes to the birth certificates of children
whose parents married after they were born. Most state laws declared that
a child born out of wedlock became legitimate if and when the child's parents subsequently married. The customary way of noting this on a child's
birth certificate had been simply to make amendatory changes directly
on the face of the birth record. "The usual procedure consists of crossing
out 'No' and inserting 'Yes'" where the standard certificate asked if the
birth was legitimate. In this way, the certificate showed the child's history,
her move from illegitimate to legitimate. From the point of view of child
welfare advocates who wanted to protect illegitimate children from the
sins of their parents, this was inadequate. Instead, reformers urged that
states adopt laws like the one passed in Illinois in 1931. The Illinois law
provided that when an illegitimate child's parents married, an entirely new
birth certificate would be issued for the child, showing that the child had
been legitimate at the time of birth. By 1938, at least ten states had similar
legislation on the books, and in many other states, parents who requested
new birth certificates for their children were granted them, "since the law
specifically states that the birth is legitimated by marriage."[23]

Issuing legitimated children new birth certificates that showed they
had been born to married parents went hand in hand with another reform
urged by child welfare advocates: to issue new birth certificates to adopted
children. Like illegitimacy, adoption was regarded as an embarrassing circumstance that should be kept confidential so as not to haunt the child
with the ghost of its past. Moreover, making adopted status confidential
was, quite often, another means of concealing illegitimacy since children
born out of wedlock comprised the vast majority of adoptees. Learning—or
having it publicized—that one was adopted was as good as learning that
one was a bastard. In 1929, the US Children's Bureau first proposed that

adopted children be issued new birth records showing that they had been born to their adoptive parents; their original birth records would be placed under seal and open to inspection or reproduction only at the request of the adoptive parents, the child herself, or by court order. This procedure, explained the Children's Bureau's Mary Ruth Colby, would spare the child "the embarrassment of explaining why his own name and the names of his parents are not the same as the names on his birth record." By 1941, thirty-five states had passed such laws.[24]

While many child welfare advocates were happy about such changes, registrars of vital statistics were less sanguine. Their concerns, like those of Florida's Thompson, centered on how such changes affected the truth value of the birth record. When the American Public Health Association's (APHA) Committee on Registration of Births Out of Wedlock took up this issue, its members cautioned against issuing new birth certificates in cases of legitimation by marriage. "From a strictly legal point of view," read one committee report, "a certificate must show the facts as they are at the time of birth." When states changed certificates to read that a child was born to married parents, when in fact the child was born to unmarried parents, they compromised the legal integrity of birth certificates. Essentially, the certificates told a lie. The lie was necessary, advocates of such changes explained, because of the social nature of birth records. "The old order has given way to the new," wrote two registrars from Illinois, "and although formerly the statements of the child or its parents as to name, age, and relationship were accepted," nowadays "the presentation of a duly authenticated birth certificate has become an almost universal prerequisite for admittance to school or employment, or for foreign travel." And while this was but a "small barrier" to the legitimate child, for the illegitimate child it carried a heavy penalty.

In order to protect both the legitimated child and the integrity of birth certificates as legal documents, the APHA approved a resolution in 1935 that called for the removal of birth status—legitimate or illegitimate— from *all* birth certificates. "Only in this way," reasoned the APHA committee, "could the stigma of illegitimacy be removed from the child born out of wedlock who is later legitimized through the marriage of his parents."[25] While the increased administrative use of birth certificates as identification was based on their legal value as prima facie evidence, the same evidentiary value threatened to bring social ruin to some users of birth certificates and, for the APHA, the only resolution to this problem was to create a new structure of legal facts in which birth status did not exist. The APHA's proposal signaled, to some, that the legal character of the birth certificate—its use as identification—had trumped its public health value.

And for many of those interested in how birth certificates were used, this made the APHA's proposal quite controversial.

The US Census Bureau's Division of Vital Statistics and many on the staff of the Children's Bureau were alarmed by the APHA's proposal. Officials from the Census believed that the APHA's position privileged the use of birth certificates for identification over their statistical or public health value. Taking inspiration from the minority report of the APHA's Committee on Registration of Births Out of Wedlock, officials from both bureaus quickly mobilized a campaign against the recommendation. The minority report had stressed that collecting information about legitimacy as part of birth registration was an invaluable source of "obtaining statistics as the to the extent of illegitimacy." Ironically, this was the position taken some twenty years earlier by child welfare advocates, who wanted not only to register all births and have accurate birth statistics, but even more pointedly, to make certain that illegitimate births in particular were registered and tracked as such so as to afford protection. As the minority report pointed out, "such statistics are of great value in planning community programs for services for the protection of children born out of wedlock."[26] This was precisely because reformers had made birth certificates the trigger for intervention; were the information on birth status to be eliminated, so too would the trigger. Luetta Magruder, the superintendent of charities in Ohio, explained that it was "valuable to know statistics on the subject. We cannot combat increase of illegitimacy or plan successfully to handle situations without knowledge of extent of groups most largely affected."[27]

The minority report and its supporters stressed, moreover, that many states already protected birth status information from public disclosure by sealing the records of illegitimate births and issuing short-form birth certificates when necessary to prove citizenship, age, or name. This bifurcation of the birth certificate into public and private versions was done in order to protect illegitimate children, but it was also part of a growing recognition that birth certificates served many masters and, as a result, had many faces. Mary Frances Smith of the Children's Bureau of Philadelphia expressed this view in a letter to Agnes Hanna of the US Children's Bureau. "The two-fold purpose of the birth certificate has to be recognized," she wrote. "It is to be used for statistical purposes, and also for informational purposes." From the point of view of statistics, information about illegitimacy was important, whereas "from the point of view of the use of the birth certificate for school, proof of age, etc., it would seem very wise that this information should not be included."[28]

The APHA's recommendation that states stop collecting information about illegitimacy was adopted by some states, but not all, likely due to the fact that both the Census Bureau and the Children's Bureau opposed the move.[29] Nevertheless, the federal government took steps to recognize what Mary Frances Smith had called the "two-fold" nature of the birth certificate. At a minimum, a Census Bureau committee responsible for designing the standard birth certificate recommended in 1938 that "vital facts" not necessary for "legal identification" be put somewhere other than the face of the birth certificate. In meetings between the Children's Bureau and the Census Bureau, administrators from the two agencies attempted to work out ways to "preserve the integrity of the birth certificate and at the same time satisfy the social pressures arising because of illegitimacy and adoption." More substantially, the Bureau addressed the problem by developing new technologies for converting the "informational" character of the birth record into a document for the verification of identity. One of these was a form that could be used by federal agencies to request the confidential verification of birth. When the US Armed Forces, the State Department (for passports), the Social Security Agency, or another federal bureaucracy needed to verify the name, age, or place of birth of an individual, the agency could directly request that information from the state division of vital statistics rather than requiring the individual to furnish a birth certificate. "The reason for the confidential verification," explained the Census Bureau's Halbert Dunn, ". . . is to protect the illegitimate child."[30] Thus, even in states that did not issue short-form birth certificates or protect birth records as confidential, federal agencies could avoid asking for— and thus avoid seeing—information about birth status.

Aside from trying to amend the way that the federal government used state birth records, during the 1940s officials from the Census Bureau, the Children's Bureau, and the American Association of Registration Executives encouraged states to adopt a short-form birth certificate that they called a birth card—a laminated, wallet-sized version of the birth record that would omit birth status (see fig. 5.2). Here was a portable identity document that an individual could carry with him to supply the facts of his identity, except, of course, for his parentage. Because parentage would be omitted from all birth cards, those of legitimate and illegitimate persons would appear identical. "A child who is asked to show a birth record to get a work permit," argued Helen C. Huffman of the US Public Health Service, "should not have to show a paper revealing that he was born out of wedlock." Many state registrars were enthusiastic about the birth cards. Tennessee's state registrar, Don Peterson, reported that he promoted them "to the work permit offices, big manufacturers, and others who routinely require proof of age." He also reported that "people who have Birth Cards are proud of them and show them around." Mississippi's state registrar

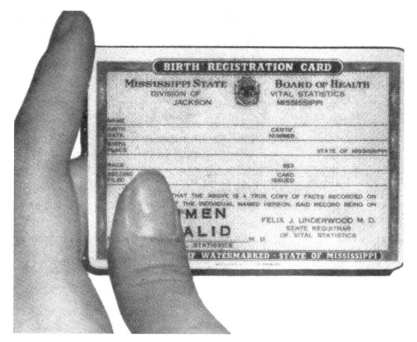

FIGURE 5.2. Birth Registration Card. The hand holding the birth card was meant to show its "convenient" size, made just to fit in a wallet as a source of ready identification. Source: Helen Huffman, "A First Protection for the Child Born Out of Wedlock," *The Child* 11 (August 1946): 34.

likewise raved about the cards. "It is one of the nicest things I have ever done in my office," gushed Richard Whitfield, who also reported that he carried his own card "with me all the time. It's the most useful thing I ever saw for cashing checks, and other needs for identification." Indeed, in some states, birth cards issued to adults contained a photograph on the back so they could better serve as identification. At a point when not all states yet issued driver's licenses, this form of pocket credential could prove useful.[31]

By 1950, seventeen states issued birth cards as an alternative to birth certificates, though their use varied widely between such states. While in North Carolina, as many as 75 percent of requests for copies of certified birth records were met by issuing a birth card, in states such as Tennessee and California, this number was less than 1 percent. In states that used the birth card, "the determining factor in most instances for issuance of birth cards rather than regular photostatic copies was the question of legitimacy." Surveys undertaken by the American Association of Registration Executives uncovered not only the uneven use of the birth card among the states, but also some of the reasons for it. The virtue of the birth card—

that it was a partial transcript—meant that it was not accepted by some federal, state, or local agencies as proof of identity. Many individuals, moreover, shied away from getting a birth card rather than a certified copy of their birth certificate precisely because the birth card did *not* contain information about legitimacy and was, therefore, "stigmatized" by its association with illegitimacy.[32] Not only were partial transcripts considered less trustworthy, but also they reproduced the problem they were designed to solve: revealing, albeit indirectly, the facts of birth status.

Finally, in 1949, the Census Bureau issued a revised Standard Certificate of Live Birth that attempted to resolve the tensions between the statistical, identificatory, and legal uses of the birth record. The new certificate was bifurcated into its public and private dimensions (see fig. 5.3). While

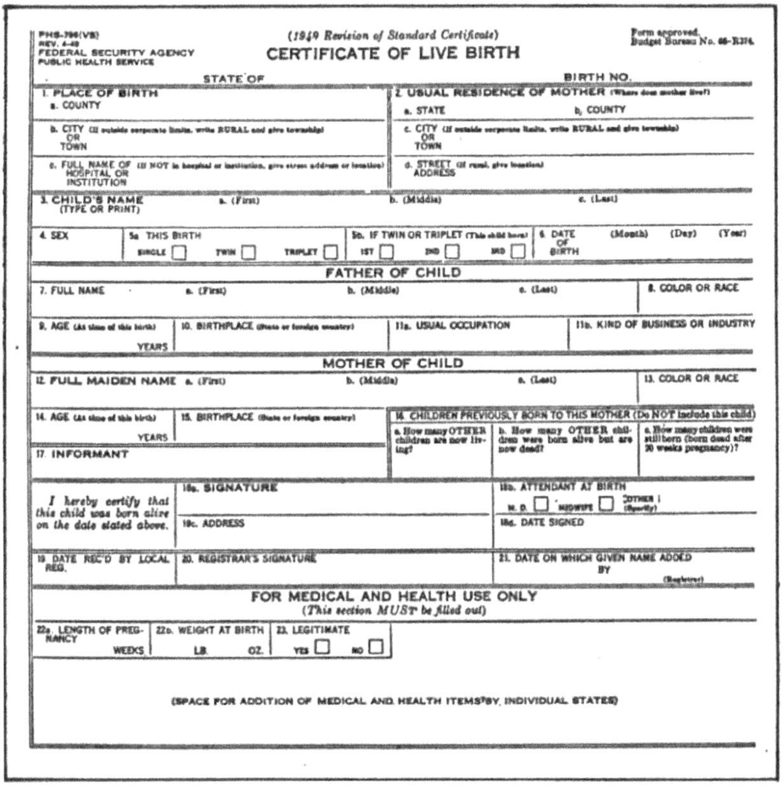

PHS-786(VS)
REV. 4-49
FEDERAL SECURITY AGENCY
PUBLIC HEALTH SERVICE

(1949 Revision of Standard Certificate)

CERTIFICATE OF LIVE BIRTH

Form approved, Budget Bureau No. 68-R374.

STATE OF

BIRTH NO.

1. PLACE OF BIRTH
a. COUNTY
b. CITY OR TOWN (If outside corporate limits, write RURAL and give township)
c. FULL NAME OF HOSPITAL OR INSTITUTION (If NOT in hospital or institution, give street address or location)

2. USUAL RESIDENCE OF MOTHER (Where does mother live?)
a. STATE
b. COUNTY
c. CITY OR TOWN (If outside corporate limits, write RURAL and give township)
d. STREET ADDRESS (If rural, give location)

3. CHILD'S NAME (TYPE OR PRINT) a. (First) b. (Middle) c. (Last)

4. SEX

5a. THIS BIRTH SINGLE ☐ TWIN ☐ TRIPLET ☐

5b. IF TWIN OR TRIPLET (This child born) 1ST ☐ 2ND ☐ 3RD ☐

6. DATE OF BIRTH (Month) (Day) (Year)

FATHER OF CHILD

7. FULL NAME a. (First) b. (Middle) c. (Last)

8. COLOR OR RACE

9. AGE (At time of this birth) YEARS

10. BIRTHPLACE (State or foreign country)

11a. USUAL OCCUPATION

11b. KIND OF BUSINESS OR INDUSTRY

MOTHER OF CHILD

12. FULL MAIDEN NAME a. (First) b. (Middle) c. (Last)

13. COLOR OR RACE

14. AGE (At time of this birth) YEARS

15. BIRTHPLACE (State or foreign country)

16. CHILDREN PREVIOUSLY BORN TO THIS MOTHER (Do NOT include this child)
a. How many OTHER children are now living?
b. How many OTHER children were born alive but are now dead?
c. How many children were stillborn (born dead after 20 weeks pregnancy)?

17. INFORMANT

I hereby certify that this child was born alive on the date stated above.

18a. SIGNATURE

18b. ATTENDANT AT BIRTH M.D. ☐ MIDWIFE ☐ OTHER (Specify)

18c. ADDRESS

18d. DATE SIGNED

19. DATE REC'D BY LOCAL REG.

20. REGISTRAR'S SIGNATURE

21. DATE ON WHICH GIVEN NAME ADDED BY (Registrar)

FOR MEDICAL AND HEALTH USE ONLY
(This section MUST be filled out)

22a. LENGTH OF PREGNANCY WEEKS

22b. WEIGHT AT BIRTH LB. OZ.

23. LEGITIMATE YES ☐ NO ☐

(SPACE FOR ADDITION OF MEDICAL AND HEALTH ITEMS BY INDIVIDUAL STATES)

FIGURE 5.3. The 1949 Standard Certificate of Birth. In contrast to the Standard Certificate in use for the first half of the twentieth century, the new record relegated information about illegitimacy to the confidential "for medical and health use only" section of the certificate. Source: *The Confidential Nature of Birth Records* (Washington, DC: GPO, 1949), 10.

the certificate retained boxes for most of the information traditionally collected on birth records—place of birth, information about the child's parents, sex, date of birth—it moved information about legitimacy to a new section that was designated "for medical and health use only." Information collected in this section would not, by definition, become part of the official transcript and thus would not be reproduced. But information contained there could, however, be used to collect aggregate statistics. In this way, the legal integrity of the birth certificate and its value as a form of identification could be preserved without compromising either the social status of those born out of wedlock or the state's desire to track information about its illegitimate population. And, by relegating legitimacy to the realm of "health and medical" information, the Census Bureau's form allowed Americans to preserve the status distinction between children born in and out of wedlock while also erasing it as an obvious basis for discrimination in the law.[33] A social and legal category became a matter of health.

The use of birth registration to construct a population—illegitimate children—that would become the object of state intervention conforms to many of the stories we tell about the creation of an expansive, modern state. Whether scholars deploy the Foucauldian concept of "biopolitics" or the Scottian metaphor of "legibility," the assumption is that the development of the modern state is a story of the creation of bureaucratic institutions to map and manage population. Knowledge is an instrument of state power whether it is used to surveil or to protect life, and as states develop their institutional capacity, their ability and desire to categorize, name, and otherwise know their populations proceeds apace. Indeed, scholars such as Ian Hacking argue that the greatest political effect of state enumeration is not the policies that result but the initial creation of categories into which populations are sorted. Naming is the ultimate power.[34] To the extent that scholars of American state building reject such accounts, it is because, as they argue, the American state displays different patterns of development. Whether it is because of its fragmented federalism or its hybrid public-private partnerships, historians and political scientists usually depict the American state as less coherent and unified, if not less powerful, than the European nation-states and colonial powers that dominate scholarly accounts of the "modern" state.[35]

Yet the rise and fall of illegitimacy as a category on birth certificates contradicts both of these accounts. As a state project, birth registration is fragmented, hybrid, *and* successful. It is an example of an increasingly intimate, "knowing" state, one that tags, sorts, and demands identification from its population and uses its power to regulate marriage, sexuality, and the family. And yet, in the face of the success of birth registration—indeed, *because* of its success—states and the federal government agreed to know *less* about the population by removing birth status from birth certificates. Tracking changes in how states recorded illegitimacy demonstrates the contradictory politics of knowledge surrounding technologies of identi-fication. To be "known" by a state is to be *both* the object of surveillance and the subject of modern rights, entitlements, and protections; in the case of recording illegitimacy, states exercised their power equally by re-vealing and concealing.[36] Birth certificates are a particularly potent site to glimpse the dynamics of this contradiction because they are technologies vested with multiple tasks: to collect aggregate population information for statistical purposes; to class individuals as members of certain groups; and to identify discrete individuals. Though these tasks could coalesce, they also clashed. As instruments of an intimate state, birth certificates did not simply reflect changes in ideas about the state's relationship to illegitimacy, but also produced some of those changes by making iden-tification clash with protection. The more states succeeded both in reg-istering births and in requiring individuals to prove their identity using birth certificates, the more the contradictory politics of state knowledge complicated the revelation of illegitimacy. In choosing to remove birth status from birth certificates, states and the federal government did not simply choose privacy over knowledge, but instead shifted tactics in an ongoing biopolitical project. As scholarship on the postwar United States has shown, illegitimacy hardly faded away as a category simply because it was no longer recorded on birth certificates. Rather, it assumed new life as part of the pathologization of Black families, where high rates of nonmarital birth and households headed by single mothers were cast by policymakers as the engines of poverty, crime, and a host of other social problems. Such children may not have been marked by their birth certifi-cates, but they were marked nonetheless.[37]

NOTES

1. Duclos to Bracken, May 1, 1915, box 26, unlabeled folders, Health Depart-ment, Correspondence and Miscellaneous Records, ca. 1904–1915, Minnesota His-torical Society (hereafter, MN-SBH-CMR, 1904–1915); Bracken to Hensler, May 27, 1915, box 26, MN-SBH-CMR, 1904–1915; Bracken to Duclos, June 7, 1915, box 26, MN-SBH-CMR, 1904–1915.

2. Sarah Igo outlines these different narratives in the introduction to her re-cent book *The Known Citizen: A History of Privacy in Modern America* (Cambridge, MA: Harvard University Press, 2018), 1–16.

3. Cressy L. Wilbur, *The Federal Registration Service of the United States: Its*

Development, Problems, and Defects (Washington, DC: GPO, 1916), 18, 39; and Sam Shapiro and Joseph Schachter, "Birth Registration Completeness United States, 1950," *Public Health Reports (1896–1970)* 67, no. 6 (1952): 513–24.

4. For a detailed account of the spread of registration laws, the ideology of nineteenth-century reformers, and the problems with the administration of such laws, see Susan J. Pearson, *The Birth Certificate: An American History*, chapter 2, book manuscript in progress. For colonial-era registration, see Robert Kuczynski, "The Registration Laws in the Colonies of Massachusetts Bay and New Plymouth," *Publications of the American Statistical Association* 7 (1900): 1–9; Robert Gutman, *Birth and Death Registration in Massachusetts, 1639–1900* (New York: Milbank Memorial Fund, 1959); and Simon Szreter, "Registration of Identities in Early Modern English Parishes and Among the English Overseas," in *Registration and Recognition: Documenting the Person in World History*, ed. Keith Breckenridge and Simon Szreter (Oxford: Oxford University Press, 2012), 67–92.

5. Pearson, "'Age Ought to Be a Fact': The Campaign Against Child Labor and the Rise of the Birth Certificate," *Journal of American History* 101 (2015): 1144–65.

6. C. L. Wilbur, *The Federal Registration Service of the United States: Its Development, Problems, and Defects* (Washington, DC: GPO, 1916), 47.

7. James C. Scott, *Seeing Like a State: How Certain Schemes to Improve the Human Condition Have Failed* (New Haven, CT: Yale University Press, 1998), 80.

8. Michael Grossberg, *Governing the Hearth: Law and the Family in Nineteenth-Century America* (Chapel Hill and London: University of North Carolina Press, 1985), 196–218.

9. Emma O. Lundberg and Katharine F. Lenroot, *Illegitimacy As a Child-Welfare Problem, Part 1* (Washington, DC: GPO, 1920), 20; and Anderson, quoted in Hastings Hart, *The Registration of Illegitimate Births: A Preventative of Infant Mortality* (New York: Russell Sage Foundation, 1916), 5.

10. Bracken to Hart, July 26, 1915, box 26, MN-SBH-CMR, 1904–1915; Hart, *Registration of Illegitimate Births*, 14–15; Lundberg and Lenroot, *Illegitimacy As a Child-Welfare Problem, Part 1*, 35; Howard Moore, *The Care of Illegitimate Children in Chicago* (Chicago: Juvenile Protective Association of Chicago, 1912); and "Birth Registration and Establishment of Paternity," speech by Louise de Koven Bowen, printed in US Children's Bureau, *Standards of Legal Protection for Children Born Out of Wedlock: A Report of Regional Conferences Held Under the Auspices of the U.S. Children's Bureau and the Inter-City Conference on Illegitimacy* (Washington, DC: GPO, 1921), 53–54.

11. E. Wayne Carp, *Family Matters: Secrecy and Disclosure in the History of Adoption* (Cambridge, MA: Harvard University Press, 1998); Ellen Herman, *Kinship by Design: A History of Adoption in the Modern United States* (Chicago: University of Chicago Press, 2008); and Regina Kunzel, *Fallen Women, Problem Girls: Unmarried Mothers and the Professionalization of Benevolence, 1890–1945* (New Haven, CT: Yale University Press, 1993).

12. Hart, *Registration of Illegitimate Births*, 15–17.

13. Emma O. Lundberg, *Children of Illegitimate Birth and Measures for Their Protection* (Washington, DC: GPO, 1926), 8–9.

14. [Emma O. Lundberg], "Legislation for Children Born Out of Wedlock," *Sur-*

vey (March 13, 1920): n.p., Box 45, Scrap Book No. 41, US Department of Labor, Edith and Grace Abbott Papers, Special Collections Research Center, University of Chicago Library [hereafter, EGAP]; and US Department of Labor, Children's Bureau, "On Legislation for the Protection of Children Born Out of Wedlock," press release, March 6, 1920, Box 45, Scrap Book No. 41, EGAP.

15. US Children's Bureau, *Standards of Legal Protection for Children Born Out of Wedlock*, 33.

16. Robyn L. Rosen, *Reproductive Health, Reproductive Rights: Reformers and the Politics of Maternal Welfare, 1917–1940* (Columbus: Ohio State University Press, 2003), 45–61; and [US Children's Bureau], *Norwegian Laws Concerning Illegitimate Children*, introduction and translation by Leifur Magnusson (Washington, DC: GPO, 1918).

17. Lundberg and Lenroot, *Illegitimacy As a Child-Welfare Problem, Part 1*, 19; and US Children's Bureau, *Standards of Legal Protection for Children Born Out of Wedlock*, 150.

18. US Children's Bureau, *Standards of Legal Protection for Children Born Out of Wedlock*, 18.

19. US Children's Bureau, *Standards of Legal Protection for Children Born Out of Wedlock*, 47.

20. Agnes K. Hanna, "Guarding Illegitimate Status," *Child Welfare League of America Bulletin* 13 (May 1934): 6.

21. Sheldon Howard and Henry Bixby Hemenway, "Birth Records of Illegitimates and of Adopted Children," *American Journal of Public Health and the Nation's Health* 21 (June 1931): 643.

22. Thompson to Pierson, February 3, 1936, Box 2, Folder: Florida Health Department and Vital Statistics Division, Correspondence with, 1936–1965, MN-VSD-SF.

23. Report of the Committee on Registration of Births Out of Wedlock, presented to the Vital Statistics Section, American Public Health Association, Milwaukee, October, 1935, Box 490, File 4-2-1-2-4, USCB-CF; "Registration of Births of Illegitimate and Adopted Children," in *American Public Health Association Year Book, 1933–1934, American Journal of Public Health and the Nation's Health* 24, Supplement 2 (1934): 86; Howard and Hemenway, "Birth Records of Illegitimates and of Adopted Children," 641–47; and US Children's Bureau, *Paternity Laws: Analysis and Tabular Summary of State Laws Relating to Paternity and Support of Children Born Out of Wedlock, in Effect January 1, 1938* (Washington, DC: GPO, 1938), 2.

24. Carp, *Family Matters*, 53–55; Mary Ruth Colby, *Problems and Procedures in Adoption* (Washington, DC: GPO, 1941), 120; and Howard and Hemenway, "Birth Records of Illegitimates and of Adopted Children," 647.

25. Report of the Committee on Registration of Births Out of Wedlock, presented to the Vital Statistics Section, American Public Health Association, Milwaukee, October, 1935, Box 490, File 4-2-1-2-4, USCB-CF; and Howard and Hemenway, "Birth Records of Illegitimates and of Adopted Children," 643.

26. Minority Report of the Committee on Registration of Births of Out of Wedlock, December 12, 1935, Box 490, File 4-2-1-2-4, USCB-CF.

27. Response from Luetta Magruder [1936], Box 490, File 4-2-1-2-4, USCB-CF.

28. Smith to Hanna, March 11, 1936, Box 490, File 4-2-1-2-4, USCB-CF.

29. It is difficult to track the precise number of states that dropped legitimacy from the birth certificate, or to determine when they did so, since the decision was often administrative rather than statutory. In 1943, the Census Bureau claimed that nine states did not follow their standard for the "legitimacy question." It does not list these states. See "A Check List of Aspects of the Vital Records System Which Require Standardization and Improvement," material prepared for the meeting of the Census Advisory Committee, January 19, 1943, Box 77, Census-CAC. A 1948 newspaper article also puts the number of states that do not record legitimacy at nine and lists them as California, Georgia, Mississippi, New Jersey, Nevada, Ohio, Oregon, Tennessee, and Washington. See "9 States' Birth Papers Leave Illegitimacy Out," *New York Herald Tribune*, February 29, 1948, A5.

30. Minutes of the Subcommittee on Revision of Standard Certificates, April 5, 1938, Box 74, Census-CAC; Memorandum from Dunn to Director, 23 October 1943, Box 85, Census-ROADSS-TPM; Meeting of the Council on Vital Records and Vital Statistics, Nov 28–30, 1944, Box 118, Folder: Vital Statistics, Council on Vital Records & Vital Statistics, Census-ROADSS-GR; Minutes of the Meeting of the Council on Vital Records and Vital Statistics, Oct 23–25, 1945, Box 118, Folder: Vital Statistics, Council on Vital Records & Vital Statistics, Census-ROADSS-GR.

31. Minutes of the Meeting of the Council on Vital Records and Vital Statistics, Held at the Bureau of the Census, Washington, DC, April 30–May 2, 1946, Box 118, Census-ROADSS-GR; Helen C. Huffman, "A First Protection for the Child Born Out of Wedlock," *The Child* 11 (1946): 35; Rose McKee, "Social Workers Urge State Solons to Approve Use of 'Birth Cards,'" *Atlanta Constitution*, November 28, 1946, 13; "Birth Record System Hides Illegitimacy," *Los Angeles Times*, February 6, 1950, 21; and James B. Rule et al., "Documentary Identification and Mass Surveillance in the United States," *Social Problems* 31 (1983): 225.

32. *Study of the Experience of States Issuing Birth Cards*, typescript memorandum, ca. 1951, Box 3, Folder: Working Group on Promoting and Testing Completeness of Vital Registration, 1949–1951, MN-VSD-SF.

33. By contrast, in Great Britain, the solution was, in 1947, to create a short-form birth certificate. This had already been in existence in most US states for several decades. Deborah Cohen, *Family Secrets: Living with Shame from the Victorians to the Present Day* (London: Viking, 2013), 144.

34. Michel Foucault, *The History of Sexuality, An Introduction, Volume 1* (New York: Vintage Books, 1978); James C. Scott, *Seeing Like a State: How Certain Schemes to Improve the Human Condition Have Failed* (New Haven, CT: Yale University Press, 1998); and Ian Hacking, "Biopower and the Avalanche of Printed Numbers," *Humanities in Society* 5 (1982): 279–95.

35. This literature is voluminous, but the most influential articulations of this complexity remain: Elisabeth S. Clemens, "Lineages of the Rube Goldberg State: Building and Blurring Public Programs, 1900–1940," in *Rethinking Political Institutions: the Art of the State*, edited by Ian Shapiro et al. (New York: New York University Press, 2006), 187–215; and William Novak, "The Myth of the 'Weak' American State," *American Historical Review* 113 (2008): 752–72.

36. Igo, *The Known Citizen*, 15–16; and Keith Breckenridge and Simon Szreter, "Recognition and Registration: The Infrastructure of Personhood in World His-

tory," in *Registration and Recognition: Documenting the Person in World History*, ed. Breckenridge and Szreter (Oxford: Oxford University Press, 2012), 1–36.

37. On the post–World War II history of illegitimacy, see Rickie Solinger, *Wake Up Little Susie: Single Pregnancy and Race Before* Roe v. Wade (New York and London: Routledge, 1992); on efforts to fight the racialized stigma of illegitimacy in law and policy, see Serena Mayeri, "Marital Supremacy and the Constitution of the Nonmarital Family," *California Law Review* 103 (October 2015): 1277–1362. Race not only played a role in the construction of the problem of illegitimacy after World War II, but of course race was also a creature of birth certificates. Racial status continued to be recorded on birth certificates after birth status was removed. Race was eventually removed after a debate similar to the one about removing birth status, where advocates for removal argued that racial classification was stigmatizing and discriminatory, and advocates for retaining racial classification argued, among other things, that racial classification provided population knowledge essential for administering programs of social welfare. In the end, the solution was the same compromise that settled the problem of birth status: race was removed to the "health" section of the certificate. These debates and the process of removing racial classification from the public face of the birth certificate are detailed in my forthcoming book, *The Birth Certificate: An American History* (Chapel Hill: University of North Carolina Press, forthcoming 2021).

6

Race, the Construction of Dangerous Sexualities, and Juvenile Justice

TERA EVA AGYEPONG

INTRODUCTION

Chicago was the home of the nation's very first juvenile court. A product of the Progressive child-saving movement, the juvenile court relied on institutional interventions to care for and reform children who broke the law. It quickly became a site through which the state regulated the intimate lives of children within its jurisdiction. Progressives' successful advocacy for a nonpunitive juvenile justice system centered on special courts was rooted in the rehabilitative ideal—the notion that children were inherently innocent and entitled to a justice system separate from adults. The emergence of Cook County Juvenile Court in Chicago in 1899 signaled the political viability of the rehabilitative ideal and the emergence of the juvenile justice system.[1]

While is it debatable whether the juvenile justice system was ever actually "rehabilitative" in practice, it is more clear that the rehabilitative intentions and discourse surrounding juvenile justice did not emerge with Black children in mind. Poor native white and European immigrant children were its intended beneficiaries. The constructions of childhood innocence, vulnerability, and rehabilitation that triggered the emergence of juvenile justice in Chicago did not apply to Black children. The state recognized Black children's childhood only to the extent that their legal status as individuals "under the age of eighteen" made them candidates for entry into the juvenile court and not the adult criminal justice system. In juvenile justice discourse and practice, childhood for African Americans was far from being an assumed marker of purity, or inspiring protection.

Instead, it subjected Black youths to particular institutional, social, and economic vulnerabilities.[2]

Looking into the ways that the Cook County Juvenile Court and the Illinois Training School for Girls at Geneva dealt with racial difference suggests that the discourse of rehabilitation and the institutional apparatus of the juvenile justice system were key components in facilitating a process of racialized criminalization. The infection of racial prejudice not only circumscribed the handling of Black children but also led to a demise of the rehabilitative ideal by the 1930s, and a turn to incarceration, ultimately changing the administration of justice for all children. Intersecting notions of race and sex and sexuality shaped differential treatment of girls and boys, as well as of Blacks and whites, by the juvenile court and the institutions to which the court sent the youths to be "trained." Examining practitioners' implementation of the rehabilitative ideal in the Illinois Training School for Girls at Geneva reveals how far a race-specific and gendered construction of delinquency operated, and shows how racialized criminalization of Black children shaped the twentieth-century juvenile justice system as a whole.

RACIAL DISPARITIES IN THE JUVENILE JUSTICE SYSTEM

The Illinois General Assembly's passage of the Juvenile Court Act of 1899 marked the political ascendance of the notion that children—because of their vulnerability, inherent innocence, and potential to be rehabilitated— needed their own separate non-adversarial court. This "Act to regulate the treatment and control of dependent, neglected and delinquent children" merged reformers' concerns about child welfare with crime control, giving the juvenile court original jurisdiction over children's cases. The juvenile court designated two categories among the individuals brought before it. A person under the age of eighteen who broke the law was labeled a "delinquent." The court applied the alternative term "dependent" to a minor who was abused, neglected, or abandoned and did "not have proper parental care or guidance." The two categories distinguished criminal behavior from noncriminal needs or circumstances.[3]

These differing diagnoses should have meant different institutional treatments of children so assessed. But the juvenile court's disposition of *dependent* Black children's cases was often indistinguishable from its disposition of *delinquent* children's cases. Racialized conceptions of childhood vulnerability affected the likelihood of children being viewed as "dependent" or "delinquent" in the juvenile justice system. Even more consequentially, the vast majority of public and private agencies in and around Chicago for poor, abused, neglected, or abandoned (i.e., "dependent") children, including maternity homes for pregnant and unmarried girls, refused to accept African American children at all.[4] This dearth of institutional resources for Black children was exacerbated as the Great Migration swelled the size of the African American population in Chicago.

Because the only institutions that readily admitted Black children were facilities for "delinquent" children, the juvenile court deemed African American children delinquent in order to have somewhere to send them, despite a large proportion being neglected or abused, not lawbreakers at all. The juvenile court thus actively participated in constructing the image of a "delinquent" child by applying the label disproportionately to Black children, inflating seeming evidence of their criminal behavior. This trend was not unique to Chicago. A national study of 1923, analyzing the distribution of Black and white children across various types of institutions, found from juvenile court records elsewhere that 50 percent of Black youths were sent to correctional facilities, while 19 percent of white youths were.[5]

The Chicago court saw a far greater proportion of African American children than of whites to begin with, because police surveillance in the city's Black neighborhoods led to extremely high arrest rates.[6] Law enforcement officials had a disposition, "conscious or unconscious," as a 1923 Commission on Race Relations concluded, "to arrest Negroes more freely than whites, to book them on more serious charges, to convict them more readily, and to give them longer sentences."[7] As a result, African American children made up a disproportionate number among those at institutions for delinquents, not because they committed more crimes than any other group of children, but because of racial discrimination at the community level, and the juvenile court's limited institutional options for the care of dependent Black children. Over time, the overrepresentation of Black children in juvenile court and conflation of Black dependency with delinquency led to a racialized process of criminalization. Black children became increasingly associated with delinquency.

THE "GIRL PROBLEM" AT THE ILLINOIS TRAINING SCHOOL

Assessments of children's delinquency depended on gender as well as race, since perceptions of what was criminal varied by gender. Many girls were arrested, or committed to the juvenile court by family members, for engaging in premarital sex, or going to dance halls, or getting rides from strange men—or many other potential slips from Victorian norms of female behavior. No boys were constrained or brought into court for such reasons. A girl who was sexually assaulted could be blamed for the crime perpetrated against her, and then labeled a "sex delinquent" in juvenile court.[8]

Not only in Chicago but in many other American cities at the turn of the century the growing autonomy of young women had become a source of alarm for experts and reformers. Reformers identified a "girl problem" in female adolescents' sexuality, which became the focus of intense public anxiety and the target of reform and control. The phrase "the girl problem" encapsulated generational anxieties prompted by young women and girls' sexual behavior and flamboyant dress, as well as by economic and sexual exploitation of them. But these notions of a "girl problem" that funneled many girls and young women into juvenile justice systems were racialized. Many experts and reformers directed their efforts at poor immigrant girls of European descent, believing that these girls' antisocial behavior or promiscuity deviated from a normal standard of behavior that could be restored through legal reforms, institutional commitments, and rehabilitative programs. They did not make the same benevolent assumptions about African American girls.[9]

The Illinois State Training School for Girls at Geneva first opened its doors in December 1893 with the purpose to protect young girls from the perils of city life, as well as from their own sexuality. Once the training school began working hand in hand with Chicago's juvenile court, it became integrated into the juvenile justice system's ideological and administrative program, and stressed its rehabilitative purpose.[10] The Geneva school accepted African American girls along with whites but did not treat the two the same. (No evidence has surfaced of other racial designations among its residents.) Their experiences diverged because of the staff's and consultants' implicitly racialized understandings of protection and delinquency.

On the surface, the Geneva school looked integrated because it accepted both white and Black girls, but in practice, within its walls, it was racially segregated. The girls living there typically fell between the ages of thirteen and eighteen, although they might be as young as nine or as old as twenty-one. The majority, who came from various cities around the state, were American-born whites or European immigrants.[11] Between 1896 and 1920, African American girls made up 10 to 15 percent of the residents. Their percentage steadily increased from about 20 percent in 1920 to 35 percent in 1928, even though African Americans composed under 2 percent of Illinois's population. Their stark overrepresentation was in part the lack of other institutional options for pregnant, poor, sick, neglected, and abused dependent girls in Chicago. The overall numbers of residents grew larger over time, averaging 450 girls in 1920 and 520 by 1950.[12]

Geneva's staff members' and administrators' primary rehabilitative goal was "to help correct" and prepare the girls for "re-adjustment as citizens" by "educating the girls to a high standard of womanhood." They utilized a family-style cottage system to make the institution less prison-like and to give the residences a "home-like atmosphere," placing a housemother, managing matron, and housekeeping matron in each cottage. Despite this cover story of Geneva being a home-like institution (and some staff members' genuine intent to make it so), reports of cruelty there and harrowing stories about the nature of confinement tainted its reputation. Some young women assigned to Geneva by the court took drastic steps to avoid going there, and others tried to escape from its harsh disciplinary regime, which included beatings and other forms of corporal punishment.[13]

After arriving at the institution, each girl was put in isolation, screened for sexually transmitted infections, given an IQ test, psychologically evaluated, and assigned a counselor. All girls were trained in the domestic arts and had to do housework and make their own stockings and clothing, while resident physicians, psychiatrists, psychologists, counselors, and nurses determined each girl's rehabilitative program individually. The emphasis on specifically sexual "delinquency" in inmates of Geneva did not occur at a parallel local institution for boys, the Training School for Boys at St. Charles. Boys were committed to St. Charles not for inappropriate sexual interaction but for crimes such as physical assault, robbery, and murder. Upon admission, boys were given a battery of physical, psychological, and intellectual tests, but they were not subject to invasive medical exams that screened them for sexually transmitted infections; the impetus for the boys' "rehabilitation" was not their sexuality.[14]

"VIOLENT ATTACHMENTS": MANUFACTURING A SEXUALLY DEVIANT AND BLACK FEMALE DELINQUENCY

As soon as African American girls crossed Geneva's threshold, admission tests reinforced the notion that they were more sexually promiscuous and diseased than their white counterparts, since their rates of pregnancy and venereal disease were higher than those of white girls. Rather than inferring that these rates showed the girls' greater vulnerability to abuse and assault, staff members assumed that the girls' own sex delinquency was to blame.[15] In spite of the fact that African American girls typically were younger than whites, and often sent to Geneva not for criminal behavior but because there were no institutions willing to take them as "dependent," staff members believed that the African American residents were the most violent, sexually deviant, and uncontrollable girls there.[16]

This belief that African American girls had an innate proclivity for violence and aggression—visible in staff members' notes, in state institutional reports, and in studies by external reviewers—had material implications for their experiences at Geneva, as it underlay the institution's unusual and strict policy of racial segregation, implemented in housing and all activities. All the cottages were reserved for white girls except two, where African Americans were housed—regardless of their growing numbers. The Illinois Association for Criminal Justice reported that "in the cottages for white girls, each has a separate room, while in the colored cottages some of the rooms are shared by two girls . . . There was anywhere from twenty-two to thirty-four girls per cottage, while in the cottages for colored there were fifty per cottage."[17] The overcrowding situation for Black girls was often worse, their numbers more than double the expected occupancy of the cottages. Institutional reports between 1910 and 1953 refer not only to segregated cottages, but also to separate choruses, musical quartets, Christmas programs, musical recitals, glee clubs, and vocational training courses. Classes for whites and Blacks met at different times.[18] Geneva's administrators even thought it necessary to separate the disciplinary cottages, which the girls referred to as "dungeons."[19]

Staff members and administrators explicitly stated that they instituted racial segregation in an effort to manage the perceived aggression on the part of African American girls. Their decision did not simply replicate wider societal practices. Rather, it reflected their view that African American girls had a unique set of problems that could be recognized and anticipated because of their race, and that they needed to be segregated from other girls because of these problems.

Staff members at Geneva were deeply unsettled by sexual interactions among the girls, contending that "efficiency and deportment in school, cottage, and the industrial room all suffer[ed]" as a result of it. Girls who were found engaging in such relationships were "taken immediately out of school and kept away from all group contacts," encouraged to read and sew, and given "plenty of exercise" along with a "new diet which had some of the richer foods removed" in an attempt to "build up interests which would be substituted for homosexual activity."[20] Among boys at the Illinois Training School at St. Charles three miles away, homosexual behavior was punished also; attempts were made to prevent it not only through continual surveillance but also by placing beds to make surveillance easier, prohibiting boys from going to cottage basements unsupervised, and creating a rigorous recreational and physical education program. When boys were found engaging in "immoral" practices, staff members punished them by making them stand silently for up to three hours, whipping them, or sending them to a detention cottage.[21] Nonetheless, institutional leaders' attention to boys' same-sex relationships at St. Charles reached nowhere near the height of staff members' concerns at Geneva.

Interracial sexual relationships among the girls provoked the most anxiety and consternation—so much so that prevention of such relationships was used to rationalize segregation. Visiting psychologist Margaret Otis noted in a 1913 report that "the difficulty [of interracial sex] seemed so great and the disadvantage of intimacy between the girls so apparent that segregation was resorted to . . . The girls were kept apart both when at work and when at play . . . and the white girls were absolutely forbidden to have anything to do with the colored."[22] Geneva's superintendent during the 1930s, Florence Monahan, said in her memoir, *Women in Crime*, "It is pretty well known that homosexuality and perversion thrive in places where the population is all of one sex. I came face to face with the problem at Geneva . . . Our biggest difficulty was the Negro and the white girls . . . By segregation we were able to eliminate the major portion of the trouble."[23]

Geneva's staff members, having embedded negative representations of Black womanhood in their approach to the sexual behavior of African American girls, believed that Black girls instigated these interracial love relationships. They were not alone in their fear of interracial sex. At other institutions for delinquent women and girls, staff and administrators were also anxious about the "love-making between the white and colored girls" and viewed it as an extension of their "perversion."[24] Criminologists, psychologists, and state officials elsewhere likewise encouraged prison and reformatory administrators to prevent relationships between Black and white women for fear that they would disrupt prison discipline.[25] In contrast, administrators at the Illinois Training School for Boys at St. Charles, where the demographic profile among boys was similar to that of girls at Geneva, did not consider racially segregating boys until the mid-1930s, despite similar prohibition of homosexual relationships.

In nearly all the descriptions of relationships between Geneva's Black and white girls, staff members and visiting professionals suggested that African American girls forcefully initiated relationships with white girls. Their construction masculinized African American girls, portraying them as the sole sexual aggressors even in the face of clear evidence of white girls' actions.[26] For example, psychologist Margaret Otis argued, reading African American girls out of common notions of femininity, that interracial sex at Geneva was different from the "ordinary form that is found among girls in high-class boarding-schools."[27] Unlike relationships between boarding-school girls presumably white, where both participants retained feminine identity, for Otis, "difference in color . . . took the place of difference in sex" in cross-racial relationships. The Black partner was not "ordinary" but embodied the characteristics of a different sex. Otis also believed that an "animal instinct" was "paramount" in Black girls and influenced their sexual relationships.[28] Social scientist Ruth Klein made a similar argument after conducting a study at Geneva in 1918: "The violent attachment of one girl for another takes on a heterosexual character, the aggressor adopting the masculine role and the other girl playing the feminine part . . . when the attachment occurs between a colored and a white girl, the former invariably assumes the masculine role."[29] An administrator interviewed as part of the Illinois Association of Criminal Justice's 1928 inquiry likewise reported that "in every case in which colored and white girls became attached to each other, the colored girl is considered the male, and is called 'daddy' or sometimes 'uncle.'"

Psychiatrist Elizabeth Stone also concluded that African American girls "were usually more aggressive" and "appealed to the weaker white in a masculine sense." Stone asserted that African American girls' aggressive prowling for interracial sex was sought through "vulgar pantomime and suggestive acts, even in broad daylight, and at school." She claimed that African American girls' attempts to gain the sexual attention of white girls might take violent physical form: a "colored girl, to attract the attention of the white, will surreptitiously expose her person" or resort to assault. She related the story of an African American girl who allegedly "choked her sweetheart into submission if she resisted, and threatened to kill her and do her all manner of bodily injury if she told of these visits."[30] Otis's reporting similarly emphasized an image of desperate African American girls who went to extraordinary lengths—by using "curious love charms made of locks of hair" and other "superstitious practices"—to gain access to white girls.[31]

Stone's and Otis's depictions of African American girls as aggressive, oversexed beings discursively linked them to similar images of violently hypersexual Black men.[32] White girls at Geneva, in contrast, were portrayed by staff as passive, devoid of any agency in their relationships with Black girls. Researchers and staff members unwittingly revealed the falsity of their own constructs, however, in their fuller descriptions of these relationships. These descriptions belie the notion that African American girls were the sole aggressors and white girls were completely passive. Several offered examples of white inmates actively seeking relationships with Black girls and defying staff members' rules in order to do so. Stone described a superintendent's frustration at a Geneva dance because "the white girls insisted in dancing with the colored."[33] She also relayed the story of a white girl who carried her Black "honey's" soiled napkin in her bosom for a week as a mark of devotion. Psychologist Margaret Otis noted that white girls who had a "habit of 'nigger-loving' . . . would congregate in one part of the dormitory to watch at the window for colored girls to pass . . . Notes could be slipped out, kisses thrown and looks exchanged . . . just 'to see the coons get excited.'"[34] Klein related an incident where white girls precipitated a "minor scandal" because they "moved into the cottage of the colored girls" despite the matrons' attempt to prevent same-sex relationships between them.[35] Some of the girls' own statements confirmed initiatives taken on both sides. When Otis asked one of the African American girls which race initiated such relationships, she responded, "It might be either way."[36] White girls' and Black girls' persistent attempts to interact with each other despite all the restraints was certainly a form of institutional resistance among them.

The researchers' and staff members' conclusion that African American girls invariably occupied an aggressive, "masculine" role, despite their own findings of contrary evidence, reveals how their pre-existing notions about African American girls were rearticulated within the framework of the institutions' protective and rehabilitative goals, adding to a longer history of masculinizing Black women. By constructing the image of an inherently deviant, masculine, unalterably hypersexual Black girl delinquent whose negative influence contaminated other girls, staff members and administrators injected the color line into their rehabilitative discourse and practice. The same behavior among Black and white girls led to drastically different conclusions. Unlike Black girls, white girls were able to retain their feminine identity despite engaging in behaviors that might be thought masculine, such as procuring a dance partner, boldly watching a potential lover walk by, or disobeying orders. Their manufacturing of an African American sexual deviant confirmed white girls' inclusion in the rehabilitative project and excluded Black girls from it.[37]

RACIALIZED CONSTRUCTIONS OF FEMALE
DELINQUENCY BEYOND GENEVA

Geneva was not alone in this approach to its residents' interracial liaisons. At other homes for delinquent girls, staff members and researchers blamed African American girls similarly for sexual "perversion." In a 1920 study of inmates at the New York State Reformatory at Bedford, psychiatrist Elizabeth R. Spaulding concluded that homosexual sex occurred because African American girls "represented a substitute for unattainable heterosexual" relationships craved by many white girls at the institution.[38] On the basis of her study of a home for delinquent girls in 1941, psychologist Theodora Abel likewise argued that white girls interpreted the "Negro aggression and dominance" as "maleness" and that their "physical characteristics seem to enhance [white girls'] attraction to Negro girls."[39]

Staff members and professionals at Geneva typically did not bother inquiring into reasons for Black girls' interest in whites, only the reverse, and they imagined that these relationships were situational and temporary. White girls held the center of their analyses of interracial relationships. Otis reported that many of them "had never seen anything of the kind outside" and engaged in the behavior only "when they saw other girls doing it." The social scientist Ruth Klein speculated that white girls who had relationships with Black girls would be more likely to become involved with Black men upon release. "Having a colored 'honey' may make it easier for white girls to have intercourse or live with colored men after they are paroled," she wrote.[40] The possibility that white inmates were naturally attracted to other girls did not occur to her. She assumed that the white girls would inevitably have relationships with men upon release—even "colored" men.[41]

There is no evidence that Klein, Otis, or staff members analyzed why Black girls engaged in same-sex relationships. Because they projected already-existing sexual deviance on to Black girls, they had no motivation to analyze and explain sexual behaviors they deemed perverse. Their analyses resulted in the construction of a racialized female delinquent that put African American girls beyond the scope of any meaningful rehabilitation. Social scientists' practice of casting Black women and girls as aggressors in interracial prison sex echoed through the twentieth century, showing up in Catherine Nelson's 1974 study of homosexuality among prison women: "Because of greater aggressiveness and domination in the general socialization process, lower class black females appear more likely to take on a male heterosexual role."[42]

Nascent juvenile justice institutions elsewhere around the country were likewise engaged in constructing racialized understandings of female delinquency. Assumptions about the masculinization and inherent sex delinquency of Black girls showed up in the Memphis juvenile court, as Jennifer Trost has shown. In Memphis, juvenile court officials dealing with white girls focused in the predictable way on their inappropriate sexual behaviors, but were more concerned with criminal activity by African American girls—the same emphasis given to African American boys in court. Memphis court officials acted as if Black girls' sexual behavior was incorrigible and did not address it, even though the girls were on average younger than white girls and more likely to have been sexually exploited.[43]

Historian Susan Cahn has shown how white Southerners' assumptions about African American girls' inherent sexual deviance led Southern states to disregard them when establishing juvenile rehabilitative institutions. Southern states established racially segregated institutions for Black boys, for white boys, and for white girls, but virtually none for Black girls through World War II. This absence implied that "deviant" sexual behavior among white girls was an uncommon and correctable condition, while in African American girls it was so deeply rooted and widespread that no institutional rehabilitation program could make a dent. One North Carolina legislator voiced his opinion that "it would take the United States army to correct the morals of all Negro girls in the state."[44] Through the 1930s, whites in North Carolina opposed founding any training school for Black girls, according to the *Charlotte Observer*, because there were simply too many who fit the description of sex delinquency.[45] African American community members in numerous Southern states, mostly club women, angry and appalled that Black girls were so typified and therefore neglected, took up rehabilitative and protective work themselves.[46]

At the Illinois State Training School for Girls at Geneva, African American girls were not excluded from the training school but subject to a discursive differentiation and physical within-institution segregation that structured administrative decisions and resulted in the construction of a race-specific image of Black female delinquency. As the rehabilitative program at Geneva focused on curing sex delinquency and creating "proper women," staff members' practices whitened the rehabilitative ideal and cast blackness as delinquency. Thus in both North and South, juvenile justice institutions participated in the discursive and practical exclusion of African American girls from notions of innocence and rehabilitation. Black girls' vulnerabilities were erased in the ascendancy of the figure of the Black female delinquent.

THE JUVENILE COURT AND THE PUNITIVE TURN

The Cook County Juvenile Court similarly played an active role in constructing the image of a "delinquent" child, disproportionately applying the label to Black children and inflating their numbers. Opponents of the court, who believed that the justice system should not mitigate punishment based on the age of the offender, voiced objections from the outset.

Racism became a powerful currency for such opponents, as the proportions of Black children among those appearing before the court increased and a racialized construction of the delinquent child hardened.

In the 1930s, with Chicago in the throes of the Great Depression and gang wars among organized crime, racialized understandings of delinquency helped fuel a public hysteria over "dangerous" children in the juvenile justice system. The popular and political sentiments that had made the juvenile court movement viable during the Progressive Era began to wane. The city's major newspapers paid new attention to Black crime and advocated a more punitive stance to children in court. The conservative *Chicago Tribune* published several articles squarely opposed to the juvenile court. One article, "Social Workers Defend Young Toughs," criticized the "citizens committee on the juvenile court" for "asking the legislature to take jurisdiction of even the most hardened young criminals away from the Criminal court and hand it over exclusively to the juvenile court."[47]

In 1935, the chief justice of Cook County's criminal court, Dennis Sullivan, launched a campaign to wrest power over children from the juvenile court, to bring those accused of crimes to criminal court instead. (The criminal court by common-law tradition had jurisdiction over anyone ten years or older, but in practice it ceded jurisdiction to the juvenile court. The 1926 case *People v. Fitzgerald* confirmed concurrent jurisdiction.) Judge Sullivan, according to the *Chicago Tribune,* "criticized the juvenile court, asserting that it attempted to take jurisdiction of young offenders, no matter how hardened and criminal minded they were," and gave them such "light sentences" that they could resume their "criminal careers" upon release. Judge Sullivan's efforts did not immediately succeed. Then he seized on the prosecution of Susie Lattimore, a sixteen-year-old African American girl accused of murder, to buttress his arguments for removing youthful offenders from the juvenile court's jurisdiction.[48]

It was a Black female delinquent's case that Sullivan successfully brought to the fore. Susie Lattimore, the youngest of seven children, had migrated to the city with her family from Atlanta, Georgia, at age four. Like many poor migrant Black families, the Lattimores struggled financially. On the night of February 23, 1935, Susie, age fifteen, stabbed sixteen-year-old Ruth Robinson during a fight at a tavern. At trial, Susie described the fight this way: "One night we were in the beer tavern on Racine and she did not want me to dance with her boyfriend and she came and pushed me away from him." Susie asked to borrow a knife from a friend there, "just in case," and got into a fight with Ruth, stabbing her in the chest. Ruth died that night. Susie was arrested, brought before the juvenile court, and then, following routine procedure, to the Institute for Juvenile Research to be examined by a psychologist. The psychologist concluded that she was a "high grade mental defective" with a mental age of only ten years and one month, and recommended that the juvenile court commit her to Dixon State Hospital for psychiatric treatment.

The presiding judge of the juvenile court ignored the institute's recommendations and transferred Susie's case to criminal court. There, she pleaded not guilty but waived her right to a trial, because her attorney, public defender Benjamin Bacharach, submitted a motion to transfer her case back to juvenile court. Bacharach contended that the criminal court did not have the jurisdiction to try her, since the juvenile court had already declared her delinquent. When Susie appeared in criminal court, she faced Judge Sullivan. Sullivan rejected her attorney's motion and found Susie guilty of first-degree murder, sentencing her to twenty-five years at the Illinois State Reformatory, an institution for adult women in Dwight, Illinois.

Her lawyer appealed the decision to the Illinois Supreme Court. For unknown (and possibly political) reasons, the state's attorney provided an incomplete record of Susie's trial to the higher court. The incomplete record led the higher court to act as if the juvenile court had contested Susie's transfer to the adult criminal justice system (though it had not done so), and therefore to consider the issue of the concurrent jurisdiction held by the juvenile and criminal courts.[49]

The "sole question" on appeal in *People v. Lattimore* was "whether the defendant, a ward of the juvenile court, who had been indicted for murder, can on such an indictment be tried in the criminal court without the consent of the juvenile court." The Supreme Court said yes, resorting to common law to affirm the criminal court's superior jurisdiction over any child aged ten or above. The court opined that "by no stretch of the imagination" was it conceivable that the legislature, in establishing the juvenile court, had intended to turn it "into a haven of refuge where a delinquent child of the age recognized by the law as capable of committing a crime should be immune for punishment for violation of the criminal laws of the State."[50] Susie Lattimore's case gave the Cook County state's attorney the authority, in effect, to prosecute children in criminal court and sentence them to adult penitentiaries. *Lattimore* likewise gave prosecutors huge discretion in deciding which children would be tried as adults—a new channel through which racial biases against Blacks could thrive in the justice system.

People v. Lattimore thus rejected the notion of children's inherent innocence and malleability, principles on which the juvenile court movement had been built. Susie Lattimore's case crystallized the state's growing impatience with rehabilitative ideals and its turn toward punishment. It is not coincidental that the watershed decision divesting the juvenile court of its primary jurisdiction and marking the beginning of the state's more punitive treatment of youthful offenders arose in the case of an African American girl. It was soon followed by another significant carceral turn, spurred by local concerns over "dangerous" youths of a marked "racial stock" at the boys' Illinois State Training School at St. Charles. A threatening image of violent Black boyhood opened a channel toward the state legislature's approval of the construction of the state's first maximum-security prison for boys in Sheridan, Illinois, in 1939. Thus the presence of Black children, and race-incriminating reactions to them, played a critical role in the short life of the state's embrace of the rehabilitative ideal, its dismantling, and the transition to a more punitive juvenile justice system.

NOTES

1. Michael Grossberg, "Changing Conceptions of Child Welfare in the United States, 1820–1935," and David S. Tanenhaus, "The Evolution of Juvenile Courts in the Early Twentieth Century: Beyond the Myth of Immaculate Construction," in *A Century of Juvenile Justice*, ed. Margaret K. Rosenheim (Chicago: University of Chicago Press, 2002), 17, 38–39, 42–74; and David S. Tanenhaus, "Degrees of Discretion: The First Juvenile Court and the Problem of Difference in the Early Twentieth Century," in *Our Children, Their Children: Confronting Racial and Ethnic Differences in American Juvenile Justice*, ed. Darnell F. Hawkins and Kimberly Kempf-Leonard (Chicago: University of Chicago Press, 2005). See also Michael Willrich, *City of Courts: Socializing Justice in Progressive Era Chicago* (Cambridge: Cambridge University Press, 2003), xxii, 78–80, 159; David W. Southern, *The Progressive Era and Race: Reaction and Reform, 1900–1917* (Wheeling, IL: Harlan Davidson, 2005); Anthony Platt, *The Child Savers: The Invention of Delinquency* (Chicago: University of Chicago Press, 1977), 45; and Steven Mintz, *Huck's Raft: A History of American Childhood* (Cambridge, MA: Harvard University Press, 2004), 176–78.

2. The concept of childhood has always connoted more than simply chronological age, since it is socially and legally constructed in intersection with other constructed categories such as race, gender, and class.

3. Juvenile Court and Juvenile Detention Home Annual Report of 1924, Municipal Reference Collection, Harold Washington Library Center, Chicago Public Library.

4. Elizabeth Lasch-Quinn, *Black Neighbors: Race and the Limits of Reform in the American Settlement House Movement, 1890–1945* (Chapel Hill: University of North Carolina Press, 1993), 15–17.

5. Tera Agyepong, *The Criminalization of Black Children: Race, Gender, and Delinquency in Chicago's Juvenile Justice System, 1899–1945* (Chapel Hill: University of North Carolina Press, 2018), 39–40, 51–53; and US Bureau of the Census, Children under Institutional Care, 1923 (Washington, DC: GPO 1927), 301–2, quoted in Thornsten Sellin, "The Negro Criminal: A Statistical Note," *Annals of the American Academy of Political and Social Science* 140 (1928).

6. E. Franklin Frazier, *The Negro Family in the United States* (Notre Dame: University of Indiana Press, 2001), 372.

7. Chicago Commission on Race Relations, *The Negro in Chicago: A Study of Race Relations and a Race Riot* (Chicago: University of Chicago Press, 1923), 328–30.

8. Earl Moses, *The Negro Delinquent in Chicago* (Washington, DC: Social Science Research Council, 1936), 1–2. Anne Meis Knupfer, "'To Become Good, Self-Supporting Women': The State Industrial School for Delinquent Girls at Geneva, Illinois, 1900–1935," *Journal of the History of Sexuality* 9 (2000): 420–46, esp. 422; and Sophonisba Breckinridge and Edith Abbott, *The Delinquent Child and the Home* (New York: Russell Sage Foundation, 1912), 314.

9. See, for example, Regina Kunzel, *Fallen Women, Problem Girls: Unmarried Mothers and the Professionalization of Social Work, 1890–1945* (New Haven, CT: Yale University Press, 1995); Mary Odem, *Delinquent Daughters: Protecting and Policing Adolescent Female Sexuality in the United States, 1885–1920* (Chapel Hill: University of North Carolina Press, 1995); Ruth Alexander, *The Girl Problem: Female Sexual Delinquency in New York, 1900–1930* (Ithaca, NY: Cornell University, 1995); and Kathy Peiss, *Cheap Amusements: Working Women and Leisure in Turn-of-the-Century New York* (Philadelphia: Temple University Press, 1986).

10. Michael Grossberg, "A Protected Childhood: The Emergence of Child Protection in America," in *American Public Life and the Historical Imagination*, ed. Wendy Gamber, Michael Grossberg, and Henrik Hartog (Notre Dame: University of Notre Dame Press, 2003); John R. Sutton, *Stubborn Children: Controlling Delinquency in the United States, 1640–1981* (Berkeley: University of California Press, 1988); Illinois State Training School for Girls, *Biennial Report of the Illinois State Home for Juvenile Female Offenders at Geneva: 1894–1896* (Springfield, IL: Hartman State Printer, 1896), 9; and Department of Public Welfare, *9th Annual Report of the Department of Public Welfare* (Springfield: Illinois State Journal Company, 1926), 263–66.

11. Charlotte Ruth Klein, "Success and Failure on Parole: A Study of 160 Girls Paroled from the State Training School at Geneva, Illinois" (master's thesis, University of Chicago, 1935), 9; and Tanenhaus, "Degrees of Discretion," 108.

12. *8th, 12th and 21st Annual Reports of the Department of Public Welfare* (Springfield: Illinois State Journal Company, 1925, 1929, 1938); Illinois Board of Administration, *The Institution Quarterly* 11 (Springfield: Department of Public Welfare, 1920); Illinois State Training School for Girls, *Seventh Biennial Report of the Trustees, 1904–1906* (Springfield: Hartman State Printer, 1906), 27–29; Chicago Commission, *Negro in Chicago*, 339; and Bertha Corman, "A Study of 446 Delinquent Girls with Institutional Experience" (MA thesis, Social Service Administration, University of Chicago, 1923), 10.

13. Illinois Board of Administration, *The Institution Quarterly* 13 (Springfield: Department of Public Welfare, 1922), 264; Department of Public Welfare, *9th Annual Report of the Department of Public Welfare*, 202; Illinois State Training School for Girls, *Biennial Report . . . 1894–96*, 8; and Geneva Illinois State Training School for Girls, *Third Biennial Report of the Trustees, Superintendent and Treasurer of the State Home for Juvenile Female Offenders at Geneva* [1898], 7.

14. *5th Biennial Report of the Trustees* [1902], 14–16; and St. Charles School for Boys, *3rd Biennial Report* (Springfield, IL, 1907), 388.

15. Letty Joyce Grossberg, "A Study of Negro Girls Committed to the Geneva State Reformatory in 1937–1938 by the Cook County Juvenile Court" (MA thesis, Social Science Administration, University of Chicago, 1940), 23, 25.

16. Michael W. Sedlak, "Youth Policy and Young Women, 1870–1972," *Social Service Review* 56, no. 3 (September 1982): 456–57.

17. Illinois Association for Criminal Justice materials, including "Juvenile Delinquency, Part 1," by Earl Myers, Ernest Burgess Papers, Box 10, folder 1, Special Collections Research Center, University of Chicago.

18. Department of Public Welfare, 21st Annual Report of the Department of Public Welfare (1938), 529; see also the *Institutional Quarterly* publications 1912–1913 and 1921–1922, and Annual Reports of the Department of Public Welfare 1928–1931 and 1936–1939.

19. Illinois Association for Criminal Justice materials; see also "24 Resign Posts after School Slaying," *Chicago Defender*, March 1, 1941, regarding disciplinary cottages.

20. Illinois Association for Criminal Justice materials.

21. Department of Public Welfare, 12th Annual Report (1929), 197; 19th Annual Report (1936), 323, 33; and 23rd Annual Report . . . December 31, 1937 (Chicago: Illinois Board of Public Welfare Commissioners, 1939), 3.

22. Margaret Otis, "A Perversion Not Commonly Noted," *Journal of Abnormal Psychology* 8 (1913): 113–16; and Illinois Association for Criminal Justice materials.

23. Florence Monahan and Lewis E. Lawes, *Women in Crime* (New York: Ives Washburn, 1941), 223.

24. Margaret Otis, "A Perversion," 113–16; and Eugenia C. Lekkerkerker, *Reformatories for Women in the United States* (Groningen, Netherlands: J. B. Wolters' Uitgevers-Maatschappij, 1931), 234.

25. Estelle B. Freedman, "The Prison Lesbian: Race, Class, and the Construction of the Aggressive Female Homosexual 1915–1965," *Feminist Studies* 22 (1996): 423; and Lekkerkerker, *Reformatories*.

26. Klein, "Success and Failure"; and Esther H. Stone, "A Plea for Early Commitment to Correctional Institutions of Delinquent Children, and an Endorsement of Training and Vocational Training in These Institutions," *The Institutional Quarterly* 9 (1918): 9, 65.

27. Otis, "A Perversion," 113.

28. Otis, "A Perversion," 114.

29. Klein, "Success and Failure," 66–67.

30. Stone, "A Plea for Early Commitment," 65–66.

31. Otis, "A Perversion," 115–16.

32. Paula J. Giddings, *Ida: A Sword Among Lions* (New York: Amistad, 2008), 221–29.

33. Stone, "A Plea for Early Commitment," 66.

34. Otis, "A Perversion," 114.

35. Klein, "Success and Failure," 66.

36. Otis, "A Perversion," 114.

37. Otis, "A Perversion," 114.

38. Edith R. Spaulding, "Emotional Episodes among Psychopathic Delinquent Women," *Journal of Nervous and Mental Disease* 54 (1921): 299–306.

39. Theodora M. Abel, "Dominant Behavior of Institutionalized Subnormal Negro Girls: An Experimental Study," *American Journal of Mental Deficiency* 67 (1943): 429–36.

40. Klein, "Success and Failure," 68.

41. Otis, "A Perversion," 113.

42. Catherine I. Nelson, "A Study of Homosexuality among Women In- mates at Two State Prisons" (PhD diss., Temple University, 1974), 156.

43. Jennifer Trost, *Gateway to Justice: The Juvenile Court and Progressive Child Welfare in a Southern City* (Athens: University of Georgia Press, 2005), 122–24.

44. Susan Cahn, *Sexual Reckonings: Southern Girls in a Troubling Age* (Cambridge, MA: Harvard University Press, 2007), 46, 69–70, quotation from "Moral Advancement in North Carolina," *Danville Register*, February 20, 1931.

45. Cahn, *Sexual Reckonings*, 46, citing *Charlotte Observer*, February 19, 1939.

46. Cahn, *Sexual Reckonings*, 69–70.

47. "Social Workers Defend Coddling of Young Toughs," *Chicago Tribune*, April 29, 1939. See also, in *Chicago Tribune,* "Escapes at St. Charles," Sept. 2, 1935; "Rules Juvenile Court No Haven for Criminals," December 21, 1935; "Oppose Juvenile Court Trials of Youths up to 21," March 13, 1938; "Five Towns Lie in Fear of 'Boys' at State School," February 1, 1939; and "Charges Boys Learn Crime at St. Charles," February 3, 1939.

48. *People of the State of Illinois v. Susie Lattimore*, Case No 23103, 362 Ill. 206, Superior Court of Cook County Records Transcript & Judgment, Illinois State Archives. See also David Tanenhaus, *Juvenile Justice in the Making* (New York: Oxford University Press, 2004), 150–53; Joan Gittens, *Poor Relations: The Children of the State in Illinois, 1818–1990* (Urbana: University of Illinois Press, 1994), 132–33; and L. Mara Dodge, "Reform Struggles and Legal Challenges: The Cook County Juvenile Court, 1924–1999. A Historical Overview," in *A Noble Experiment? The First 100 Years of the Cook County Juvenile Court, 1899–1999*, ed. Gwen Hoerr McNamee (Chicago: Chicago Bar Association, 1999), 85.

49. "Social Workers Defend Coddling of Young Toughs." See also "Escapes at St. Charles"; "Rules Juvenile Court No Haven for Criminals"; "Oppose Juvenile Court Trials of Youths up to 21."

50. Transcript, and Brief for Defendant in Error, *People of the State of Illinois v. Susie Lattimore*.

7

Eugenic Sterilization as a Welfare Policy

MOLLY LADD-TAYLOR

In May 1927, the US Supreme Court handed down one of its most notorious decisions: the state of Virginia could surgically sterilize a young "feeble-minded" mother without her consent.[1] Carrie Buck was just seventeen years old when she had a baby out of wedlock, was designated feeble-minded in Juvenile and Domestic Relations Court, and wound up in the Virginia Colony for Epileptics and Feeble-minded. Her mother, an alleged prostitute, was already an inmate, and her baby, after a brief examination, was pronounced feebleminded too. Virginia's Eugenical Sterilization Act of 1924 permitted the sterilization of feebleminded, insane, or epileptic inmates who were the "probable potential parent of socially inadequate offspring," and the Colony superintendent thought Carrie's family history of feeblemindedness and immorality made her an ideal test case for the new law.[2] The Supreme Court upheld her sterilization three years later. Writing for the majority, Justice Oliver Wendell Holmes Jr. argued that the state already called on the "best citizens" to give up their lives during war, so it would be strange not to ask those who "already swamp the strength of the State" to make the lesser sacrifice of sterilization. He added: "It is better for all the world, if instead of waiting to execute degenerate offspring for crime or to let them starve for their imbecility, society can prevent those who are manifestly unfit from continuing their kind. . . . Three generations of imbeciles are enough."[3]

Holmes's words expose the court's disdain for unmarried mothers with few resources, and Carrie's personal tragedy illustrates the state's power over reproduction, the most intimate decision in people's lives. The *Buck* opinion has few defenders today, and most Americans are repelled by the eugenic creed of improving the human population by sterilizing the "unfit." Yet between 1907 and 1937, thirty-two US states passed eugenic laws, resulting in the sterilization of more than 63,000 Americans.[4] *Buck v. Bell* has never been overturned.

There is a vast scholarly literature on eugenics, and the disturbing story of Carrie Buck has been told in dozens of books and films. Most accounts emphasize Carrie's victimization at the hands of eugenic experts and a coercive state. They point out that she was neither unintelligent nor immoral, just a poor young woman who became pregnant after being raped.[5] As legal historian Paul Lombardo has demonstrated, eugenicists "manufactured evidence to fit the state's case against Carrie Buck," and her own lawyer, a founding member of the Colony's board of directors, colluded with the state against his client.[6] Carrie's case was never about her intellectual abilities, biologist Stephen Jay Gould wrote in 1984; "it was always a matter of sexual morality and social deviance. The annals of her trial and hearing reek with the contempt of the well-off and well-bred for poor people of 'loose morals.'"[7] As another recent book contends, Carrie was "not a threat to society, but its victim."[8]

Carrie's sterilization was horribly cruel and unjust, but the one-dimensional narrative of an elite, eugenics-inspired "war against the weak" is too simple.[9] It exaggerates the influence of eugenic ideas, overlooks other motivations for sterilization, and ignores the abuses perpetrated by non-elites, including family members such as Carrie's foster parents and their nephew, who raped her. John and Alice Dobbs initiated the petition to institutionalize Carrie in order to protect their nephew from a rape charge (or forced marriage) and avoid the shame of illegitimacy. After Carrie was sterilized and the Colony superintendent made plans to discharge her, they tried to keep her in the institution for life. The Dobbses also kept Carrie's baby and raised her as their own, failing to inform either Carrie or Colony officials when the little girl died from a complication of measles at the age of eight.[10] Clearly, surgical sterilization was not the only wrong Carrie Buck suffered, and she was not victimized only by eugenicists and a repressive state. Poor women's lives are filled with coercion. Focusing on a single aspect of Carrie's mistreatment—the eugenic crusade to build a better race—draws attention away from the suffering caused by poverty, the sexual double standard, and a punitive welfare system. It also creates a false distinction between an enlightened "us" of today and a mean-spirited, prejudiced "them."

In reality, US sterilization policies had as much to do with concerns about welfare dependency as with eugenic ideas about heredity and human improvement. While Holmes's chilling phrase "three generations of imbeciles are enough" has generated the most attention, his decision also quoted the Virginia law saying that many feebleminded persons, "if incapable of procreating, might be discharged with safety and become self-supporting with benefit to themselves and society."[11] As the Supreme Court understood, state sterilization policies were a practical way to reduce the apparent burden of "socially inadequate" persons who relied on public relief.

The state was not only a perpetrator of eugenic abuse; the "state," in the form of the welfare state and the courts, also functioned at times as a bulwark against abuse. State officials and institution superintendents typically initiated sterilization proceedings, often at the behest of local welfare workers. Yet federal welfare measures enacted during and after the New Deal, by reducing extreme poverty and the stigma of dependency on government aid, enabled some poor people to resist eugenic institutionalization and sterilization.[12] Moreover, court decisions were not consistent. Although *Buck* was never overturned, the Supreme Court struck down the compulsory sterilization of criminals in *Skinner v. Oklahoma* (1942), a precedent-setting decision that recognized a right to marriage and procreation and formed the basis for crucial later rulings overturning prohibitions on interracial marriage, birth control, abortion, and same-sex marriage.[13] A federal court cited *Skinner* when in 1974 it prohibited the use of federal family planning funds for involuntary sterilization and the sterilization of minors and "mental incompetents" legally unable to consent to the operation.[14]

SCIENCE, STERILIZATION, AND WELFARE POLICY

The British scientist Francis Galton coined the term *eugenics* from the Greek for *well-born* in 1883; the American eugenicist Charles Davenport defined it nearly thirty years later as "the science of the improvement of the human race by better breeding."[15] One of the first US scientists to apply the Austrian monk Gregor Mendel's laws of inheritance to human heredity, Davenport believed that personal qualities like intelligence and criminality were biological traits transmitted unchanged across generations in a predictable pattern. Since heredity was fixed and environmental factors were inconsequential, he theorized, the only way to improve the human population was through "better" breeding. People with good genes should be encouraged to have more children, and people with bad genes should have fewer.[16]

In 1910, Davenport established the Eugenics Record Office (ERO) in Cold Spring Harbor, New York, and it quickly became the institutional center of eugenic education and research in the United States. A private agency financed primarily by philanthropist Mary Harriman and the Carnegie Institution, the ERO facilitated research on human heredity, collected information on inherited family traits, and promoted eugenic legislation and policies—especially sterilization. Its superintendent, Harry Laughlin, became one of the nation's most influential eugenic experts. He was called upon by the House Committee on Immigration and Naturalization and, as a consultant, played a key role in the federal Immigration Act of 1924, which restricted European immigration based on a national origins quota and barred East Asian immigrants entirely. Laughlin also wrote a Model Sterilization Law, which became the basis for Virginia's sterilization statute, and provided a deposition supporting the sterilization of Carrie Buck.[17]

"Eugenics" is often equated with Harry Laughlin's hardline views and the racial policies of Nazi Germany, but it actually encompassed a variety of political agendas and perspectives.[18] While Laughlin and Davenport associated undesirable traits with Blacks and immigrants, and supposed that immigration restriction and sterilization would improve the nation's health, others put eugenics to work for a different purpose. Progressive maternalists drew on eugenic language about "better babies" to promote prenatal and infant care and a higher standard of living. Feminists led by Margaret Sanger campaigned to legalize birth control, claiming both that it was essential to women's self-determination and sexual health, and that it would lead to fewer "defectives." African American leaders such as W. E. B. Du Bois used eugenic language about healthy childhood and the "talented tenth" to advance the cause of racial justice. As historian Frank Dikötter observes, eugenics was "not so much a clear set of scientific principles as a 'modern' way of talking about social problems in biologizing terms."[19]

Eugenicists themselves divided their field into two distinct strategies. Positive eugenics, such as better baby clinics and marriage counseling, encouraged people with seemingly desirable traits to have more children. Negative eugenics, such as sterilization and permanent "segregation" in a public institution, sought to reduce the propagation of those considered unfit. In the United States, most historians agree, negative eugenic policies had the greatest legislative success.[20] Indeed, the drive for sterilization was so effective that many people mistakenly conflate "eugenics" and "sterilization."

Histories of eugenic sterilization often emphasize the impact of Harry Laughlin's Model Sterilization Law, first written in 1914 but revised and republished in 1922. Laughlin's law contained due process procedures designed to withstand a court challenge, but its targeted population— "persons who because of degenerate or defective hereditary qualities are potential parents of socially inadequate offspring"—was horribly broad. A socially inadequate person was one who "fails chronically in comparison with normal persons, to maintain himself or herself as a useful member of the organized social life of the state." The "socially inadequate classes" encompassed the feebleminded, insane, epileptic, inebriate, criminalistic, diseased, blind, deaf, deformed, and dependent (the last group specifically included "orphans, ne'er-do-wells, the homeless, tramps, and paupers").[21]

Laughlin's callous references to "degenerate or defective hereditary qualities" and "socially inadequate offspring" are certainly unsettling. Yet state sterilization policies emerged as much from longstanding efforts to limit public responsibility for the poor and control out-of-wedlock sexuality as from eugenicists' hereditarian ideas. As criminologist Lizzie Seal points out, Laughlin's capacious understanding of a socially inadequate person "displayed a biological register of 'inheritance lines', but also an economic register that emphasized the dependency of the socially inadequate who were maintained by 'public expense.'"[22] Socially inadequate persons were a seemingly endless burden on the public purse, and even policymakers and welfare officials who disagreed with Laughlin's hardline eugenic views supported sterilization as a welfare policy because it was more humane than permanent institutionalization and cheaper than long-term financial support.

Analyzing sterilization policies' deep roots in America's locally oriented public welfare system helps explain how sterilization arose as a tool of intimate governance and why it persisted long after "eugenics" went out of fashion. State sterilization programs replicated two fundamentals of welfare practice rooted in English poor law: the principle of local responsibility and the distinction between deserving and undeserving poor. From the 1600s until the 1900s, the smallest unit of government—the parish, township, or county—was legally responsible for the care of destitute residents whose families could not support them. Local property taxes paid for the upkeep of county poorhouses and orphanages, and local taxpayers paid a portion of the cost of maintaining indigent county residents in state institutions. Even during the New Deal, when the federal government provided aid to the aged and unemployed, public assistance for "unemployables"— dependent children, single mothers, and people considered to have mental disabilities—remained largely a local responsibility. The practice of sending vagrants out of town—and/or refusing to support poor people whose legal residency was in dispute—remained an important part of welfare practice into the 1930s.[23]

Charity officials had long drawn a distinction between the "worthy" poor, whose economic problems were not of their own making, and "unworthy" paupers, whose dependency on public relief was attributed to their own indolence or degeneracy. In many ways, the historian Michael Katz observes, eugenics simply "tossed the mantle of science over the ancient distinction between the worthy and the unworthy poor."[24] From the 1870s on, chronic poverty was increasingly seen through a scientific lens as hereditary or innate, rather than as a religious or moral failing as it had earlier been viewed. Drawing on the Lamarckian theory of the inheritance of acquired characteristics and the popular science of degeneration, charity officials proposed that immorality and dependency on relief could trigger anatomical changes transmitted to subsequent generations, causing reversion to a less civilized state. Clean living and self-support were necessary to prevent degeneration, they claimed.[25]

VARIETIES OF STERILIZATION LAWS

State sterilization statutes, like the public welfare systems of which they were a part, differed enormously. They were so different, in fact, that the author of a 1940 study said he used the adjective *eugenic* as "only a general appellation" to distinguish nonpunitive sterilization laws from statutes permitting sterilization as punishment for convicted criminals.[26]

"Eugenic" sterilization laws varied in their timing, statutory provisions, and administrative intensity. Indiana enacted the first sterilization law in 1907, twenty years before *Buck v. Bell*. By the time the Supreme Court issued its ruling, twelve states had eugenic sterilization laws, and about eight thousand persons had been sterilized.[27] Seven more states legalized sterilization after the Supreme Court decision; the state of Georgia and territory of Puerto Rico enacted the last US sterilization laws in 1937. In the end, thirty-two states legalized eugenic sterilization at some point, but eighteen did not, and the number of recorded sterilizations in states that enacted eugenic laws ranged from zero (in Nevada and New Jersey) to more than twenty thousand (in California). Nearly one-third of America's eugenic surgeries took place in California, but for many years tiny Delaware, which sterilized "only" 945 people, had the highest per capita sterilization rate in the country.[28]

Although Laughlin's Model Sterilization Law provided a basis for the Virginia law under which Carrie Buck was sterilized, most states did not follow the Laughlin model. James E. Hughes, the author of the 1940 study, emphasized the "great diversity" in the statutory basis on which individuals were sterilized. Of the twenty-nine state sterilization laws in effect in 1940, only eight used Laughlin's phrase "probable potential parent of socially inadequate offspring." Twelve more states contained eugenic language about the inadvisability of procreation due to inherited deficiencies. Twelve state laws referred to the welfare of society, and an astonishing twenty-two sterilization statutes—three-quarters of the total—cited, as a basis for sterilization, that it would be beneficial to or in the best interest of the patient.[29] Of course, sterilization administrators, not patients, decided what was "beneficial."

One way administrators thought sterilization would benefit patients was by facilitating their release from a state institution. In 1940, nearly three-quarters of sterilization laws applied exclusively to institutionalized persons, demonstrating that the policy of eugenic sterilization was inseparable from compulsory institutionalization—eugenic segregation.[30] Psychiatrists sometimes recommended sterilization as a therapeutic procedure that would ease the suffering of individual patients and facilitate their discharge from a mental hospital, but many administrators simply viewed it as a means of institutional population control. As a precondition for release from a state institution, sterilization was the "price of freedom" for institutionalized persons.[31]

The classes of persons subject to sterilization differed from state to state. Every state sterilized individuals who were designated feebleminded, and all but two sterilized the insane. Two-thirds of state sterilization laws applied to people with epilepsy, one-third targeted habitual criminals, and one-quarter applied to people considered sexual perverts or moral degenerates. Three states specifically authorized the sterilization of people with syphilis, but only one (Georgia) provided for the "eugenic" sterilization of people with a *physical* disability or disease.[32]

The sex and race of the sterilized population changed across space and over time. Prior to 1921, men accounted for 57 percent of recorded sterilizations, and 80 percent of surgeries were performed on the insane.[33] In 1963, the last year for which cumulative state-level statistics are available, women accounted for 61 percent of sterilizations and the feebleminded for 52 percent.[34] In Southern states, an initial focus on white female "sex delinquents" shifted dramatically at midcentury, when Black welfare recipients became the principal targets.[35] African Americans were underrepresented in North Carolina's sterilization program in the 1930s and 1940s, but they accounted for 64 percent of sterilizations in the mid-1960s, more than twice their proportion of the state population.[36] In California, institutionalized men with Spanish surnames were 23 percent more likely to be sterilized than their non-Latino counterparts, and women with Spanish surnames were sterilized at a rate 59 percent higher than non-Latinas.[37] Poor people of color, stereotyped as licentious, hyper-fertile, and an economic burden, were disproportionately classified defective and condemned as the undeserving poor.

Still, the relationship between racism and eugenic policies was complex. Eugenics was "never *not* about race," historians Alison Bashford and Philippa Levine observe, but prior to the 1950s sterilization policies generally targeted "marginalized insiders," white people reviled as disabled and degenerate, rather than people of color.[38] During the interwar years, more sterilizations took place in "white" Midwestern states like Kansas and Minnesota than in all the former Confederate states combined.[39] Moreover, legal, administrative, and budgetary considerations shaped sterilization practice in every locale. A brief comparison of California, North Carolina, and Puerto Rico, which actively sterilized large numbers of persons of color, brings the importance of statutory language and administrative processes into view.

California had by far the most active US sterilization program. It sterilized more than twenty thousand persons, one-third the national total, largely because its far-reaching sterilization law operated for decades without a serious legal test. Men accounted for 50 percent of California sterilizations, and those designated insane were 58 percent.[40] California's first sterilization statute, passed in 1909, applied to institutionalized persons for their "physical, moral, or mental welfare." A second law added a reference to heredity and an explicitly eugenic rationale. A third law, enacted in 1917, expanded the groups subject to sterilization to include inmates "suffering from perversion or marked departures from normal mentality or from disease of a syphilitic nature." In addition to the statutes' expansive language, California lacked the protections for patients' rights found in most other states, making it difficult to challenge a sterilization order in court. When in 1951 the state finally narrowed the categories of persons subject to sterilization and instituted an appeal process, the number of operations plummeted. Less than 2 percent of California's recorded sterilizations took place after 1951.[41]

Under California law, institution superintendents initiated the sterilization process. Just three of California's eleven state institutions for the feebleminded and insane—Patton, Stockton, and Sonoma—accounted for 68 percent of sterilizations.[42] The superintendents of these institutions advocated sterilization for both eugenic and therapeutic reasons, but historian Alexandra Minna Stern points out that their surgical enthusiasms likely also related to managerial concerns. Sterilization, a precondition for release, helped officials control the problem of overcrowding.[43]

North Carolina differed from California because of the large percentage of sterilizations performed on noninstitutionalized persons after World War II. The state's first two sterilization laws, enacted in 1919 and 1929, were rarely used, but in 1933 new legislation spelled out appeals procedures, extended sterilization to noninstitutionalized persons, and established a eugenics board within the Department of Public Welfare to hear sterilization cases. North Carolina became the only state to allow social workers to initiate sterilization petitions. Ellen Winston, commissioner of public welfare from 1944 to 1963 and a member of the state's eugenic board, worked fervently to extend the supposed benefits of sterilization to noninstitutionalized welfare recipients, many of whom were Black. In her view, sterilization protected unmarried welfare mothers from having more children and thus deepening their dependency, and should be available to Blacks as well as whites. North Carolina eventually sterilized nearly 7,600 persons; most were women, and a disproportionate percentage were Black. The large number of welfare recipients sterilized underscores the blurred line between "eugenic" sterilization, which aimed to improve the genetic quality of future generations, and the routine implementation of sterilization as a welfare policy thought to protect poor women and children from destitution while lessening the burden on the public purse. Moreover, as historian Johanna Schoen has demonstrated, a small but significant number of sterilizations were contraceptive in purpose. Nearly 6 percent of petitions to the eugenic board between 1937 and 1966, and up to 20 percent in the 1960s, concerned clients seeking contraceptive sterilization.[44] Ironically, Schoen observes, "The eugenic program [was] one of the few resources available to poor and minority women who sought greater reproductive control."[45]

Poverty, racism, and women's limited reproductive options also shaped the history of sterilization in Puerto Rico, where a staggering 35 percent of women of reproductive age were sterilized by the 1980s.[46] Puerto Rico came under US authority in 1898, following Spain's defeat in the Spanish-American War, and its high sterilization rate is often attributed to a eugenics-inspired US government plan to reduce the problems caused by poverty and unemployment by ridding the island of its "surplus" population.[47] Puerto Rico enacted two sterilization bills in 1937. Law 116 established a eugenics board to authorize the sterilization of persons suffering from mental illness, retardation, epilepsy, or sexual perversion if it would improve their condition or prevent the procreation of children with inherited deficiencies; the board could also approve "contraceptive instruction" for couples who requested it.[48] Law 136 authorized the commissioner of health to promote "eugenic principles" by providing maternal health and contraceptive services in public health units and hospitals.[49] With these two bills, Puerto Rico legalized both voluntary contraceptive sterilization and involuntary eugenic sterilization at a time when the former was illegal everywhere on the mainland.

The history of sterilization in Puerto Rico is inseparable from the battle over birth control. In the 1920s and 1930s, Puerto Rican feminists and health professionals promoted birth control as an essential component of modernization using eugenic language about maternal health and overpopulation. The Catholic Church and Nationalist Party, in contrast, portrayed birth control as an American imposition that threatened Puerto Rican identity and survival. During the New Deal, the US government provided financial support for birth control clinics in Puerto Rico, but Catholic opposition quickly led to the withdrawal of federal funds. This created an opening for private initiatives. Clarence Gamble, a eugenicist, philanthropist, and heir to the Procter & Gamble soap fortune, became the major funder of Puerto Rico's birth control program. His hardline eugenic views, promotion of ineffective foam powders, and zeal for sterilization reverberated for decades. Even so, Puerto Rico's Eugenics Board authorized only ninety-seven involuntary sterilizations between 1937 and 1950, and Law 116 was repealed in 1960. The overwhelming majority of sterilizations in Puerto Rico were legally voluntary and contraceptive in purpose.[50]

Sterilizations in Puerto Rico increased dramatically after World War II, along with hospital births and women's labor-force participation. Sterilizations in district hospitals doubled between 1944 and 1950. Sterilization became the leading form of contraception on the island, and by 1965 about one-third of mothers aged twenty to forty-nine were sterilized, double the percentage a decade earlier. Most sterilized women already had several children.[51] They "chose" the operation in the context of limited access to birth control and the constraints of poverty, colonialism, and US economic power. Although some later regretted the operation, the overwhelming majority said they made the decisions themselves. Ironically, political opposition to birth control likely contributed to Puerto Rico's high sterilization rates by making it more difficult to obtain other forms of contraception.[52]

In the first half of the twentieth century, eugenicists waged a fervent and racially coded campaign against the propagation of the "unfit." Yet US sterilization policies varied widely and served a variety of social, economic, and administrative purposes that are obscured by a too-narrow focus on abhorrent eugenic theories about human heredity and better breeding. When California eugenicists described sterilization as a "protection, not a penalty," they expressed a paternalistic side of state sterilization policies that is often overlooked.[53]

STERILIZATION IN OPERATION: THE CASE OF MINNESOTA

Most histories of sterilization focus on the worst abuses, making states like California and North Carolina seem the norm. An analysis of a comparatively modest program like Minnesota's expands our understanding of the range of sterilization policies and underscores the importance of poverty and welfare in shaping sterilization practice.

Minnesota's sterilization law, passed in 1925, differed from most other states because it was voluntary—at least on paper—and applied only to individuals already under court-ordered guardianship as feebleminded or insane. Lawful sterilizations in Minnesota required the written consent of an insane person who had been hospitalized for six months or, in the case of feeblemindedness, consent from the next of kin. (The feebleminded person, having been declared legally incompetent in court, could not provide consent for herself.) The state's sterilization program peaked during the late 1930s, when relief rolls expanded because of the Depression. The number of operations dropped off during World War II, but the law remained on the books until 1975. Ultimately, Minnesota reported 2,350 sterilizations.[54]

The complicated intersections of child welfare and a supposed "menace of the feebleminded" shaped Minnesota's sterilization program from the beginning. The foundation for Minnesota's sterilization law was its 1917 Children's Code, a legislative package that modernized the state's child welfare apparatus and joined the common-law doctrine of *parens patriae*—the state as parent—to the state's police power. Among its provisions, the code empowered judges to commit dependent or neglected children—and any person "alleged to be feeble minded, inebriate or insane"—to state guardianship *without* the approval of parent or kin. Once someone was committed as feebleminded, the State Board of Control as legal guardian decided whether to institutionalize the person or, after 1925, recommend sterilization.[55]

The statutory definition of a feebleminded person was vague: "any person, minor or adult, other than an insane person, who is so mentally defective as to be incapable of managing himself and his affairs, and to require supervision, control and care for his own or the public welfare." Any "reputable citizen" could initiate commitment proceedings, and the broad definition of feeblemindedness gave local judges wide latitude to make the designation.[56] Since judicial commitment—and the ensuing institutionalization—shifted a portion of the cost of supporting the "feebleminded" dependent poor from the county to the state, it was a convenient means of reducing local welfare costs and ridding communities of troublesome individuals who did not fit the criteria for insanity.[57] Feeble-mindedness was the basis for 82 percent of sterilizations in Minnesota, higher than the national proportion of 52 percent.[58]

Historians have described feeblemindedness as a "catchall term" rooted in crude scientific theories about heredity and elitist assumptions about the inferiority of certain groups. Immigrants, people of color, poor whites, criminals, individuals with mental and physical disabilities, and sexual minorities—in short, anyone who "behaved in ways that offended the middle-class sensibilities of doctors, judges, or social workers"—risked the feebleminded label.[59] "Feebleminded" was more than a derogatory term, however; it was also a definitive legal category, since individuals so designated in court had to surrender the right to vote, own property, and make their own medical decisions in exchange for the state's "protection."[60]

Minnesota officials described the feebleminded persons they targeted for sterilization as "children" in need of protection; they did not simply disparage them as innately inferior stock. Many women targeted for sterilization *were* young, and social workers thought they were protecting them from the stresses of parenting, while also protecting the unborn from being raised by an incompetent (and childlike) parent. Feebleminded Minnesotans were also childlike in a legal sense; regardless of age, they were legal wards of the state deprived of the citizenship rights of adults.[61]

Minnesota's three-step eugenic sterilization process—judicial commitment, institutionalization, and finally surgery—began at the local level. First, a school official, child welfare worker, or police officer identified an individual who was truant, disabled, or sexually delinquent as possibly feebleminded and petitioned the court to commit the person to guardianship. Then a probate or district judge, a local elected official not required to have any legal or medical training, decided whether the person met the legal criteria for feeblemindedness and, if so, committed the individual to state guardianship. Although the judge could appoint an examining board to assist with the diagnosis, if the person was "obviously feebleminded" he could, with the consent of the county attorney, make the designation on his own. The State Board of Control, acting as the feebleminded person's legal guardian, made decisions about institutionalization and recommended sterilization. A three-person panel composed of a member of the Board of Control, the superintendent of the state school for the feebleminded, and a psychologist authorized the surgery. *A family member had to provide written consent.* Specific sterilization decisions were thus shaped by numerous individuals and an assortment of factors, including the inadequacy of local welfare funding, concerns about overcrowding in the state institution, electoral politics (since judges were elected), and family dynamics. No single authority exercised full control over the sterilization authorization process. As a result, judgments about commitment and sterilization were unpredictable. Even the chief administrator of Minnesota's sterilization law could not understand why some sexually delinquent women were adjudged feebleminded and sterilized, while others with very similar IQ, background, and behavior were not. In the 1930s, she conducted a study. She found no consistent criteria for judicial assessments, only the shocking arbitrariness of sterilization practice.[62]

Nearly everyone sterilized in Minnesota had one thing in common, however: they were poor. Most were dependent on some form of public aid, and their personal stories reveal a litany of hardship and abuse. Consider the case of June Boyd. Like Carrie Buck, she got pregnant as a teenager and gave birth to an illegitimate child. Unlike Carrie, June was not designated feebleminded right away. She and her baby were initially sent to the state reform school for delinquent girls; only later was June transferred to the Faribault School for the Feebleminded, where she was eventually sterilized and discharged. Her baby was sent to the state orphanage.[63]

What made June feebleminded in the eyes of the Board of Control? Like many other sterilized Minnesotans, she was uneducated, sexually misbehaving, and came from a "broken" home. Social workers described her father and stepmother as shiftless and illiterate, and her home as "one of the poorest ever seen, filthy and hardly any bedding or furniture." June herself used vile language and admitted to having sex with four different boys. Social workers said she was "practically a prostitute." The judge declared her a "menace to the county." Convinced that June would be a bad mother, the authorities "protected" her baby by taking him away. He was almost certainly placed for adoption.[64] As June's case suggests, eugenic sterilization policy was as much about preventing allegedly feebleminded women from rearing their own children as about preventing the transmission of hereditary defects.

June brazenly flouted conventional moral codes, and it is possible to see her feebleminded diagnosis as an attempt by the state to punish and control her sexual rebelliousness. Yet many "feebleminded sex delinquents," including Carrie Buck, were victims of sexual abuse or assault. Some had physical, mental, or learning disabilities that left them vulnerable to sexual violence and exploitation. A disproportionate number came from dysfunctional or abusive families—or no families at all, which is surely one reason they were vulnerable to the state's intrusions. Lucille Johnson, for example, had a life filled with tragedy. Her mother died when she was a child, and she had two illegitimate children, the result of intercourse with her father and brother. (Her father served time in the state prison for incest.) One of Lucille's babies died as an infant, and she lost the other to adoption. The superintendent recognized that Lucille's sex delinquencies were "beyond her control," but it never occurred to him that her "feeble-mindedness" might stem from the trauma of incest and the loss of her mother and children. He simply assumed that her mental deficiency was inherited and incurable.[65]

Next to illegitimacy, being the mother of a large family on public relief was the principal motivation for sterilization in interwar Minnesota. At a time when social workers treated most troubled welfare families with a combination of casework, environmental improvements, and monetary aid, feeblemindedness provided a compelling explanation for the failure of social work interventions to return a family to social and economic respectability. In a truly painful vicious circle, troubled families were assumed to be feebleminded, and families with a feebleminded designation were assumed to be troubled and unfit.[66]

Most people assume that families resented the feebleminded label and resisted state-imposed sterilization. In fact, some families turned to welfare boards or the courts when they wanted help controlling troublesome sons or daughters, even consenting to sterilization to avoid the stain (or cost) of illegitimacy. Others saw sterilization as a way to control their own reproduction when other forms of birth control were inaccessible. Institutional records show that some mothers entered the institution "for sterilization" and expected to return home after surgery. As a Twin Cities social worker observed, the sterilization program "worked out well in families where there were already enough children and the mother and father were convinced that there should not be any more."[67] Yet a poor woman seeking eugenic sterilization for contraceptive purposes was extremely vulnerable. As a feebleminded ward of the state, she had to spend weeks or months in the state institution, surrender her civil rights, and risk losing her children to child protection authorities because feebleminded mothers were by definition unfit. Tragically, some women were so desperate for contraceptive health care that they were willing to take that risk.

Of course, many families fiercely resisted the state's eugenic policies. One took its legal challenge to the Minnesota Supreme Court. Rose and Fred Masters were poor tenant farmers who struggled to support their six children during the Depression and applied for county relief. Despite regular visits from county welfare workers, they had four more children while they were receiving public assistance. A frustrated welfare board concluded that the Catholic couple's "unrestricted fertility . . . was not consistent with their economic and social capacities" and recommended sterilization. The couple was committed to state guardianship as feeble-minded, and Mrs. Masters was institutionalized a few months after the birth of her tenth child. Her neighbors immediately petitioned for her release. In 1944, the Minnesota Supreme Court reversed her commitment and sent the case back to the lower courts.[68]

The state's claim that Mrs. Masters was feebleminded centered on her housekeeping and mothering. The county welfare board claimed that she was a poor housekeeper and neglected her children. The family home was rundown. Mrs. Masters never made proper meals; the only food on the table was bread and syrup, and the bread was never sliced, just torn off in the middle. The children's hair was long, their clothes were in tatters, and they were often absent from school. Social workers attributed Mrs. Masters's neglect of her children to feeblemindedness, but her neighbors insisted that she was neither feebleminded nor a bad mother. Her children were "just as normal as anyone's children," one neighbor testified. "She wasn't probably as good a housekeeper as some people," another explained, "but she was a very good mother." The Minnesota Supreme Court reversed Mrs. Masters's commitment. "Even in this modern age of birth control and social welfare agencies," the court ruled, "the circumstance of being the mother of an unusually large family, as measured by present standards, should not label a woman as a moron." Mrs. Masters should not have to demonstrate her own mental competence; the burden of proof should fall on the state. The decision had no effect on her children, however. A court had declared them "neglected," and they remained wards of the state. Restoration of custody would necessitate another court proceeding.[69]

The *Masters* case is a stunning example of the state as perpetrator of eugenic abuse. It also demonstrates that the "state"—in this case, the Minnesota Supreme Court—was often the best vehicle for defending against that abuse. By the 1940s, an array of social programs and the courts' enlarged authority over children and the so-called feebleminded had markedly extended state intervention into poor people's intimate lives. Yet social work practices varied and, as the reversal of the lower court's commitment order in *Masters* reveals, court judgments were not monolithic.[70] Although most poor people resisted eugenic institutionalization and sterilization by running away, at times poor families and communities turned to the courts and social workers they trusted to challenge eugenic threats to their personal freedom and bodily integrity—and end unwanted governmental interference in their intimate lives.

County welfare boards initiated most sterilization petitions in Minnesota, but the police often started the commitment process for men, who accounted for 20 percent of the state's sterilizations. Men were often committed following a sexual offense or a vagrancy charge. Minnesota had a relatively small proportion of vasectomies compared to California, both because its sterilization program was administered through the child welfare system and because of its consent requirement. While not coming close to current standards of informed consent, Minnesota's consent provision gave parents and spouses some say in the sterilization process. Many families balked at sterilizing men because of concerns about the operation's impact on masculinity and sexual performance. As well, state officials were less likely to recommend sterilization for men because sterilization was a step toward discharge, and many communities were vocal in their opposition to the release of "defective" men. As a result, feebleminded women were regularly sterilized and released, but their male counterparts had to remain in the institution.[71]

STERILIZATION AND WELFARE AFTER WORLD WAR II

In Minnesota, as in most states outside the South, eugenic surgeries peaked during the Depression and dropped off during World War II. Although the number of operations increased slightly after the war as state institutions returned to normal, eugenic sterilization ceased being a routine welfare policy, except in the South. New Deal entitlement programs and the GI Bill reduced chronic poverty and the denigration of (white) families who depended on government aid, just as better access to birth control, improved treatments for venereal disease, and the modern adoption market undermined the eugenics-era association between unwed mothers and feeble minds. The civil rights and mental health reform movements further challenged the perceived link between race, class, and low intelligence.[72]

Yet sterilizations continued and even increased in some states. Nationwide, nearly 30 percent of eugenic surgeries took place between 1945 and the end of 1963, when reporting stopped. A disproportionate percentage occurred in Southern states with sizable Black populations. For example, 60 percent of North Carolina's sterilizations took place after 1950, compared to just 5 percent of Minnesota's.[73]

In the 1960s and 1970s, the vast majority of sterilizations—both voluntary and involuntary—were performed under the auspices of federal family planning programs rather than eugenic laws. A series of Supreme Court rulings legalized birth control and abortion, hospitals eased restrictions on elective sterilization, and the federal government began to provide some family planning services to low-income women as part of the War on Poverty. The US Office of Economic Opportunity began to fund "volun-

tary" contraceptive sterilizations (but not abortions) in 1971. Amid growing concerns about the long-term safety of birth control pills and other
contraceptive measures, the number of sterilizations skyrocketed. Within
a few years, as many as 100,000 to 150,000 low-income women had been
sterilized. Federally funded sterilizations were supposed to be voluntary,
but hospitals promoted them aggressively. Many women were pressured
to sign the consent forms, especially if they were on welfare, and the Nixon
administration blocked the distribution of guidelines meant to ensure
voluntariness.[74]

The problem of sterilization abuse burst into public consciousness
when two young African American girls, twelve-year-old Minnie Lee Relf
and her fourteen-year-old sister Mary Alice, sued the federal government
for their involuntary sterilizations. The Relf sisters were not sterilized under Alabama's eugenic statute, but their story fit the standard narrative of
eugenics: workers at the Montgomery Family Planning Clinic identified
the girls as "mentally retarded" and tricked their mother into consenting to the operations by putting her X on a consent form she was unable
to read. The Relf suit inspired dozens of other women to come forward,
exposing and challenging sterilization abuse across the US mainland and
Puerto Rico. To many critics, the use of federal funds to sterilize large numbers of indigenous women and low-income women of color was evidence
of a deliberate policy of racial genocide and social engineering, which saw
eugenicists work with and within Planned Parenthood and the US government to impose their bigoted notions of reproductive fitness on poor Black
and brown communities. As an influential 2013 book concluded, "Eugenics and old-style eugenicists were at the heart of birth control and welfare
policy in the early 1970s."[75]

The emphasis on eugenics-inspired doctors and social workers pur-
posefully sterilizing "unfit" women of color is too simple. It ignores the
mundane sources of sterilization abuse, such as poverty, the structures
of Medicaid and hospital funding, and the limited contraceptive choices
of poor women. It sidesteps allegations of mental disability and the issue
of racial bias within the "mentally retarded" label. It plays down the fact
that the most egregious sterilization abuse coincided not with the expansion of federal welfare measures during President Lyndon Johnson's War
on Poverty, but with the increasingly anti-welfare climate of the early 1970s,
when Nixon scaled down federal anti-poverty agencies, states cut welfare
budgets, and a proposed Family Assistance Program, consisting of benefits
for male-headed households and work requirements for welfare recipients, amplified and racialized the divide between the "deserving" and "undeserving" poor.[76] Finally, it evades the reality that while many individuals

were forcibly "sterilized by the state," other parts of the "state"—especially the courts—placed limits on sterilization and became an important tool for stopping the abuse. The Relfs sued the federal government, presented their case in congressional hearings, and had a big impact. In *Relf v. Weinberger* (1974), Judge Gerhard Gesell prohibited the use of federal funds for nonconsensual sterilizations and ordered new guidelines to ensure that federally funded contraceptive sterilizations were truly voluntary.[77]

We should look back on America's history of eugenic sterilization with revulsion. Yet state sterilization policies were never only about improving the human race by "better" breeding. From the beginning, eugenic sterilization was part of a chronically underfunded and locally variable public welfare system that stoked public scorn for the poor and disparaged families who depended on government assistance as immoral, incompetent, and undeserving. Public aid to the US poor has always been bound up with moral judgments and intrusions into recipients' intimate lives, yet state power was more diffuse and the justifications for sterilization more varied than most histories of eugenics presume. Today, when reproductive rights are at risk, racism, poverty, and health disparities are increasing, and a battle over public spending is raging, it is time to broaden our thinking about the lessons of eugenic sterilization.

NOTES

1. In this chapter, I regularly use offensive words such as *feebleminded* and *defective* without quotation marks. These words are more expansive than present-day terms like *intellectual disability,* and while using them is problematic, no other phrasing so vividly conveys the scientific and cultural assumptions behind state sterilization laws.

2. Paul A. Lombardo, *Three Generations, No Imbeciles: Eugenics, the Supreme Court, and* Buck v. Bell (Baltimore: Johns Hopkins University Press, 2008), 101–3, 290.

3. *Buck v. Bell,* 274 U.S. 200 (1927).

4. Molly Ladd-Taylor, *Fixing the Poor: Eugenic Sterilization and Child Welfare in the Twentieth Century* (Baltimore: Johns Hopkins University Press, 2017), 229.

5. In addition to Lombardo, see Adam Cohen, *Imbeciles: The Supreme Court, American Eugenics, and the Sterilization of Carrie Buck* (New York: Penguin, 2016); Philip R. Reilly, *The Surgical Solution: A History of Involuntary Sterilization in the United States* (Baltimore: Johns Hopkins University Press, 1991); Harry Bruinius, *Better for All the World: The Secret History of Forced Sterilization and America's Quest for Racial Purity* (New York: Knopf, 2006); and Mark A. Largent, *Breeding Contempt: The History of Coerced Sterilization in the United States* (New Brunswick, NJ: Rutgers University Press, 2008).

6. Lombardo, *Three Generations,* xi.

7. Stephen Jay Gould, "Carrie Buck's Daughter," *Natural History* 93 (July 1984): 14–18.

8. Cohen, *Imbeciles*, 7.

9. Edwin Black, *War Against the Weak: Eugenics and America's Campaign to Create a Master Race* (New York: Four Walls Eight Windows, 2003).

10. Cohen, *Imbeciles,* 14–17, 285–86, 291–92.

11. *Buck v. Bell*, at 205–6.

12. Ladd-Taylor, *Fixing the Poor,* 173–80.

13. Lombardo, *Three Generations,* 268–74.

14. *Relf v. Weinberger*, 372 F. Supp. 1196 (D.D.C. 1974).

15. Quoted in Alexandra Minna Stern, *Eugenic Nation: Faults and Frontiers of Better Breeding in Modern America* (Berkeley: University of California Press, 2005), 11.

16. Mark Haller, *Eugenics: Hereditarian Attitudes in American Thought* (1963; repr., New Brunswick, NJ: Rutgers University Press, 1983), 61–68; and Daniel J. Kevles, *In the Name of Eugenics: Genetics and the Uses of Human Heredity* (1985; repr., Cambridge, MA: Harvard University Press, 1998), chapter 3.

17. Garland E. Allen, "The Eugenics Record Office at Cold Spring Harbor, 1910–1940: An Essay in Institutional History," *Osiris* 2 (1986): 225–64.

18. The classic work on eugenics and Nazism is Stefan Kühl, *The Nazi Connection: Eugenics, American Racism, and German National Socialism* (New York: Oxford University Press, 1994). Recent works that take a different approach include Philippa Levine, *Eugenics: A Very Short Introduction* (New York: Oxford University Press, 2016); and Marius Turda, *Modernism and Eugenics* (New York: Palgrave Macmillan, 2010).

19. Frank Dikötter, "Race Culture: Recent Perspectives on the History of Eugenics," *American Historical Review* 103 (April 1998): 467. See also Alison Bashford and Philippa Levine, eds., *The Oxford Handbook of the History of Eugenics* (New York: Oxford University Press, 2010); and Paul A. Lombardo, ed., *A Century of Eugenics in America* (Bloomington: Indiana University Press, 2011).

20. Molly Ladd-Taylor, "Eugenics, Sterilisation, and Modern Marriage in the USA: The Strange Career of Paul Popenoe," *Gender and History* 13 (August 2001): 298–327.

21. Harry H. Laughlin, *Eugenical Sterilization in the United States* (Chicago: Psychopathic Laboratory of the Municipal Court of Chicago, 1922), 446–47; and Lombardo, *Three Generations,* xii, 51.

22. Lizzie Seal, "Designating Dependency: The 'Socially Inadequate' in the United States, 1910–1940," *Journal of Historical Sociology* 26 (June 2013): 147.

23. Ladd-Taylor, *Fixing the Poor,* 11–12.

24. Michael B. Katz, *In the Shadow of the Poorhouse: A Social History of Welfare in America* (New York: Basic Books, 1986), 183.

25. Ladd-Taylor, *Fixing the Poor,* 13.

26. James E. Hughes, *Eugenic Sterilization in the United States: A Comparative Summary of Statutes and Review of Court Decisions* (Washington, DC: GPO, 1940), 1.

27. E. S. Gosney, "Operations for Eugenic Sterilization Performed in State Institutions Under State Laws Up to January 1, 1928," Sterilization Statistics, series 7,

Association for Voluntary Sterilization Records, 1929–1981, Social Welfare History Archives, University of Minnesota Libraries (hereafter AVS Records); and Hughes, *Eugenic Sterilization,* 25–29.

28. Ladd-Taylor, *Fixing the Poor,* 121.

29. Hughes, *Eugenic Sterilization,* 16–17.

30. Hughes, *Eugenic Sterilization,* 5–7.

31. Joel T. Braslow, *Mental Ills and Bodily Cures: Psychiatric Treatment in the First Half of the Twentieth Century* (Berkeley: University of California Press, 1997), 70; James Trent, *Inventing the Feeble Mind: A History of Intellectual Disability in the United States* (New York: Oxford University Press, 2016), 190; and Ladd-Taylor, *Fixing the Poor,* 165.

32. Hughes, *Eugenic Sterilization,* 3, 16.

33. Laughlin, *Eugenical Sterilization,* 96. The large number of male sterilizations in the early period partly reflects the imbalanced sex ratio in California.

34. Human Betterment Association, "Sterilizations Performed under U.S. State Sterilization Statutes through December 31, 1963," AVS Records.

35. Susan K. Cahn, *Sexual Reckonings: Southern Girls in a Troubling Age* (Cambridge, MA: Harvard University Press, 2012), 163.

36. Johanna Schoen, "Reassessing Eugenic Sterilization: The Case of North Carolina," in *A Century of Eugenics in America,* 149–50. African Americans were 29 percent of the state population in 1930, but accounted for only 23 percent of sterilizations. By 1960, the Black population was only 24.5 percent of the state's total population. Campbell Gibson and Kay Jung, *Historical Statistics on Population Totals by Race, 1790 to 1990, and by Hispanic Origin, 1970 to 1990, for the United States, Regions, Divisions, and States,* Working Paper No. 56, Table 48, https://www.census.gov//content/dam/Census/library/working-papers/2002/demo/POP-twps0056.pdf.

37. Nicole Novak et al., "Disproportionate Sterilization of Latinos Under California's Sterilization Program, 1920–1945," *American Journal of Public Health* 108 (May 2018): 611–13.

38. Bashford and Levine, "Introduction: Eugenics and the Modern World," in *Oxford Handbook,* 6.

39. Human Betterment Foundation, "Table of Sterilizations Done in the United States under State Sterilization Laws, up to January 1, 1942," AVS Records.

40. "Sterilizations Performed . . . through December 31, 1963."

41. Stern, *Eugenic Nation,* 99–100; Alexandra Minna Stern, "From Legislation to Lived Experience: Eugenic Sterilization in California and Indiana, 1907–79," in *A Century of Eugenics in America,* 101–2; and Human Betterment Association of America, "Sterilizations Reported in the United States to January 1, 1952," AVS Records.

42. Alex Wellerstein, "States of Eugenics: Institutions and Practices of Compulsory Sterilization in California, in *Reframing Rights: Bioconstitutionalism in the Genetic Age,* ed. Sheila Jasanoff (Cambridge, MA: MIT Press, 2011), 38.

43. Stern, "From Legislation to Lived Experience," 105–6.

44. Johanna Schoen, *Choice and Coercion: Birth Control, Sterilization, and Abortion in Public Health and Welfare* (Chapel Hill: University of North Carolina Press, 2005), chapter 2.

45. Schoen, *Choice and Coercion,* 138.

46. Annette B. Ramírez de Arellano and Conrad Seipp, *Colonialism, Catholicism and Contraception: A History of Birth Control in Puerto Rico* (Chapel Hill: University of North Carolina Press, 2011), 176.

47. Bonnie Mass, *Population Target: The Political Economy of Population Control in Latin America* (Toronto: Canadian Women's Educational Press, 1976).

48. Laws of Puerto Rico 1937, No. 116, 267–71.

49. Laws of Puerto Rico 1937, No. 136, 294–95.

50. Laura Briggs, *Reproducing Empire: Race, Sex, Science, and U.S. Imperialism in Puerto Rico* (Berkeley: University of California Press, 2002), chapter 5; and Ramírez de Arellano and Seipp, *Colonialism,* 204n3.

51. Harriet B. Presser, *Sterilization and Fertility Decline in Puerto Rico* (Berkeley: University of California Institute of International Studies, 1973), 28–29, 61.

52. Ramírez de Arellano and Seipp, *Colonialism,* 140–44; and Briggs, *Reproducing Empire,* 158.

53. Stern, *Eugenic Nation,* 99.

54. Ladd-Taylor, *Fixing the Poor,* 16.

55. Ladd-Taylor, *Fixing the Poor,* 55.

56. Laws of Minnesota 1917, chap. 344, sec. 1.

57. Ladd-Taylor, *Fixing the Poor,* 84–87.

58. "Sterilizations Performed . . . through December 31, 1963."

59. Cohen, *Imbeciles,* 16.

60. For an extended discussion of this topic, see Ladd-Taylor, *Fixing the Poor,* chapter 3.

61. Ladd-Taylor, *Fixing the Poor,* 8.

62. Mildred Thomson, *Prologue: A Minnesota Story of Mental Retardation* (Minneapolis: Gilbert, 1963), 89.

63. "June Boyd," Home School for Girls, Case Files, Minnesota Historical Society, St. Paul (hereafter MHS); and Faribault State School and Hospital (hereafter FSSH), *Record of Sterilization Cases,* no. 318, MHS. June Boyd is a pseudonym.

64. "June Boyd," Home School for Girls, Case Files.

65. "Possibilities for Clubhouse (Sterilized 9/29/28)," enclosed in J. M. Murdoch to Mildred Thomson, November 13, 1928, FSSH Superintendent Correspondence, MHS.

66. Molly Ladd-Taylor, "The 'Sociological Advantages' of Sterilization: Fiscal Politics and Feebleminded Women in Interwar Minnesota," in *Mental Retardation in America: A Historical Anthology,* ed. Steven Noll and James W. Trent Jr. (New York University Press, 2004), 281–99.

67. Chas. E. Dow, "The Problem of the Feeble-Minded III," typescript, August 9, 1934, Department of Public Welfare Library, MHS.

68. *In re Masters*, 216 Minn. 553, 13 N.W.2d 487 (1944); and Ladd-Taylor, *Fixing the Poor,* 170–73.

69. *In re Masters*, 216 Minn at 490, 492, 489.

70. See Michael J. Willrich, "The Two Percent Solution: Eugenic Jurisprudence and the Socialization of American Law, 1900–1930," *Law and History Review* 16 (Spring 1998): 63–111.

71. Ladd-Taylor, *Fixing the Poor,* 108–15. See also Molly Ladd-Taylor, "The Eugenic Origins of Minnesota's Psychopathic Personality Act of 1939," *Journal of Policy History* 32 (April 2019): 192–216.

72. Ladd-Taylor, *Fixing the Poor,* 173–80. For a different view, see Randall Hansen and Desmond King, *Sterilized by the State: Eugenics, Race, and the Population Scare in Twentieth-Century North America* (Cambridge: Cambridge University Press, 2013).

73. Human Betterment Association of America, "Sterilizations Officially Reported to January 1, 1951," AVS Records; and Ladd-Taylor, *Fixing the Poor,* 229.

74. Rebecca M. Kluchin, *Fit to Be Tied: Sterilization and Reproductive Rights in America, 1950–1980* (New Brunswick, NJ: Rutgers University Press, 2009), 94–98; and Hansen and King, *Sterilized by the State,* 244–49.

75. Hansen and King, *Sterilized by the State,* 257. On the *Relf* case, see Gregory Michael Dorr, "Protection or Control? Women's Health, Sterilization Abuse, and *Relf v. Weinberger*," in *A Century of Eugenics in America,* 161–90; and Molly Ladd-Taylor, "Contraception or Eugenics? Sterilization and 'Mental Retardation' in the 1970s and 1980s," *Canadian Bulletin of Medical History* 31 (2014): 189–211.

76. Dorr, "Protection or Control?," 168–69.

77. Ladd-Taylor, *Fixing the Poor,* 211–15.

8

"Land of the White Hunter"

Legal Liberalism and the Shifting Racial
Ground of Morals Enforcement

ANNE GRAY FISCHER

Late one night in October 1961, Los Angeles police officers V. C. Dossey and C. H. Watson thought they had made a legitimate arrest when they charged Betty, a white woman, with disorderly conduct. The officers were in their radio car, patrolling a predominantly Black neighborhood in South Los Angeles—an area, according to police, "plagued by females" engaging in suspect sexual practices—when they observed Betty "cruis[ing] in a manner designed to attract" the attention of men. When Dossey and Watson stopped to question Betty, she became "hostile" and refused to identify herself. A search of Betty's belongings turned up more evidence of her sexual criminality, including a "contraceptive kit." Later, when officers interrogated Betty at the police station, she delivered in "the most vulgar and profane language . . . her opinion of 'blue coats.'"[1]

Prior to World War II, the incriminating combination of a white woman in a Black neighborhood carrying items associated with nonreproductive sex and daring, above all, to disrespect police officers would very likely have been sufficient to yield a conviction. But, in a surprising twist, the charges against Betty were dismissed by the city attorney's office. A deputy for the city prosecutor advised the police department "to be very restrictive and conservative" in their enforcement of this morals misdemeanor—in other words, officers should lean on the side of nonenforcement because the city prosecutor was newly "reluctant" to pursue these cases. In a rare admission of error, the chastened Los Angeles Police Department (LAPD) leadership admitted that "it would have been wiser to have released" Betty without pressing charges. Betty's case is emblematic of an important turning point in the twentieth-century history of sexual policing: it marked a deepening racial inequity of morals enforcement, through the gradual decriminalization of white women's presumed nonmarital straight sexual practices, and the intensifying targeting of Black women for allegedly engaging in the same.[2]

In 1964, three years after Betty's arrest, very different law enforcement practices were on display when Los Angeles County supervisor Kenneth Hahn declared "an all-out war against narcotics and open prostitution" in his predominantly Black district in South Los Angeles. Coordinating with the sheriff and district attorney, Hahn orchestrated "accelerated enforcement activities" in the neighborhood. The campaign was kicked off in April with a weekend vice raid during which over one hundred "suspects" were arrested, rounded up, and loaded onto buses. Despite the different jurisdictions of city and county, these two episodes—the city prosecutor indicating his office's reluctance to enforce morals misdemeanors in 1961 and the coordinated mass morals misdemeanor arrests just a few years later—illuminate the divergent racial trajectories that sexual policing took after this formative midcentury moment in the United States.[3]

Unequal police practices were a longstanding problem in Los Angeles's Black neighborhoods, but as California morals laws relaxed during a period of legal liberalism from the mid-1950s through the early 1960s, the racial inequity of morals law enforcement deepened. Arrest statistics in Los Angeles confirm the widening racial disparity in midcentury morals enforcement: between 1954 and 1963, the number of white women arrested for prostitution-related offenses decreased by 22 percent, while the number of arrested Black women increased by 23 percent. To Black residents of Los Angeles, morals enforcement in Black neighborhoods was a flagrant example of police discrimination. Many residents were particularly outraged that a nightly caravan of "white hunters" (white men soliciting for sex) drove into Black neighborhoods accosting Black women with impunity, and Black women continued to be harassed by police—even as white women were conspicuously immunized from police action. By the mid-1960s, Black protestors challenged the racial disparity in morals enforcement in Los Angeles and residents engaged in violent battles with police attempting to arrest Black women on morals charges.[4]

Los Angeles reveals two critical dimensions of the postwar racial history of morals law enforcement. First, midcentury processes of sexual liberalization in social science and legal reform shaped law enforcement authorities' "reluctance" to pursue white women like Betty while preserving police officers' discretionary power to disproportionately target Black women. Second, the city's Black communal violence was touched off in part by this racial inequity in morals enforcement. Presenting a history of midcentury morals law reform alongside morals crackdowns and confrontations between Black people and police officers in segregated Los Angeles exposes an understudied site of mounting police repression and Black protest in a period of ascendant sexual liberalism. The racial inequity in morals policing—exacerbated by liberalizing morals laws—was a powerful, if heretofore unrecognized, factor in the many clashes between police and Black residents that culminated in the 1965 communal violence in the Black neighborhood of Watts.

Intimate governance in this moment of liberal reform did not simply mean the state punishment of women on the social margins. Rather, law enforcement served as a mechanism to redraw the margins themselves, recasting white women's nonmarital straight sexual practices as legal and, if not yet normal, then at least private and beyond the reach of criminal law. As a result, white and Black women presumed to be engaging in the same sexual practices experienced an unequal density and velocity of state power. This decisive shift in midcentury sexual policing demonstrates the power of law enforcement to rewrite social scripts and produce new forms of intersectional oppression.

As the country's changing sexual mores became an increasingly mainstream fact of twentieth-century life, social scientists, lawyers, and civil libertarians successfully mounted challenges to morals laws. These laws, which were chiefly deployed against women, encompassed a suite of broad, sexualized misdemeanors, including disorderly conduct and vagrancy. Social scientists and legal reformers argued, in particular, that the draconian prohibitions on widely practiced nonmarital heterosexual sex threatened to criminalize otherwise normal sexual relationships. In 1961 the California legislature, manifesting the spirit of legal liberalism coursing through American law in this period, revised the state's vagrancy statute, which covered the disorderly conduct charge that police pinned on Betty—one reason for the prosecution's disinclination to press these charges. That same year, the Supreme Court of California struck down Los Angeles municipal morals ordinances in the *In re Lane* ruling. While these reforms effectively decriminalized nonmarital straight sex, they preserved law enforcement's discretionary authority to police public affronts to morality—a legal turn that increasingly shielded white women from citywide morals enforcement, but had ominous consequences for residents of Black neighborhoods roundly policed as zones of immorality.

Morals law reform did not proceed in a race-neutral vacuum. Rather, it took shape within the postwar context of segregated urban neighborhoods and the police response to the growing Black population. Throughout the postwar period, two massive population shifts changed the racial meaning and experience of American cities. First, beginning in World War II and continuing throughout midcentury, millions of Southern Black migrants moved to cities in the West. This tremendous movement converged with the rapid proliferation of racially restricted, federally subsidized suburbs as white male breadwinners and their families were drawn to cheap mortgages for homes outside the cities. By 1965, Black people in the United States were more urbanized than whites, with nearly three-quarters of the total Black population living in cities. In Los Angeles, where twentieth-century development was driven by white, Protestant, and Republican interests, these population shifts unleashed powerful political pressures to contain the Black population. Despite the city's racial and ethnic diversity, Black people specifically were targeted for urban control during this period. In 1960, Black residents outnumbered "Spanish-surname" residents in the city by more than 74,000, and because they experienced more acute forms of housing exclusion than any other nonwhite group, the majority of Black Angelenos were visibly concentrated in just nine neighborhoods in South Los Angeles (an area made up of thirty neighborhoods). Policing the city in this period, then, meant protecting whiteness by containing blackness. Given this context, it is reasonable to take the words of LAPD chief William Parker literally when he said in his opening address as chief in 1950 that "Los Angeles is the white spot of the great cities of America today. It is to the advantage of the community that we keep it that way."[5]

As white suburbs expanded and white urban majorities declined amid the accelerating movement of Black migrants to cities, white midcentury observers increasingly saw cities as threatening sites of racial and sexual disorder. Racist hierarchies of sexual morality—of white suburban normality and Black urban deviance—were mapped onto spatial segregation. The criminological and popular discourse of this period linked a decades-old association of blackness and criminality with urban moral decay. Black sexuality was understood as a public and group-wide disorder, intimately connected with the presumed space of Black life, namely the "ghetto," while white sexuality was increasingly reconceived within the private, individualized, and domestic sphere—a development closely related to the legal retreat from regulating nonmarital straight sex. Enterprising politicians, police leaders, and conservative activists channeled white fears of urban "moral breakdown" by pouring racial content into midcentury urban code words, such as "street crime" and "immorality," and less subtle euphemisms for cities, such as the routinely deployed "jungles."[6]

The police in Los Angeles played a crucial role in buttressing a white narrative that conflated urban blackness with immorality and criminality, especially through the common police practice of funneling vice to the city's segregated Black neighborhoods. White men were permitted by police to engage in vice activities in Black neighborhoods while police disproportionately targeted Black people for morals offenses. These police practices strengthened the myth that Black people were immoral and criminal, and that Black neighborhoods were the primary sites of lawbreaking. Even as police leaders lashed out at the putative constraints imposed by liberal court rulings, officers retained broad discretionary power in Black neighborhoods to conduct vice raids, crackdowns, and mass arrests for morals offenses. At the very moment when the scope and purpose of police discretion was under revision, Los Angeles law enforcement authorities weaponized sexual policing to assert their dominion over outraged Black residents.

REDEFINING SEXUAL CRIMINALITY, DEEPENING RACIAL DIVISIONS

An onslaught of postwar statistics, including rates of premarital pregnancy, single motherhood, and venereal disease infection, delivered inescapable evidence that Americans were increasingly having sex beyond the legal sanction of marriage. Alfred Kinsey's *Sexual Behavior in the Human Female*, published in 1953 to a storm of publicity (no doubt primed by his 1948 bestseller on the "human male"), detailed the frequency, variation, and partners in Americans' sexual careers, ultimately exposing the myth of extramarital chastity that governed official norms. "Kinsey demonstrated that much of Americans' sexual activity took place outside of marriage," historian Miriam Reumann argues, "and that the majority of the nation's citizens had violated accepted moral standards as well as state and federal laws in their pursuit of sexual pleasure."[7]

Morals laws across the country created a broad class of "law abiding law breakers," according to the authors of the 1950 edition of *Social Disorganization*, a social science textbook. In this period of acute contradictions—when more white women were engaging in nonmarital sex, but domestic white womanhood was prized with a renewed vengeance—the gap between sexual practices and sexual laws was magnified and held up to broad critique. Reproductive rights attorney Harriet Pilpel argued in 1952 that American morals laws "are honored more in the breach," and popular author Christopher Gerould had more colorful language for the moral legal code: "American sex laws are a vast garbage heap of discarded attitudes and worn-out prejudices, piled up and preserved over centuries in the statute books." A gathering force of legal scholars, social scientists, and popular critics challenged the wasteful and misguided deployment of "overcriminalization" to effect moral suasion.[8]

At the heart of these postwar challenges to overbroad morals laws was an effort to redraw the line that separated a "law abiding law breaker" from a criminal. Which women were "overcriminalized"? Which were sufficiently criminalized—or perhaps even undercriminalized? Concepts of female deviance had certainly not disappeared. But what counted as deviant, and among whom, and what kind of deviance registered as a social problem, was undergoing a significant recalculation. Social scientific explanations, suffused with a mélange of spatial, biological, and pathological narratives, guided definitions of women's criminality. As women's sexuality was reappraised within the context of distinct racial spaces— the "home" for white women and the "slum" for Black women—white women's nonmarital sexuality was redefined as a private, individual sickness, requiring, in the popular social science and social hygiene literature of the period, psychoanalytic treatment rather than intervention by the criminal justice system. Black women's nonmarital sexuality, however, was reaffirmed—by way of a glancing sociological recognition of structural urban deprivation—as a public, community-wide criminal tendency requiring stiff morals enforcement. When social scientists, lawyers, and judges pushed for legal reforms to narrow the gap between sexual practices and sexual laws, they ultimately, if indirectly, deepened the divide between white sexual legality and Black sexual criminality.

The terms with which liberal critics built their case for an updated moral code highlighted the particular injustice of the laws against middle-class white behaviors. Many challengers of morals laws couched their critiques in expressions of sexual liberalism that—not unlike the traditional morality that these critics rejected—prized marriage as the source of "mature" and "normal" sexual pleasure. Indeed, a key tenet of this sexual liberalism held that mutually satisfying sex was a necessary cornerstone of fulfilling marriages; and, although growing numbers of midcentury liberal reformers were tentatively warming to the possibility of noncriminal sexual relations outside marriage, wedlock remained the unequivocal site of the most well-adjusted sex. Kinsey, along with his colleagues and readers who applauded a frank airing of pervasive sexual practices, believed that greater education and transparency in matters of sex would promote healthier relations between the sexes and, therefore, healthier marriages. The criminalization of sex, and the attendant moral stigma and shame, frustrated efforts to forge strong marital bonds through sexual openness.[9]

What most exercised these social scientists was overbroad sex laws' affront to otherwise respectable people, and these laws' injurious effect on marital stability. By framing their critique of sex laws as a threat to marital happiness, liberal social scientists and legal scholars revealed the limits of sexual liberalism to substantially remedy the racial, gender, and class inequities built into morals law enforcement. "As sexual liberalism took hold among the white middle class, it raised new issues for the maintenance of sexual order," historians John D'Emilio and Estelle Freedman argue. "In particular, how could the legitimation of heterosexual eroticism remain within 'responsible' limits?" The emphasis on marital sexual fulfillment did not necessarily imply the strengthening of gendered or raced stratifications within the moral order. However, in a midcentury culture fixated on the cleaving of suburbanizing white patriarchal nuclear families and urbanizing Black families in segregated cities allegedly fraught with "social disorganization," sexual liberalism became a vehicle for widening the racial discrepancy between normalized sexual practices and sexual criminalization. "[A]s black urban communities grew, the black family and black sexual mores appeared as a convenient counterpoint, identifying the line between what was permissible and what was not," D'Emilio and Freedman conclude.[10]

Social science in this period played an important role in establishing Black people and the neighborhoods to which they were confined as the "counterpoint" to white normality. So-called environmental criminology—an influential school of thought that held that people's socioeconomic conditions produced their behaviors—was applied almost reflexively to Black people during this period. Indeed, this iteration of social science perpetuated a long-twentieth-century sociological project that bound blackness with criminality. The authors of *Social Disorganization* claimed that "the deteriorated social areas in which the Negro is forced to live are conducive neither to high standards of conduct nor to law-abiding behavior." Spatial explanations for Black criminality drew on sociological and structural factors to explain Black people's supposed deviance. However, by focusing exclusively on Black behaviors and forms of crime most visible in Black neighborhoods and by ignoring or downplaying the prevalence of white criminality, this midcentury worldview accommodated blanket generalizations about the Black community. These explanations sustained group-wide appraisals of Black people as latently criminal and immoral because of the "pathology" of their segregated neighborhoods. The white myth of Black sexual deviance, in particular, provided a direct route from the systemic degradation of Black neighborhoods to the inherent sexual criminality of blackness. Contrary to widely publicized evidence that sexual norms were loosening across all social strata, a 1949 California Special Crime Commission Report insisted that "the more illicit sexual and immoral codes are often perpetuated and practiced" in the "slums" where Black people lived.[11]

Postwar social science did more than ratchet up the association between blackness, immorality, and criminality. It also attenuated the relationship between white womanhood and sexual criminality. Another influential school of thought circulating during this period—the psychiatric worldview—argued that white women who engaged in nonmarital sexuality were not criminals, but rather individuals who were "maladjusted" to their otherwise healthy domestic environment. White women who deviated from prevailing codes of sexual morality were not criminals in need of punishment; instead, they were "neurotics" suffering from a "pathology of sex" who required "treatment" so they could be reabsorbed back into their "normal" surroundings. White women, then, became increasingly seen as individual psychological subjects whose nonmarital sexual practices, while not necessarily morally acceptable, were also not appropriately considered criminal.[13]

While both Black and white female sexual offenders in this period were cast as prone to deviance—Black women through their environment and white women through their personal maladjustments—only Black women's sexuality remained latently criminal. White women's sexual "abnormality," social scientists, psychiatrists, and criminologists argued, should be understood as a psychological, rather than criminal, condition. As nonmarital straight sex became the practiced norm among women, a question remained for legal reformers to sort out: to what extent was nonmarital sex criminal behavior? Racialized interpretations of social science would help determine which women would be considered pathological offenders requiring psychiatric treatment and which women would remain sexual criminals requiring state intervention.

CRIMINALIZING BLACK NEIGHBORHOODS: THE RACIAL LIMITS OF MORALS LAW REFORM

Critics of morals laws were increasingly committed to relaxing the laws prohibiting nonmarital straight sex. But many reformist liberals remained ambivalent about relinquishing legal control over morals altogether. "The criminal law should be based upon the moral law," reporter Sara Harris and New York City judge John Murtagh affirmed in *Cast the First Stone*, their popular 1957 account of prostitution; but, they added, "It does not follow, however, that all moral offenses should be designated as crimes." Legal reformers sought to resolve the tension between easing criminal sanctions on sex while preserving police authority. As they set to work, they operated from the social scientific presumptions of white normality and Black deviance. In compromises that took place in courts, conference

rooms, and state legislatures across the nation, when legal reformers rewrote the penal code, they retained the race-neutral crime of "public immorality." Through this ambiguous language, these reformers helped create the conditions for white women to benefit unequally from the gradual
legal permissions of sexual liberalization.[13]

The midcentury tensions and outcomes in morals law reform were best
illustrated in the American Legal Institute's massive multiyear project to
produce a Model Penal Code (MPC). When the MPC was finally released
in 1962, it was merely a suggested framework that states eager to modernize their penal code could borrow. The MPC was the culmination of what
Louis Schwartz, an MPC co-reporter and University of Pennsylvania law
professor, called "a new pitch in intensity" over the debate around "legal
moralism," or the appropriate role of the state in the enforcement of morals. Many MPC reporters were "uneasy about [the attempt] to regulate
private sexual behavior." They agreed that the threat of legal punishment
was an ineffective deterrent to crimes against morality—including "alcoholism, narcotic addiction, prostitution, and deviant sexual activity"—
arguing instead that "therapy is necessary and may be effective" for this
category of crime. However, a vocal faction held fast to the "outright regulation of morality." So the reporters reached a compromise: while the MPC
proposed that "promiscuous noncommercial sexuality" be decriminalized,
it affirmed the repression of "open flouting of prevailing moral standards
as a sort of nuisance in public thoroughfares and parks."[14]

The space that MPC reporters, in their compromise, left available for
police discretion to determine violations of "public morality" was precisely
where Black women continued to be vulnerable to sexual criminalization.
MPC drafters knew well that, especially in the realm of morals enforcement, "prosecutions for sexual derelictions are arbitrarily selected," and
that morals offenses "facilitate . . . police discriminations more often than
general compliance with legal norms." Indeed, many legal and criminological critics of the existing moral penal code recognized that the discrepancy between the letter of the law and prevailing practice fell hardest on
Black women. Police officers played a central role in determining whether
a presumed sexual offender was arrestable, and race played a central role
in informing the officer's judgment.[15]

By upholding the power of law enforcement to police public morality,
MPC reporters effectively, if unintentionally, ratified officers' suspicion
of Black women in the women's own neighborhoods. As criminologist
Jerome Skolnick argued, legal moralism strengthened police officers' "to-
talitarian tendencies by 'criminalizing' the environment." And by criminalizing the urban space in which Black people were segregated, morals laws

"incline the police to a more rigid conception of order which heightens both the perception and presence" of crime in the area. Because Black women, according to white myth, were agents of hypersexuality, their very presence in the city was read as a "deviation" from white public morality. In this context, when states updated their laws in the spirit of the MPC, Black women would likely be excluded from the legal permissions of sexual liberalism.[16]

The midcentury flurry of legal analysis and reform proposals translated into material changes to morals laws. In the final weeks of 1961, the California State Supreme Court struck down Los Angeles's capacious municipal morals ordinances. Carol Lane—a white woman variously described by the press as a "Hollywood model," a dancer, and other suggestive labels—was at the center of the challenge case. She had been arrested by Los Angeles police in her home in a white neighborhood and charged with "resorting" to engaging in illicit sex. The "resorting" law under challenge empowered police to arrest any person found in any physical place, public or private, with the alleged purpose of "performing or participating in any lewd act with any such person." Municipal judge Kathleen Parker convicted Lane after hearing police testimony that an officer had "watched through a window as men on two different occasions visited Miss Lane in the bedroom of her apartment." Lane appealed her case up to the California Supreme Court, which decided in her favor.[17]

In the ruling, the justices reasoned, first, that police had not supplied any proof that Lane had accepted money "or other consideration" in her rendezvous. Next, the majority argued that, while laws against commercial sex were abundantly developed in the state penal code, "neither simple fornication or adultery alone nor living in a state of cohabitation and fornication" was a crime in the state. The Los Angeles ordinance, which effectively criminalized nonmarital straight sex, conflicted with the higher power of state law and was, on those grounds, struck down. This single ruling also felled a host of other Los Angeles morals ordinances that deployed similarly overbroad language. The court's argument that nonmarital straight sexual practices—which, significantly in this case, took place in a white domestic context—were not and could not be made a criminal offense in the state of California reflected the liberalizing conceptions of women's sexual privacy being developed during this period. That the early beneficiaries of this new privacy were white women reveals the racial limits of sexual privacy as a substantial right.[18]

Because *In re Lane* hinged on the conflict between municipal and state legal authority, the court did not specifically address police power in its decision. However, police discretion was a crucial mechanism in the enforcement of the interchangeable and broad suite of public order offenses, such as disorderly conduct and vagrancy, which provided an additional weapon for law enforcement to police the presumed sexual behavior of women. Historian Risa Goluboff argues that determining the limits of this police discretion was at the heart of efforts to reform vagrancy laws in the early 1960s. Legal reformers seeking to tame police excesses in vagrancy law enforcement were distinct from the social scientists and lawyers taking aim at sex laws; however, the work of the two groups overlapped in the enforcement of vagrancy laws against women. Targeted women may have been only one class in a larger universe of challengers emboldened through the midcentury to take aim at vagrancy laws, but each targeted group's argument contributed to an escalating debate over the appropriate scope of police power.[19]

When California legislators set out to reform the state's vagrancy law in 1961, they faced a tricky, and perhaps impossible, challenge: to strike a balance between, on the one hand, protecting the discretionary power of police to enforce public order, and, on the other hand, curbing the police tendency to use this discretion to target racially and economically marginalized people. How could a vagrancy law stop police officers from arresting people based on "looks, not acts" while still preserving police officers' power to arrest "suspicious" individuals? Along with trying to balance these cross-purposes, legislators knew as well that a previous legislative attempt to overhaul the state's vagrancy law had been vetoed by the governor. Not surprisingly, the eventual reform law delivered mixed results. A "loitering" provision authorized an arrest "if the surrounding circumstances . . . [indicate] to a reasonable man that the public safety demands" apprehension of a suspicious target. The emphasis on a spatial judgment to justify police discretion provided race-neutral language that made the continued criminalization of Black neighborhoods lawful. This reformed vagrancy law that Governor Pat Brown signed into law in 1961 showcased the liberal potential of the courts and legislatures in this period—and the racist, illiberal results that remained a definite possibility.[20]

These legal reforms, in political and practical intent, were designed to modulate police officers' discretionary power. But when these reforms were put into practice in the context of segregated cities, they indirectly sustained an intensification of racial inequity in the realm of morals enforcement. Los Angeles police arrest statistics for 1962, the year after the *In re Lane* ruling and the vagrancy statute revision, illustrate this shift: between 1961 and 1962, arrests of white women dropped by 12 percent, while those of Black women rose 18 percent. As police practices shifted to accommodate the new legal terrain created by morals law reforms, the racial and gender logics that underwrote morals enforcement were exposed—fueling anger within Black neighborhoods.[21]

BLACK PROTEST AND THE RACIAL POLITICS
OF MORALS ENFORCEMENT

As Black people came to constitute a larger percentage of the American urban population, a new generation of Black residents experienced an enduring twentieth-century dynamic: the simultaneous underpolicing and overpolicing of their neighborhoods. This dynamic, as in earlier decades, was especially visible in the discretionary enforcement of morals laws. The "Negro districts" to which Black people were confined by vigilant police— the frontline enforcers of de facto segregation—served as the city's vice playgrounds for slumming white men, or "white hunters." But even as police permitted vice activities in Black neighborhoods at their discretion, they also disproportionately targeted Black people for morals arrests (gambling for men and sex offenses for women in these years). "Much of the commercialized vice is foisted upon the colored community by virtue of the larger community's willingness to permit such activities to flourish there," one police manual noted in 1947. Throughout the twentieth century, the white myth of Black hypersexuality enabled a vicious tautology: police restricted vice to Black neighborhoods because of prevailing white beliefs about the immorality of blackness; and because vice was pushed into Black neighborhoods, these were the primary sites of morals arrests directed at Black residents.[22]

For Black residents, the racial discrimination in morals enforcement was an especially combustible issue because it was made possible by, and reflected, a meshwork of urban oppression: residential segregation; white myths of Black sexual deviance and criminality; and the unequal delivery of state goods, including police protection, which was experienced instead as police predation. Unequal police practices were not new to Black neighborhoods, but as California morals laws on their face relaxed during this period of legal liberalism, the racial inequity of morals law enforcement was exacerbated.

The decriminalization of white women presumed to be engaging in nonmarital heterosexual sex was a visible legal trend in the years surrounding the *In re Lane* ruling. White women in Los Angeles were granted an unprecedented measure of sexual freedom from the law. One Hollywood sheriff explained to a *Los Angeles Times* reporter that "today's liberal judicial interpretations" shielded sexually suspect white women from legal punishment. To Black residents, the conspicuous removal of white women from police officers' list of sexually profiled women threw into sharp relief the racial disparities in morals enforcement. "An investigation of any neighborhood, regardless of its racial complexion, will disclose prostitution in some form," a Black community leader and short-lived member of the Los Angeles Police Commission protested. "To point out the [Black] district as a vice area because colored people live there, without naming other sections where similar conditions exist, seems biased to me and designed to discredit Negroes."[23]

Another result of the racial disparities in morals enforcement was especially infuriating to Black residents: white men enjoyed license to come to Black neighborhoods to solicit Black women. "Invading hordes of Caucasian motorists" trolled Black city streets nightly, one columnist wrote in the *Los Angeles Sentinel*, a Black newspaper. Black residents zeroed in on the hypocrisy of white men, "well clad, driving expensive automobiles" in Black neighborhoods "cruising for dates" during a period of stark urban racial segregation—a time when, as one LAPD officer recalled, Black people "could not venture" into the white districts of the city "without a strongly documented purpose." The spatial affront of Black residential exclusion, segregated vice, and cruising white hunters was a problem for Black people living in cities across the country. In an article on a Black neighborhood dubbed "the land of the white hunter" by the newspaper, a resident was quoted linking restrictive housing with vice segregation: "What we do resent . . . is the white man who drives here under the cover of darkness to solicit women, who if they moved next door to him would see him sell his house the next day."[24]

Black residents also protested that white men—white hunters and police officers alike—compounded the insult of white people's freedom of movement by entering Black neighborhoods and accosting Black women simply "because they happen to be walking in their own neighborhood," a writer for the *Sentinel* fumed. Police officers, like the white cruisers they ignored, shared the white men's presumption that any Black woman they saw in a Black neighborhood was a likely prospect, and they felt justified to automatically presume a woman's sexual guilt. During the early 1960s, many women brought their experiences of being arrested on morals charges simply because they were on city streets to local chapters of the National Association for the Advancement of Colored People (NAACP) and the American Civil Liberties Union (ACLU). One such woman was Roxie Williams, who was arrested after she sought police protection from white men who solicited her and loitered outside her home. The police, Williams testified, were going to have to "change their attitude," because "the younger generation is not going to tolerate what we took." The vulnerability of Black women to unchecked police action highlighted for a new generation the exposure of all Black residents to arbitrary arrest and violence.[25]

In previous decades, Black people used their respectability as the basis of their protests against police practices and pursued their goals through good-faith requests to police leaders for dignity and equity in morals enforcement. This strain of activism did not disappear at midcentury. When Black critics of the police dared to publicly take on the delicate matter of prostitution in a political culture where the myth of Black hypersexuality prevailed, many were compelled in their negotiations with white authorities to pledge their commitment to middle-class sexual morality—and, through this respectability, to justify safe and dignified policing in their neighborhood. However, as the racial disparity in sexual policing was thrown into even sharper relief in the early 1960s, the enduring register of respectability protest collided with an emboldened brand of resistance. Protestors directly challenged both the sexual license of white hunters and the political authority of discriminatory police. They began delivering public indictments of, and even physical resistance to, morals enforcement.

One confrontation between sheriff's officers and Black people indicated that some Black residents were increasingly willing to physically deny the legitimacy and value of morals policing. In September 1963, plainclothes sergeant John Barwicki lingered on the corner of Central Avenue and Sixty-Seventh Street, where he baited two women—Gloria, an unemployed waitress, and another unknown woman ("Suspect #3")—to offer him sex for money. "After grasping both suspects by the arms," Barwicki walked them toward his unmarked car. At this point, "approximately 20 unidentified male Negroes . . . began crowding around blocking the sidewalk," according to the sheriff's report. Barwicki tried to push through the gathering audience when James, an unemployed Black cook, called out, "That blue-eyed white man is mistreating those women. Make him turn those women loose." As James and other men in the group pushed and distracted Barwicki, both women "wrenched free" and ran down the street. James held Barwicki back as the officer tried to go after the women. When Barwicki managed to pull out his gun, James gave chase. Backup swiftly arrived, and Barwicki was joined by deputy Kenneth Jones. Together the officers cornered James inside a nearby hotel: "necessary force was used to restrain him." While the officers were beating James, another nearby deputy caught up to Gloria, cuffed her, and charged her with disorderly conduct. "Suspect #3," however, got away. The sheriff's department later recorded—in highly mediated language—that James, dazed and battered after the ordeal, said: "I knew you were a sheriff and I knew that the girls were prostitutes, but I didn't want to see you arrest them. I thought those other guys would help me, but it didn't work out that way." By late 1963, courageous residents started pushing back when police arrested women off the street—an indication of the frustration that was coming to a boil.[26]

As episodes of Black communal violence began spreading across the nation's urban map, observers worried that the police-sanctioned racial inequity in morals policing was kindling for a furious conflagration in Black neighborhoods. The *Los Angeles Times*, the voice of white, business-aligned residents, warily turned its gaze to the "highly volatile situation" in Black neighborhoods: "Because of the inter-racial nature of this vice problem, an explosive situation could be developing," a journalist reported. In 1964 Mrs. John Richardson—a white property owner who inherited a duplex her parents had purchased in South Los Angeles in 1934, "while the area was a white neighborhood"—wrote a concerned letter to Kenneth Hahn, her county supervisor. Watching the rapidly deteriorating "reputation" of the neighborhood, Richardson sounded a note of alarm, not only because of her increasing property taxes but also due to the looming threat she saw of a "bad race riot" if vice conditions persisted apace.[27]

In 1964 Kenneth Hahn was up for reelection. Particularly in election years, authorities dreaded public uproar over vice. During these years, the anxiety over losing the confidence of white property owners such as Richardson was compounded by rising fears of a "bad race riot." Hahn convened law enforcement representatives from the offices of the district attorney and the county sheriff to discuss the Black neighborhood in which Richardson owned property along Central Avenue. At this meeting, the undersheriff informed the authorities that "we have intelligence reports" indicating that "school people, mothers, and other citizens in the area" were planning "public demonstrations" to protest the presence of vice and the way it was policed (or not) in their neighborhood. The undersheriff "pointed out the undesirability to all concerned of such demonstrations." When Hahn flexed his considerable muscle from the County Board of Supervisors to try to preempt these protests, he drew from a widely circulated and well-worn playbook among local authorities: he called for more vice raids and more arrests in Black neighborhoods. By exploiting the political currency of police vice raids targeting Black residents, Hahn was at once reinscribing the presumed criminality of Black people while purporting to improve conditions in Black neighborhoods. He hoped the raids would appeal to political constituencies that might otherwise be opposed: residents, both white and Black, who were glad to see authorities at last taking action after decades of police neglect; and white voters in general, who agreed that the criminalization of blackness was a necessary feature of well-ordered urban governance and applauded stronger policing of Black people.[28]

In April 1964, as described in the introduction, Hahn kicked off his "all-out war against narcotics and open prostitution" with mass round-ups of Black residents. But the heightened tension between Black people and police inflamed residents' reactions to this round of crackdowns. The weekend that Hahn launched his vice raid coincided with a series of violent confrontations between police and Black people. At least three clashes erupted in instances where vice was otherwise absent. Yet "all three incidents," the *Los Angeles Times* observed, "occurred in the same area where shortly after midnight deputy sheriffs conducted vice raids that resulted in 110 arrests." In each confrontation, as police moved in to handcuff men, "a crowd closed in," as the *Los Angeles Sentinel* reported, and people disrupted an arrest by throwing rocks and bricks, or obstructed the arrest by chasing the officers, tripping them, or trying to "wrestle the handcuffed prisoner from the officers." When the school-community coordinator of a local high school delivered his response to the weekend battles at a "somber" City Hall press conference the following Monday, the racial inequity of morals enforcement was the first grievance he listed. The *Los Angeles Sentinel* reported that he spoke the "consensus of the community": "The climate of today is an explosive one. The [community] knows that vice, prostitution and gambling are participated in by other communities which are overlooked by the police. [So] they respond explosively when the vice squad raids Central Los Angeles."[29]

For decades, Black residents' serious grievances of police disrespect, harassment, abuse, and murder were regularly dismissed, denied, ignored, or belittled; or the residents were treated to even more doses of the hostile, racist policing that outraged people in the first place. The August 1965 violence that broke out in the Watts neighborhood did not involve morals enforcement. Rather, it was ignited by another source of police harassment and Black frustration: routine stops for alleged traffic infractions (in this case, by the California Highway Patrol). However, the many confrontations between police and Black people that punctuated the months leading up to the Watts Riot demonstrate that the discriminatory sexual policing of Black women was a major and underappreciated factor in the violence. Discriminatory morals law enforcement was a substantial motor of police power and Black anger.[30]

CONCLUSION

In the aftermath of the Watts Riot, Los Angeles politicians and law enforcement authorities reaffirmed their investment in the aggressive morals policing that had in part triggered Black communal violence in the first place. Significantly, these officials pointed to *In re Lane* and liberalizing morals laws as a key source of racial disorder. In the fall of 1965, just weeks after Watts, Los Angeles County supervisor Warren Dorn floated a proposal to place a "decency amendment" on the statewide ballot that would "restore local determination over laws on crimes which were taken away in 1961 by the California Supreme Court." Los Angeles district attorney Evelle Younger endorsed the Dorn amendment. Fusing law enforcement authorities' hostility to relaxed morals laws with white fears of racialized crime, Younger made his case for mass morals policing in Black neighborhoods: the "recent riots have . . . supplied [the] proof," he argued, that Los Angeles needed "a return to the law as it was prior to the Carol Lane decision." By linking the Watts Riot with a need for tougher morals laws, the district attorney's call for stricter morals enforcement was clearly not intended as an effort to recriminalize white women's nonmarital sexual practices. It was, rather, an effort to double down on the criminalization of residents in Black neighborhoods, and in this particular valence, the sexual criminalization of Black women. In this way, the freshly recalibrated racial logics of sexual policing consolidated around the notion that mass morals misdemeanor arrests in Black neighborhoods were an important way to contain Black violence specifically, and Black people generally.[31]

Dorn eventually withdrew support for his own "decency amendment," but his proposal to nullify *In re Lane*—and the enthusiastic endorsement it received from Los Angeles law enforcement authorities—demonstrated the powerful traction of white myths of Black sexual criminality, and signaled that morals policing would continue to be central to white law-and-order politics targeting Black neighborhoods. Indeed, when Ronald Reagan gave his first gubernatorial message to the state legislature in 1967, he outlined a six-point agenda for his "crime war." Returning "lawmaking authority over vice to cities and counties" was the first item on his list. The law enforcement politics of post-Watts Los Angeles would become foundational to the nationwide development of a highly discretionary and discriminatory police program prioritizing low-level morals misdemeanors as a technique to justify, legalize, and impose expanding police power.[32]

Sexual policing has historically meant more than simply enforcing sexual norms. Rather, political authorities wielded sexual policing as a tool of urban governance. Morals laws were deployed to enforce a patriarchal, white supremacist urban order—but this order was not merely enforced for its own sake. As this episode demonstrates, the enforcement of moral order was bound up with power struggles for political authority. More importantly, the dominant vision of urban order was revised across the twentieth century as white women were, to a certain degree, released from the punishing intervention of the state. In the face of liberal reforms, police power was a nimble shapeshifter, recalculating its targets and methods while tightening its grip on Black neighborhoods and lives.

The liberal revision of morals enforcement had a material impact on women's long-contested right to the city: white women's spatial mobility—and, to a lesser extent, sexual freedom—expanded as Black women were subject to intensifying state surveillance, harassment, arrest. By considering the changing meanings of white and Black womanhood amid the transformations in racial, gender, and sexual politics in the postwar period, it becomes clear that women's freedom is not increased linearly or distributed equally: one woman's relative sexual freedom can exist alongside another woman's sexual criminalization.

NOTES

1. For more extensive citations, see Anne Gray Fischer, "'Land of the White Hunter': Legal Liberalism and the Racial Politics of Morals Enforcement in Mid-century Los Angeles," *Journal of American History* 105, no. 4 (March 2019): 868–84. Betty was arrested along with two other white women; the charges against all three were dismissed. There is some evidence that the police officers used force on Betty. W. H. Parker, "Intra-Department Correspondence," December 4, 1961, folder 1, box C–248, December 6, 1961, Board of Police Commission (BOPC) Agenda Packets (Los Angeles City Archives).

2. Through legal changes and the recalibration of the exercise of police discretion during the period under review, white women's straight nonmarital sexual practices were subject to a confluence of court-level—and street-level—legal reforms that amounted to something that resembled, but certainly did not guarantee, decriminalization. Parker, "Intra-Department Correspondence."

3. Press release, April 13, 1964, Sheriff, Vice, 1963–1964 folder 3, box 143.2.18.1–3, Kenneth Hahn Collection (Huntington Library, San Marino, CA); "Deputies Arrest 110 in Central Ave. Vice Raids," *Los Angeles Times*, April 12, 1964, p. C2.

4. In statistical reports, the LAPD breaks down arrests by sex and the following racial categories: Caucasian, Negro, Indian, Latin, Chinese, Japanese, and Other. White and Black arrests constitute the majority of prostitution-related arrests during this period. LAPD annual reports stop listing arrests by sex and race after 1949. However, statistical digests exist for the years 1954–1963. For consistency, I work exclusively with statistical digests. It is important to note that after 1954, Black women were a numerical majority of women arrested, clear evidence of their disproportionate arrests after World War II. This disproportion becomes more acute across the following decade. The early 1960s, then, mark a culmination of a racial shift in LAPD practices that was developing throughout the postwar period in the city. Los Angeles Police Department Statistical Digests, 1954–1963 (Los Angeles City Archives).

5. Kelly Lytle Hernández writes that between 1920 and 1960, Black residents

were central to California's carceral regime. See Hernández, *City of Inmates: Conquest, Rebellion, and the Rise of Human Caging in Los Angeles, 1771–1965* (Chapel Hill: University of North Carolina Press, 2017), 185–94. On race and the postwar migrations of people and capital, see Robert O. Self, *American Babylon: Race and the Struggle for Postwar Oakland* (Princeton, NJ: Princeton University Press, 2005); Max Felker-Kantor, "Fighting the Segregation Amendment: Black and Mexican American Responses to Proposition 14 in Los Angeles," in *Black and Brown in Los Angeles: Beyond Conflict and Coalition*, ed. Josh Kun and Laura Pulido (Berkeley: University of California Press, 2013), 145–46; and William H. Parker, quoted in *Parker on Police*, ed. O. W. Wilson (Springfield, IL: Charles C. Thomas, 1957), 8.

6. On midcentury presumptions of Black criminality, see Elizabeth Hinton, *From the War on Poverty to the War on Crime: The Making of Mass Incarceration in America* (Cambridge, MA: Harvard University Press, 2016), esp. 27–95. On the establishment of the linkage between blackness and criminality in an earlier period, see Khalil Gibran Muhammad, *The Condemnation of Blackness: Race, Crime, and the Making of Modern Urban America* (Cambridge, MA: Harvard University Press, 2010).

7. Alfred C. Kinsey et al., *Sexual Behavior in the Human Female* (Philadelphia: W. B. Saunders Company, 1953); Amanda Littauer, *Bad Girls: Young Women, Sex, and Rebellion Before the Sixties* (Chapel Hill: University of North Carolina Press, 2015), 85–86; and Miriam G. Reumann, *American Sexual Character: Sex, Gender, and National Identity in the Kinsey Reports* (Berkeley: University of California Press, 2005), 1.

8. Mabel Elliott and Francis Merrill, *Social Disorganization* (New York: Harper, 1950), 107; Pilpel, quoted in Littauer, *Bad Girls*, 141; and Christopher Gerould, *Sexual Practices of American Women* (New York: Lion Books, 1953), 133.

9. On midcentury marriage and sexual liberalism, see Elaine Tyler May, *Homeward Bound: American Families in the Cold War Era* (New York: Basic Books, 1988).

10. John D'Emilio and Estelle B. Freedman, *Intimate Matters: A History of Sexuality in America* (Chicago: University of Chicago Press, 1998), 298.

11. Elliott and Merrill, *Social Disorganization*, 647; and *Final Report of the Special Crime Study Commission on Social and Economic Causes of Crime and Delinquency* (Sacramento: State of California, 1949), 12.

12. I draw on William Moore's formulation of midcentury criminology for my argument. See William Howard Moore, *The Kefauver Committee and the Politics of Crime, 1950–1952* (Columbia: University of Missouri Press, 1974), vii–viii; and Edward Glover, "The Abnormality of Prostitution," in *Women: The Variety and Meaning of Their Sexual Experience*, ed. A. M. Krich (New York: Dell, 1953), 247–73.

13. John M. Murtagh and Sara Harris, *Cast the First Stone* (New York: McGraw-Hill, 1957), 299.

14. Louis B. Schwartz, "Morals Offenses and the Model Penal Code," *Columbia Law Review* 63 (April 1963): 670n1; Herbert Wechsler, "The Challenge of a Model Penal Code," *Harvard Law Review* 65 (May 1952): 1112; and Schwartz, "Morals Offenses and the Model Penal Code," 673, 682, 683.

15. Schwartz, "Morals Offenses and the Model Penal Code," 671; and Elliott and Merrill, *Social Disorganization*, 135–37.

16. For a discussion of hypersexuality and Black womanhood, see Patricia Hill Collins, *Black Feminist Thought: Knowledge, Consciousness, and the Politics of Empowerment* (New York: McGraw-Hill, 1991), chapter 6; and Jerome H. Skolnick, *Justice without Trial: Law Enforcement in Democratic Society* (New York: Wiley, 1966), 206–7.

17. "Court Hears Carol Lane 'Sex Case,'" *Hollywood Citizen News*, April 16, 1962; "'Resorting' Ordinance in L.A. Ruled Invalid," *Los Angeles Times*, December 27, 1961; "58 District Attorneys to Meet on Vice Laws," *Los Angeles Times*, January 12, 1962, p. 26; and "Yorty, City Attorney Tangle on Vice Laws," *Los Angeles Times*, December 29, 1961, p. 1.

18. *In re Carol Lane*, 367 P.2d 673 (CA, 1961).

19. Risa Goluboff, *Vagrant Nation: Police Power, Constitutional Change, and the Making of the 1960s* (New York: Oxford University Press, 2016), 147–85.

20. Goluboff, *Vagrant Nation*, 71, 204.

21. Los Angeles Police Department Statistical Digest, 1962 (Los Angeles City Archives).

22. On the twentieth-century relationship between vice, race, segregation, and police, see especially Chad Heap, *Slumming: Sexual and Racial Encounters in American Nightlife, 1885–1940* (Chicago: University of Chicago Press, 2009); and Kevin J. Mumford, *Interzones: Black/White Sex Districts in Chicago and New York in the Early Twentieth Century* (New York: Columbia University Press, 1997). Joseph D. Lohman, *The Police and Minority Groups: A Manual Prepared for Use in the Chicago Park District Police Training School* (Chicago: Chicago Park District Police Training School, 1947), 101.

23. "Crime's Golden Egg: Sin and Glamour Pave Sunset Strip," *Los Angeles Times*, January 31, 1965, p. F1; and "Negro Leaders Hit Vice Probe with Bias," *Los Angeles Mirror News*, September 9, 1957, clipping, Prostitution, ONE Subject Files Collection (ONE National Gay and Lesbian Archives at the USC Libraries, University of Southern California, Los Angeles).

24. A. S. "Doc" Young, "Prostitution: It's a Recurring Problem," *Los Angeles Sentinel*, March 31, 1960, p. 8A; "Perspective on the LAPD: A Simple Time, in Black and White," *Los Angeles Times*, October 12, 1995, p. B9; Walter Ames, "Western-Adams Vice Stirs Fears," *Los Angeles Times*, January 30, 1961, p. 1; William Buchanan, "South End: A Slice of Life," *Boston Globe*, July 18, 1965, p. A7; and "Westside Vice War Renewed," *Los Angeles Sentinel*, January 4, 1962, p. A1.

25. "Policemanship," *Los Angeles Sentinel*, November 17, 1960, p. A6; and "Police Malpractice and the Watts Riot: A Report by the ACLU of Southern California," Appendix C, 1966, box 162, ACLU of Southern California (ACLUSC) Records (Charles E. Young Research Library, University of California, Los Angeles).

26. For encouraging others to resist the police, James was charged with lynching. "Sheriff's Department Complaint Report," September 29, 1963, Hahn, Sheriff, Vice, 1963–1964 folder 2, Hahn Collection.

27. Paul Coates, "Vice Casts Its Shadow on West Adams District: White Men on Prowl for Negro Streetwalkers," *Los Angeles Times*, April 11, 1965; and Letter from Mrs. John F. Richardson to Hahn, April 25, 1964, Sheriff, Vice, 1963–1964 folder, box 1.43.2.18.3, Hahn Collection.

28. C. E. Roos, Chief Patrol Division, to Peter J. Pitchess, Sheriff, "Meeting to Discuss Enforcement Problems at 68th and Central," April 9, 1964, Hahn, Sheriff, Vice, 1963–1964 folder 3, box 143.2.18.1–3, Hahn Collection.

29. "Crowds Attack Police Here for Third Time," *Los Angeles Times*, April 12, 1964, p. 1; and L. M. Meriwether, "Citizens, Police in Head-On Clash: Incidents Alarm Public," *Los Angeles Sentinel*, April 16, 1964, p. A1.

30. In this essay, I use the word "riot" in the spirit that Kwame Holmes theorizes in "Beyond the Flames: Queering the History of the 1968 D.C. Riot," in *No Tea, No Shade: New Writings in Black Queer Studies*, ed. E. Patrick Johnson (Durham, NC: Duke University Press, 2016), 306–7.

31. "Drive Opens to Place Decency Law on Ballot," *Los Angeles Times*, October 19, 1965; "Wise Action on 'Decency' Proposal," *Los Angeles Times*, January 5, 1966; Tom Goff, "Dorn Ready to Give Up on 'Decency,'" *Los Angeles Times*, January 4, 1966, p. 3; and Evelle Younger to Warren Dorn, "In re: Proposed Addition of Section 11.5 to Article 11 of the California Constitution," August 25, 1965, "Decency" Initiative folder, box 135, ACLU of Southern California Records.

32. Goff, "Dorn Ready to Give Up on 'Decency,'" 3; "Wise Action on 'Decency' Proposal"; and Ray Zeman, "Reagan Outlines 6-Step Crime War: Asks Local Ordinances to Control Sex and Public Decency Offenses," *Los Angeles Times*, January 18, 1967, p. 3.

9

Sex Panic, Psychiatry, and the Expansion of the Carceral State

REGINA KUNZEL

In 1949, George Raymond was brutally beaten by two men he and a friend picked up for sex. After the assault, he ran toward the road, hailed a car, and asked to be taken to the police. "I don't recall why I did this," he stated, "for later I had every reason not to call the police."[1] Rather than chasing down Raymond's assailants, the police took Raymond to jail. He was later examined by two psychiatrists, who, when they learned of his sexual history with men and adolescent boys, determined him to be a sexual psychopath. So diagnosed, and without a criminal charge, much less a conviction, he was committed indefinitely to Saint Elizabeths Hospital, the federal institution for the mentally ill in Washington, DC.

Raymond was carcerally institutionalized under what became known as the Miller Law, passed in 1948 in the District of Columbia and named for its sponsor, Nebraska representative Arthur Miller. The new law increased the punishment for sexual offenses with minors as well as for sodomy, defined in the law as penetration "however slight" of the mouth or anus of one person with the sexual organs of another. To that anatomically precise definition, and in strategically vague language, the Miller Law added to its list of criminalized sexual offenses "any other unnatural or perverted sexual act with any other person or animal."[2]

The aspect of the Miller Law that most radically enlarged its purview was its inclusion of behavior characterized sweepingly as "inviting for the purpose of immorality."[3] Under the Miller Law, a person identified as a "recidivist" in any of these categories of sexual offense was examined by two psychiatrists to determine whether they were a sexual psychopath—in the law's definition, "a person, not insane, who by a course of repeated misconduct in sexual matters has evidenced such lack of power to control his sexual impulses as to be dangerous to other persons."[4] If so identified, they would be committed indefinitely to Saint Elizabeths Hospital.

While proponents of the Miller Law most often cited the dangers posed by sexual psychopaths to children, the law was used primarily to criminalize consensual sex between adult men (as were sexual psychopath laws passed in twenty-nine states by the late 1950s).[5] Although not a pioneering law (by the time it was introduced in 1948, seven states already had similar laws on the books), the Miller Law was distinguished by the fact that it was initiated and passed at the federal level by the US Congress.[6] And so while it governed the relatively small geographical territory of the District of Columbia, the law bore the imprimatur of the federal state. Passed in the period known to historians for witnessing the height of hostility toward sexual and gender nonconformity, the Miller Law was part of a national wave of sexual psychopath laws that vastly expanded the criminalization of nonnormative sex, especially sex between men, and part of a larger state project of regulating and policing homosexuality.

The midcentury sexual psychopath scare has been analyzed by historians George Chauncey, Estelle Freedman, and others who have tracked the way in which panics were sparked by sensationalizing media reporting on sex crimes, usually involving the brutal murder of a child. Bills criminalizing a range of sexual offenses were promoted by grassroots citizens groups and then sponsored by state legislators and enacted into law. Historians have exposed those scares' exaggerated imaginings of risk and the ways in which panic about sexual psychopaths functioned as proxies for other postwar social anxieties: about the hypermasculinization and potential violence of returning World War II veterans, the wartime disruption of sexual and gender norms, Cold War threats to national security, shifting boundaries of sexual normality, and the heightened visibility of postwar gay and lesbian urban subcultures.[7]

This essay joins those examinations of how nonnormative sex became the focus of state regulation in the postwar United States, with an interest in understanding how an alliance between psychiatry and the state worked to criminalize sexual difference. It is not incidental that George Raymond and others committed under sexual psychopath laws were incarcerated in mental hospitals rather than prisons. The regulation, surveillance, and criminalization of intimate life was facilitated (and also masked) by the discourse of medicine and the language of illness, treatment, and cure. Looking closely at the extensive congressional debate over the Miller Law reveals psychiatric authority to be at the center of its justifying logics.

The Miller Law was passed at a moment when psychiatric power was ascending. Psychiatry's enhanced cultural authority and prestige in the wartime and postwar United States derived, in large part, from psychiatrists' successful claim to expertise beyond chronic mental illness, to what psychiatrist Harry Stack Sullivan called "problems in living."[8] Key among those problems were those presented by gender and sexual difference. Psychiatrists staked their claim to expertise on homosexuality in particular over the course of the 1940s, '50s, and '60s, decades that have been characterized as psychiatry's "golden age."[9] Claiming expertise over issues of sexual and gender difference was not incidental to psychiatry's burgeoning authority, nor was it a sideshow to psychiatry's larger professional agenda or to the flourishing of a broader postwar American therapeutic culture. Psychiatric jurisdiction over the problems believed to be constituted by and ensuing from sexual and gender nonconformity was a crucial driver of the field's enhanced power at midcentury and central to the expansion of psychiatric authority.

Psychiatrists derived new authority as well from the strategic alliances they made with law and the government, and many of those alliances were made through psychiatry's claim to expertise over issues of sexuality. Psychiatrists received an enormous boost in authority when they persuaded the federal government to incorporate psychiatric assessment in the screening of military inductees as part of the Selective Service Act of 1940. Washington, DC, psychiatrist Harry Stack Sullivan and Saint Elizabeths supervisor Winfred Overholser formulated guidelines for the psychological screening of military inductees in an attempt to weed out those who might be most vulnerable to the psychic stresses of military service and combat. Though Sullivan dissented from the midcentury psychiatric consensus that homosexuality was a mental disorder (he was himself in a long-term secret relationship with a man), homosexuality was listed in the regulations as a disqualifying factor for military service. Psychiatrists also oversaw a shift in policy, whereby active-duty members of the armed services could be discharged for homosexuality. From 1941 to 1945, nearly 10,000 sailors and soldiers, most though not all men, were discharged for homosexuality.[10]

Psychiatrists also made themselves useful to the state by offering their endorsement, however ambivalent, of sexual psychopath legislation. They provided the justificatory medical language in which the laws were cast, they agreed to serve as expert assessors of sexual psychopathy, they oversaw the carceral institutionalization and treatment of people committed under the new laws, and they certified the success of recovery and "cure" for safe release as required by law. Psychiatric discourse, even when disavowed or qualified by psychiatrists, helped usher in sexual psychopath legislation; it also mystified the laws' criminalization of sexual difference in ways that would make them difficult to challenge, both at the time and by gay and lesbian activists who struggled to dissociate homosexuality from attributions of mental illness decades later.

THE MILLER LAW, MEDICALIZATION, AND CRIMINALIZATION

When the Miller Law was proposed in Washington, DC, in 1948, the context of sexual panic that made laws like it seem so necessary and made the rationales for the expansion of criminal categories and policing of deviant sexuality so persuasive was already part of the national commonsense, set in legal precedent and declared constitutional in higher courts. The Minnesota sexual psychopath statute upon which the Miller Law was modeled had survived constitutional challenge in the state's highest court in 1939, and the US Supreme Court upheld its constitutionality in 1940. When the Miller Law was proposed in 1948, seven states already had sexual psychopath laws on the books.

While the solidifying consensus around the virtue and legitimacy of sexual psychopath laws made it highly likely that the bill would move quickly through Congress, some lawmakers expressed concerns about the law's dramatic expansion of state power. In the congressional subcommittee hearings on the bill, Iowa congressman Joseph O'Hara poked fun at the awesome reach of the proposed law and its structuring paranoia, remarking that its broad and vague definition of sexual psychopaths as persons who lacked the power to control their sexual impulses reminded him "of a little quip. 'All the world is queer but thee and me, and even thou art a little queer.'"[11] Saint Elizabeths psychiatrist Benjamin Karpman, invited to testify before Congress as an expert in the psychiatric treatment of criminals, raised a hypothetical question about the husband and wife who, "to prevent having more children . . . indulge in what [the Miller Law termed] sodomy." What if the wife were to sue for divorce and charge her husband with violation of the law? he asked. "Are you going to send him to St. Elizabeths?" Anticipating claims about privacy that would come to be so important in arguments for the decriminalization of homosexuality more than half a century later, Karpman asked about the man "who is a pervert in the strictest sense of the word, but makes it a business of his own?"[12]

These voices of skepticism were quickly stifled. Representative George MacKinnon, sponsor of the Minnesota sexual psychopath law passed nearly a decade earlier, shot down Karpman's suggestion that there was such a thing as a harmless pervert. Although the imperiled child was the privileged subject of community outrage and media reporting on sex crimes and often characterized by historians as the instigating subject of these laws, MacKinnon responded to Karpman's criticisms not by referencing the child sex-murderer, but rather, and revealingly, the person who "is a constant menace to society, particularly to younger boys and young men." That person was particularly dangerous, MacKinnon insisted, in contexts of hierarchical relations among men such as the military and the labor force: "They go around and they may not force them, but the fact that they may have a superior rank, they may be a chief petty officer where the boy is in a subordinate capacity; and the same thing exists out in the ordinary, everyday life where somebody may be an employer. . . . And while it is true there is no act of force, such a person is a substantial menace to society."[13] While historians have sometimes characterized gay men as the collateral victims of midcentury sexual psychopath laws that targeted violent sexual crimes against children, the congressional debate on the Miller Law reveals them to have been a key and deliberate target. The virtue of the Miller Law, in the eyes of its proponents, was in criminalizing such acts of "social menace" that were not captured by existing criminal law but were newly understood as indicative of dangerous sexual psychopathy.

In early drafts of the bill, sexual deviance was cast in criminal terms, emphasizing the law's punitive aims. In calling to order the hearing of the congressional subcommittee on February 20, 1948, Representative Miller described the bill as one "to provide for the *commitment, detention, and treatment of criminal sexual psychopaths.*"[14] But as the bill was discussed and revised, references to criminality, detention, and punishment were whittled away. In the law's final form just three months later, passed on May 20, 1948, it was described as providing for "the treatment of sexual psychopaths in the District of Columbia, and for other purposes."[15]

Advocates of the Miller Law succeeded in both expanding the criminalization of nonnormative sex and effectively mystifying and hiding that expansion by describing sexual deviance in the language of medicine. The question of the law's intent with respect to issues of punishment and treatment came up repeatedly in subcommittee hearings. When Kentucky representative Frank Chelf asked for clarification about the "penalty" or "final punishment" for a person charged under the Miller Law in order to be certain that the proposed law would not weaken punishment for sexual crimes, Congressman MacKinnon explained that it "does not provide for any criminal penalty. It provides that such persons shall be considered as sick persons, and they are to be handled in that way rather than as criminals."[16] Saint Elizabeths superintendent Overholser, called upon to testify in the hearings, offered his professional authority to support this position, stating that "As a physician I would rather see them dealt with outside the criminal law."[17]

In line with the Miller Law's medicalized conception of sexual psychopathy, the person charged under its statutes was not referred to as "the defendant" or "the accused," but rather a "patient." "This is in accordance with the theory that the title essentially provides treatment rather than punishment," its authors explained.[18] The virtue of the law, in Overholser's understanding, was in recognizing "a very large group of offenders as essentially sick people rather than vicious ones."[19]

The Miller Law's definition of the sexual psychopath as a "patient" rather than a "defendant" and its medical language of treatment instead of incarceration and punishment had several important effects. Since it mandated the hospitalization and ideally the rehabilitation of the sexual psychopath rather than punitive incarceration, it allowed supporters to characterize the law as progressive and humane. The description of the bill that went before Congress touted it as being "in conformity with the most up-to-date thinking in the fields of psychiatry and criminal law."[20] MacKinnon described the Miller Law as "dealing in what you might call a more modern way with these psychopathic personalities."[21] Overholser praised the proposed legislation "as progressive, as practical, as indicating a closer union of the law with medicine, and as indicating that the law is ready to take advantage of the scientific knowledge concerning behavior."[22] Medical language aligned sexual psychopath laws rhetorically with modernity and progress.

The medicalization of the sexual psychopath had important juridical effects as well. In taking the determination of sexual psychopathy out of the courtroom and into the psychiatric clinic, the Miller Law effectively evaded the requirement of due process. While people formally defined as "defendants" were guaranteed a trial by jury, privilege against self-incrimination, and protection against double jeopardy, people defined as "patients" did not. "Since the proceedings here in question are not of a criminal character," MacKinnon stated, "the constitutional right to a jury trial does not apply to proceedings of this type."[23] This was the case even for what members of Congress and Overholser acknowledged would potentially result in lifelong carceral institutionalization.

A generous (if overly trusting) reading of the Miller Law might take the law at its progressive word, viewing its investment in treatment and cure as part of a more general swing of the pendulum of US penal history away from retribution and toward rehabilitation. The postwar period is characterized by historians of incarceration as a time when the "rehabilitative ideal" held sway, and sexual psychopath laws were heralded by some at the time as the pinnacle of progressive thinking about crime as psychologically motivated and the offender as rehabilitatable. But the psychiatric language of treatment and cure did not evade what Michel Foucault called "the sordid business of punishing."[24] Removing the language and apparatus of criminal law in sexual psychopath laws at once mystified their expansion of criminalization and facilitated the expansion of the powers of the state over sexuality. The Miller Law's advocates recognized and valued that expansion. Overholser identified the intention and aim of the law as the "widening . . . of the scope as to the group of persons who are recognized by the law as needing treatment for their benefit and for the benefit of society."[25] In proposing changing the law's subject from "criminal sexual psychopath" to "sexual psychopath," MacKinnon rejected the language of "criminal" not simply as unmodern in its punitive implications, but as "too restrictive." He continued, explaining that "A lot of these acts of a sexual nature are not what might be classed as criminal. . . . I think if you are going to make it necessary to show that there is a criminal propensity, that is too strict a burden."[26]

When the bill came to a vote, MacKinnon referred to a tacit common understanding of the purpose of this expansion of the law, stating that "I am sure we are all familiar with a great many of the circumstances surrounding many of these offenses, or breaches of good conduct, and I don't think . . . that it is desirable to make it necessary to first file a criminal charge before you can subject the individual to treatment."[27] MacKinnon made clear that while the bill included "some provisions dealing with what may be classed as sex crimes" and that the law "provides for increased penalties" for those crimes, the proposed law "adds additional offenses and penalties therefore for breaches of public decorum that have not previously been covered by District statutes."[28] The virtue of this kind of legislation, two psychiatrists noted shrewdly several years after its passage, was that it "satisfied the diverse strivings and tendencies of both the treatment-minded and the punishment-minded."[29] When the Miller Law was presented in Congress, the main line of questioning had to do with whether it would weaken or strengthen the sex laws in the District. With the reassurance from its sponsors that it would strengthen them "very much," it passed.[30]

The Miller Law's medicalized mystification of criminalization is especially striking given the ambivalence on the part of psychiatrists regarding sexual psychopath laws and the psychiatric concepts on which they were based. As lawmakers knew, the term "sexual psychopath" connoted medical authority. It was a more purportedly scientific term than the terms "sex pervert," "sex deviate," or "sexual degenerate" that circulated around the same time in the press and popular culture (although vernacular references to the "sex pervert" did appear in congressional discussion of the bill).[31] As MacKinnon pointed out, "It is true that the term 'psychopathic' is not a part of the working vocabulary of most people. Yet the reasonably well informed recognize it as having reference to mental disorders."[32] In fact, that was the term's great advantage: it sounded more like an objective psychiatric diagnosis than an expression of moral judgment or contempt.

It seemed to matter little to legislators that many psychiatrists had long dismissed the diagnostic category of the "psychopath" as a "wastebasket diagnosis."[33] As early as 1924, the distinguished psychiatrist William Alanson White proclaimed that the category of the psychopath had become "a sort of middle ground for the dumping of odds and ends" and was not a meaningful clinical category.[34] Believing that mental disorder was at the root of all crime and envisioning a future when mental hospitals would replace prisons, Karpman stated provocatively in congressional subcommittee hearings on the Miller Law, "I object to the use of the word 'criminal,' and I object to the use of the word 'psychopath.'"[35] Although Karpman was recognized as an expert in the study of the psychopathic criminal and authored some of the earliest work in the 1930s linking criminality to sexual deviance, he came in later years to the conclusion that "[t]he terms 'sexual psychopath' and 'sexual psychopathy' have no legitimate place in psychiatric nosology or dynamic classification."[36] Two years before the debate about the Miller Law, in 1946, Karpman expressed his disagreement "with the view that some psychopaths are homosexuals . . . as if the two go together. There is absolutely nothing in common between psychopaths on the one hand, and homosexuals and sexual perverts on the other."[37] The first edition of the American Psychiatric Association's *Diagnostic and Statistical Manual of Mental Disorders* (*DSM*) in 1952 did not include sexual psychopathy as a diagnostic category.

Psychiatrists were especially critical of the portion of the Miller Law and other sexual psychopath laws that compelled defendants under penalty of law to answer questions asked by psychiatrists charged by the court with determining whether they met the statutory standard for sexual psychopathy. As Overholser observed, "you cannot expect to get the truth from him when you are holding a club over his head."[38] Psychiatrists were also less optimistic than legislators about a "cure" for sex offenders. Overholser expressed his reservations about the Miller Law's imperative that sexual psychopaths would be institutionalized until they were deemed "'fully and permanently recovered.'"[39] Nearly a decade later, in 1956, psychiatric experts reported in a public forum on sex offenders that "neither a prison term nor surgery may make him change his ways."[40] Such a determination of cure was especially difficult "if not impossible to render," psychiatrist Karl Bowman later claimed, in the case of homosexuals.[41]

The expanded criminalization of nonnormative sex, then, was promoted, justified, and effectively erased as such through the discourse of medicine. The carceral and criminal expansion sanctioned by new sexual psychopath laws was accomplished through the language of illness, treatment, and cure. Medicalized language and the support, however ambivalent, of psychiatrists, emboldened by their new prestige after the war and eager to expand their professional purview into the criminal justice system, licensed this carceral expansion. So empowered, psychiatrists overcame their hesitations. As Saint Elizabeths superintendent Overholser told members of Congress about sexual psychopaths, "[i]t is an interesting group from a therapeutic point of view and we should welcome the opportunity to deal with them."[42]

NON-PATIENT HOMOSEXUALS

In 1948, the year that the Miller Law was passed and as the postwar policing of homosexuality intensified, Harry Hay first conceived of an activist group committed to reconceptualizing homosexuality as constituting a minority group worthy of protection from persecution and discrimination rather than an individual problem or pathology. With a group of friends in Los Angeles in 1950, Hay founded the Mattachine Society, and local branches were formed across the country in the years that followed.

Mattachine organizations often courted professionals and experts as allies and invited them to speak at their meetings, and in 1964, former US attorney Sidney Sachs met with members of the Mattachine Society of New York to discuss the Miller Law, then sixteen years in operation. Sachs had helped draft the legislation, and he noted that in the ten years between 1954 and 1964 there had been ninety-three Miller Law admissions to Saint Elizabeths Hospital, averaging between nine and ten people per year. At the time of his talk, he reported, there were forty-nine people on the hospital's rolls listed as sexual psychopaths committed under the Miller Law.[43] Since this number was very small in relation to the number of people arrested in the District for same-sex sex, rounded up routinely by the US park police who patrolled gay cruising spots, Sachs reassured Mattachine members that "the statute is very seldom used," and he encouraged them to take comfort in the fact that "everything on the books that is oppressive to homosexuals is not carried out to the letter."[44]

The responses of Mattachine members to Sachs's presentation captured the complex and critical relationship that gay men and lesbians were forging in the 1960s to psychiatric authority and to the pathologization and criminalization of homosexuality that it sanctioned. Members in attendance at Sachs's talk seemed to understand that the terrorizing and criminalizing effects of the Miller Law and other sexual psychopath laws—naming homosexuality a form of sexual psychopathy and identifying it as a social menace, erasing distinctions between consensual same-sex sex and violent sexual assault, conflating the gay man and the pedophile, and licensing a massive upsurge in the policing of gay cruising areas—had a much longer reach than the law itself. Some reasonably imagined themselves to be the potential victims of such laws. One man in attendance countered Sachs's efforts to de-dramatize the significance of the Miller Law and to minimize its effects, observing that "the weight of these laws is such that homosexuals per se can be hospitalized by some arbitrary decision, that somehow this status falls within the purview of the law."[45] That comment was an astute one, capturing the way that sexual psychopath laws targeted a "status"—a kind of personality or type defined by a lack of control over sexual impulses—rather than a particular offense. Another noted that, in the terms of the law, he was clearly a "recidivist": "I am a homosexual," he stated boldly, and "I commit the act habitually."[46] (When Sachs spoke about the Miller Law at the conference of East Coast Homophile Organizations later that year, an audience member made the same point, asking "Would I, as a habitual practicing homosexual, be called a sexual psychopath?" "I think you would be," Sachs replied.)[47]

Others in attendance at the New York Mattachine Society meeting, however, were eager to put some distance between themselves and the public targets of sexual psychopath laws: people who were sexually sick, those who were sexually uncontrolled and impulsive, and especially adults who had sex with children. Those stigmas had powerfully criminalizing and exclusionary effects, and the associations of pedophilia, predation, and sexual compulsion were particularly adhesive when it came to gay men. One man declared to Sachs that he was "in sympathy with the general concept of the sexual psychopath laws." His only concern, he stated, was "in the possibility of their misuse."[48]

That distancing move—approving of sexual psychopath legislation while seeking to remove gay men from its criminalizing purview—aligned with the broader effort on the part of gay activists beginning in the 1960s to dissociate themselves from attributions of sexual pathology and to dislodge homosexuality from its classification as a mental illness. In 1952, four years after the passage of the Miller Law, psychiatrists codified their understanding of homosexuality as a mental disorder in the first edition of the *DSM*, the taxonomic and diagnostic catalog of mental disorders published by the American Psychiatric Association. The *DSM* identified homosexuality and transvestism (alongside pedophilia, fetishism, and sexual sadism, and including rape, sexual assault, and mutilation) as pathological sexual deviations under the larger category of "Personality Disorders" in its first edition in 1952 and its second in 1968.[49] Beginning in the 1940s and continuing through the 1970s, American psychoanalysts such as Edmund Bergler, Irving Bieber, and Charles Socarides popularized an understanding of homosexuality as a dangerous expression of psychopathology and a curable mental disorder.[50]

Beginning in the 1960s, and with increasing boldness in the early 1970s, gay and lesbian activists challenged reigning psychiatric orthodoxies and worked to sever the associative connection between mental illness and homosexuality. The person most closely associated with that position was Frank Kameny, a World War II veteran and astronomer who was fired from his position with the US Army Map Service in 1957 when a background check turned up a record of his past arrest on a charge of "lewd conduct" for soliciting sex in a public restroom. He went on to dedicate his life to gay activism, founding the Mattachine Society of Washington, DC, in 1961. To Kameny, the argument against conceiving of homosexuality as a form of mental illness was a grounding political move, essential to the political intelligibility of gay people. "'The entire homophile movement is going to stand or fall upon the question of whether homosexuality is a sickness," Kameny wrote, "and upon our taking a firm stand on it.'"[51] That position was stated boldly in Washington, DC, Mattachine's "anti-sickness" resolution, approved in 1965, that "in the absence of valid evidence to the contrary, homosexuality is not a sickness, disturbance, or other pathology in any sense, but is merely a preference, orientation, or propensity, on par with, and not different in kind from, heterosexuality."[52]

Kameny did not underestimate the extent to which the understanding of homosexuals as sick undergirded a larger structure of stigma, exclusion, discrimination, and criminalization. Recognizing the importance of medicalized discourse to sexual psychopath laws allows us to see the broader stakes and political edge of gay activists' anti-sickness stance, aimed not only at the stigma created by psychiatry's position on homosexuality or the damage done to individuals who were led to understand themselves as mentally ill, but also at the codification of psychiatric stigma in law. Kameny and others were aware of the ways in which psychiatric authority over homosexuality enabled the expansion of the criminalization of non-normative sexuality under the guise of progressive, humane, and medical treatment. They understood as well that the insidious reach of the medical model went beyond the power of psychiatry to undermine the "self-respect, self-esteem, self-confidence, and self-image" of individual homosexuals, and beyond the promotion of a cultural climate of homophobia by fostering an understanding of homosexuality as a curable mental disorder.[53] The labeling of homosexuality as pathological supported a range of discriminatory laws and restrictions, including sexual psychopath laws. The fight against sickness, then, was also a fight against criminalization, and a fight for recognition and citizenship.

The American Psychiatric Association's declassification of homosexuality as a mental illness in 1973 was celebrated by gay activists at the time and by historians since as a milestone in the history of social justice. I conclude, though, by pondering the possible narrowing of political vision produced by the move to distance homosexuality from a larger group of "sexual psychopaths" and more generally from "sickness." That question runs so counter to familiar and triumphalist stories of the victory of gay activists over psychiatric stigma that it is difficult to frame. But it was a question that Kameny himself anticipated. Clear-eyed in his appraisal of the costs of psychiatric stigma, Kameny insisted that "Whatever definitions of sickness one may use, sick people are NOT EQUAL to well people in any practical, meaningful sense. . . ."[54] He seemed to comprehend (and to peremptorily excuse) the exclusionary effects of his own anti-sickness position when he wrote that "Properly or improperly, people ARE prejudiced against the mentally ill. Rightly or wrongly, employers will NOT hire them. Morally or immorally, the mentally ill are NOT judged as individuals, but are made pariahs. If we allow the label of sickness to stand, we will then have *two* battles to fight—that to combat prejudice against homosexuals per se, and that to combat prejudice against the mentally ill—and we will be pariahs and outcasts twice over. One such battle is quite enough."[55]

Kameny articulated the pragmatic strategy of organizing around a single axis of oppression. His words also suggest an awareness of the stigmatizing dynamics that Erving Goffman described in moments of "mixed encounter," when, as Jonathan Metzl notes, an "affirmation of one's own health depends on the constant recognition, and indeed the creation, of the spoiled health of others."[56] Queer and disability studies scholar Robert McRuer identifies the removal of homosexuality from the third edition of the *DSM* in 1973 as "one of the founding moments of contemporary gay liberation," and also "a distancing from disability."[57] The long history of attributions of mental illness and the criminalization those attributions sanctioned made it crucial for lesbian and gay activists to distance themselves from so-called "sexual psychopaths." That political project required distancing queer people from a long history of injury and illness, disentangling "gay" from the most stigmatized subjects. The title of a panel organized by gay activists in 1971 at the meeting of the American Psychiatric

Association, "Lifestyles of Non-Patient Homosexuals," spoke powerfully to the desire to separate healthy gays from sick ones.

The anti-sickness agenda required gay and lesbian activists to shear off the rights-deserving homosexual from other forms of stigmatized and criminalized sexual difference. That made it difficult to challenge the criminalization of same-sex sex, facilitated as it was by psychiatric language and authority. In disaggregating gay and lesbian from the sick and the criminal, gay activists lost the possibility of understanding the expansion of the criminalization of sexual offenders, and criminalization more broadly, as issues of importance to queer people.[58] Sexual psychopath legislation licensed tactics that would be essential to what we would come to recognize as those of the carceral state—the use of decoys and plainclothes strategies in the policing of cruising areas, the criminalization of identity and incarceration based on the prediction of risk, and indefinite sentences under civil commitment statutes—experiments in incapacitation and perpetual criminalization that are now common practices in the era of mass incarceration.[59] Those criminalizing and carceral strategies were pioneered in the policing and criminalization of sex and intimate life, masked and mystified as such through the use of psychiatric language and through the marshalling of psychiatric authority.

NOTES

1. George Raymond (pseudonym), "My Life History," 29–30, Benjamin Karpman papers, University of Minnesota.

2. "A Bill to Provide for the Treatment of Sexual Psychopaths," H.R. 6071, 4–5.

3. It went on to prohibit such invitations "upon any avenue, street, road, highway, open space, alley, public square, enclosure, public building or other public place, store, shop, or reservation at any public gathering or assembly in the District of Columbia, to accompany, go with, or follow him or her to his or her residence, or to any other home or building, enclosure, or other place," for prostitution "or any other immoral or lewd purpose" (H.R. 6071, 2).

4. "A Bill to Provide for the Treatment of Sexual Psychopaths," H.R. 6071, 5–6.

5. See Morris Ploscowe, *Sex and the Law* (New York: Prentice-Hall, 1951), 216; and Estelle B. Freedman, "'Uncontrolled Desires': The Responses to the Sexual Psychopath, 1920–1960," *Journal of American History* 74, no. 1 (June 1987): 83–106.

6. Prior to World War II, California, Illinois, Michigan, and Minnesota had enacted laws for the civil commitment and psychiatric treatment of sexual psychopaths. By the end of 1947, Massachusetts, Vermont, and Wisconsin had also enacted similar provisions.

7. See George Chauncey, "The Postwar Sex Crime Panic," in *True Stories from the American Past*, ed. William Graebner (New York: McGraw-Hill 1993), 160–78;

Freedman, "'Uncontrolled Desires'"; Simon Cole, "From the Sexual Psychopath Statute to 'Megan's Law': Psychiatric Knowledge in the Diagnosis, Treatment, and Adjudication of Sex Criminals in New Jersey, 1949–1999," *History of Medicine and Allied Sciences* 55, no. 3 (2000): 292–314; Elise Chenier, *Strangers in Our Midst: Sexual Deviancy in Postwar Ontario* (Toronto: University of Toronto Press, 2008); Fred Fejes, "Murder, Perversion, and Moral Panic: The 1954 Media Campaign against Miami's Homosexuals and the Discourse of Civic Betterment," *Journal of the History of Sexuality* 9, no. 3 (June 2000): 305–47; and Philip Jenkins, *Moral Panic: Changing Concepts of the Child Molester in Modern America* (New Haven, CT: Yale University Press, 1998). A critique of the sexual psychopath laws was articulated at the time by Edwin H. Sutherland, "The Diffusion of Sex Psychopath Laws," *American Journal of Sociology* 56 (1950): 142–48.

8. Harry Stack Sullivan, *Conceptions in Modern Psychiatry* (Washington, DC: William Alanson White Foundation, 1947), 4.

9. Nathan G. Hale Jr., *The Rise and Crisis of Psychoanalysis in the United States: Freud and the Americans, 1917–1985* (New York and Oxford: Oxford University Press, 1995), 276.

10. See Allan Bérubé, *Coming Out Under Fire: The History of Gay Men and Women in World War Two* (New York: Free Press, 1990), 147. On "blue discharges" during World War II, see Margot Canaday, *The Straight State: Sexuality and Citizenship in Twentieth-Century America* (Princeton, NJ: Princeton University Press, 2009), 145–46, 150–54.

11. H.R. 2937—H.R. 5264, Criminal Sexual Psychopaths, U.S. House of Representatives, Committee on the District of Columbia, February 20, 1948, 99.

12. H.R. 2937—H.R. 5264, Criminal Sexual Psychopaths, 112.

13. H.R. 2937—H.R. 5264, Criminal Sexual Psychopaths, 114. When Rep. Miller introduced the bill to Congress, on the other hand, he observed that "The present laws of the District of Columbia do not seem adequate to handle sex crimes against children" (H.R. 6061, Treatment of Sexual Psychopaths in the District of Columbia, Congressional Record, April 26, 1948, 4886).

14. Congressional Record—House, February 3, 1948, 1038.

15. H.R. 6071, 80th Congress, 2nd Session, May 21, 1948, 1.

16. Congressional Record—House, April 26, 1948, 4887.

17. H.R. 2937—H.R. 5264, Criminal Sexual Psychopaths, 101.

18. "Providing for the Treatment of Sexual Psychopaths in the District of Columbia," 80th Congress, 2nd Session, Report No. 1377, 6.

19. H.R. 2937—H.R. 5264, Criminal Sexual Psychopaths, 103.

20. "Providing for the Treatment of Sexual Psychopaths in the District of Columbia," 80th Congress, 2nd Session, Report No. 1377, 8. Elise Chenier makes a similar argument, tracing the genealogy of sexual psychopath laws in Canada to Progressive Era laws that named the "defective delinquent," in her analysis, a "medicalized version of the habitual criminal" (Chenier, *Strangers in Our Midst,* 21). Chenier writes that "It is . . . useful to see criminal sexual psychopath legislation as one point on a century-long trajectory of psycho-medical thinking about criminality, sexual, and legal responsibility, and as part of a long tradition of social reform that took a dim view of punishment and repression" (40).

21. H.R. 2937—H.R. 5264, Criminal Sexual Psychopaths, 7.

22. Hearings on "Criminal Sexual Psychopaths," 97.

23. H.R. 2937—H.R. 5264, Criminal Sexual Psychopaths, 39–40. In the discussion of the bill in the Committee on the District of Columbia, O'Hara noted that the Committee "endeavored in considering this subject, realizing the danger which might exist in a wave of hysteria of social workers or anything of that nature, that the right of the accused or the rights of an individual are safeguarded to the greatest extent that we could do so, even to the right of counsel, to insist upon counsel to appear before him in any and all of these cases" (H.R. 6071, 80th Congress, 2nd session, March 31, 1948, 16–17).

24. Michel Foucault, *Abnormal: Lectures at the Collège de France, 1974–1975*, trans. Graham Burchell (New York: Picador, 2003), 23.

25. H.R. 2937—H.R. 5264, Criminal Sexual Psychopaths, 103.

26. H.R. 2937—H.R. 5264, Criminal Sexual Psychopaths, 83.

27. H.R. 2937—H.R. 5264, Criminal Sexual Psychopaths, 64.

28. Congressional Record—House, April 26, 1948, 4887.

29. Frederick J. Hacker and Marcel Frym, "The Sexual Psychopath Act in Practice: A Critical Discussion," *California Law Review* 43, no. 5 (December 1955): 767.

30. H.R. 6061, "Treatment of Sexual Psychopaths in the District of Columbia," *Congressional Record*, April 26, 1948, 4887; Sutherland, "The Diffusion of Sexual Psychopath Laws," 146.

31. In response to Chelf's question about the law's penalty for the "sexual pervert," MacKinnon responded: "Title II of the bill is not aimed at the ordinary sexual pervert, nor is it limited to perverts" (H.R. 6061, "Treatment of Sexual Psychopaths in the District of Columbia," *Congressional Record*, April 26, 1948, 4885–87).

32. H.R. 2937—H.R. 5264, Criminal Sexual Psychopaths, 34.

33. "The Psychopathic Individual: A Symposium," *Mental Hygiene* 8 (1924): 175. See also Hacker and Frym, "Sexual Psychopath Act in Practice," 770.

34. "The Psychopathic Individual: A Symposium," *Mental Hygiene* 8 (1924): 175.

35. H.R. 2937—H.R. 5264, Criminal Sexual Psychopaths, 117.

36. Benjamin Karpman wrote that "Psychopaths exhibit a combination of hypersexuality with a strong homosexual component. Despite their intellectual capacity, they are unable to foresee the consequences of their acts since their primitive emotional organization presses for immediate release" (*The Individual Criminal; Studies in the Psychogenetics of Crime* [Washington, DC: Nervous and Mental Disease Publishing, 1935], 26); see also Karpman, "The Sexual Psychopath," *Journal of Criminal Law & Criminology* 42 (1951–1952): 185.

37. Karpman, "A Yardstick for Measuring Psychopathy," *Federal Probation* 10 (1946): 29.

38. H.R. 2937—H.R. 5264, Criminal Sexual Psychopaths, 107.

39. U.S. House of Representatives, Committee on the District of Columbia, discussion of H.R. 2937—H.R. 5264 Criminal Sexual Psychopaths, Feb. 20, 1948, 115; H.R. 2937—H.R. 5264, Criminal Sexual Psychopaths, 105.

40. "2,000 Hear Experts on Sex Deviates at Star Forum," *ONE* 4, no. 3 (1956): 13.

41. Karl M. Bowman and Bernice Engle, "A Psychiatric Evaluation of the Laws of Homosexuality," *American Journal of Psychiatry* 112, no. 6 (February 1956): 577–83.

42. H.R. 2937—H.R. 5264, Criminal Sexual Psychopaths, 104.

43. The law was used even less frequently in the years immediately after its passage. The Saint Elizabeths Hospital Annual Report in 1951 noted that "very few sexual offenders are being committed under this act; it is doubtful, in fact, just how great an added sense of security the community should feel on the basis of the operation of this law" (4). The hospital's annual report of 1952 stated that "For the moment the act seems to have lapsed into a state of desuetude," noting that only three sexual offenders had been committed under the act during the fiscal year (Saint Elizabeths Hospital, *Annual Report*, 1952, 4).

44. David K. Johnson points out that despite the passage of the Miller Sexual Psychopath Law in 1948, most men arrested for same-sex sex in the District of Columbia were charged with disorderly conduct, allowed to post a $25 fine, and released (Johnson, *The Lavender Scare: The Cold War Persecution of Gays and Lesbians in the Federal Government* [Chicago: University of Chicago Press, 2004], 117). The Miller Law was not unusual in this regard. Sutherland wrote in 1950 that "the states which have enacted such laws make little or no use of them" (Sutherland, "The Diffusion of Sexual Psychopath Laws," 142). As such, as Matthew Gambino points out, the Miller Law "became the basis for an expanded campaign of harassment and intimidation aimed at gay men in the District" (Matthew Gambino, "Mental Health and Ideals of Citizenship: Patient Care at St. Elizabeths Hospital in Washington D.C., 1903–1962," PhD diss. [University of Illinois, 2010], 237; see also Johnson, *Lavender Scare*, 55–63).

45. Sidney S. Sachs, "A Short Discussion of the Miller Act," 1964, Mattachine Society of New York papers, IGIC, New York Public Library, Box 4, Fol. 1 ("Legal Matters"), Reel 11.

46. Sachs, "A Short Discussion of the Miller Act."

47. Lily Hansen and Barbara Gittings, "East Coast Homophile Organizations—Report '64. Part Two: Highlights of ECHO," *The Ladder* 9, no. 4 (January 1965): 10–11.

48. Sachs, "A Short Discussion of the Miller Act."

49. *Diagnostic and Statistical Manual of Mental Disorders* (1952), 38–39.

50. See Edmund Bergler, *One Thousand Homosexuals* (Patterson, NJ: Pageant Books, 1959); Bergler, *Homosexuality: Disease or Way of Life?* (New York: Hill and Wang, 1956); Charles Socarides, *The Overt Homosexual* (New York: Grune and Stratton, 1968); and Irving Bieber et al., *Homosexuality: A Psychoanalytic Study of Male Homosexuals* (New York: Basic, 1962).

51. Frank Kameny, "Speech," quoted in John D'Emilio, *Sexual Politics, Sexual Communities: The Making of a Homosexual Minority in the United States, 1940–1970* (Chicago: University of Chicago Press, 1983), 163.

52. "Policy of the Mattachine Society of Washington," adopted March 4, 1965, reprinted in *Eastern Mattachine Magazine* 10, no. 4 (May 1965): 22–23.

53. Kameny, "Gay Liberation and Psychiatry," in *The Homosexual Dialectic*, ed. Joseph A. McCaffrey (Englewood Cliffs, NJ: Prentice-Hall, 1972), 189.

54. Kameny, "Emphasis on Research Has Had Its Day," *The Ladder* 10, no. 1 (1965): 13.

55. Kameny, "Does Research into Homosexuality Matter?" *The Ladder* 9, no. 8 (1965): 16–17.

56. Jonathan Metzl, "Why Against Health?," in *Against Health: How Health Became the New Morality*, ed. Jonathan Metzl and Anna Kirkland (New York: New York University Press, 2010), 5. See Erving Goffman, *Stigma: Notes on the Management of Spoiled Identity* (Englewood Cliffs, NJ: Prentice-Hall).

57. Robert McRuer, "Shameful Sites: Locating Queerness and Disability," in *Gay Shame*, ed. David Halperin and Valerie Traub (Chicago: University of Chicago Press, 2009), 184.

58. Roger N. Lancaster suggests as much in his study of the cultural phenomenon of sex panic and its manifestations in criminal law, when he proposes that because of "current political strategies for evading stigma and managing unspoken accusations," especially circulating around the figure of the pedophile, mainstream LGBT rights cannot speak to the "absent presence" or spectral figure of the homosexual in the current sex panic. "When, as the price of entry into the 'properly political sphere,' mainstream gay rights organizations promote a hypernormal image of homosexuality, maintain silence about sex offender registries and 'child safety zones,' and . . . avoid discussions of age-of-consent laws," Lancaster writes, "they reinforce a dynamic that Lee Edelman has described: everyone wants to offload the burden of queerness onto someone else; no one wants to be holding the stigma" (Lancaster, *Sex Panic and the Punitive State* [Berkeley: University of California Press, 2011], 233).

59. On the importance of the use of decoy policing to the carceral buildup, see Elizabeth Hinton, *From the War on Poverty to the War on Crime: The Making of Mass Incarceration in America* (Cambridge, MA: Harvard University Press, 2017). On the importance of sex and sexuality to the history of the carceral state, see "History of Sexuality and the Carceral State," *Notches: (re)marks on the history of sexuality*, part 1: http://notchesblog.com/2016/03/10/histories-of-sexuality-and-the-carceral-state-part-1/; part 2: http://notchesblog.com/2016/07/05/histories-of-sexuality-and-the-carceral-state-round-2/; and part 3: http://notchesblog.com/2016/11/22/histories-of-sexuality-and-the-carceral-state-part-3/.

10

The Fall of Walter Jenkins and the Hidden History of the Lavender Scare

TIMOTHY STEWART-WINTER

In 1964, with the arrest and resignation of presidential assistant Walter Jenkins, the Cold War lavender scare reached into the highest echelons of government and briefly threatened the reelection campaign of President Lyndon B. Johnson. Just before 4 PM on October 14 of that year, Johnson learned that Jenkins, his longest-serving and most trusted aide, had been arrested one week earlier by plainclothes police officers while having sex with another man in a YMCA basement men's room two blocks from the White House. Not only that, Jenkins had been arrested previously in the same men's room in 1959. In the scandal that ensued, the US presidency collided with the state's preoccupation with deviant forms of same-sex intimacy. This essay uses the archive produced by the Jenkins affair to open a unique window onto sexual policing in the 1960s. That archive reveals in microcosm the workings of the lavender scare, as historians have defined the period from 1953 to 1975 when homosexuals were excluded categorically from all federal government jobs.

The Jenkins case represented the lavender scare at its pinnacle. As David K. Johnson has shown, the midcentury state persecution of gay men and lesbians developed out of both the nation's Cold War preoccupation with espionage and partisan Republican hostility toward the growing post–New Deal federal bureaucracy. A Senate subcommittee reported in 1950 that "one homosexual can pollute a government office," and President Dwight Eisenhower enshrined that concept in an executive order soon after becoming president in 1953.[1] State and local governments undertook their own crackdowns. An investigation sponsored by the Florida legislature to hound Black civil rights activists in the wake of the 1954 *Brown* decision expanded its purview by the early 1960s into a statewide purge of gay schoolteachers and professors.[2]

By the late 1950s, Lyndon Johnson was the preeminent legislator in a capital where loyalty endured unless and until a man was "guilty of a morals conviction or a murder rap or membership in the Communist Party," in the words of a character in Allen Drury's bestselling 1959 novel of Washington, *Advise and Consent*.[3] The possibility of discrediting oneself through exposure in a homosexual act—whether by police action or otherwise— had increasingly organized the lives and careers especially of men who worked in government. A morals charge was the ultimate political weapon, one that could render its victim "reduced in our minds from a whole and usual person to a tainted, discounted one."[4] Never had such a grenade been lobbed so high into the halls of American government.

The Jenkins affair was sui generis: a routine arrest in a "tearoom," as gay men called public toilets where they cruised for sex, that was reported on the front page of every major US newspaper, dissected and reanalyzed by a massive FBI investigation, and all but universally familiar to Americans. In a nationwide poll conducted that October, 88 percent of Americans had heard of "the Jenkins case."[5] "Ribald cracks and unprintable jokes raced around," one journalist wrote, "jumping via telephone from city to city, and jetting around like travelling salesmen."[6] This essay exploits two distinctive bodies of documentation the Jenkins case produced, much of it during the twenty-six days of his hospitalization for "nervous exhaustion," about the architecture and dynamics of intimate governance in the lavender scare era. The first is the FBI's ninety-four-page "Report on Walter Wilson Jenkins," together with its ten attached exhibits, for which at least 436 people were interviewed during an eight-day period.[7] The second is the avalanche of mail that Walter and Marjorie Jenkins received in the fall of 1964—over four thousand letters, Walter later wrote a friend—including telegrams, reflective dispatches, get-well cards, and a few items that someone set aside in a folder marked "Mean Letters."[8]

The evidence that accumulated around the Jenkins case illuminates three points about the lived experience of the lavender scare. First, the hammer of antigay sexual policing came down not solely on men who had a gay identity already or would understand themselves as gay in the future, nor even the many more whose intimate lives put them at risk of surveillance and arrest. Rather, the state punished a much broader cast of characters: the dependents, neighbors, wives, children, and friends of the purged, and all those forced to recalibrate their personal ties to the outcast. In the case of Jenkins, these included the president of the United States, who was forced to conceal future contact with Jenkins for the duration of his presidency. Their tie was another male intimacy policed and pressed into a closet. The Jenkins case was not only or even primarily an episode in queer history. It was also a family story, as the First Lady drove home in an unusual public statement drawing attention to Jenkins's vulnerable wife and children.

Second, the harshest punishments we associate with the lavender scare's dragnet, including the canonical one of dismissal from a job, were employed unsystematically and even infrequently. Cruising a tearoom was something a federal employee might get away with *even* if he was arrested, as Walter Jenkins learned—perhaps overlearned—in 1959. The worst penalties were terrifying but also far from certain to be meted out. If the purging of homosexuals was scripted by the state, the performers flubbed lines, missed cues, and ad-libbed with notable frequency. Jenkins was the highest profile of the thousands purged from the US government during the lavender scare, but his fate was terrifying partly because it was so unusual for someone widely respected to be expunged so spectacularly. Compassionate exceptions could not be expected, but they were made often enough to be hoped for. The state's most powerful accomplices, including the press and the police, at times stretched the mesh of surveillance and widened its holes enough to let someone wriggle out.

Third, the state not only purged men but also sought to repair them and restore them to the designated breadwinner role. State agents saw the marital household as a powerful construct for resolving deviance and rehabilitating even men who strayed far from sexual norms. Precisely because of this pro-marital bent, the state and its accomplices exerted a powerful disciplinary effect, pushing men into, or back into, marriage. Authorities assigned wives the task of repairing men tarnished by arrests and restoring them as fathers and breadwinners. As Lauren Gutterman has argued, "the state's willingness to usher those with same-sex desires or experiences into marriage was compatible with—and perhaps even essential to—the goal of removing homosexuality from public view."[9]

For a man in a government job, a tearoom arrest would likely pull him into a police station. If he was lucky, he would avoid a courtroom or jail cell. Yet even wriggling out of the net would enroll him in a secret drama of concealment or correction. He would almost certainly not tell his wife, but if doing so was unavoidable, she was likely to keep the secret from others as well. State power could be exerted without the bulk of Americans noticing. Rather than being a behemoth, intimate governance often occurred out of sight.

Where historians of the lavender scare have often read official records against the grain or used materials made by people who understood themselves as gay, Jenkins's mail offers a counter-archive, a rare window onto the perceptions of men and women who saw in his personal crisis a mirror of their own lives. In central Connecticut, a woman sat down at her type-writer and wrote to Marjorie Jenkins, "I feel a compulsion that will not be stilled until I have written you; for I, too, have been through the shadow of the same horror as yours." Though her own husband's transgression had not received national publicity, it was widely known in her circles. "Three times I have been through the hell of public exposure (each time in a different place). Twice it was possible to keep the story from the chil-dren. The third time, they shared the agony as young adults, one still in the teens." She added, "I never knew another woman with the same prob-lem, never confided the trouble to anyone. . . . There are probably many of us."[10] Such letters let us see intimate governance through a new lens. What comes into focus is a lavender scare both harsher and gentler than we have known: gentler in that the state's dragnet was porous and many transgressions slipped through, but harsher in its tendency and power to summon disciplinary authorities and accomplices to shore up and correct the marital household.

Very few of those caught by the mid-twentieth-century anti-homosexual state apparatus resisted its domination. Far more often they accepted their fate, doubled down on compliance with norms, and disappeared into the fog of history. It is those hidden experiences—that hidden history—that I have tried here to reconstruct.

"SOMEBODY GOES WRONG IN EVERY FAMILY"

Lyndon Johnson was in the presidential suite at New York's Waldorf-Astoria Hotel when his longtime personal lawyer Abe Fortas telephoned him with shocking news. That morning a journalist, acting on anonymous tips, had obtained the reports of Jenkins's two arrests and telephoned the White House seeking comment. A panicked Jenkins had driven to Fortas's house and, distraught, explained the outlines of the situation. One week earlier, on the evening of Wednesday, October 7, two plainclothes officers of the Metropolitan Police Department's Morals Squad had placed a ladder outside the men's restroom of the downtown G Street YMCA and taken turns climbing up to peer over the transom and watch Jenkins and another man having oral sex in a doorless toilet stall. The two men were arrested and driven to the police station, where they were questioned, each forfeited $50 collateral, and were let go.

The Jenkins news was shocking because it involved a man in a high position brought so low, from the apex of US global power to a place

"This sort of thing could give my organization a bad name!"

FIGURE 10.1. Editorial cartoon by Paul Conrad, *Los Angeles Times*, October 16, 1964. Used with permission of the Conrad estate.

associated with dirt and contamination. One editorial cartoonist showed LBJ slumped over his desk in the Oval Office while a Washington YMCA official leans over the president, shaking his finger and telling him, "This sort of thing could give my organization a bad name!" (see fig. 10.1). "For a week to ten days that's really what official Washington unofficially talked about," recalled Bill Moyers, whom Jenkins had first hired to work for Johnson in the summer of 1954. "It was *everywhere*."[11] As one woman wrote to Jenkins, "It is the tragedy for you that your 'failures' have been too graphically depicted for people to disregard them."[12] The dingy basement men's room, drawing together strangers of unknown social strata with indeterminate intentions, was a physical tableau that the US public did not see but vividly imagined.

By 1964, the Johnson and Jenkins families had been intertwined for a quarter century; Walter had been working for Mr. Johnson, as he called his boss, for longer than he had known Marjorie. Born on a farm in rural north Texas, the youngest of six, Jenkins attended junior college in Wichita Falls and transferred to the University of Texas at Austin. In 1939, Johnson, then a thirty-one-year-old congressman, hired the twenty-one-year-old Jenkins partly on the basis of the latter's ability to take rapid shorthand. Except for his service in North Africa and Italy during World War II and an unsuccessful 1951 congressional campaign, Jenkins had worked for Johnson ever since, often serving as Johnson's conduit to the sprawling political world of Texas Democrats (see fig. 10.2). As LBJ rose to be the youngest Senate majority leader in history and then gained unprecedented control over the chamber, Jenkins was at his side. The Jenkins children, like Johnson's, spent half the year in school in Washington while the Senate was in session and the other half in Austin (see fig. 10.3). Nothing about Walter seemed deviant. His "only unusual mannerism," a *Time* correspondent wrote, is that "Jenkins has a habit of locking his hands together, thumbs up, when talking to persons in his office."[13]

The assassination of John F. Kennedy suddenly made Jenkins the right-hand man to the president (see fig. 10.4). From Love Field in Dallas, while waiting for Kennedy's body to be loaded onto the airplane, Johnson had called Jenkins in Washington to ask whether the nation now faced a broader or continuing threat.[14] Jenkins met the plane at Andrews Air Force

FIGURE 10.2. Congressman Lyndon B. Johnson (seated) and staff members including Walter Jenkins (standing, fourth from left), in Johnson's House of Representatives office, 1948. LBJ Library photo by unknown.

FIGURE 10.3. Walter and Marjorie Jenkins and their children by the pool at the LBJ Ranch outside Johnson City, TX, ca. 1958. Courtesy of Beth Jenkins Bromberg.

Base and rode in the president's helicopter back to the White House.[15] On December 7, 1963, the night the Johnsons moved into the White House, they were the Jenkinses' guests for dinner, and Luci Baines Johnson had Beth Jenkins for a sleepover on her first night in the White House.[16] For eleven months, Jenkins handled the president's most delicate tasks. When Johnson chose Hubert Humphrey as his running mate, Jenkins placed the call to Humphrey.[17] He knew all of Johnson's secrets. And when J. Edgar Hoover sent the White House a three-page memorandum marked both "obscene" and "top secret" describing the fruits of his electronic surveillance of Martin Luther King Jr., Jenkins scrawled in pencil an instruction to his assistant Mildred Stegall to file it under Martin Luther King.[18]

Now, with the help of Clark Clifford, another lawyer and Johnson adviser, Fortas had spent the day secluding Jenkins and pleading for editors to delay publication of the Jenkins story. "We thought [under] the circumstances that certainly Walter ought not to be around the White House," Fortas told Johnson, "and that the best way to handle it was for him to go to a hospital, which has been done. He's at George Washington [University]

FIGURE 10.4. Walter Jenkins and President Lyndon B. Johnson in the Oval Office, January 1964. LBJ Library photo by Yoichi Okamoto.

Hospital, with instructions to have no phone calls, no visitors, no nothing, and he'll be kept there under sedation." The two men had visited the offices of the city's three daily newspapers in turn, pleading on humanitarian grounds for each editor to hold back the story until Jenkins's resignation could be arranged. Fortas advised Johnson that he had told the editors Jenkins had had too much to drink and "had a complete blackout about it, and that he couldn't remember anything." Fortas added that this account, "our version," was false: "He *does* remember." Johnson was dumbfounded. "Just tell me: Could this be true?"[19] Johnson sent Fortas to remove sensitive documents from Jenkins's office safe and then visit him in the hospital to obtain his resignation.

Johnson had made his steady control of the country's nuclear codes his leading argument for why voters should choose him over Senator Barry Goldwater. Now it appeared he had harbored on his staff a "security risk"—a man with access to government secrets whose homosexuality, under official US policies, made him vulnerable to blackmail by Soviet agents.[20] Even more embarrassing was the fact that police records showed he had been arrested previously in 1959. In the following days Johnson was at pains to emphasize that he had not known of the earlier arrest. But his *not* knowing posed a political problem of its own: since the Kennedy assassination, Jenkins had regularly attended National Security Council meetings, lending credence to Goldwater's assertion that the incident was a "clear indication of lax security" in the administration.[21] Either White House procedures had let someone slip through who should have been screened out, and thus the administration's security procedures were not stringent enough, or else an exception had been made for someone personally close to Johnson. Either one would be damaging.

Making matters worse, Johnson feared that the Jenkins news would aid Goldwater's effort to make character and "morality" campaign issues. Another former member of Johnson's inner circle—Bobby Baker, the secretary to the majority leader when Johnson was master of the Senate—faced credible charges of financial corruption, the subject of an ongoing Senate committee inquiry that Johnson was struggling to contain. What is more, Jenkins had already been implicated in January 1964 when a witness in the Baker matter testified that Jenkins had accepted a kickback on Johnson's behalf. Jenkins had denied the allegation, but Republicans were pressing for him to testify about it.[22] Johnson had reason to fear the two scandals would blur in the public mind into an image of a president surrounded by shady characters.

Johnson sought the advice of confidants late into the night about how to confront this grave new political crisis, including Texas governor John Connally, who like Jenkins had begun his political career working for Congressman Johnson in 1939. "Now, they'll be digging up the Sumner Welles thing," Connally advised, referring to a diplomat whose forced resignation in 1943 over a rumored gay sex scandal prefigured the postwar lavender scare—"and talking about communists and homos and everything else that infiltrated the government." He further suggested that LBJ "draw your family as close to you as you can. You travel together as a unit, you appear together as a unit, you're photographed together as a unit, particularly in the light of what's happened here tonight."[23] The way to beat back the image of a sordid basement encounter was to place his normal, heterosexual, nuclear household on display.

In the first day after the bombshell, Johnson ruminated about how to talk about his tie to Jenkins. In the price Democrats had paid for Secretary of State Dean Acheson's infamous 1950 statement about a friend accused as a Soviet spy, "I do not intend to turn my back on Alger Hiss," Johnson saw a cautionary tale. He told Fortas, "I don't think it does much good to talk compassion. I think you just get into kind of a Dean Acheson turn my back statement." Any "semblance of being protective or defensive" must be avoided.[24] He told the First Lady, "The average farmer just can't understand your knowing it and approving it or condoning it, any more than he can Acheson not turning his back."[25] He considered giving an off-the-record interview positioning Jenkins not as a friend but as family. He floated the phrasing "some of us have mentally retarded brothers and some of us have alcoholic brothers and somebody goes wrong in every family";[26] and later, "if none of you have ever had anything like this in your family why you wouldn't understand it, but nearly every family has had some problem and we regret it very much."[27] The next morning, he told Attorney General Nicholas Katzenbach that he had been as shocked as if "you and Lady Bird had been living together every night" or "my daughter committed treason."[28] That evening, on the plane back to Washington, he told reporters in an off-the-record exchange that it was "as if his wife had run off with another man or one of his children had come home pregnant."[29]

Jenkins *was* family, as the First Lady signaled in an unusual public statement that figuratively returned him to his marital household. Lady Bird Johnson had proposed offering Jenkins a job at the LBJ ranch or her Austin radio station, in effect to shift Jenkins from the Johnsons' public household to their private one. Lyndon told her that they should "let them know" privately that they would provide for the Jenkins family, but "I don't see any reason to 'know' publicly." Lady Bird said she would make a statement of support for Walter, and Lyndon tacitly acquiesced. Her statement, released that morning, began, "My heart is aching today for someone who has reached the point of exhaustion in dedicated service to his country," and called Jenkins a family man who "has been carrying incredible hours and burdens since President Kennedy's assassination" and had thus undergone a nervous breakdown. She predicted that his "recovery" would be helped not only by "the medical attention that he needs," but by "his wife and six fine children and his profound religious faith."[30] By preceding her husband in commenting, the First Lady labeled the matter as a private sorrow rather than a matter of public consequence.

The Johnsons did help Jenkins provide for his family while being careful to keep these efforts concealed. At Johnson's request, the philanthropist and Democratic donor Mary Lasker sent Jenkins a substantial check at Christmas with a letter saying, "I know how expensive your illness must have been and want to send you this gift in order to help with the costs of it."[31] In January 1965, Jenkins's brother Charles complained about LBJ's failure to make "a statement to the nation clearing your good name" to the effect that "this terrible thing is not true."[32] Walter replied, "I can assure you that the President has done everything possible to be helpful and will continue to do so."[33] In March, Jenkins moved his family back to Austin[34] and launched a new career as a management consultant. He opened an office in Austin's Brown Building, owned by Johnson's patrons Herman and George Brown. Texas firms in industries close to Johnson, such as aviation, hired Walter without having to place him on their permanent payroll. Marjorie remained, as she had long been, on the KTBC payroll, receiving $4,800 in salary in 1965.[35] "They came in under the shelter of the Johnson family," recalled a friend who socialized with Walter and Marjorie in Austin.[36]

For the remainder of his presidency, LBJ never acknowledged Jenkins publicly. At the same time, White House staff remained in close touch with Jenkins through back channels. Indeed, in April 1965, he was still speaking to his former secretary Mildred Stegall on the telephone "nearly every day."[37] Stegall replied to some of his letters sent to the White House by hand-writing short replies across the bottom and mailing them back, which ensured no government record of the exchange would exist. In 1966, when Luci Baines Johnson and Beth Jenkins served as bridesmaids at each other's weddings, only the mothers and the bride's father attended each wedding, averting the spectacle of the two men appearing in public together.[38] Johnson's "faithful retainer became a nonperson," Clark Clifford would later observe.[39]

"THE GOOD FORTUNE TO ESCAPE PUBLIC NOTICE"

If October 14, 1964, is a clear boundary in the vast records of LBJ's long political career, the date when the ubiquitous name of Walter Jenkins vanishes from countless files, for the FBI it was the beginning of an investigative frenzy. Just eight days later, the bureau completed its "Report on Walter Wilson Jenkins" and released a short summary stressing its major finding that no breach of national security had occurred. The full, classified report rehearsed the failure of anyone who knew Jenkins to suspect that he had homosexual tendencies; for example, Cartha "Deke" DeLoach, Hoover's deputy, "stated Mr. Jenkins is an above average golfer and at no time has exhibited 'sissy' or effeminate mannerisms."[40]

Beyond this, however, the report reconstructs the mesh of sexual surveillance surrounding Jenkins stretching back to his adolescence. What emerges in the pages of the report is a capital city filled with sexual secrets where the exercise of compassion is, in a sense, another secret. As a father of four wrote Jenkins anonymously from Cleveland, there were, in fact, "many thousands of other good, church-going family men who have lived your torture but who have had the good fortune to escape public notice."[41] Indeed, the report brings to mind Foucault's suggestion that punitive regimes also incorporate a "margin of tolerated illegality," a space characterized by "the non-application of the rule."[42] It delineates both the extent of the lavender scare and its limits.

The FBI investigation's official purpose, of course, was to determine if national security had been jeopardized. But Johnson also clearly meant for the FBI to police the police by checking their work. Had the recent arrest of Jenkins been routine? It had been: Jenkins had been swept up during ordinary enforcement in a public restroom where, in the preceding six months, forty-four other men had similarly been "picked up on morals charges."[43] Johnson was skeptical, suspecting a Republican dirty trick even after DeLoach explained that the reason plainclothes policemen had spied on Jenkins in a public toilet was that they were paid to spy there on a daily basis.[44] That the *arrest* was routine did not mean Goldwater's campaign or the RNC had not learned of it and leaked the story; indeed, there is evidence suggesting they could have. For example, on October 13 a Goldwater campaign staffer had called Republican senator John J. Williams of Delaware, a Johnson antagonist who had relentlessly pursued the Bobby Baker inquiry, to let him know about a phone call from someone with "a lot of information on Walter Jenkins."[45] According to *Newsweek* editor Ben Bradlee, the FBI believed but could not prove that a pro-Goldwater park police officer had leaked the arrest report to Burch and the *Star*. The FBI report offers hints consistent with this.[46]

Both times the arresting offers belonged to the Metropolitan Police Department's Morals Division, a specialized unit that mainly targeted sex work and gay cruising. Such units proliferated in the 1950s and were often under pressure to justify their existence by arrests.[47] On the day of Jenkins's 1959 arrest, Morals Division officers citywide arrested five Black women on charges relating to prostitution, six white and two Black men on gay-related charges, and one Black man on drug charges.[48] White men such as Jenkins were then unlikely to be arrested under any circumstance *except* by the Morals Division in a tearoom. By contrast, as Kwame Holmes has shown, Black men faced sexual regulation not only from specialized units but also from precinct cops on the beat in Black neighborhoods, who monitored their potential or actual interactions with white women.[49] The gay-related arrests mostly happened near Lafayette Park, across the street from the White House—the longstanding hub of white gay life in a segregated city.[50]

Jenkins's two arrests would seem to imply a role for chance in whether a particular arrest brought down the hammer on a government worker. Yet chance was in part a pattern of nonenforcement in the name of "compassion" that had arisen in response to the severity of punishment associated with morals charges. Because such charges "are so damaging to the reputation of a man," the city's newspapers "ordinarily do not report the mere allegation of an offense, where an ordinary citizen is involved."[51] Yet the Morals Division, for its part, turned prominent citizens into "ordinary" ones, retaining the original arrest record in its confidential files while producing a sanitized one for the department's Identification File, available to any police officer and to the FBI. The sanitized arrest reports "downgraded the occupations of persons in high-level posts . . . because of what disclosure might mean to the suspect's family and livelihood." For Jenkins's 1959 arrest, the sanitized report altered his employer from "Senate of the U.S.A." to "unemployed," replaced graphic details with a description of Jenkins's behavior as merely "loitering," and altered his charge from "Investigation (Pervert)" to "Investigation (Suspicious Person)."[52] The head of the Morals Division called this "standard procedure [in] cases of this nature."[53] When Johnson asked the Secret Service to issue Jenkins a White House pass in 1961, the Secret Service received from the FBI only the fact that there had been an arrest for "Investigation (Suspicious Person)." The Secret Service simply "did not evaluate the FBI criminal report as involving a serious matter."[54] And so the hammer did not come down.

The FBI report suggests that for every case involving homosexual charges that was dismissed, there were many quiet resignations and close calls. One section, "Alleged Association With Other Persons With Possible Homosexual Tendencies," describes ten men who were all known to Jenkins and at some point suspected of such "tendencies." No single pattern emerges. One man, a friend of Jenkins's from UT-Austin, became a district court judge and then, in 1954 and on the cusp of statewide office, was "'caught' in a hotel room" with "a young man." He withdrew from a runoff campaign in progress (the press reported his cover story that he had insufficient funds to mount a second statewide effort), then a month later resigned quietly from the district court.[55] Another man, however, employed by a US senator "answering legislative mail and conducting research for the Senator's speeches" since 1958, had been arrested in a Washington tearoom in January 1963 and, like Jenkins, had forfeited $50 collateral. Yet the senator had not learned of the arrest, and the man had simply remained in his job.[56]

In two instances, Walter Jenkins himself is the one identified as showing compassion toward a male colleague suspected of homosexual tendencies. In the spring of 1949, a fellow member of Johnson's Senate staff, N., had been arrested on a morals charge in Lafayette Park and "telephoned Mr. Jenkins at his home" from the police station. Jenkins paid N.'s $25 collateral and drove him home. N. quickly resigned from Johnson's staff and moved to New York City, and Jenkins avoided telling Johnson the reason for N.'s departure.[57] In the second instance, Bob Waldron—technically an administrative assistant to Representative J. J. "Jake" Pickle of Texas, but frequently loaned to Johnson's office to assist him on trips—sought a position on the National Aeronautics and Space Council. In January 1964, Jenkins learned that the FBI had determined that Waldron had engaged in homosexual acts. Waldron was denied the Space Council slot—but kept his job and remained in the president's orbit.[58] In truth, Waldron's queerness had never been a secret. He was "terrifically effeminate,"[59] swishy in "appearance and mannerisms,"[60] the kind of man who "would show up at a party in a cutaway coat, a white tie, and shorts that kind of thing."[61] Only during the Jenkins investigation did the FBI's scrutiny of Waldron force his resignation from the staff of Jake Pickle.[62]

"BRING YOUR FAMILY TOGETHER BACK INTO THE SUN"

During the twenty-six days he spent in George Washington University Hospital, Walter Jenkins did not disappear. Hundreds of Americans were moved to write to him and his family. Some pieces were mailed care of the White House, others to the hospital, and still others to the Jenkins home address. Items addressed to "Walter Jenkins, Washington, DC," found their way to him. Civil servants wrote that their high esteem for him was unchanged, Catholics that they would pray a novena for his family, Republicans that they admired his public service. Countless strangers wished his children well. People sent bits of Henry James, Oscar Wilde, and scripture (especially "Let him who is without sin cast the first stone"). A group of neighbors in St. Louis attached their names and addresses on numbered lines to a formal petition praising his service to the nation.

Even J. Edgar Hoover pushed to designate Jenkins as a man who was undergoing a recovery from illness, in an unprecedented public approbation from the nation's premier symbol of both law enforcement and anticommunism: he sent a bouquet of flowers to Jenkins in the hospital, a story broken by the society columnist Betty Beale.[63] Hoover was masterful at dispensing and collecting favors, and in a crucial turn in their long-standing transactional relationship, Johnson had early in 1964 exempted the director from age-based mandatory retirement. Hoover's floral gift locked in the idea that Jenkins's resignation was a tragedy and signaled to Americans that he was not dangerous—which enraged some right-wing

Republicans.[64] It limited Goldwater's ability to benefit politically from the fall of Walter Jenkins.

Marital advice poured in, from the practical to the highfalutin. A New Jersey man jotted, "Get a good psychiatrist, also be more religious, and discuss relocation with your wife and children, as you will get the 'cold shoulder' from many former very good friends." In February he wrote again with an update: "I have a new job now, and it's not always easy but one has to brave the storm."[65] From Tennessee, a man wrote that he had been the full-time pastor of a large Baptist church. "Then there was a circumstance similar to yours in which I was relieved." Just over a year later, he was no longer preaching full-time, but "I came back and have a small church and am teaching here in our high school." He said he was "happier than I have ever been" and that his wife and six children "are well adjusted to our new way of life."[66]

Powerful people sent good wishes. Ben Bradlee, the editor of *Newsweek*, wrote Marjorie that "we pray for the strength and courage that will bring your family together back into the sun."[67] Charles Luckman, the "boy wonder" former president of Pepsodent and Lever Brothers, said that "the single most important thing is to regain your health," and that if he did so, his public "stature" would be secured.[68]

Some men wrote anonymously to recount their own secret experiences of being arrested on morals charges. "I walked in your shoes once myself," wrote a man from Alexandria, Virginia, "being also married with a growing family and a responsible job in the Federal Service only to have it blow up in my face following an arrest for disorderly conduct."[69] From Arizona: "I was forced to resign my job with the Department of the Interior last July."[70] From Canada: "I have a personal understanding of your problem."[71] From New York State: "I, too, was in a similar position nine years ago this past February."[72] From Long Island: "Seven years ago, here in New York, I was arrested under similar circumstances and with a similar charge."[73] Some sent reassurance that such desires could be conquered: "I eventually put myself in the care of a psychiatrist, and, after nine years of psychoanalysis, I can safely say that I have come through the ordeal rather well," wrote one man.[74] Men pointed to psychiatry and religious faith as avenues to repair.

In letters to Marjorie Jenkins, wives expressed sympathy for her humiliation and grief. "In time," promised a friend, "family, love, and care and medical assistance can mend the pieces into a whole, healthy, happy man, husband, father and citizen again."[75] Wives poured out their suffering, sadness, wisdom, and resolve. "I have experienced exactly what you are going through—a husband who was high in government, who lost everything because of disorderly charges," wrote one woman in a letter mailed from

Washington, DC.[76] From a New Jersey suburb, another promised, "It will be a rough road, but I am sure you must be a strong American woman who will be able to handle this newest problem. (I did.)"[77]

A few condemned the antigay state regime that had hurt Jenkins. "As one who also has your tendencies I sympathize with you," wrote a Staten Island man. "It is very unfortunate that you were caught. I hope I never [am]."[78] A woman in California denounced the lavender scare for "the vicious circularity of the federal government—in labeling homosexuality a crime, creating the opportunity for blackmail, and then firing the homosexual because he *could* be blackmailed."[79] A man from Cincinnati said "there are thousands of homosexuals in the U.S. alone" and complained, "and even though we are susceptible to blackmail—there is no law to protect us from such a crime."[80] Another man wrote, "People just don't understand us," before offering a critique of the state's accomplices, suggesting that it was not gay men who needed fixing, but their critics: "But I have noticed in my own office that the men who talk about your case the most are all latent homosexuals, although they don't realize it."[81]

Relieved by Johnson's landslide victory, Walter embraced the project of repair. According to a family friend, Marjorie had complained not long before his arrest that "if she had not been a Catholic she might as well be divorced because she never saw her husband."[82] Now, in Texas, even as Walter became a better breadwinner than ever—the household's taxable income nearly tripled from 1964 to 1966—he finally had time, too, for family life.[83] In April, at the end of his children's spring break, he wrote his brother Bill, "I bought a small boat Saturday morning, and we spent all afternoon Saturday and all day Sunday water skiing on Lake Austin. I think the Noxzema Co. is going to declare a dividend based on the amount everybody had to use last night before we could stop itching and burning from the sun."[84] A month later he wrote friends, "One of the great pleasures of the last few months has been getting to know my children."[85] Lyndon Johnson had famously demanded that his staff reply to *all* mail on the day it arrived. Now Jenkins, altogether appropriately, took some time off before replying to his hospital mail.

The Jenkins scandal is usually portrayed as a bump in the road to LBJ's 1964 landslide victory, "dramatically sharp at the moment of impact and now only a detail," as the journalist Theodore H. White put it in his bestselling book about the campaign, first published in the summer of 1965.[86] The scandal was quickly pushed off the front pages by foreign policy crises when Soviet premier Nikita Khrushchev was ousted and China detonated its first nuclear bomb. More recently, David K. Johnson has called it a "setback" to the effort of gay activists in the Mattachine Society of Washington to challenge the ban on gay federal employees.[87] The group's founder, Frank Kameny, framed this effort as a fight waged on behalf of a minority group he defined as "the homosexual American citizen"; to him, a tearoom arrest was not the kind of case that would be useful.[88] Kameny told Barbara Gittings that homophile groups should avoid commenting publicly because the "circumstances of arrest do not warrant test case," according to what appear to be notes that she took during a telephone call.[89]

Jenkins was publicly silent about the web of antigay surveillance that ruptured his life—not only on October 7, 1964, when he forfeited $50 collateral instead of challenging police allegations, and on October 14 when he cooperated with his hospitalization and seclusion, but for all of his remaining twenty-one years of life. Only once did he write in detail about what the events meant to him, in a written reply to the FBI's October 22 summary of its report that he drafted and revised at least four times. The reply made three points. First, he did not agree that he had "admitted having engaged in the indecent acts"; in case the sedation had caused the FBI agents to misunderstand him, he clarified that he simply did not know whether or not he had had sex with men in the YMCA toilet. Second, the assertion attributed to him that any homosexual experiences "had occurred after extreme fatigue and imbibing in alcohol" was flawed; rather, he had "no recollection of such instances." To a queer historian drawn to Jenkins precisely by his nonnormative sexuality, this much is disappointing, but understandable. Of a man whose secrets have been so painfully ripped from him, it is too much to ask that he elect to unburden himself of whatever secrets remained his to tell.

In his third and strongest objection to the FBI summary, Jenkins declared that he was troubled by the statement that he "has had limited association with some individuals who are alleged to be, or who admittedly are, sex deviates."[90] In one version of his reply he made the intriguing assertion, "I suppose this sentence could be said with truth about many employees of the United States Government." But this was deleted from later drafts. In what remained, he wrote: "I am particularly disturbed that a person reading this report in the future may be led to believe that I have knowingly associated with Government employees who, to my knowledge, are or were sex deviates." For posterity, he wished to record, "to the contrary, in every instance where any file I received provided [a] basis for suspecting the applicant engaged in homosexual practices, I recommended against the appointment of the applicant."[91]

At first glance, it is both disappointing and puzzling that Walter Jenkins, in his only formal response to the travails visited on him by the lavender scare, asked to be recorded as having been diligently complicit in its persecution. Yet there is a lesson in our puzzlement, which says as much about us as about him. It helps restore the non-inevitability—indeed, the improbability—of the fact that Kameny's view of the midcentury antigay state regime as unjust discrimination would become, half a century later, the dominant one. There were many more Jenkinses than Kamenys in 1964. They had no way to know that this David would someday slay that Goliath. There was little reason to think the hammer that had come down on men like them during the Cold War would ever be lifted.

NOTES

For feedback on earlier versions of this work, thank you to the editors and the participants in the Intimate States workshop, the 2017–2018 Harvard Warren Center seminar, the American Political History Institute at Boston University, David K. Johnson, John Alexander Burton, Alison Lefkovitz, and particularly Justin Glasson. I also wish to thank Beth Jenkins Bromberg, Bill Moyers, Rick Valelly, and the archivists at the Lyndon B. Johnson Presidential Library, especially Brian McNerney, Jennifer Cuddeback, and Christopher Banks.

1. US Congress, Senate, Committee on Expenditures in the Executive Departments, *Employment of Homosexuals and Other Sex Perverts in Government*, Senate Doc. 241, 81st Cong., 2nd sess., 1950, 4.

2. David K. Johnson, *The Lavender Scare: The Cold War Persecution of Gays and Lesbians in the Federal Government* (Chicago: University of Chicago Press, 2004); Stacy Braukman, *Communists and Perverts under the Palms: The Johns Committee in Florida, 1956–1965* (Gainesville: University Press of Florida, 2012); Margot Canaday, *The Straight State: Sexuality and Citizenship in Twentieth Century America* (Princeton, NJ: Princeton University Press, 2009); John Howard, *Men Like That: A Southern Queer History* (Chicago: University of Chicago Press, 1999); and Charles Francis, "Freedom Summer 'Homos': An Archive Story," *American Historical Review* 124, no. 4 (October 2019): 1351–63.

3. Allen Drury, *Advise and Consent* (Garden City, NY: Doubleday & Company, 1959), 308. Drury's novel was likely inspired by the 1954 suicide of Senator Lester Hunt of Wyoming. Among other personal and political difficulties Hunt faced at the time of his death, allies of Joseph McCarthy were threatening to expose the arrest of Hunt's son on a morals charge. In *Advise and Consent*, a senator's suicide stems not from a recent arrest but from a political enemy mailing his wife copies of the letters he had written to a male lover during World War II. A Hollywood adaptation of the book was released in 1962. On Hunt, see "Senator's Son Convicted on Morals Charge," *Washington Post*, October 7, 1953; Marquis Childs, "Smears and Tears Plague the Senate," *Washington Post*, July 6, 1954; and Rick Ewig, "McCarthy Era Politics: The Ordeal of Senator Lester Hunt," *Annals of Wyoming* 55 (Spring 1983): 9–21.

4. Erving Goffman, *Stigma: Notes on the Management of Spoiled Identity* (Englewood Cliffs, NJ: Prentice-Hall, 1963), 2.

5. Horace Busby memo, October 17, 1964, box 30, Pre-Election Material—Oct [1 of 2] folder, Office Files of Bill Moyers, Lyndon B. Johnson Presidential Library, Austin, Texas [hereafter LBJL].

6. From Gart and the Chicago Bureau to Parker, October 16, 1964, box 31k, Johnson, Lyndon (13 of 22) folder, Theodore H. White Papers, John F. Kennedy Presidential Library, Boston, Massachusetts [hereafter THWP].

7. "Report on Walter Wilson Jenkins" [hereafter "RWWJ"], 27–52. All quotations from this report are either from the copy in box 29B, Office Files of Mildred Stegall, LBJL, or from a copy obtained by the author from the FBI via the Freedom of Information Act (request 1390108–000). The two versions contain different, partially overlapping sets of redactions.

8. Walter Jenkins to Roberta Forbes, April 9, 1965, box 41, Dallas folder, Personal Papers of Walter Jenkins, LBJL [hereafter PPWJ]. This unprocessed collection is in the process of being reorganized and re-boxed by LBJ Library archivists; citations here refer to the box numbers in use prior to the reorganization.

9. Lauren Jae Gutterman, *Her Neighbor's Wife: A History of Lesbian Desire Within Marriage* (Philadelphia: University of Pennsylvania Press, 2019), 16. See also Alison Lefkovitz, "'The Peculiar Anomaly': Same-Sex Infidelity in Postwar Divorce Courts," *Law and History Review* 33, no. 3 (August 2015): 665–701: "By denying fault divorces, or at least alimony, to the wives of men who had cheated with men, judges kept potentially gay men in the marriage market on the assumption that marriage itself could cure them" (669).

10. "A friend indeed" to Marjorie Jenkins (postmarked Naugatuck, CT), October 24, 1964, box 39, Connecticut folder, PPWJ.

11. Interview with Bill Moyers, January 18, 2018, New York City, transcript in possession of the author.

12. Mab Ashforth Goldman to Walter Jenkins, November 3, 1964, box 51, New York folder, PPWJ.

13. Kent Demaret to Parker, October 15, 1964, box 31k, Johnson, Lyndon (16 of 22) folder, THWP.

14. Transcript, Marie Fehmer Chiarodo Oral History Interview II, August 16, 1972, LBJL.

15. William Manchester, *The Death of a President: November 20–November 25, 1963* (New York: Harper and Row, 1967), 402.

16. Lady Bird Johnson, *A White House Diary* (New York: Holt, Rinehart and Winston, 1970), 16; interview with Beth Jenkins Bromberg and Walt Jenkins Jr., Bee Cave, Texas, June 4, 2016, transcript in author's possession.

17. Robert Dallek, *Flawed Giant: Lyndon Johnson and His Times, 1961–1973* (New York: Oxford University Press, 1998), 158; and Robert A. Caro, *The Path to Power: The Years of Lyndon Johnson, Volume 1* (New York: Vintage, 1981), 654.

18. David J. Garrow, *The FBI and Martin Luther King, Jr.: From "Solo" to Memphis* (New York: W. W. Norton, 1981), 117–18; J. Edgar Hoover to Walter W. Jenkins, July 17, 1964, box 32, Martin Luther King 1 of 2 folder, Office Files of Mildred Stegall, LBJL; and Kenneth O'Reilly, *Racial Matters: The FBI's Secret File on Black America* (New York: Free Press, 1989), 154.

19. Telephone conversation #5876, sound recording, LBJ and ABE FORTAS,

10/14/1964, 3:56 PM, Recordings and Transcripts of Telephone Conversations and Meetings, LBJ Presidential Library, accessed June 29, 2020, https://www .discoverlbj.org/item/tel-05876. I have reversed the sequence of Fortas's account for clarity.

20. James J. Kilpatrick, "Johnson and the Jenkins Case," *Washington Evening Star*, October 22, 1964.

21. Thomas W. Ottenad, "Goldwater Says Jenkins Report Is Not Enough," *St. Louis Post-Dispatch*, October 22, 1964.

22. Cabell Phillips, "Kickback Linked to Johnson Aide," *New York Times*, January 22, 1964.

23. Telephone conversation #5882, sound recording, LBJ and JOHN CONNALLY, 10/14/1964, 8:45 PM, Recordings and Transcripts of Telephone Conversations and Meetings, LBJ Presidential Library, accessed June 29, 2020, https://www .discoverlbj.org/item/tel-05882.

24. Telephone conversation #5889, sound recording, LBJ and ABE FORTAS, 10/15/1964, 1:13 AM, Recordings and Transcripts of Telephone Conversations and Meetings, LBJ Presidential Library, accessed June 29, 2020, https://www .discoverlbj.org/item/tel-05889.

25. Telephone conversation #5895, sound recording, LBJ and LADY BIRD JOHNSON, 10/15/1964, 9:12 AM, Recordings and Transcripts of Telephone Conversations and Meetings, LBJ Presidential Library, accessed June 29, 2020, https:// www.discoverlbj.org/item/tel-05895. See Robert D. Dean, *Imperial Brotherhood: Gender and the Making of Cold War Foreign Policy* (Amherst: University of Massachusetts Press, 2001), 73–76; and K. A. Cuordileone, *Manhood and American Political Culture in the Cold War* (New York: Routledge, 2005), 40–45. Johnson also tried to link Jenkins to Goldwater, claiming falsely and repeatedly that as a result of Goldwater's being technically the commander of an Air Reserve Squadron made up of members of Congress and their staffers, he had vetted Jenkins and even given him efficiency ratings. "RWWJ," 94; and John Barron, "Didn't Know Jenkins' Record, Johnson Says," *Washington Evening Star*, October 16, 1964.

26. Telephone conversation #5880, sound recording, LBJ and ABE FORTAS, 10/14/1964, 8:02 PM, Recordings and Transcripts of Telephone Conversations and Meetings, LBJ Presidential Library, accessed June 29, 2020, https://www .discoverlbj.org/item/tel-05880.

27. Telephone conversation #5886.

28. Telephone conversation #5891, sound recording, LBJ and NICHOLAS KATZENBACH, 10/15/1964, 7:26 AM, Recordings and Transcripts of Telephone Conversations and Meetings, LBJ Presidential Library, accessed June 29, 2020, https:// www.discoverlbj.org/item/tel-05891.

29. Sidey to Parker, October 16, 1964, box 31k, Johnson, Lyndon (14 of 22) folder, THWP.

30. Statement of Mrs. Lyndon B. Johnson, October 15, 1964, box 86, EX FG 11-8-1/ Jenkins, Walter folder, White House Central Files, LBJL.

31. Mary Lasker to Walter Jenkins, December 23, 1964, box 70, Lasker, Mary folder, PPWJ; and Mary Lasker to Lyndon B. Johnson, December 23, 1964, copy in

box 276, Lyndon Baines Johnson folder, Mary Lasker Papers, Columbia University Library, New York.

32. Charlie Jenkins to Walter Jenkins, January 28, 1965, box 157, Charles H. Jenkins folder, PPWJ.

33. Walter Jenkins to Charles H. Jenkins, February 5, 1965, box 157, Charles H. Jenkins folder, PPWJ.

34. "Jenkins Taking Up Residence in Texas," *New York Times*, March 12, 1965.

35. Income tax returns, box 105, PPWJ.

36. Telephone interview with Sandy Silver, August 22, 2016, transcript in author's possession.

37. Walter Jenkins to Frances Forbes, April 1, 1965, box 70, Miss Frances Forbes folder, PPWJ.

38. Interview with Beth Jenkins Bromberg and Walt Jenkins Jr., Bee Cave, Texas, June 4, 2016, transcript in author's possession.

39. Clark Clifford with Richard Holbrooke, *Counsel to the President: A Memoir* (New York: Random House, 1991), 402.

40. "RWWJ," quotation at 45.

41. Unsigned letter to Walter Jenkins, October 15, 1964, box 51, Ohio folder, PPWJ.

42. Michel Foucault, *Discipline and Punish: The Birth of the Prison*, trans. Alan Sheridan (New York: Vintage, 1995 [1977]), 82.

43. Morton Mintz and Alfred E. Lewis, "Jenkins Case Was Handled Routine Way," *Washington Post*, October 16, 1964; and "'Y' Closes Its Public Rest Room," *Washington Post*, October 18, 1964.

44. Telephone conversation #5884, sound recording, LBJ and CARTHA "DEKE" DELOACH, 10/14/1964, 9:00 PM, Recordings and Transcripts of Telephone Conversations and Meetings, LBJ Presidential Library, accessed June 29, 2020, https://www.discoverlbj.org/item/tel-05884.

45. Untitled memo, October 13, 1964, box 32, folder 112, John J. Williams Papers, University of Delaware Library.

46. Memo #28, from Benjamin C. Bradlee to "Nation, Elliott, Manning, Bernstein," n.d., box 6, folder 4, Benjamin C. Bradlee Papers, Harry Ransom Center, University of Texas at Austin.

47. Anna Lvovsky, "Cruising in Plain View: Clandestine Surveillance and the Unique Insights of Antihomosexual Policing," *Journal of Urban History* (2017), https://doi.org/10.1177/0096144217705495, 4. Two modes of antigay policing occurred in "tearooms" and other public places: decoy operations, in which plainclothes officers lured men to solicit them for sex, and clandestine surveillance, in which police watched men having sex through vents or peepholes or over transoms. Jenkins was caught by the former in 1959 and the latter in 1964. Public restrooms were the most common site for arrests of both types. Jon J. Gallo et al., "The Consenting Adult Homosexual and the Law: An Empirical Study of Enforcement and Administration in Los Angeles County," *UCLA Law Review* 13, no. 3 (March 1966): 643–832, here 707n138.

48. This snapshot covers all arrests citywide conducted between 12:10 AM on Thursday, January 15, 1959, and 1:00 AM the next day. "RWWJ," exhibit F. See Anne

Gray Fischer, "'Land of the White Hunter': Legal Liberalism and the Racial Politics of Morals Policing in Midcentury Los Angeles," *Journal of American History* 105, no. 4 (2019): 868–84.

49. Kwame Holmes, "Beyond the Flames: Queering the History of the 1968 D.C. Riot," in *No Tea, No Shade: New Writings in Black Queer Studies*, ed. E. Patrick Johnson (Durham, NC: Duke University Press, 2016), 304–22, quotation at 308.

50. Genny Beemyn, *A Queer Capital: A History of Gay Life in Washington, D.C.* (New York: Routledge, 2015), 120–24, 140.

51. J. R. Wiggins, "The Famous Have Less Protection," *Bulletin of the American Society of Newspaper Editors* 481 (December 1, 1964), 1, 15, in box 155, folder 87, Abe Fortas Papers, Yale University Library, New Haven and Steele and Hannifin to Parker, October 15, 1964, in Johnson, Lyndon (16 of 22) folder, box 31k, THWP. See also "Reporting on the Jenkins Case," *Washington Evening Star*, October 17, 1964.

52. "RWWJ," exhibit A.

53. Scott E. Moyer memo, October 16, 1964, in "RWWJ," exhibit E. In response to the FBI report, Moyer pledged to close the gap that "compassion" had opened up in enforcement by ensuring that reports of morals arrests would henceforth "include accurate descriptions of suspects' occupations." Whether or not this occurred, the division nonetheless backed off from morals arrests in public places, which decreased by half from 1964 to 1965. Alfred E. Lewis and Willard Clopton, "Changes in Police Rules Follow Jenkins Arrest," *Washington Post*, October 24, 1964; and "Morals in the Parks," *Washington Post*, January 1, 1966.

54. Douglas Dillon to Nicholas Katzenbach, October 16, 1964, in National Security File—Intelligence File, Box 10, F: Walter Jenkins, Presidential Papers, LBJL

55. "RWWJ," 65–66. I have withheld A.'s name and identifying details, since I have found no published report of this story.

56. "RWWJ," 64.

57. "RWWJ," 77–78.

58. Telephone conversation #5880.

59. "RWWJ," 81.

60. "RWWJ," 36.

61. Interview with Lloyd Hand, telephone, February 16, 2020, notes in author's possession.

62. "RWWJ," 72.

63. Betty Beale, "Friends Console the Jenkinses," *Washington Evening Star,* October 21, 1964.

64. Jenkins wrote Hoover, "Considering all the trouble your flowers to me caused you, the least I can do is to tell you of my deep and sincere gratitude." Walter Jenkins to J. Edgar Hoover, December 16, 1964, box 85, Hoover, J. Edgar folder, Washington, PPWJ.

65. W. J. H. to Walter Jenkins, n.d. but fall 1964, and W. J. H. to Walter Jenkins, February 5, 1965, box 51, New Jersey folder, PPWJ.

66. J. B. D. to Walter Jenkins, October 26, 1964, box 51, Tennessee folder, PPWJ.

67. Ben Bradlee to Marjorie Jenkins, October 17, 1964, box 42, Bradlee, Ben folder, PPWJ.

68. Charles Luckman to Walter Jenkins, October 27, 1964, box 215, Charles Luck-man folder, PPWJ.

69. "An understanding friend" to Walter Jenkins, October 19, 1964, box 51, Vir-ginia folder, PPWJ.

70. Charles C. Tucker to Walter Jenkins, November 3, 1964, box 70, Arizona folder, PPWJ.

71. "Don" to Walter Jenkins, October 24, 1964, box 39, Foreign folder, PPWJ.

72. W. D. to Walter Jenkins, October 22, 1964, box 51, New York folder, PPWJ.

73. B. V. to Walter Jenkins, October 18, 1964, box 51, New York folder, PPWJ.

74. W. D. to Walter Jenkins, October 22, 1964.

75. Minnie Lee Wire to Marjorie Jenkins, October 18, 1964, box 70, Virginia folder, PPWJ.

76. Unsigned letter to Marjorie Jenkins, October 24, 1964, box 39, D.C. folder, PPWJ.

77. Mary Byrnes to Marjorie Jenkins, October 17, 1964, box 51, New Jersey folder, PPWJ.

78. "An understanding friend" to Walter Jenkins, October 19, 1964.

79. Karen S. Kendler to Walter Jenkins, October 26, 1964, box 71, California folder, PPWJ.

80. Unsigned letter to Marjorie Jenkins, October 19, 1964, box 51, Ohio folder, PPWJ. I have silently corrected spelling errors.

81. "A friend" to Walter Jenkins, October 28, 1964, box 51, New York folder, PPWJ.

82. "RWWJ," 31.

83. Income tax returns, box 105, PPWJ.

84. Walter Jenkins to Mr. and Mrs. W. R. Jenkins, April 19, 1965, box 70, Miscel-laneous Cities—Texas folder, PPWJ.

85. Walter Jenkins to Mr. and Mrs. Reginald C. Martin, May 14, 1965, box 70, Miscellaneous Cities—Texas folder, PPWJ.

86. Theodore H. White, *The Making of the President 1964* (New York: Atheneum, 1965), 386.

87. Johnson, *Lavender Scare*, 199.

88. In fact, Kameny, like Jenkins, had had *two* tearoom arrests—and the sec-ond one meant he "could no longer claim that the [first] had been a fluke." Eric Cervini, *The Deviant's War: The Homosexual vs. the United States of America* (New York: Farrar, Straus & Giroux, 2020), 44.

89. Handwritten notes [n.d. but October 1964], box 97, folder 7, Barbara Git-tings/Kay Lahusen Papers, New York Public Library. I thank Marcia Gallo for con-firming that the handwriting is Gittings's.

90. Telephone conversation #5948, sound recording, LBJ and J. EDGAR HOOVER, 10/23/1964, 6:00 PM, Recordings and Transcripts of Telephone Conver-sations and Meetings, LBJ Presidential Library, accessed June 29, 2020, https://www.discoverlbj.org/item/tel-05948.

91. Untitled statement by Jenkins, n.d., box 29A, Jenkins Investigation folder, Office Files of Mildred Stegall, LBJL. In one conversation, DeLoach seems to tell

Johnson that on receiving Jenkins's statement, the FBI "let him think it was being put in [its files]" without this actually occurring. Telephone conversation #6368, sound recording, LBJ and CARTHA "DEKE" DELOACH, 11/16/1964, 4:40 PM, Recordings and Transcripts of Telephone Conversations and Meetings, LBJ Presidential Library, accessed June 29, 2020, https://www.discoverlbj.org/item/tel-06368.

11

The State of Illegitimacy after the Rights Revolution

SERENA MAYERI

Between 1960 and the early 1980s, social movements and social change transformed state regulation of marriage, family status, and sexuality. Movement-driven victories in courts and legislatures vanquished the remnants of coverture; decriminalized contraception, abortion, and interracial intimacy; and abolished the most severe legal discrimination against "illegitimate" children. The no-fault revolution eased access to divorce; rates of nonmarital cohabitation and childbearing soared. Federal and state laws prohibited employment discrimination based on race, sex, and eventually pregnancy. Yet these vast changes—occurring within a remarkably compressed period of time—did not unseat the privileged place of heterosexual marriage in the eyes of the state. Even as marital status increasingly correlated with race, education, and income, the law continued to regard marriage as the gateway to public and private benefits and the normative site for bearing and raising children.[1]

Focusing on the legal treatment of nonmarital families, this essay examines the changing contours of state regulation of sexuality and family status during and after the "rights revolutions" (as the 1960s–1970s constitutional interpretations benefiting individual rights are often called). Before the 1960s the state routinely penalized nonmarital sex and childbearing, using various formal and informal mechanisms, most of them economic. States excluded "illegitimate" children from paternal inheritance, workers' compensation, wrongful death recovery, and public assistance. Federal law rendered nonmarital children ineligible for many social welfare benefits. Employers and landlords discriminated against pregnant women, unmarried parents, and nonmarital families with impunity. Racialized fears of moral contagion and antagonism to civil rights activism often motivated these discriminations. In response, civil rights, feminist, and welfare rights advocates produced new legal and constitutional weapons meant to eliminate family status discrimination. Principles of equality, privacy, liberty, and due process, embodied in constitutional, statutory, and administrative law but newly articulated from the late 1960s into the 1970s, began to force state and federal officials to justify exclusionary and discriminatory practices.

Plaintiffs in the early "illegitimacy cases"—all of them African American women and their children—often argued that legal disadvantages based on birth status violated constitutional guarantees of equal protection of the law because they discriminated against poor people of color. State actors denied any racial motivation, and instead cited moralistic justifications for penalizing nonmarital childbearing. For example, states claimed that legal burdens on illegitimate children were rational deterrents to adults' illicit sexual relationships and incentives for legal marriage. Schools that excluded unmarried cohabitants and parents from teaching positions cited educators' responsibility to model high moral standards. Other defenders of these policies often linked sexual morality to (white) morale. For instance, employers maintained that unwed mothers degraded their workforce by alienating self-governing, desirable (white) employees. Welfare officials argued that (white) taxpayers would not support public assistance if it meant funding "illegitimacy" in communities of color.

Despite these defenses of illegitimacy penalties, plaintiffs' constitutional challenges, beginning in the late 1960s, gradually impelled lagging states to modernize their regulations.[2] Modernization did not occur evenly or comprehensively, but patterns are discernible. First, the "whitewashing" of "illegitimacy" cases by courts is a consistent theme. Race—so central to political debates over nonmarital childbearing and also to many early plaintiffs' arguments—remained virtually invisible in most judicial opinions, although the mid-level bureaucrats and state officials who defended illegitimacy penalties did not always hide their racial motivations well. That racial subtext may have nurtured sympathy for plaintiffs among some federal judges, especially those very familiar with white Southern officials' recalcitrance in resisting the desegregation of schools and public accommodations. When unmarried Black parents advanced expansive visions of sexual privacy, co-parenting, and extended family care, courts sometimes ruled in their favor, but ignored plaintiffs' larger claims about racial, sexual, and economic injustice. The Supreme Court squelched illegitimacy penalties in outlier states, but never did so on race discrimination grounds.

Second, ascendant legal and constitutional norms of nondiscrimination and sexual privacy devalued the moralistic arguments that had once dominated the discourse regarding nonmarital childbirth. Judicial scrutiny of penalties placed on illegitimacy increasingly compelled states to find more pragmatic, functional rationales. Distinctions between "legitimate" and "illegitimate" families most often survived if based on ostensibly neutral grounds, such as the difficulty of proving paternity, or the desire to encourage parents to "legitimate"—and take financial responsibility for—their nonmarital children. When constitutional rulings forbade states from punishing "innocent" children for the "transgressions" of their parents, state actors increasingly couched their penalties for nonmarital childbearing in terms of children's welfare. States could, for example, force mothers to reveal the identity of their children's fathers on pain of losing public assistance, fines, or even incarceration, on the grounds that children deserved paternal knowledge and support.

Yet while moralizing rhetoric became less acceptable, the motivations underpinning state action remained relatively constant. Indeed, underlying both the old moralistic justifications and the newly sanitized pragmatic rationales lurked a common state imperative: the privatization of economic dependency within the family. Southern states, often with federal government cooperation, had long excluded African Americans from social insurance and public assistance programs. As Aid to Families with Dependent Children (AFDC) became available to single mothers of color in the 1950s and 1960s, anxieties about out-of-control welfare spending and sexual "immorality" fueled a growing backlash that helped realign American politics. Interwoven "war on welfare" and "tough on crime" agendas captured American politics by the early 1970s.[3]

Unsurprisingly, then, plaintiffs who challenged burdens on nonmarital families were most successful when the change they sought protected the public fisc. For instance, employers' formal barriers to hiring unmarried mothers succumbed to constitutional challenge by plaintiffs who emphasized that access to good jobs would keep them off the welfare rolls. But women lost their battle to use constitutional privacy law as a shield against paternity disclosure as a mandatory requirement for receiving public assistance.

In short, state regulation of "illegitimacy" evolved from moralistic formalism to fiscal functionalism: states were willing to render marital status less important if doing so promoted private familial support and care for children. Fiscal concerns had long animated family law and policy, of course. But moralistic formalism only worked to the extent that it successfully discouraged nonmarital families from forming. In the 1960s and 1970s, rates of cohabitation and nonmarital births accelerated. An already fragile consensus that sex should take place only between married heterosexual couples and that "illegitimate" children should be given up for adoption splintered. The increasing numbers of nonmarital families pushed states to find new pathways to confirm legitimate family relationships. They did so still with the aim of assuring private family support.

MORALISTIC FORMALISM AND CHILDREN'S WELFARE

Laws discriminating against "illegitimate" children and their parents littered the statute books at midcentury, some of them the remnants of common law, others the more recent product of resistance to racial desegregation.[4] When plaintiffs animated by the civil rights and anti-poverty movements began to challenge illegitimacy penalties on constitutional grounds, their lawsuits confronted states with charges of discrimination based on race, poverty, and birth status. The first such cases to arrive at the Supreme Court came from Louisiana in 1968. Because the children of Louise Levy were "illegitimate," a Louisiana law prevented them from recovering damages from the hospital for their mother's wrongful death from undiagnosed hypertensive uremia. In another case, Louisiana state law prevented Minnie Brade Glona from suing for the wrongful death of her nonmarital son Tommie, killed in an automobile accident in Texas. Both parties challenged the state.

In *Levy v. Louisiana*, ACLU and NAACP Legal Defense Fund (LDF) lawyers elaborated on arguments first advanced in 1960 when Louisiana had infamously purged thousands of African American families from welfare rolls for bearing children "out of wedlock"—a move widely seen as retaliation for protests against racial segregation. Discrimination against illegitimate children, advocates argued, violated the Fourteenth Amendment's equal protection guarantee. They compared discrimination based on birth status to discrimination based on race. And they emphasized its hugely disproportionate impact on "poor Negro children" in the South, who, they contended, should not suffer because of circumstances utterly beyond their control.[5]

Louisiana insisted that the exclusion of illegitimate children from a statute allowing legitimate children to recover for a parent's wrongful death had nothing to do with race or any punitive intent. Rather, the state merely wished to promote the institution of marriage. Privileging the legal formality of marriage, or at least formal legitimation of children, served the goal of social stability and provided a bulwark against communism and totalitarianism. The likes of Russia, China, and Nazi Germany blurred the lines between legitimate and illegitimate families; Louisiana was not about to follow suit.[6]

Similarly, the insurance company seeking to avoid a payout in Tommie Brade's death adopted the Louisiana Supreme Court's rationale that the state had "a legitimate interest in protecting the general welfare and morals of its citizens, in preserving the family unit, and in discouraging 'bringing children into the world out of wedlock.'"[7] No recognized legal or constitutional principle prevented Louisiana from "discouraging . . . promiscuity, bigamy, adultery, illegitimacy, and other undesirable consequences of uncontrolled sexual conduct."[8] Indeed, if the state could criminalize fornication, surely it could discourage such immoral behavior through less drastic means.[9] Faced with accusations of race- and poverty-based discrimination, Louisiana framed illegitimacy penalties in terms of ostensibly race-neutral morality and governance.

Outside of court, ACLU lawyers questioned the state's prerogative to regulate consensual sexual conduct.[10] But they avoided challenging marital primacy in their submissions to the Court in *Levy*.[11] The local Louisiana attorney who initiated the lawsuit portrayed Louise Levy as a pious, hardworking woman who scraped together enough money from her work as a domestic laborer to send her children to Catholic school. Excluding her children from recovery, he emphasized, would burden public coffers and let the tortfeasor off scot-free.[12]

In contrast, in an Alabama case, Mrs. Sylvester Smith and her attorney, Martin Garbus, directly challenged that state's "substitute father" law, which denied public assistance to mothers found to have an intimate relationship with a man, by calling the law an invasion of mothers' sexual privacy. Smith proclaimed her sexual independence, declaring her personal life "none of [her social worker's] business." Smith said she would pursue intimate relationships as long as she was young enough to enjoy the company of men.[13]

Alabama disclaimed any interest in punishing nonmarital families or in making a "moral judgment about the sexual behavior of the poor." The state hoped to distinguish substitute father laws from "suitable home" regulations, which had come under fire for intolerably invading the privacy of poor mothers.[14] Alabama cited a desire to ensure fairness for marital families, in which husbands had an automatic legal responsibility to support their children.[15] And presuming "men in the house" to be potential providers ostensibly avoided intrusive case-by-case determinations of which men were in fact providing for their intimate partners' children.

The assertion that substitute father laws avoided intrusion into the intimate lives of the poor was laughable, of course: (white) social workers routinely invaded (Black) mothers' privacy to determine who was known to be involved with a man. But Alabama's lawyers insisted that the state was "not urging a morality crusade. . . . Just because cohabitation out of wedlock may also carry with it a theological connotation of 'sin' and by law be 'illegal,' [Alabama should not be] accused of making moral judgments."[16] State welfare department head Ruben King famously proclaimed that "if a man wants to play, he should pay"—which sounded in terms of moral disapprobation more than fairness. Alabama officials also argued that substitute father laws were necessary to maintain the already precarious taxpayer support that made AFDC possible. White citizens, they warned, would not countenance a subsidy for "illegitimacy."

King v. Smith exposed the blurry line between moralistic or religious rationales for discouraging nonmarital cohabitation, and the ostensibly pragmatic goal of incentivizing marital and nonmarital families alike to avoid bearing children they could not afford to raise. Put another way, the moral taboo against nonmarital births itself stemmed in large part from practical concerns about protecting the public fisc and rewarding "responsible" sexuality. The gradual demise of moralistic arguments for discrimination based on marital or family status was a shift in justificatory rhetoric more than a substantial change in motivation.

Understanding how and why this shift occurred nonetheless sheds light on what were genuine challenges to the logic that underpinned marital supremacy. States did not immediately abandon moralistic justifications. Even though subsequent plaintiffs in Louisiana emphasized the racially disproportionate impact of illegitimacy discrimination and highlighted its punishment of blameless children, when Louisiana defended its inheritance statute from constitutional challenge as late as 1970, the state claimed its prerogative to "strengthen the idea of a family unit to discourage the promiscuous bearing of children out of wedlock."[17] But that case, *Labine v. Vincent*, was the last time a moralistic argument won the day.[18]

Faced with plaintiffs' claims to rights of privacy and to freedom from discrimination based on race, sex, and poverty, the Supreme Court never rescinded states' prerogative to regulate sexual conduct or to promote marriage. Rather, when plaintiffs prevailed, it was because the court majority believed that discriminatory laws did not effectively deter nonmarital sex and childbearing but rather caused "hapless and innocent children" to suffer "illogical and unjust" disadvantage. In a passage cited time and again, Justice Lewis F. Powell Jr. wrote in *Weber v. Aetna Casualty* in 1972:

> The status of illegitimacy has expressed through the ages society's condemnation of irresponsible liaisons beyond the bonds of marriage. But

visiting this condemnation on the head of an infant is illogical and unjust. . . . [N]o child is responsible for its birth and penalizing the illegitimate child is an ineffectual—as well as unjust—way of deterring the parent.[19]

The court's focus on children obscured and minimized the claims of adults who argued that illegitimacy penalties perpetuated racial, sexual, and economic subordination. In the 1970s, feminists developed a critique that emphasized how illegitimacy penalties infringed on women's reproductive and sexual freedom. They protested the economic injustice suffered by women who shouldered primary responsibility for the care and support of nonmarital children. The Court ignored these arguments, just as it resisted acknowledging the racially disparate impact of illegitimacy penalties. Many of the illegitimacy statutes challenged came from Southern states that had mightily resisted desegregation, which influenced social movement strategies and enlisted the sympathies of some lower court judges—but not the opinions of the Supreme Court.[20]

Opponents of illegitimacy penalties did force the government to justify family status discrimination on different grounds, however. Certain patterns are apparent. State and federal governments generally succeeded in defending laws that distinguished between "legitimate" and "illegitimate" children and parents when they could present a plausible functional justification for the discrimination, such as avoiding the difficulty of ascertaining paternity; encouraging parents to "legitimate" their children formally; or prioritizing support to children who had lived with or depended financially upon a parent who died. Courts were more skeptical when the state rationalized discrimination as enforcing morality, deterring illicit conduct, or rendering marriage the only means of legitimating nonmarital childbirth. Plaintiffs were most successful in cases where they could credibly claim that invalidating the challenged law or practice would advance children's welfare *and* maintain private support for dependent children.

LEGITIMATION AS A SUBSTITUTE FOR MARRIAGE

Although they varied by state, several paths to "legitimation" existed by midcentury.[21] Many states allowed a father to legitimate his child by marrying her mother. Others enacted "legitimation by acknowledgment" statutes, providing procedures whereby a father could formalize a legal relationship with his child.[22] The legal consequences of legitimation varied from state to state, creating a confusing patchwork of laws that defied generalization. For reformers like Harry Krause, who prioritized the formalization of legal paternal relationships, the proposed Uniform Legitimacy Act—later the Uniform Parentage Act (UPA)—held out the promise of providing consistent standards. Not all states embraced the UPA's guidelines, however, nor did they uniformly resolve second-order questions about how legitimation would affect the rights and duties of nonmarital parents and children.

Once most states made formalizing a parent-child relationship easier, the Court became more sympathetic to the claims of plaintiffs who lived in states that conditioned legal paternity on formal marriage. Two of the landmark 1970s cases involving nonmarital father/child relationships originated in Illinois, a state whose family laws deliberately drew sharp lines between marriage and nonmarriage. In the first of these cases to reach the US Supreme Court, Peter Stanley successfully challenged an Illinois law that divested him of parental rights over children he had lived with since birth, because he had never married their now-deceased mother Joan. The resulting Court decision for the first time recognized a nonmarital father's due process right to notice and a hearing before his parental rights could be terminated.[23]

A few years later, Deta Mona Trimble claimed a constitutional right to inherit from her father, Sherman Gordon, a young man who died without a will, the victim of a homicide. Trimble and her mother successfully challenged an Illinois law providing that an illegitimate child could not inherit from a father who died intestate, unless he subsequently "legitimated" them by marrying. Deta Mona's mother, Jessie, alleged discrimination based on birth status, race, and sex, but the Court focused again on the harm to blameless children:[24] "The parents have the ability to conform their conduct to societal norms, but their illegitimate children can affect neither their parents' conduct nor their own status."[25] Justice Powell acknowledged the state's interest in avoiding the difficulties of proving the paternity of a deceased putative father. But proof problems, Powell wrote, could not justify the exclusion of *all* illegitimate children, including those whose fathers had, like Gordon, acknowledged and supported their children.[26]

When states provided easier paths to "legitimate" paternal relationships and parents failed to follow them, however, the Court proved less sympathetic. In *Lalli v. Lalli*, the plaintiff was an adult son whose father, Mario Lalli, had lived with and acknowledged him and his late sister as his children. When Mario died a violent death, his biological son Robert challenged the New York law that disinherited him because Mario had never signed a formal legitimation order. Several factors distinguished the Lalli case from *Trimble*: a less needy and sympathetic plaintiff (Lalli was a white, well-off adult with apparent family ties to organized crime) compared to an impoverished African American child and her mother; the background presence of Mario's legal (and perhaps wronged) wife who stood to inherit if her son did not; and little hint of race-, sex-, or class-based discrimination. Justice Powell, whose vote determined the result in both 5–4 decisions, attributed the difference in outcome to the fact that New York—unlike Illinois—allowed fathers easily to legitimate their children. Mario need not have married Robert's mother, but rather could simply have filed an order of filiation formally acknowledging his paternity.[27]

Neglected opportunities to legitimate also cost fathers access to their nonmarital children. When Leon Quilloin sought to block the adoption of his eleven-year-old biological son Darrell by Darrell's mother's husband, the Court unanimously rejected his plea to retain parental rights and visitation, despite evidence that Quilloin had developed a significant relationship with his son during the first several years of Darrell's life. While Darrell's mother Ardell worked in New York, Darrell lived in Savannah, cared for by his maternal and paternal grandmothers with help from Quilloin. Darrell expressed his wish to be adopted by Ardell's husband *and* to maintain a relationship with Quilloin; a poignant exchange in court made clear that the eleven-year-old boy did not understand that the two were mutually exclusive. Under Georgia law, Justice Thurgood Marshall wrote, Quilloin could simply have petitioned for legitimation and gained the right to veto the adoption—and the duty to support Darrell. Georgia could, consistent with the US Constitution, provide divorced fathers with greater rights than never-married fathers who had not lived with and continually supported their children.[28]

Georgia law also ensnared Curtis Parham, whose six-year-old son Lemuel died tragically in a car accident alongside his mother, Cassandra Moreen. Richmond County superior court judge Franklin H. Pierce found that Parham had "in every respect treated [Lemuel] as his own," visiting with him daily, caring for him on many weekends, providing consistent financial support and care.[29] But in 1979, the US Supreme Court upheld the state law that denied Parham any right to recover for his child's wrongful death. Justice Potter Stewart wrote that Parham, "as the natural father, was responsible for conceiving an illegitimate child and *had the opportunity to legitimate the child but failed to do so*."[30] Parham was not a child "for whom the status of illegitimacy is involuntary and immutable," so it was "neither illogical nor unjust for society to express its 'condemnation of irresponsible liaisons beyond the bonds of marriage'" by excluding fathers from recovery.[31]

Quilloin's and Parham's claims arose from caregiving arrangements that departed from the marital nuclear family ideal but reflected the reality of many families of color: cooperation between extended family members (the grandmothers who helped care for Darrell while his parents worked in different states) and non-cohabiting parents who did not live in marriage-like households but nevertheless participated in what we would now call co-parenting (Parham and Moreen).[32] The Court, however, reaffirmed the superiority of marital parenthood and the state's prerogative to discriminate against unmarried fathers by withholding rights from men who did not take available steps to "legitimate" their children and assume responsibility for their support.

MARRIAGE AS A PROXY FOR DEPENDENCY

States invented alternative processes for legitimation precisely because they wished to hold putative fathers financially responsible for their non-marital children. Unsurprisingly, then, among the outlier state laws the Court struck down in the early 1970s was Texas's exemption of nonmarital fathers from civil and criminal liability for child support.[33] Child support exclusions were an easy case: exempting nonmarital fathers from financial obligations hardly seemed designed to discourage illicit sex—at least on the part of men. Children and their mothers both suffered from the denial of support. And eliminating biological fathers as a potential source of funds threatened additional public welfare expenditures. As the prototypical nonmarital father shifted from unfaithful married patriarch to irresponsible and impecunious unmarried man, the Court's professed concern for children's welfare dovetailed with the desire to alleviate burdens on public resources. A similar impulse drove the Court's subsequent willingness to declare that short statutes of limitations for determining paternity were unconstitutional.[34]

More puzzling to many observers were the distinctions the justices drew between various federal statutes that treated legitimate and illegitimate children differently for purposes of awarding social insurance benefits. Reforms under President Lyndon Johnson had begun to mitigate a regime that used discriminatory state laws to justify excluding "illegitimate" children from federal benefits.[35] Still, several significant discriminations persisted, such as one that put legitimate children ahead of illegitimate children in gaining survivors' benefits after a wage-earning parent's death. Constitutional challenges ensued in the early 1970s.

A Maryland case illustrated the injustice: James T. Hall died in 1969, having earned for his survivors a total family payment of almost $300 per month. Just ten months earlier, James had married Bernice, who had four children from prior relationships. Though James and Bernice lived together as husband and wife for only a few weeks before separating for the rest of his life, her children (his stepchildren) shared in the Social Security benefits. By contrast, Barbara Griffin, James's nine-year-old biological daughter whom he was legally obligated to support—and did support—until his death, received no benefits at all. James's stepchildren's entitlement exhausted the family limit.[36] In a 1972 ruling, a three-judge federal district court declared the provision unconstitutional, because it discriminated on the basis of birth status.[37] The Supreme Court apparently agreed, affirming the lower court without issuing its own opinion.

Ramon Jimenez, too, won a favorable ruling on his constitutional claims. Jimenez had lived in Chicago with Elizabeth Hernandez and their three children. Hernandez left the family in 1968, leaving Jimenez caring for five-year-old Magdalena, three-year-old Alicia, and Eugenio, an infant. Disabled since 1963, Jimenez had previously claimed Social Security benefits for his legal wife, Filomena, and their five children, all of whom lived in Puerto Rico. But when he applied for benefits for his three nonmarital children, only Magdalena was eligible, because only she was born before the onset of her father's disability. The Social Security Administration defended its denial of benefits to Alicia and Eugenio on the grounds that the exclusion prevented "spurious claims" by "unscrupulous" fathers claiming paternity to collect "additional cash." The Supreme Court held that ensuring support for children who in fact were dependent on a parent remained a legitimate government goal, but any legal distinction among children had to be rationally related to that objective.[38]

By 1975, the remaining discriminatory Social Security laws also seemed unlikely to withstand constitutional scrutiny.[39] One required illegitimate children whose paternity had not been formally established to prove they depended on their father for financial support in order to receive benefits. Legitimate children received benefits automatically. Critics noted that this exclusion effectively targeted the poorest and most vulnerable children. As a welfare rights advocate and law professor wrote in 1969, "It hardly seems rational to deny benefits only to that group of deserted illegitimate children who have been unfortunate enough not to have some public authority or adult pursue his father and obtain a judicial degree or written acknowledgement of paternity."[40] Further, he pointed out, the excluded children were "most likely to be receiving" AFDC, so that the "denial of Social Security benefits submits them to the indignity of the public assistance system and . . . shifts approximately half the cost of their support from the federal government to the states."[41]

Litigation challenging this requirement foregrounded poignant examples of its impact. The parents of Gregory Norton Jr. were unmarried high school students, aged fourteen and sixteen, when he was born in 1964. They lived separately with their respective parents, and his maternal grandmother cared for Gregory Jr. "Being so young, and unemployed," Gregory Norton Sr. could not afford to contribute more than a few dollars and some clothing for the baby. He joined the military when his son was a year old, and was killed in Vietnam fifteen months later at age nineteen. Though Gregory Sr. had begun gathering the documents necessary for his son to receive a dependent child's military allotment, he "failed . . . to complete the required procedures before he was killed."[42] Gregory Jr.'s grandmother filed an application for Social Security survivors' benefits on her grandson's behalf in 1969, to no avail: Gregory Jr. could not prove, as required, that he was dependent upon his father for financial support.[43]

Belmira Lucas had lived in Providence with Robert Cuffee for almost twenty years, and they had two children together, Darin and Ruby. Unable to divorce her legal spouse because of his severe disabilities, Lucas knew she was not "free to marry" and so could not prove that her relationship with Cuffee was a common-law marriage under Rhode Island law, though he had given her a ring symbolizing marriage four years after they began living together.[44] Robert supported Darin and Ruby during the several years they lived together, and they called him "Daddy." But when Belmira's legal husband, Raymond, died in 1965, Belmira did not marry Robert—perhaps out of embarrassment at having lived so long out of wedlock, as she told the court, or perhaps because of Robert's drinking and violent behavior, which led their relationship to dissolve shortly thereafter. Robert left to live with his mother in 1966, visited the children two or three times per week, and occasionally gave them money. Meanwhile, Belmira provided most of her family's support, working for the local electric company. When Robert died in 1968, Darin and Ruby were ineligible for Social Security survivors' benefits because they could not prove their dependency upon Robert at the time of his death. Belmira and her children lost out, in other words, because she—not Robert—had shouldered primary responsibility for breadwinning as well as caregiving in the eighteen months prior to his death.[45]

Lower courts ruled this discrimination unconstitutional, but the Supreme Court upheld it, citing "administrative convenience."[46] Justice John Paul Stevens wrote in dissent that the law was "the product of a tradition of thinking of illegitimates as less deserving persons than legitimates."[47] The majority's decision seemed to Stevens and many observers like an abrupt departure from established precedents.[48] But the Court's ruling also reflected a persistent vision tying dependence to marriage, allowing

Congress (constitutionally) to presume that marriage produced dependent spousal and parent-child relationships.[49]

Sometimes this presumption of dependence worked against married couples: in 1976, the Court unanimously held that Congress could withhold disability benefits from an otherwise eligible individual who married a nondisabled person, on the assumption that a married person could and should depend upon his or her spouse for support.[50] But more often, the equation of marriage with dependency worked to exclude unmarried or divorced individuals and their families from benefits.[51] Earlier cases had established that Congress could not deny benefits to all illegitimate *children*. But *Lucas* confirmed that the Congress *could* require proof of actual dependency as a prerequisite for children's eligibility for benefits. And the Congress remained free to assume unmarried *adults'* lack of dependency and deny them benefits.

Poverty lawyer Herbert Semmel had long criticized illegitimacy-based discrimination in the Social Security Act and found in Margaret Gonzales's experience a perfect illustration of another discrimination: unmarried mothers' exclusion from mothers' Social Security benefits. Gonzales lived with Norman W. Boles in Georgetown, Texas, from 1963 to 1966 without marrying him and gave birth to Norman J. Boles in 1964. In 1967, Norman Sr. left for Tennessee, where he married another woman and had two more sons with her. When Norman Sr. died in 1971, all three of the Boles children received children's insurance benefits. But only Nancy Boles, Norman's legal widow, was eligible for mothers' benefits under the Social Security Act. Gonzales and her son filed a class action lawsuit in 1974 challenging the exclusion, with the help of Texas legal aid attorneys and the Center for Law and Social Policy (CLASP).[52]

When the *Boles* litigation began, only mothers (meaning mothers of "legitimate" children) could receive "mothers' insurance" benefits under the Social Security Act when a wage-earning father died. The following year, the Supreme Court ruled that excluding widowed fathers from these benefits violated equal protection: widowed fathers as well as mothers ought to gain benefits to support a child deprived of one parent. In *Weinberger v. Wiesenfeld*, ACLU attorney and law professor Ruth Bader Ginsburg persuaded even the inveterate sex-equality skeptic Justice William Rehnquist that children should not be deprived of the care of a living parent simply because that parent was a father rather than a mother. The Court majority also accepted her argument that denying insurance benefits to fathers who cared for their children after a mother's death devalued both the mother's wage *and* the father's caregiving labor.

Now the *Boles* plaintiffs had their argument on a silver platter. Litigants and judges alike understood the outcome of *Boles* to depend upon whether mothers or children were the primary intended beneficiaries of "mothers' insurance" benefits. Federal district court judge Jack Roberts agreed with the plaintiffs that "Mother's Benefits are not . . . to support the mother but rather stem from the statutory purpose to assist the children." He condemned the provision as "the classic case of visiting the sins of the parents on the child."[53] The government, however, prevailed in the Supreme Court by arguing that Congress had merely used marriage as a proxy for the *mother's* dependence on the father for support. The justices thought it perfectly reasonable to assume that unmarried mothers were "significantly less likely to have been dependent on the wage-earner."[54] Once again, the equation of marriage with dependency—and nonmarriage with mothers' and children economic independence from their father underwrote marital families' privilege at the expense of nonmarital parents and their children.

WORK AND (CHILDREN'S) WELFARE

A similar shift from morality-based to functional justifications for discrimination is visible in litigation challenging the exclusion from public employment of women who became pregnant or bore children outside marriage. In the late 1960s and early 1970s, employers often cited the immorality of nonmarital sex as grounds for excluding unmarried women from occupations such as teaching when they became pregnant. In a few short years, however, emerging legal norms of nondiscrimination and sexual privacy impelled a justificatory shift, elevating functional justifications above moralistic rationales for exclusion.

School districts had often defended their exclusion of unmarried mothers from employment on moralistic grounds. Like homosexuality, nonmarital pregnancy and childbearing was per se evidence of moral unfitness to teach the next generation of young people. Officials expressed concern that impressionable children who viewed teachers as role models would infer that illicit sexual relationships were to be condoned or even celebrated, rather than censured. In school districts that had resisted racial desegregation and sustained white flight to private "segregation academies," officials defended restrictions on unmarried parents' employment as essential to retaining (white) taxpayer support for the public schools. The perception that public schools were sanctioning sexual immorality, they warned, threatened to deepen white parents' suspicions that desegregation would lead, inevitably, to moral decay.

Against these charges of immorality, plaintiffs in *Andrews v. Drew Municipal Separate School District* advanced an alternative vision of responsible sexual citizenship that valorized single mothers' efforts to seek education and employment in order to care for and support themselves and their children. The mothers excluded from jobs as teachers and teachers' aides in Drew, Mississippi, schools could have depended upon stingy and stigmatized welfare benefits from the state; instead, they sought to become self-sufficient taxpaying citizens. Women such as Katie Mae Andrews had graduated from college against all odds; they were upstanding, churchgoing pillars of the community—positive, not negative, role models for the children they sought to teach. Punishing single mothers for choosing to bear and raise their nonmarital children encouraged either abortion or dependence on public assistance. Andrews's lawyers and supportive amici curiae argued that principles of sexual and racial equality, as well as reproductive freedom, should preclude the exclusion of unmarried mothers from employment as schoolteachers.

In his 1973 decision holding the Drew school district's policy unconstitutional, Judge William Keady did not address many of the plaintiffs' expansive constitutional arguments.[55] Nevertheless, he resisted the view that bearing a nonmarital child was per se evidence of immorality, noting the "multitudinous circumstances under which illegitimate childbirth may occur" with "little, if any, bearing, on the parent's present moral worth."[56] Moreover, Keady condemned the sexual double standard: "[A] male who sires an illegitimate child is equally the partner to the sexual act and is equally the parent of the child, even though the mother may be 'stuck with the result,'" as the rule's enforcer, Superintendent George F. Petty, himself put it.[57]

The aspiring schoolteachers' successful constitutional challenge meant that they could provide for themselves and their children without relying on the state. Unmarried mothers who sought public assistance through AFDC fared less well; a victory for them would have imposed a greater burden on the public fisc. As state and federal governments limited welfare benefits and accelerated child support enforcement efforts in the late 1960s and 1970s, states enacted requirements that unmarried mothers seeking aid divulge the name of their children's fathers or face penalties. Connecticut enacted one of the more draconian laws, prescribing fines and imprisonment for up to one year for mothers who refused to identify fathers in court. Plaintiffs, many of them impoverished women of color, challenged the Connecticut law in 1973 with the help of the Connecticut Civil Liberties Union as a violation of their rights to privacy and equal protection.

Connecticut officials defended the mandatory paternity disclosure law in terms by now familiar to courts considering family status–based classifications. Compelling mothers to name their sexual partners, the state insisted, vindicated children's interest in developing relationships with their fathers. "Why," the state attorney general demanded, "should a mother be permitted, by her inaction, to cast her child into the eternal caverns of illegitimacy?"[58] Federal district court judge M. Joseph Blumenfeld lamented the "anguish suffered by illegitimate children denied the satisfaction of knowing their paternity," and declared the interests of "recalcitrant mothers" diametrically opposed to those of their "innocent children."[59]

Mothers offered a range of reasons for refusing to disclose paternity, including well-founded fears of physical violence from their children's fathers; concerns about ruining fragile relationships children had established with their biological fathers or with new father figures; and worries about censure from religious communities.[60] Child psychiatrist Albert Solnit, coauthor of classic family law texts such as *Beyond the Best Interests of the Child*, testified that the punishment of incarcerating a mother would be "catastrophic" for her child, and argued that mothers, primary caregivers, should be considered champions, not enemies, of their children's well-being.[61] Plaintiffs also contended that the state's real interest in paternity disclosure was not, in fact, the welfare of blameless nonmarital children, but rather protection of the public fisc—at best. At worst, the law was an attempt to expose and humiliate mothers who gave birth to children outside marriage, since the fathers of children whose mothers sought public assistance could rarely fulfill their child support obligations and save public expenditure. The Connecticut law was ultimately superseded by federal regulation. The Supreme Court thus never passed judgment on the constitutionality of mandatory paternity disclosure laws, which enjoyed a resurgence in the 1996 Personal Responsibility and Work Opportunity Act.[62]

CONCLUSION

Various strands of jurisprudence operated in distinctive ways to shape the kinds of arguments that lost and retained the power to persuade courts as moralistic grounds for discriminating against nonmarital families lost currency. Everyone understood the midcentury moral panic about nonmarital childbirth as inextricably linked to race. Most of the plaintiffs whose birth status discrimination cases reached the Supreme Court in the 1960s and 1970s were African Americans or other individuals and families of color. But although some lower court judges engaged plaintiffs' race discrimination arguments, none of the birth status or welfare rights decisions of the late 1960s mentioned race. By the early 1970s, political shifts on and off the Court undermined race discrimination arguments.[63] Some plaintiffs continued to argue along those lines; others relied on birth status and sex discrimination only. Even where race seemed utterly central to the protagonists on the ground—as in Katie Mae Andrews's or Sylvester Smith's cases—the Court avoided ruling on these grounds, or even recognizing the racially charged context.

The contemporaneous burgeoning of sex-equality law tended primarily to undermine discrimination against unmarried mothers where the government enforced a sexual double standard: punishing women for nonmarital childbirth but allowing men to escape scot-free. Sexual privacy jurisprudence called into question—but did not eradicate—the state's ability to infringe upon sexual freedom and to intrude into individual reproductive decision-making.

As older rationales lost potency, what remained were ostensibly neutral justifications that served the same goal: protecting public coffers. The state could enact laws that pushed parents who did not marry to find other means of privatizing their families' support. If the state provided a pathway to "legitimacy," parents could incur penalties for failing to take it. Illegitimate children should not suffer for their parents' "sins," but the state could use marriage as a proxy for dependency. It remained constitutional for the state to prioritize the needs of marital families or to withhold benefits from family members who had no formal legal status. For the most part, employers could no longer discriminate against unmarried mothers engaged in or seeking gainful employment, but single parents who called upon the state for financial assistance faced resistance that defied constitutional challenge.

As antidiscrimination and sexual privacy challenges pushed states to modernize the regulation of birth status, courts often used antidiscrimination law selectively, to mitigate birth status discrimination mostly where that discrimination did not serve a clear fiscal objective. Some remaining illegitimacy penalties served fiscal goals and promoted marriage; others did not. Still others placed burdens on state coffers that might be borne by the federal government.

When states could no longer rely upon traditional morality, overt white supremacist rationales, sexual double standards, or prejudice against nonmarital children, the justifications left standing laid bare a dilemma: full equality for nonmarital families posed a profound threat to a legal order that relied on marriage to privatize the costs of dependency and to channel government benefits to a particular sort of nuclear family. To the extent that nonmarital families could act as functional equivalents of their marital counterparts, states were willing to dispense with the formalities of marriage. But to question the status of families—rather than individual citizens, or caregiver/dependent dyads—as a basic economic unit of government would require an expansion of state capacity and a redistribution of resources that seemed less likely than ever by the late twentieth century.

NOTES

1. On the legal privileging of marriage in the twentieth-century United States, see Margot Canaday, "Heterosexuality as a Legal Regime," *Cambridge History of Law in America*, ed. Michael Grossberg and Christopher Tomlins (Cambridge: Cambridge University Press, 2008); Nancy F. Cott, *Public Vows: A History of Marriage and the Nation* (Cambridge, MA: Harvard University Press, 2000); and Alice Kessler-Harris, *In Pursuit of Equity: Women, Men, and the Quest for Economic Citizenship in Twentieth-Century America* (Oxford: Oxford University Press, 2001).

2. On the modernization of legal status regimes and the phenomenon of "preservation through transformation," see Reva B. Siegel, "Why Equal Protection No Longer Protects: The Evolving Forms of Status-Enforcing State Action," *Stanford Law Review* 49 (1997): 1111–48.

3. See, for example, Marisa Chappell, *The War on Welfare: Poverty and Politics in Modern America* (Philadelphia: University of Pennsylvania Press, 2010); Elizabeth Hinton, *From the War on Poverty to the War on Crime: The Making of Mass Incarceration in America* (Cambridge, MA: Harvard University Press, 2017); Julilly Kohler-Hausmann, *Getting Tough: Welfare and Imprisonment in 1970s America* (Princeton, NJ: Princeton University Press, 2017); and Jennifer Mittelstadt, *From Welfare to Workfare: The Unintended Consequences of Liberal Reform* (Chapel Hill: University of North Carolina Press, 2005).

4. For a catalogue of illegitimacy penalties circa 1970, see Harry D. Krause, *Illegitimacy: Law and Social Policy* (Indianapolis: Bobbs Merrill, 1971). On the use of illegitimacy penalties to resist racial desegregation, see Anders Walker, *The Ghost of Jim Crow: How Southern Moderates Used* Brown v. Board of Education *to Stall Civil Rights* (New York: Oxford University Press, 2009).

5. Serena Mayeri, "Marital Supremacy and the Constitution of the Nonmarital Family," *California Law Review* 103 (2015): 1291.

6. Brief for the Louisiana Attorney General, *Levy v. Louisiana*, 391 U.S. 68 (1968)

7. Brief of Respondents, *Glona v. American Guar. & Liab. Ins. Co.*, 391 U.S. 73 (1968), 13.

8. Brief of Respondents, *Glona*, 23.

9. Brief of Respondents, *Glona*, 23.

10. John C. Gray Jr. and David Rudovsky, "The Court Acknowledges the Illegitimate: *Levy v. Louisiana* and *Glona v. American Guarantee & Liability Insurance Company*," *University of Pennsylvania Law Review* 118 (1969): 15–18; and Norman Dorsen and David Rudovsky, Comment, "Equality for the Illegitimate?," *Welfare Law Bulletin*, May 1967, at 15. Whether or not plaintiffs challenged the state's privileging of marriage in court may also have affected how states justified their discriminatory laws.

11. As then law student, later distinguished feminist legal scholar Sylvia Law wrote: "We have not questioned the value of family (legitimate system). We have shown that the discrimination here is *wholly ineffectual* in deterring illegitimacy or securing legitimate families." Sylvia Law, Notes on Reply Brief to Louisiana Attorney General, February 22, 1968, Norman Dorsen Papers, Bobst Library, New York University, Box 32, Folder 15.

12. Mayeri, "Marital Supremacy," 1290.

13. I discuss *King v. Smith* in similar terms in Mayeri, "Marital Supremacy," and Mayeri, "Intersectionality and the Constitution of Family Status," *Constitutional Commentary* (2017). For more on *King v. Smith*, see Rickie Solinger, "The First Welfare Case: Money, Sex, Marriage, and White Supremacy in Selma, 1966, A Reproductive Justice Analysis," *Journal of Women's History* 2, no. 3 (Fall 2010): 13–38; Elizabeth Pleck, *Not Just Roommates: Cohabitation After the Sexual Revolution* (Chicago: University of Chicago Press, 2012); Karen M. Tani, "Administrative Equal Protection: Federalism, the Fourteenth Amendment, and the Rights of the Poor," *Cornell Law Review* 100 (2015): 825–99; and Alison Lefkovitz, *Strange Bedfellows: Marriage in the Age of Women's Liberation* (Philadelphia: University of Pennsylvania Press, 2018), chapter 4.

14. "Suitable home" laws denied public assistance to families in which mothers were found to have engaged in nonmarital sexual relations or given birth to children outside marriage.

15. Brief for Appellants, *King v. Smith*.

16. Brief for Appellants, *King v. Smith*, 50.

17. Brief of Attorney General of Louisiana as Amicus Curiae, *Labine v. Vincent*, 3.

18. See *Labine v. Vincent*, 401 U.S. 532 (1971).

19. Powell continued: "Courts are powerless to prevent the social opprobrium suffered by these hapless children, but the Equal Protection Clause does permit us to strike down discriminatory laws relating to status of birth where . . . the classification is justified by no legitimate state interest. . . ." *Weber v. Aetna Casualty*, 406 U.S. 164, 175–76 (1972).

20. On welfare rights' advocates "Southern Strategy," see Martha Davis, *Brutal Need: Lawyers and the Welfare Rights Movement, 1960–1973* (New Haven, CT: Yale University Press, 1993).

21. Krause, *Illegitimacy*. The process of enacting schemes for the "legitimation" of children born outside marriage occurred over several decades.

22. Kristin Collins, "Bureaucracy as the Border: Administrative Law and the Citizen Family," *Duke Law Journal* 66 (2017): 1738–39; Ernst Freund, US Department of Labor, Children's Bureau, *Illegitimacy Laws of the United States and Certain Foreign Countries* (1919), 22–23.

23. *Stanley v. Illinois*, 405 U.S. 645 (1972). For more on *Stanley*, see Serena Mayeri, "Foundling Fathers: (Non)Marriage and Parental Rights in the Age of Equality," *Yale Law Journal* 125 (2016): 2309–24.

24. Justice Powell wrote for a closely divided Court that while "no one disputes the appropriateness of Illinois' concern with the family unit, perhaps the most fundamental social institution of our society," the justices had firmly "rejected the argument that a State may attempt to influence the actions of men and women

by imposing sanctions on the children born of their illegitimate relationships." *Trimble v. Gordon*, 430 U.S. 762, 769 (1977).

25. *Trimble v. Gordon*, 430 U.S. at 770.

26. *Trimble v. Gordon*, 430 U.S. at 762.

27. *Lalli v. Lalli*, 439 U.S. 259 (1978).

28. The Court did not "rest its decision" on the fact that Quilloin did not legitimate Darrell; Marshall noted that Quilloin may not have been aware of the legitimation procedure until after Darrell's prospective stepfather petitioned for adoption. For more, see Mayeri, "Foundling Fathers," 2341–42.

29. Order, *Parham v. Hughes*, Findings of Fact, in Joint Appendix at 6, *Parham v. Hughes*, 447 U.S. 347 (1979).

30. *Parham v. Hughes*, 441 U.S. 347, 353 (1979).

31. *Parham v. Hughes*, 441 U.S. 347, 353 (1979).

32. I described these cases similarly in Mayeri, "Intersectionality and the Constitution of Family Status," 408.

33. *Gomez v. Perez*, 409 U.S. 535 (1973); *Linda R.S. v. Richard D.*, 410 U.S. 614 (1973). For more on these cases, see Mayeri, "Marital Supremacy," 1313–17.

34. See *Mills v. Habluetzel*, 456 U.S. 91 (1982), and subsequent cases.

35. See Krause, *Illegitimacy*, 39–40. Prior to 1965, nonmarital children's eligibility for Social Security benefits depended primarily upon whether the child would have the right to inherit from her biological father (if he did not leave a will) under the law of the state in which she lived. Because state laws often excluded nonmarital children from paternal inheritance, and many mothers had insufficient earnings at the time of the father's death or disability to qualify for benefits themselves, most illegitimate children remained ineligible for Social Security funds to which their legitimate counterparts were entitled. The 1965 amendments to the Act expanded eligibility by providing that the children of workers who acknowledged their paternity in writing, had paternity recognized by a court through a support order or otherwise, or lived with their nonmarital children and contributed financially were eligible for some survivors' and disability benefits.

36. See *Griffin v. Richardson*, 346 F. Supp. 1226, 1228–29 (D. Md. 1972).

37. *Griffin v. Richardson*, 346 F. Supp. 1226, 1228–29 (D. Md. 1972).

38. *Jimenez v. Weinberger*, 417 U.S. 628 (1974).

39. The Supreme Court's record on illegitimacy was mostly pro-plaintiff at mid-decade. Further, the Court had recently decided key sex discrimination cases involving the allocation of government benefits to marital families. See *Frontiero v. Richardson* 411 U.S. 677 (1973); *Weinberger v. Wiesenfeld* 420 U.S. 636 (1975).

40. Herbert Semmel, "Social Security Benefits for Illegitimate Children after *Levy v. Louisiana*," *Buffalo Law Review* 19 (1969): 297.

41. Semmel, "Social Security Benefits," 296.

42. *Norton v. Mathews*, 427 U.S. 524, 525–26 (1976).

43. *Norton v. Mathews*, 427 U.S. at 525–26.

44. Rhode Island was one of only a handful of states that still recognized common-law marriage in 1975.

45. The facts of *Mathews v. Lucas* are discussed using similar language in Mayeri, "Marital Supremacy," 1324–35.

46. *Mathews v. Lucas*, 427 U.S. 495 (1976). Unlike in past cases, the majority agreed with the government about the provision's purpose—"to replace the support lost by a child when his father . . . dies"—not generally to provide for needy children after a parent's death. Powell noted the purpose in the margins of Blackmun's draft: *Mathews v. Lucas*. Supreme Court Case Files Collection, Box 33, Powell Papers, Lewis F. Powell Jr. Archives, Washington & Lee University School of Law, Virginia.

47. *Lucas*, 427 U.S. at 523 (Stevens, J., dissenting).

48. *Lucas* arguably did depart from decisions more closely scrutinizing discrimination based on birth status. Internal documents suggest that at least some of the justices thought that an intervening decision in *Weinberger v. Salfi* had "cut back" on Jimenez. *Mathews v. Lucas*, Supreme Court Case Files Collection, Box 33, Powell Papers.

49. Because the Court's decision in *Trimble v. Gordon* forced states to revise their discriminatory intestacy laws that provided the basis for many federal family law definitions, *Mathews v. Lucas* had less impact than it otherwise would have.

50. *Califano v. Jobst*, 434 U.S. 47 (1977).

51. Also in 1976, the justices upheld the exclusion of divorced women under age sixty-two from Social Security benefits available to married women, finding it reasonable for Congress to assume that a former spouse was less likely to be dependent than was a presently married individual. *Mathews v. deCastro*, 429 U.S. 181 (1976).

52. The facts of *Califano v. Boles* are similarly described in Mayeri, "Marital Supremacy," 1335–36.

53. *Boles v. Califano*, 464 F. Supp. 408, 411–13 (W.D. Texas 1974). The reference to "mothers' benefits" reflects that the Court had not yet extended these benefits to fathers in *Wiesenfeld*, which was decided the following year.

54. Brief for Appellant at 10–11, *Califano v. Boles*, 443 U.S. 282 (1979) (No. 78-808); *Califano v. Boles*, 443 U.S. 282 (1979). For more on the Court's internal deliberations in *Boles*, see Mayeri, "Marital Supremacy," 1337–39.

55. For more on the Andrews case, see Serena Mayeri, *Reasoning from Race: Feminism, Law, and the Civil Rights Revolution* (Cambridge, MA: Harvard University Press, 2011), chapter 5; Mayeri, "Marital Supremacy," 1316–20.

56. *Andrews v. Drew Mun. Separate Sch. Dist.*, 371 F. Supp. 27, 33 (N.D. Miss. 1973).

57. *Andrews*, 371 F. Supp. at 37.

58. Brief of the Appellee at 10, *Roe v. Norton*, 422 U.S. 391 (1975) (No. 73-6033).

59. *Doe v. Norton*, 365 F. Supp. 65, 72, 79 n.23 (D. Conn. 1973). I use similar language to describe the state's position in Mayeri, "Marital Supremacy," 1320.

60. I describe mothers' arguments in greater detail in "Race, Sexual Citizenship, and the Constitution of Nonmarital Motherhood," in *Heterosexual Histories*, ed. Rebecca L. Davis and Michelle Mitchell (New York: NYU Press, 2021).

61. Mayeri, "Marital Supremacy," 1321.

62. See Anna Maria Smith, *Welfare Reform and Sexual Regulation* (Cambridge: Cambridge University Press, 2007).

63. See Mayeri, "Intersectionality and the Constitution of Family Status"; and Mayeri, *Reasoning from Race*, chapters 3–5.

12

What Happened to the Functional Family?

Defining and Defending Alternative Households
Before and Beyond Same-Sex Marriage

STEPHEN VIDER

In 1985 Rose Ann Baer went to court against the Town of Brookhaven, Long Island, after she was charged with violating a local zoning ordinance restricting the number of unrelated people who could live together in a single-family residential zone. At the time, Baer was living in a single-family house with her sons and four women with psychiatric disabilities. The town ordinance was initially upheld, but the New York State Court of Appeals struck it down in 1989, observing that the town could not restrict the number of people in a "functionally equivalent family" simply because they were unrelated by blood, marriage, or adoption. The court did not define "functionally equivalent family" in detail, but Baer's lawyers elaborated in a letter to the *New York Times* that important distinctions included eating together and sharing cooking responsibilities and household chores. They also pointed to more subjective measures, including the women's emotional, social, and financial interdependence.[1]

The *Baer* case, and the framework of the "functionally equivalent family," was cited as precedent in the ACLU's argument for another New York appellate case a month later: *Braschi v. Stahl Associates*. Miguel Braschi had lived for over a decade with his partner, Leslie Blanchard, but their landlord threatened to evict Braschi from their rent-controlled apartment after Blanchard died from medical complications related to AIDS. The appellate court ruled in Braschi's favor—the first time a state court recognized a gay couple as a family, albeit a "functional" one.[2]

The *Braschi* case has been widely recognized as a crucial turning point in the legal recognition of gay and lesbian relationships, on the road toward domestic partnerships and same-sex marriage.[3] Braschi's lawyers, however, took a radically different approach than advocates for same-sex marriage would in the decades to come. The case was argued by William Rubenstein, a young gay lawyer who had recently been hired by the ACLU's Lesbian and Gay Rights and AIDS Projects. Rubenstein's oral argument before the court, however, made little explicit reference to Braschi and Blanchard as a gay couple, or, at Braschi's request, to the cause of Blanchard's illness and death. Rubenstein also made no specific appeal to the equality or dignity of same-sex relationships—the kinds of arguments that would become central in later same-sex marriage cases.[4] Rather, Rubenstein developed a universalist argument based on the framing of the *Baer* case: Braschi and Blanchard should be treated as a family because they behaved like a family.

Yet while *Baer* and a related line of zoning cases were critical in the *Braschi* argument and decision, the *Baer* case itself has received virtually no extended historical discussion. Moreover, the significance and ongoing potential of the legal frame of the "functionally equivalent family," or simply the "functional family," that *Baer* highlighted and *Braschi* drew upon has largely been forgotten by LGBT historians and advocates. This essay revisits *Baer v. Town of Brookhaven* in order to reconsider the social and legal history of "nontraditional" families since the 1970s and how this history connects with and diverges from better-known battles around same-sex marriage.

Centering *Baer* and the framework of functional family in this history enables two key interventions. First, rereading the influence of the *Baer* case on *Braschi* provides a broader frame for understanding the history and significance of same-sex relationship recognition, not solely through arguments for romantic equivalency (i.e., "love is love") but for family self-determination. Scholars including Katherine Franke and Nancy Polikoff have argued that the push for state and federal recognition of same-sex marriage since the early 1990s represented a new heteronormative direction in gay and lesbian advocacy—upholding the conventional legal divide between married and unmarried people. This move, in their reading, entailed a turn away from feminist and queer critiques of marriage, as well as newer and more open forms of relationship recognition they championed, such as domestic partnership.[5] Douglas NeJaime has recently critiqued these positions, arguing that domestic partnerships effectively idealized the romantic couple in precisely the ways advocacy for same-sex marriage would.[6] The functional family represents an alternative legal lineage for thinking about the past and future of family, sexual relationships, and romantic expression.

Second, a turn to the functional family in zoning and rent law draws our attention to the ways local laws and courts have frequently operated to enact, enforce, and encourage normative forms of sexual relation and family formation. Local and state laws around sodomy, gender "masquerade," "lewd vagrancy," and disorderly conduct have typically been treated as a crucial context for uncovering and understanding the history of marginalized sexual and gender expression.[7] Scholars have only begun, however, to analyze more explicitly how local laws have shaped sexual practices and identities—how local governments, police departments, courts, and community watch groups consolidated power and reshaped social norms through the regulation of sexuality, gender, and family.[8]

Housing and land-use laws have been crucial arenas of state intervention and power since the early twentieth century. Legal and urban history scholars have traced how housing law and lending practices have supported urban and suburban racial segregation and class stratification since the 1930s—typically with a focus on federal policy and programs, although some scholars have begun to address local practices as well.[9] Scholars of sexuality and LGBT history, by comparison, have been slow to trace the impact of housing law. Clayton Howard and Ian Baldwin are among the few who have, demonstrating how federal housing policies following World War II privileged the "traditional" family—the nuclear, reproductive, male-breadwinner, female-homemaker household—and how those policies began to change.[10] When scholars of sexuality have looked at zoning, meanwhile, it has been exclusively in the realm of business. Lauren Berlant and Michael Warner's essay "Sex in Public," for example, points to a zoning law passed, nearly unanimously, by the New York City Council in 1995, that created dramatic new restrictions on the location and size of adult businesses in the name of "family values."[11] This relative inattention to housing reflects an ongoing tendency in histories of LGBT life and sexuality to prioritize public space and public expressions of sexuality and gender over private ones.[12]

Disputes around housing and land-use law, however, can provide a powerful lens on the history of sexuality and family—focusing as much on the ideals proliferated in the law as the ways intimacy is organized in everyday life. Examining housing disputes also provides a critical lens on the unexpected ways oppression based on race, class, sexuality, disability, and family form have intersected. In her 1997 essay "Punks, Bulldaggers, and Welfare Queens," Cathy Cohen called on queer activists and scholars to resist an identitarian heterosexual/queer divide and work to build "a new political identity . . . inclusive of all those who stand on the outside of the dominant constructed norm of state-sanctioned white middle- and upper-class heterosexuality."[13] Looking at the *Baer* and *Braschi* cases together uncovers a critical juncture in LGBT legal history when the links between lesbian and gay households and a broader coalition of alternative households were made visible. This legal lineage of functional families exposes how local housing laws have been wielded as both a shield and a sword to defend and enforce a narrow model of heteronormative domestic citizenship—empowering communities, municipalities, and property owners to selectively and unpredictably marginalize those who failed to meet white, middle-class family ideals.[14]

ZONING TRADITION

The case against Rose Ann Baer and the four women who lived with her in Lake Ronkonkoma in Suffolk County on Long Island, New York, began in 1984 but had its roots over a decade earlier. In the early 1970s, Baer's mother began renting out rooms in her home to other women, many of them recently released from state mental hospitals. Baer moved into the house with her four sons shortly after her mother died in 1977, and she continued to operate the house as a group home for women with mental illness or intellectual disabilities.[15] This unconventional setup reflected much larger shifts in care for people with mental illness or disabilities. In 1955, state mental hospitals in Suffolk County were home to 34,000 patients. That number dropped by roughly 25,000 by 1985—the result of decades of state and national policies aimed at closing mental institutions in favor of community mental health centers. Those patients discharged often had no family to support them, making group homes of the kind Baer ran a necessity.[16]

By October 1984, Baer had four women living with her and her sons in her Cape Cod–style home in Lake Ronkonkoma, a village of the larger Town of Brookhaven. Dorothy Belli, age fifty-two, had lived with Baer for two years; Doris Scheimler, age fifty-four, for five years; Jessie Esposito, age seventy, for three years; and Ilona Hudak, age seventy-one, for two months. Together they shared two bedrooms and a bathroom on the second floor, and each paid Baer between $260 and $350 a month. Baer did all the shopping, prepared group meals, and, in her own words, "took care" of the women. Belli, Scheimler, Esposito, and Hudak also provided support to one another and more largely developed a sense of home and belonging. As Baer's lawyers later argued, the four women who lived with Baer were "emotionally attached to one another and to Rose Ann Baer."[17] The shared household also provided a sense of stability and relative autonomy. Hudak, for example, explained that she had a history of psychiatric hospitalizations and found living with Baer a better option than any other: "I have been living in rooming houses for the past fifty years. This is one of the

FIGURE 12.1. Rose Ann Baer (right) with Jessie Esposito (center) and Sandy Meddaugh (left) in front of their home in Lake Ronkonkoma, NY, 1989. Photograph by Vic Delucia, used by permission of the *New York Times*/Redux Pictures.

best that I have ever lived in. I have my own bed and a sufficient amount of privacy for the first time."[18]

Yet while little had changed since Baer's mother first began taking in other residents in the 1970s, Baer was charged in November 1984 with violating a town zoning code defining "family" as either "one or more persons related by blood, adoption or marriage" or "a number of persons, but not exceeding four, living and cooking together as a single housekeeping unit though not related by blood, adoption or marriage." One solution Baer considered was to convert the second floor into an "accessory apartment"—a second "single family" unit—but that would have required turning one of the bedrooms into a kitchen and evicting two of the current residents. It also would have meant allowing an inspector to come in to ensure the apartment was being used as claimed.[19] A few months later, Baer's lawyer moved for a preliminary injunction, but in June 1985, the case moved forward and Baer was found guilty.

Zoning codes, like the one in Brookhaven, that determine how land can be used have their origins in the early twentieth century. In 1916, New York City became the first municipality in the United States to pass citywide zoning laws, determining how tall and wide buildings in various sections of the city could be constructed, and dividing the city into various types of zones: residential, commercial, unrestricted, and undetermined. The city's zoning regulation quickly influenced policy nationwide: in 1921, Secretary of Commerce, and later President, Herbert Hoover formed the Advisory Committee on Zoning, to encourage local land-use ordinances.[20]

Such zoning laws were, on the surface, race-neutral—policing the kinds of homes that could be built, not the kinds of people who could live there—but racial segregation was undoubtedly a goal. In the 1910s, many Southern cities passed "segregation ordinances," later termed "racial zoning," to define Black and white residential blocks, with the stated goal of preventing racial "conflict and ill-feeling," as well as a "too close commingling of the two races."[21] In 1917, the Supreme Court struck down such ordinances as police overreach, interfering with the property rights of both seller and buyer. Race-neutral zoning, on the other hand, was largely upheld. The first major test came in 1926: a real estate company sued the village of Euclid, Ohio, over new zoning regulations that restricted where two-family homes, apartment houses, and businesses could be built. The Supreme Court upheld the regulations, finding that zoning was a reasonable use of police power in the name of public welfare, health, or morals. By limiting where apartment houses and two-family homes could be built, zoning codes divided communities by class and effectively gave cover for ethnic and racial segregation, since immigrants and people of color were more likely to have lower incomes and live in multifamily dwellings.[22]

Most municipalities nevertheless left the definition of "family" ambiguous in zoning laws, leaving room for local and state courts to interpret the family functionally. That shifted in the 1960s and 1970s, as more and more cities and towns began to enact more restrictive definitions of family, allowing an unlimited number of people if related by blood, marriage, or adoption, but a limited number if not. The new codes were a direct response to rising numbers of "nontraditional" (that is, non-nuclear) families in the 1960s and 1970s, communes among the most visible.[23]

These more restrictive definitions of family were soon affirmed by the US Supreme Court, with the 1974 case of *Belle Terre v. Boraas*. A landlord challenged a zoning law of the village of Belle Terre, Long Island, which restricted residence to "single families"—either a group related by blood, marriage, or adoption, or an unrelated couple "living and cooking together as a single housekeeping unit." The Supreme Court upheld the ordinance, finding, in the words of Justice William Douglas, that "family values, youth values, and the blessings of quiet seclusion and clean air" were a worthwhile use of police power.[24] The ruling cleared the way for more restrictive zoning laws throughout the country.

At roughly the same time, the Supreme Court also issued a landmark ruling recognizing "extended families" as constituting a single household. In 1977, in the case of *Moore v. City of East Cleveland*, the court ruled in favor of Inez Moore, an African American woman living with two grandsons from different parents, in violation of a local zoning code that defined family narrowly to exclude grandchildren who were not siblings.[25] The law was aimed at restricting the neighborhood by class, not race: residents of the predominantly African American city of East Cleveland had sought to preserve their neighborhood's middle-class character, excluding non-nuclear families understood as "deviant."[26] The court, however, recognized extended families as an "equally venerable" tradition. In a concurring opinion, Justice Brennan went further to identify extended family households as a "a prominent pattern—virtually a means of survival—for large numbers of the poor and deprived minorities of our society."[27] In recognizing extended families, the court moved toward acknowledging the race and class bias implicit in many zoning codes, yet it still upheld the primacy of family relationships based on blood or law. The court bowed to racial and economic liberalism but left intact zoning's social and sexual conservatism.

The *Belle Terre* and *Moore* decisions also left unchallenged that zoning restrictions on family were selectively enforced—typically when neighbors found reason for complaint. Inez Moore, for example, had already been caring for her grandson John for six years when she was charged with a zoning violation, shortly after trying to register John for public school. The four women living with Baer, too, may not have been brought to the town's attention were it not for a more public incident: at a town hearing, several of Baer's neighbors lodged complaints against her for allowing unruly young men to stay at the house. One neighbor complained that at three in the morning, he saw as many as eighteen "motorcycles" outside—with young men revving up, doing "wheelies," and drag-racing on the street. Another member of the neighborhood watch complained that cars were triple parked in front of Baer's house, and that his home was robbed multiple times. Baer explained that the people causing the trouble were other kids from the neighborhood, and that she sometimes let her sons' friends stay over if they had been drinking, but that she did not rent to anyone but the four other women.[28] Baer seems not even to have known she was violating the zoning code until neighbors and the town objected. Ultimately, neighbors seem to have held Baer responsible for the actions of her sons' friends. Baer, a single mother, was an easy scapegoat, and the zoning law an easy means to pursue a complaint against her.

The *Baer* case is only one example of the many ways "single family" zoning codes have been used to selectively penalize those perceived to violate the nuclear family ideal. In the 1990s and 2000s, for example, cities in Illinois, Virginia, and Georgia introduced zoning restrictions limiting households to "immediate relatives" in order to prevent "overcrowding," resulting in hundreds of complaints by community members against other households—the majority of them Latinx immigrants.[29] Single-family zoning codes may be presented as race- and class-neutral attempts to protect neighborhood character, yet they have left vulnerable those groups less likely to conform to normative models of the bio/legal family—including people of color, immigrants, working-class people, unmarried people, and people with disabilities. Baer herself may have been white, but her household was placed at risk, first, because Baer was a single mother, and second, because the four women she cared for were socially and economically disadvantaged by psychiatric disability and illness.

The case might have ended with a guilty plea, but soon after the town hearing, Baer contacted the Nassau/Suffolk Law Services' Mental Health Law Project, a legal advocacy program founded in 1979 to provide free counsel to people with mental illness.[30] By the summer, Jane Reinhardt, a senior staff attorney at the Mental Health Law Project, officially took over the case, joined by a new law clerk, Robert Briglio, then a student at CUNY School of Law. For Reinhardt and Briglio, the zoning code was clearly discriminatory, as demonstrated by the code's history: up until 1974, the Town of Brookhaven zoning code defined family as a "functional" unit. What mattered was *how* a group related to one another, not the nature of their relationship. It was only in 1974—shortly after the *Belle Terre* decision—that the Town of Brookhaven voted to update their zoning laws to restrict single-family households either to those people "related by blood, adoption or marriage," or to households consisting of no more than four unrelated people.[31]

The immediate impetus for the change was anxiety about so-called "groupers." As early as 1969, the Town of Brookhaven considered amending their zoning laws specifically to prevent groups of young people from living communally in single-family zones. The initial target was college students from the State University at Stony Brook, as in *Belle Terre*, but by the mid-1970s, long-term residents also had their eye on young straight singles who shared summer rental homes in the villages of Fire Island, most of them under the jurisdiction of Brookhaven. Local residents and legislators may have had LGBT vacationers in mind, too. By the 1970s, two

Fire Island communities—Cherry Grove and its neighbor, the Pines—were well known as queer vacation spots.[32]

The change to Brookhaven's zoning law, however, was not without controversy: 150 people came for a ninety-minute public hearing in July 1974 to debate the new requirements. One proponent, a representative of a local civic association, explained that the new definition of family was an effort by proponents to "retain the identity of their neighborhood." Another supporter quoted at length from the decision in *Belle Terre*. But many other residents objected to the measure, for fear it would place unfair restrictions on elderly people who wished to rent out rooms in their home for extra income, families who wished to take in foster children, young students and professionals who could not afford other types of housing, and elderly people who wished to live together. One unidentified woman objected, "Ten years from now you'll be limiting the number of children a family could have."[33]

The history of the town's zoning law, Reinhardt and Briglio argued, demonstrated that there was nothing obviously "traditional" about the traditional family the law was presumed to uphold. Reinhardt and Briglio returned ironically to the original complaint that launched the case: after all, it was Baer's sons who were responsible for the late-night noise on their street, not the four women who resided upstairs. They concluded, "One might reasonably ask whether banning appellant Baer's naturally related teenage children from their home would not better accomplish the purpose which respondents intend by their prosecution of appellant Baer."[34] In other words, "traditional" family relationships were no more or less likely to disrupt a neighborhood's "quiet seclusion" than nontraditional functional family relationships. In the end, Reinhardt and Briglio argued, Brookhaven's zoning law was a violation of due process, as it treated "traditional families" and "functionally equivalent families" differently.

Reinhardt and Briglio were not alone in making this case. By the mid-1980s, the New York Court of Appeals had heard a line of "functional" challenges to restrictive blood-, marriage-, or adoption-based zoning codes. In 1974 and again in 1978, it ruled in favor of a pair of group homes established for foster children.[35] Those cases, in turn, became the basis for a 1985 decision in the case of *McMinn v. Town of Oyster Bay*: the Court of Appeals struck down a town zoning law that restricted any two unrelated or unmarried people from living together, unless they were over the age of sixty-two, finding the law violated the due process clause of the state constitution.[36]

That line of argument still placed the burden on Reinhardt and Briglio to prove that the five women in Baer's household constituted the "functional and factual equivalent of a family"—a point which the town's lawyers disputed, on the basis that Baer collected rent. But Reinhardt countered that foster care is typically funded by the state, and this did not undo the family function of a group home. What mattered, once more, was that the women were emotionally attached to one another, regarded their home as permanent, shared household responsibilities, and ate meals together. As Reinhardt and Briglio put it, "The Baer household . . . reflects traditional character in its internal dynamics."[37]

The court's eventual decision was brief but noted widely in the media for its potential significance. In 1989, the court found that the Brookhaven zoning law violated the state constitution. They applied their judgment in *McMinn* that restrictions on the numbers of unrelated people in a single-family home violated due process when the residents functioned as a family. The case was quickly heralded in newspapers as a major hit to zoning. As a counsel to the New York State Conference of Mayors told the *New York Times*, "We are going to advise all our towns that they redo their zoning laws. . . . This decision is going to make a difference. It will allow more students to live together, more group homes and more nontraditional families."[38]

For her part, Rose Ann Baer seemed relieved the case was over. Since she was first cited for violating the zoning law in 1984, three of the original co-residents had moved out. One of the original four co-residents, Jessie Esposito, remained, and Baer had taken in one new resident, Sandy Meddaugh. Meddaugh told reporters she had been in and out of psychiatric hospitals for the last twenty years, and Baer's house was the first place she lived that felt "like a family." "When it was my birthday," Meddaugh said, "she invited my friends over and surprised me with a great big birthday cake. . . . And on Christmas, they had presents for me. I haven't had them since my grandmother was alive." Baer said she planned to take in two more women now that the case was decided. "They made me feel like I was a criminal," she said. "But I don't think I was doing anything wrong."[39]

BRASCHI'S QUEER COALITION

The *Baer* decision was quickly cited in other zoning cases to argue on behalf of other group homes and alternative families in New York, but perhaps the most unexpected citation came within a few months of the court's decision, in the case of *Braschi v. Stahl Associates*. Miguel Braschi and Leslie Blanchard first met in December 1975 in Puerto Rico. Braschi was twenty years old, on a tennis scholarship at Ohio State University, and back home visiting family for Christmas. Blanchard was forty-one years old, a nationally known hairdresser and hair colorist, on vacation in San Juan. The following summer, Braschi left Ohio State just before his senior year and moved in with Blanchard in his rent-controlled apartment on E. 54th Street in Manhattan. In October 1977, the two men exchanged Cartier bracelets as a symbol of their relationship. Blanchard was not out as a gay man publicly, but both men's friends and family accepted and regarded them as a couple. They remained together until Blanchard passed away from AIDS-related illness in September 1986. Shortly after, the landlord of the apartment they shared, Stahl Associates, moved to evict Braschi, as his name was not on the lease.[40]

The dilemma was that the city rent-control guidelines allowed the eviction of residents following the death of a leaseholder except for "the surviving spouse of the deceased tenant or some other member of the deceased tenant's family who has been living with the tenant." That language was widely (and for landlords, conveniently) understood to exclude gay couples: by the mid-1980s, stories of gay men who had been evicted from rent-controlled or rent-stabilized apartments after their partners had died were increasingly common. What was unusual was bringing the landlord to court. As Miguel Braschi's sister, Giannina Braschi, recently recalled, "[Miguel] was a very sheltered guy, and all of a sudden he finds himself in the world with nothing, naked, not knowing what to do. But his dignity was the measurement of his liberty—so he found the best lawyer in New York and . . . fought with all his mighty heart for what he thought

FIGURE 12.2. Miguel Braschi with his Scottish terrier Katie at Yellow Iris Farm, NJ, ca. 1983, courtesy of Giannina Braschi.

FIGURE 12.3. Leslie Blanchard with Miguel Braschi's mother, Edmee Braschi, Los Angeles, CA, ca. 1982, courtesy of Giannina Braschi.

was right."[41] *Braschi* quickly emerged as a key test case. The county court had initially ruled in Braschi's favor, halting the eviction, but the landlord filed an appeal. The ACLU, at William Rubenstein's urging, filed an amicus brief, but this time, Braschi lost. Rubenstein pushed to take over the case from Braschi's lawyer and appeal again.[42]

The rent-control regulation stressed familial bonds, and Braschi's affidavit in the case followed similar contours. In seeking preliminary injunction against the eviction, he emphasized that he and Blanchard lived as spouses in all but a legal sense. "Like spouses, we began our partnership with expectations of sexual fidelity. During our ten-year relationship I did not date or live with anyone else, and I believe that Leslie was also faithful to me." Braschi also emphasized that the apartment was their home together. "The apartment became the center of our lives. It was the place we shared our love and commitment to each other. Like any married couple, Leslie and I shared household responsibilities." They traveled together, shared bank accounts and credit cards, and the vast majority of Blanchard's five-million-dollar estate was left to Braschi. Braschi's affidavit also emphasized the role he played as caretaker during Blanchard's illness. Blanchard first grew sick in spring 1986, and he was hospitalized twice over the next several months. "I—and I alone," Braschi explained, "undertook all the arrangements for Leslie's care, as Leslie wished. Leslie expired in my arms, with my brother Juan also at his bedside. I had not left Leslie's bedside for the previous 48 hours. Words cannot express the tremendous loss I suffered and continue to suffer now. When I lost Leslie, I lost a part of myself." Braschi emphasized the stability and depth of his relationship with Blanchard and pointed to his caretaking role during Blanchard's illness as the ultimate sign of their bond.[43]

While Braschi's affidavit seemed to point to an argument about the equality of gay relationships to heterosexual ones, Rubenstein ultimately framed the case differently. His brief did not emphasize discrimination against gay men but discrimination against functional families. Rubenstein pointed specifically to the two recently decided zoning cases—*McMinn* and *Baer*—as precedent for looking beyond legal and biological bonds to consider whether a household operated as a family. The rent-control law was, in fact, vaguer than the zoning laws: it never defined what constituted a family in the first place. The importance of this argument became only clearer in Rubenstein's oral argument before the Court of Appeals: Rubenstein made virtually no mention of Braschi and Blanchard as a gay couple but emphasized that they were a "functional family," not unlike the women in *Baer*.[44]

Extending the "functional family" argument to a gay couple was a radical move, though there were some precedents in rent-control law. New York courts had previously protected individuals from eviction in rent-control cases when the relationship with the tenant of record resembled that of a parent and child or a heterosexual spouse.[45] This move toward more "functional" definitions of family—whether the tenants acted like or "held themselves out" to be a family—fit with a larger functional turn in family law in the 1970s and 1980s, for example, in palimony and parentage cases.[46] Still, there was virtually no precedent in gay or lesbian cases, and the language of "functional family" rested heavily on the zoning cases.

The connection to *Baer* was hardly intuitive. The *Braschi* and *Baer* cases, on their surface, seemed to have little in common, not only because one concerned rent control and the other zoning, or because one concerned a gay couple and the other a household of five women, presumed straight by the courts and media. The other key difference was financial: Blanchard's estate upon his death was valued at five million dollars.[47] Baer relied principally on the income from renting rooms; the women who rented from her, in turn, were supported largely from government disability or widow's benefits. Connecting *Braschi* to *Baer* and the line of functional family cases looked past these differences to present a coalition of nontraditional households broad enough to encompass both, highlighting how housing laws of various kinds could be a source of estrangement—literally making legal strangers of families that strayed too far from the heterosexual, nuclear family norm.[48]

Braschi's queer coalition was made imaginable in part because of HIV/ AIDS. By the late 1980s, LGBT activists, social service organizations, and advocacy groups in New York had come to recognize the broad population impacted by HIV/AIDS, well beyond gay men. This was made explicit in accompanying case documents. Paula Ettelbrick, writing for Lambda Legal, argued that failing to expand rent law's definition of family would have impact on the surviving partners of those in New York City most impacted by AIDS—"gay men, black and Hispanic women, and poor people"—leaving them vulnerable to harassment and eviction.[49] A group of AIDS service organizations, including Gay Men's Health Crisis, People with AIDS Coalition, and Brooklyn AIDS Task Force, issued an amicus brief outlining the emerging crisis of homelessness among people with AIDS, and listing a long series of cases where landlords had sought to evict surviving partners under rent law. The majority of those cases involved gay male couples, but the brief was clear that the case impacted a wide range of marginalized communities.[50] An attorney with the Harlem office of the Legal Aid Society also wrote in support of Braschi's case, arguing that "the recognition of functional family units is particularly important to low-income and minority communities," whose households often represented "augmented" rather than nuclear families.[51] HIV/AIDS revealed not only the vulnerability of gay male couples but the vulnerability of any nontraditional households facing illness and eviction. At the same time, Braschi's own position, as a Latino man living with AIDS, was left unspoken in the case documents, perhaps because it would have been difficult to demonstrate that discrimination based on race or illness was an additional factor in the landlord's effort to evict him.

Rubenstein's framing of Braschi and Blanchard as a functional family ultimately proved persuasive to the court. As the court found, "The term family . . . should not be rigidly restricted to those people who have formalized their relationship by obtaining, for instance, a marriage certificate or an adoption order. The intended protection against sudden eviction should not rest on fictitious legal distinctions or genetic history, but instead should find its foundations in the reality of family life." Determining whether or not another tenant counted as a family member in any individual case was left to the lower courts, though the court's decision singled out factors including "the exclusivity and longevity of the relationship, the level of emotional and financial commitment, the manner in which the parties have conducted their everyday lives and held themselves out to society"—or, more largely, "the totality of the relationship as evidenced by the dedication, caring, and self-sacrifice of the parties."[52] The case would quickly be cited a year later in a decision recognizing nontraditional families in rent-stabilization law, while New York State amended its own housing regulations to acknowledge broader forms of family life.[53] Braschi himself returned to San Juan and died in 1991 from AIDS-related illness, without public notice.

While the *Braschi* team had worked to place gay and lesbian couples within a broader coalition of nontraditional households, however, the case was covered in mainstream media almost exclusively as a victory for gay rights. Immediately after the case was decided, the ACLU put out a press release explaining, "Today's decision is a ground breaking victory for lesbians and gay men. . . . This is the first time that a state's highest court has recognized a gay couple to be the legal equivalent of a 'family.'" The release ended by noting that the ruling would protect low-income families as well, where there were "economic barriers to divorce and adoption" obstructing access to legal ties between household members.[54] Both mainstream and gay media, nevertheless, seized principally on the immediate case of a gay couple with headlines like "New York Court Defines Family to Include Homosexual Couples," and "Family Right Given to Gays."[55] The broader implications of the case were largely lost. This was a distinct contrast to *Baer*, which prompted both excitement and anxiety about the suburban spread of so-called "groupers" and rooming houses as well as the collapse of zoning laws, well beyond the specific context of homes for people with mental illness or disability. *Braschi* was interpreted as a case about gay couples and is widely remembered; *Baer* was interpreted as a case about all kinds of unconventional families and has been largely forgotten.

THE FUNCTIONS OF THE FUNCTIONAL FAMILY

One reason *Braschi*'s connection to *Baer* and functional family legislation has been largely ignored by historians of sexuality and LGBT politics is that the case looked more and more like an anomaly in the years to come. Less than a year after *Braschi*, in March 1990, a New York appellate court heard the case of a lesbian mother who sought visitation rights with her child after separating from her same-sex partner, although she was not related to the child biologically. The court recognized the mother's "close and loving relationship" with the child but declined to interpret "parent" functionally, rejecting outright the legal team's comparison to *Braschi*. That same year, a Kings County court found that a gay man could not be considered "a surviving spouse," and so could not dispute his partner's will. That court, too, rejected the comparison to *Braschi*, writing, "There is a great distinction between being part of a family entitled to the protection of rent-control laws because of public policy and legislative intent, and in being a surviving spouse of a decedent."[56] A later case, which established the right to second adoption by unmarried partners of biological mothers, both gay and straight, also rejected any reliance on *Braschi* as precedent, as "these are very different cases with very different issues and operative policies."[57] LGBT advocates expected *Braschi* would open new pathways to recognition of LGBT families, yet courts proved unwilling to extend functional family arguments to LGBT cases beyond rent law. The failure of functional family arguments likely made domestic partnership recognition, civil unions, and same-sex marriage appear more attractive and expedient means of securing protections for LGBT families. Yet this also meant extracting gay and lesbian couples from the broader coalition of alternative households *Braschi* began to forge.

That shift in strategy is ironic given the continued and successful appeal to *Braschi* in a wide range of New York City and state rent-control and rent-stabilized housing cases. In the three decades since the case, *Braschi* had been cited as precedent to recognize a diverse set of nontraditional family relationships, including unmarried heterosexual life partners; two elderly women who lived together as "sisters"; an aunt and nephew; and an older straight couple who were no longer romantic partners but still living together.[58] Many other nontraditional families have also undoubtedly been protected by the expanded definition of family in New York City's rent-regulation codes. The *Braschi* ruling may not have gone as far in LGBT rights as advocates at the time had hoped, but in rent law, it has worked to protect the larger coalition of functional families *Braschi* brought with it.[59] The move away from functional family arguments in advocacy for LGBT relationships is more striking still, given what Melissa Murray has identified as a larger "functional turn" in family law. Since *Braschi*, courts and policymakers have increasingly understood family in functional terms, particularly in cases around parentage, child custody, and relationship dissolution.[60]

Nevertheless, the state's embrace of the functional family remains ambivalent at best. Murray shows how California courts moved toward more functional definitions of parenthood when it meant privatizing childhood dependency. Similarly, the courts were arguably sympathetic to Baer because it meant keeping the care of the four women who lived with her privatized: evicting two of the women in the house would have placed additional burden on the state. New York City housing authorities, too, could rationalize recognizing nontraditional family members under rent law, since evicting them would have forced many tenants into homelessness. For the court, those risks seem to have outweighed the potential risks of recognizing alternative families. The burden of proving that any given household is a "functional family" has also largely fallen on homeowners and tenants themselves.[61] The functional family is not declared or recognized proactively; it is defended, when and where communities, landlords, and the state find cause for intervention.

In this sense, the state has been largely passive in seeking to recognize functional families, leaving many households open to discrimination and bias. Zoning laws, for one example, continue to disadvantage many unconventional families. In 2014, for instance, Hartford, Connecticut, issued a cease-and-desist order after a group of eight friends (three couples and two single people) purchased a mansion to live together with their children. The group, which considered themselves a family, was told they were in violation of a city zoning law that prohibited more than two unrelated people from living together.[62] The city ultimately dropped the suit but made no change to their zoning code. Other cities have been more responsive: Oneonta, New York, altered its zoning code to include a definition of "functional family," following another recent dispute.[63] These codes still, however, treat nontraditional families as an aberration, privileging the bio/legal family as the norm.

The history of the functional family ultimately exposes the limits of existing law to recognize and protect family life in its diverse forms. Sociologist Elisabeth Sheff, for example, argues that policies should be updated to accommodate multiple-partner relationships and polyamorous families with children.[64] Some families have run into custody challenges where one parent is not biologically related to a child, a challenge that a concept of functional family could help frame in the courts.[65] Gay and lesbian couples may also find that legal marriage recognition may prove no guarantee of equal treatment under the law: in 2017, the Texas Supreme Court ruled that the state was not required to extend insurance benefits to same-sex spouses of state employees (the US Supreme Court declined to hear the case).[66] Making the functional family, rather than the marital couple or biological/adoptive parent, the basis of legal recognition of a family relationship might expand possibilities for family forms and prevent discrimination based on household difference.[67]

The question remains how the legislature and courts should define family functionally. Both *Baer* and *Braschi* circled around this question, emphasizing the longevity and depth of the relationships. The two families appear, on the surface, quite distinct, as were the legal challenges they confronted. What the families shared was a commitment to caregiving. Braschi's role as a caregiver during Blanchard's illness stood out as a measure of their relationship—and the court's decision cites "care" as a signature of family life—the affective and material practices that presumably distinguished Braschi and Blanchard from mere roommates. Similarly, Baer's role went beyond that of a landlord specifically because of the ways she cared for the four women in her home. Caregiving is often overlooked as a form of material and affective labor, principally because it happens within the privacy of home (and is primarily done by women). Yet care is also an essential task of family, friends, and community, at once encompassing and expanding beyond the conventional limits of marriage and reproduction. For those who do not or choose not to fit within existing bio/legal frameworks of family, recognizing bonds of care in the law would make it possible for both the state and communities to acknowledge the diverse, often unremarked interdependencies that structure everyday life and the common links between families of all kinds.[68]

The underlying challenge remains that the intimate state does not speak with one voice. Rather, the history of family and housing law reveals the vast discretion local and state agencies, legislators, and courts have held, and still hold, to define family, and how structurally and strategically resistant those authorities have been to arriving at a universal definition. Family may be defined differently not only from town to town or state to state, but often within the same municipality or state in different arenas of family, land use, and housing law. The resistance of courts to taking *Braschi* as precedent outside rent law reflects this balkanized landscape: in any given case, family is defined less by the functions it fulfills for its members than by the function it serves for the state.[69] What looks queer about the *Braschi* case today is not only how it sought to broaden a concept of functional family but how it sought to bridge zoning and rent law. Courts have typically treated these two legal arenas as separate because their ends were understood as distinct—preserving "neighborhood character" on the one hand, home and shelter on the other. In drawing on *Baer*, the *Braschi* team asked the courts to recognize the preservation of families as the more fundamental goal within both legal canons. Nontraditional households, without legal or biological ties, remain uniquely vulnerable to the discretion of various state agents to delegitimate their relationships. And they may also bear a unique burden to prove the significance of their relationship to the state when faced with eviction, separation, loss, or a need for support. At the same time, the history of the functional family ultimately suggests the ways all forms of family life unfold in dialogue with the state, whether as a source of affirmation or estrangement, both when households and families align with state categories and interests and when they do not.

NOTES

Thank you to the editors and the participants of the *Intimate States* workshop for all of their feedback on earlier versions of this essay, with particular thanks to Serena Mayeri. I would also like to thank the librarians at the New York State Library and Seeley G. Mudd Manuscript Library at Princeton University; David S. Byers, Anna Lvovsky, and Tess O'Dwyer for their help at various stages of the project; and especially Giannina Braschi, William Rubenstein, Jane Reinhardt, and Robert Briglio for speaking with me about the cases.

1. *Baer v. Town of Brookhaven*, 73 N.Y.2d 942, 943 (1989); Robert Briglio and Jane C. Reinhardt, "'Equivalent' Families," Letters to the Long Island Editor, *New York Times*, July 30, 1989.

2. *Braschi v. Stahl Associates Co.*, 74 N.Y.2d 201 (1989).

3. For example, see Carlos A. Ball, *From the Closet to the Courtroom: Five LGBT Rights Lawsuits That Have Changed Our Nation* (Boston: Beacon Press, 2009); and Nathaniel Frank, *Awakening: How Gays and Lesbians Brought Marriage Equality to America* (Cambridge, MA: Belknap, 2017).

4. See Jeffrey Rosen, "The Dangers of a Constitutional Right to 'Dignity,'" *The Atlantic*, April 29, 2015, https://www.theatlantic.com/politics/archive/2015/04/the-dangerous-doctrine-of-dignity/391796/.

5. Katherine Franke, *Wedlocked: The Perils of Marriage Equality* (New York: New York University Press, 2017); and Nancy D. Polikoff, *Beyond (Straight and Gay) Marriage: Valuing All Families Under the Law* (Boston: Beacon Press, 2008).

6. Douglas NeJaime, "Before Marriage: The Unexplored History of Nonmarital Recognition and Its Relationship to Marriage," *California Law Review* 102 (2014): 87–172.

7. For example, Nan Alamilla Boyd, *Wide Open Town: A History of Queer San Francisco to 1965* (Berkeley: University of California Press, 2003); and George Chauncey, *Gay New York: Gender, Urban Culture, and the Making of the Gay Male World, 1890–1940* (New York: Basic Books, 1994).

8. Anna Lvovsky, "Cruising in Plain View: Clandestine Surveillance and the Unique Insights of Antihomosexual Policing," *Journal of Urban History* 46, no. 5 (2020), 980–1001; Risa Goluboff, *Vagrant Nation: Police Power, Constitutional Change, and the Making of the 1960s* (New York: Oxford University Press, 2016); and Nayan Shah, *Stranger Intimacy: Contesting Race, Sexuality and the Law in the North American West* (Berkeley: University of California Press, 2011).

9. See especially Richard Rothstein, *The Color of Law: A Forgotten History of How Our Government Segregated America* (New York: Liveright Publishing, 2017); and David M. P. Freund, *Colored Property: State Policy and White Racial Politics in Suburban America* (Chicago: University of Chicago Press, 2007). On the broader impact of local governance on racial and economic discrimination, see Colin Gordon's discussion of local citizenship in "Introduction," *Citizen Brown: Race,*

Democracy, and Inequality in the St. Louis Suburbs (Chicago: University of Chicago Press, 2019), 1–20.

10. Clayton Howard, "Building a 'Family-Friendly' Metropolis: Sexuality, the State, and Postwar Housing Policy," *Journal of Urban History* 39, no. 5 (2013): 933–55; and Ian M. Baldwin, "Rethinking the 'Era of Limits': Equitable Housing, Gay Liberation, and the Opening of the American Family in Greater Los Angeles during the Long 1970s," *California History* 91, no. 3 (2014): 42–59.

11. Lauren Berlant and Michael Warner, "Sex in Public," *Critical Inquiry* 24, no. 2 (1998): 547–66.

12. For recent work that highlights private space as sites of LGBT relationships and politics in the United States, see Lauren Jae Gutterman, *Her Neighbor's Wife: A History of Lesbian Desire Within Marriage* (Philadelphia: University of Pennsylvania Press, 2019); Stephen Vider, "'Oh Hell, May, Why Don't You People Have a Cookbook?': Camp Humor and Gay Domesticity," *American Quarterly* 65, no. 4 (2013): 877–904; and Stephen Vider, "Lesbian and Gay Marriage and Romantic Adjustment in the 1950s and 1960s United States," *Gender & History* 29, no. 3 (2017): 693–715.

13. Cathy J. Cohen, "Punks, Bulldaggers, and Welfare Queens: The Radical Potential of Queer Politics?," *GLQ: A Journal of Lesbian and Gay Studies* 3, no. 4 (1997): 441.

14. I borrow the language of shield and sword from the court decision in *Matter of Jacob*, 86 N.Y.2d 651, 669 (1995).

15. Town of Brookhaven Accessory Apartment Review Board meeting transcript, January 24, 1985, in Appendix for Defendants-Appellants at A-132, *Baer*, 73 N.Y.2d 942.

16. Statistics on mental hospitals in Suffolk County in Amended Complaint, May 10, 1985, in Appendix for Defendants-Appellants at A-215, *Baer*, 73 N.Y.2d 942. On deinstitutionalization, see E. Fuller Torrey, *American Psychosis: How the Federal Government Destroyed the Mental Illness Treatment System* (New York: Oxford University Press, 2014).

17. Amended complaint, May 10, 1985, in Appendix for Defendants-Appellants at A-211 to A-213, and Accessory Apartment Review Board meeting transcript in Appendix for Defendants-Appellants at A-149, *Baer*, 73 N.Y.2d 942.

18. Affidavit by Ilona Hudak, April 5, 1985, in Appendix for Defendants-Appellants at A-203, *Baer*, 73 N.Y.2d 942.

19. Accessory Apartment Review Board meeting transcript.

20. On the history of race and zoning law, see Freund, *Colored Property*; and Rothstein, *Color of Law*, 39–57.

21. T. B. Benson, "Segregation Ordinances," *Virginia Law Register* 1, no. 5 (1915): 330.

22. *Village of Euclid v. Ambler Realty Co.*, 272 U.S. 365 (1926); and Michael Allan Wolf, *The Zoning of America: Euclid V. Ambler* (Lawrence: University Press of Kansas, 2008).

23. Adam Lubow, "'. . . Not Related by Blood, Marriage, or Adoption': A History of the Definition of 'Family' in Zoning Law," *Journal of Affordable Housing & Community Development Law* 16, no. 2 (2007): 144–221.

24. *Belle Terre v. Boraas*, 416 U.S. 1, 9 (1974).

25. *Moore v. City of East Cleveland*, 431 U.S. 494 (1977).

26. Angela Onwuachi-Willig, "Extending the Normativity of the Extended Family: Reflections on *Moore v. City of East Cleveland*," *Fordham Law Review* 85 (2016): 2655–64.

27. *Moore,* 431 U.S. 494, 504 and 508.

28. Accessory Apartment Review Board meeting transcript.

29. Solangel Maldonado, "Sharing a House but Not a Household: Extended Families and Exclusionary Zoning Forty Years After *Moore*," *Fordham Law Review* 85 (2016): 2641–53; Daniel Edwardo Guzman, "There Be No Shelter Here: Anti-immigrant Housing Ordinances and Comprehensive Reform," *Cornell Journal of Law & Public Policy* 20 (2010): 399–439.

30. On the history of the Mental Health Law Project, see "Mental Health: LI Mental Health Programs Honored," *Newsday,* November 28, 1984.

31. Reply Brief for Plaintiffs-Respondents at 6 and 15, *Baer,* 73 N.Y.2d 942. Belle Terre's zoning victory would have had particular impact on Brookhaven: Belle Terre is a village of the Town of Brookhaven.

32. Howard Schneider, "Students Fight 'Grouper' Ban," *Newsday*, December 10, 1969; and Barbara Delatiner, "Long Island Draws the Line on 'Groupers,'" *New York Times,* August 31, 1975.

33. Pamela Warrick, "A Lively Bunch Debates Brookhaven Grouper Law," *Newsday*, July 3, 1974; and Town of Brookhaven public hearing, July 2, 1974, transcript, in Appendix for Defendants-Appellants at A-225, *Baer,* 73 N.Y.2d 942.

34. Brief for Appellants at 17, *Baer v. Town of Brookhaven*, 137 A.D.2d 472 (1988).

35. *City of White Plains v. Gennaro Ferraioli et al.*, 34 N.Y.2d 300 (1974); *Group House of Port Washington v. Board of Zoning and Appeals of the Town of North Hempstead*, 45 N.Y.2d 266 (1978).

36. *McMinn v. Town of Oyster Bay*, 66 N.Y.2d 544 (1985).

37. Brief for Appellants at 24, *Baer,* 137 A.D.2d 472.

38. Philip S. Gutis, "Court Upsets L.I. Zoning Law on Unrelated People in Home," *New York Times,* March 24, 1989. See also Adam Horvath, "Court Bolsters Group Homes: Rejects Local Law on 'Family' Occupancy," *Newsday,* March 24, 1989.

39. Ann Nowak, "Boarders Grateful Court Lets Them Stay," *Newsday* (Brookhaven ed.), March 24, 1989.

40. Ball, *From the Closet to the Courtroom*; Affidavit of Miguel Braschi, January 27, 1987, in Record on Appeal at 25–32, *Braschi,* 74 N.Y.2d 201.

41. Remarks by Giannina Braschi at "The Braschi Breakthrough: 30 Years Later, Looking Back on the Relationship Recognition Landmark," hosted by the Richard C. Failla LGBTQ Commission of the New York Courts, June 3, 2019, archived at https://history.nycourts.gov/the-braschi-breakthrough-30-years-later-looking-back-on-the-relationship-recognition-landmark/.

42. Ball, *From the Closet to the Courtroom.*

43. Braschi affidavit in Record on Appeal at 25–32, *Braschi,* 74 N.Y.2d 201.

44. Brief of Plaintiff-Appellant, January 25, 1989, and Reply Brief of Plaintiff-Appellant, April 13, 1989, *Braschi,* 74 N.Y.2d 201; and video of oral argument, New York Court of Appeals, April 26, 1989, courtesy of William Rubenstein.

45. For example, *Zimmerman v. Burton*, 434 N.Y.S.2d 127 (Civ. Ct., 1980) (marriage-like heterosexual relationship); and *2–4 Realty Associates v. Henry Pittman et al.*, 523 N.Y.S.2d 7 (1987) (parent-child-like relationship).

46. Kate Redburn, "Zoned Out: How Zoning Law Undermines Family Law's Functional Turn," *Yale Law Journal* 128, no. 8 (2019): 2412–73.

47. Braschi affidavit in Record on Appeal at 29, *Braschi*, 74 N.Y.2d 201.

48. On the concept of estrangement, see Nayan Shah, "Queer of Color Estrangement and Belonging," in *Routledge History of Queer America,* ed. Don Romesburg (New York: Routledge, 2018), 262–75.

49. Affirmation of Paula L. Ettelbrick, Lambda Defense and Education Fund, Inc., in Support of Motion for Leave to Appeal, 4, *Braschi*, 74 N.Y.2d 201.

50. Amicus Brief of the Gay Men's Health Crisis et al., *Braschi,* 74 N.Y.2d 201.

51. Affirmation of Mary Marsh Zulack, Harlem Neighborhood Office of the Civil Division of the Legal Aid Society, in Support of Motion for Reargument for Leave to Appeal, 4, *Braschi*, 74 N.Y.2d 201. See also Paris Baldacci's discussion of amicus briefs in the case, "Protecting Gay and Lesbian Families From Eviction From Their Homes: The Quest for Equality for Gay and Lesbian Families in *Braschi v. Stahl Associates*," *Texas Wesleyan Law Review* 13, no. 2 (2006–2007): 619–44.

52. *Braschi*, 74 N.Y.2d 201, 211, 212, and 213. Rubenstein notes that the Court of Appeals specifically avoided the term "functional family" to distinguish the zoning and eviction cases—even as they defined family functionally. This also allowed the court to avoid connecting Braschi to the equal protection clause of the state constitution. William B. Rubenstein, "We Are Family: A Reflection on the Search for Legal Recognition of Lesbian and Gay Relationships," *Journal of Law & Politics* 8 (1991): 89–105.

53. Baldacci, "Protecting Gay and Lesbian Families." On the impact of the case, see also Carol Levine, "AIDS and Changing Concepts of Family," *Milbank Quarterly* 68 (1990): 33–58.

54. ACLU Press Release Re: Victory, *Braschi v. Stahl Associates*; 1988–1990; American Civil Liberties Union Records: Subgroup 4, Box 5154, Folder 2, Department of Rare Books and Special Collections, Princeton University Library.

55. Philip S. Gutis, "New York Court Defines Family to Include Homosexual Couples," *New York Times,* July 7, 1989; and Marianne Arneberg, "Family Right Given to Gays," *Newsday,* July 7, 1989. See also Peter Freiberg, "Two Gays Can Be a Family, Court Says," *The Advocate,* August 15, 1989; and Jim Whelan, "NY Les/Gay Lovers Are 'Family,'" *Outweek,* July 24, 1989, 16, 74.

56. *Alison D. v. Virginia M.*, 155 A.D.2d 11, 16 (1990), affirmed by 77 N.Y.2d 651 (1991); and *Matter of Estate of Cooper*, 564 N.Y.2d 684, 688 (1990), affirmed by 592 N.Y.S.2d 797 (1993).

57. *Matter of Jacob*, 86 N.Y.2d 651, 675.

58. *WSC Riverside Drive Owners LLC v. Williams*, 3 N.Y.S.3d 342 (N.Y. App. Div. 2015); *Colon v. Frias*, 615 N.Y.S.2d 618 (Civ. Ct. 1994); *Blue Star Properties, Inc. v. New York State Division of Housing*, 19 N.Y.S.3d 285 (2015); and *530 Second Ave. Co., LLC v. Zenker*, 74 N.Y.S.3d 41 (NY App. Div. 2018).

59. For the ongoing significance of the *Braschi* case in succession rights, see Baldacci, "Protecting Gay and Lesbian Families."

60. Melissa Murray, "Family Law's Doctrine," *University of Pennsylvania Law Review* 163 (2014): 1985–2018.

61. Serena Mayeri, "The Functions of Family Law," *University of Pennsylvania Law Review Online* 163 (2015): 377–82.

62. Vanessa De la Torre, "Legal Battle Possible; 'Scarborough 11' Might Push Issue; Hartford Zoning Dispute," *Hartford Courant,* February 19, 2015.

63. Jake Palmateer, "City Loses Suit, Aims to Redefine 'Family,'" *The Daily Star,* August 3, 2009, regarding *Martella, Juravlea v. Oneonta.*

64. Elisabeth Sheff, *Polyamorists Next Door: Inside Multiple-Partner Relationships and Families* (Lanham, MD: Rowman & Littlefield, 2013).

65. Jennifer Peltz, "Modern Family: More Courts Allowing 3 Parents of 1 Child," *AP Worldstream,* June 18, 2017.

66. Amita Kelly, "Texas Supreme Court Rules Against Benefits For Same-Sex Couples," *NPR,* June 30, 2017, https://www.npr.org/2017/06/30/535021154/texas -supreme-court-rules-against-benefits-for-same-sex-couples, regarding *Pidgeon v. Turner,* 538 S.W.3d 73 (Tex. 2017).

67. For additional perspectives on decentering marriage in family law, see Tamara Metz, *Untying the Knot: Marriage, the State, and the Case for Their Divorce* (Princeton, NJ: Princeton University Press, 2010); and Melissa Murray, "*Obergefell v. Hodges* and Nonmarriage Inequality," *California Law Review* 104 (2016): 1207–58.

68. On caretaking, see Eileen Boris and Jennifer Klein, *Caring for America: Home Health Workers in the Shadow of the Welfare State* (New York: Oxford University Press, 2015). On precedent and the potential to extend legal recognition to nonparental caregivers, see Melissa Murray, "The Networked Family: Reframing the Legal Understanding of Caregiving and Caregivers," *Virginia Law Review* 94, no. 2 (2008): 385–455.

69. On the functions of family law for the state, see Murray, "Family Law's Doctrine"; and Mayeri, "The Functions of Family Law." On discrepancies between zoning law and family, see Redburn, "Zoned Out."

13

Abortion and the
State after *Roe*

JOHANNA SCHOEN

On January 22, 1973, the US Supreme Court legalized abortion in its decision in *Roe v. Wade*. Minutes after the news was broadcast, Susan Hill,
then a twenty-four-year-old social worker in Miami, Florida, received a
call from physician Sam Barr. Would she like to join him in opening an
abortion clinic, Barr inquired? Two weeks later, the new clinic opened its
doors in Winter Park, Florida, just outside Orlando. Modeling his new
practice after a Washington, DC, preterm clinic that had offered outpatient
abortion services since 1969, Barr hired two other physicians and several
counselors and began to provide abortion services to women from Florida,
Georgia, South Carolina, Alabama, Louisiana, and Mississippi. The clinic
was part of an emerging network of women's health services in Florida:
in Miami, a physician offered abortions until the twentieth week of pregnancy; there was also a new clinic in Fort Lauderdale, just north of Miami;
in Tallahassee, a feminist clinic was preparing to open; and Tampa had a
feminist health center that offered education and referred women needing
abortions to other clinics. The staffs of these clinics closely followed each
other's progress and referred patients to one another. Barr sent patients
whose pregnancies were beyond twelve weeks to the doctor in Miami who
was willing to treat them, for instance. And the feminist clinics in Tallahassee and Tampa frequently sent patients to Barr.[1]

With the legalization of abortion and the simultaneous introduction of
vacuum aspiration machines to perform first-trimester abortions, a previously clandestine and dangerous procedure became safe, quick, and inex-
pensive. As the network of clinics grew across the nation, abortions that
had once been invisible, performed secretly by underground providers or
behind the curtains of private physicians' offices, became visible. And if

the illegal or quasi-legal nature of abortion had earlier stifled research, legalization opened the procedure to scientific inquiry and debate. Abortion became one of the most studied procedures in the United States. Some physicians and journalists had spoken and written about abortion well before the procedure became legal, discussing methods, estimating morbidity and mortality rates, and arguing for legalization.[2] But now they began systematically to collect data on pregnancy termination procedures and to publish the results in medical journals. The ability to collect and compare data in turn fostered the development and introduction of new procedures and quickly contributed to the refinement of physicians' techniques. While the systematic persecution of illegal abortionists in the 1950s and 1960s had driven abortion underground and turned it into a risky or even deadly procedure for most women, legalization made abortion into the safest and most widely performed surgical procedure in the United States.[3]

But the provision of abortion care met immediate resistance. Indeed, the *Roe v. Wade* decision signified the beginning, rather than the end, of a protracted battle over access to abortion. As the antiabortion movement gained strength in the 1970s, antiabortion activists set out to countermand the *Roe v. Wade* decision by introducing a Human Life Amendment to the constitution. They eliminated public funding for any aspect of abortion care and, on the state and local level, antiabortion legislators proposed laws to limit women's access to abortion, imposed rules and regulations to prevent clinics from opening their doors, and made operation of an abortion clinic cumbersome and expensive. Still, throughout the 1970s and 1980s, the US Supreme Court protected abortion as a private choice. The justices pondered two questions: First, did the right to an abortion require states to support access to the procedure for women who found it difficult to actually obtain an abortion? And second, what limitations on abortion are permissible under *Roe*?

Despite the historic decision in *Roe*, four developments over the following two decades rendered access to abortion unevenly distributed across the country and made the procedure increasingly difficult to obtain. First, by eliminating public funding for abortion services for the poor, the federal government privatized the interest in abortion. As a result, a woman's ability to obtain an abortion depended on her financial resources, turning a right into a privilege. Second, many states drafted laws that restricted women's access to abortion, and many cities and townships turned to local ordinances, building codes, and zoning restrictions to prevent the opening of abortion clinics. Third, around the country, a vocal and aggressive wing of the antiabortion movement organized protests in front of abortion clinics, targeting clinic staff and the women who sought their services. Fourth, with the election of President Ronald Reagan, the Religious Right gained significant prominence and political influence. By the late 1980s, Reagan's appointments had shifted the composition of the Supreme Court. As a consequence, starting in the early 1990s, Supreme Court justices let stand regulations restricting access to abortion that justices had previously struck down.[4]

Abortion is—and always has been—a key arena for contesting power relations between women and men. While the decriminalization of abortion made the procedure legal and safe, women were never able to fully control their access to it. The Supreme Court decision in *Roe* was a conservative decision that left the ultimate control over women's choice in the hands of mostly male authorities—physicians, legislators, and the judiciary. Women's choices were circumscribed by physicians, who decided whether or not to offer abortion procedures, and legislators, who determined when and under what circumstances those procedures could be performed. The framing of abortion as a private decision to which women had a fundamental—but negative—right rather than a positive right that the state had to guarantee left access to abortion vulnerable to restrictions about where, when, and under what circumstances women might be granted access to the procedure. Supported by an overwhelmingly male judiciary, judges upheld hurdles and restrictions, suggesting that women were not fully emancipated adults capable of moral decision-making. Over the course of four decades, women's access to abortion care was slowly undermined as the state granted a nominal right but kept women's autonomy in check. A nominal right granted under *Roe v. Wade* became, over the course of four and a half decades, a privilege tightly controlled on the state and local level.

When the Supreme Court in *Roe* declared all criminal abortion laws unconstitutional, feminists and abortion providers expected that abortion services would become legal, widely accessible, integrated into modern medicine, and generally uncontroversial. And, indeed, while the development of abortion services around the country was uneven, by the end of the 1970s most women were able to access legal abortions. Mortality rates, which had hovered between 60 and 80 deaths per 100,000 cases in the decades prior to legalization, sank to 1.3 by 1976–1977.[5]

Abortion services were initially provided largely in hospitals. This was particularly true for public and municipal hospitals, which considered it an obligation to make abortion services available to women unable to obtain the procedure from a private physician, and for university hospitals, many of which were at the forefront of abortion research and medical reform. At the Department of Obstetrics and Gynecology at the University of Iowa Hospitals, for instance, Charles deProsse established abortion services during the months immediately after *Roe*. By May 1973, the University of Iowa Hospital offered vacuum aspirations and saline abortions to women from across the state. The department allowed deProsse to hire his own staff to ensure that all staff members supported the new program.[6]

But it was the proliferation of outpatient clinics that provided abortions in a nonhospital location that shaped the setting of abortion care for decades to come. In 1973, 81 percent of abortion providers were offering abortions in a hospital setting; by 1979, that number had dropped to 56 percent. The number of physicians performing legal abortions climbed by 76 percent, from 1,550 in 1973 to 2,734 in 1979.[7] The rapid spread of vacuum aspiration accelerated these changes. Prior to the introduction of this procedure, physicians seeking to terminate a pregnancy performed a dilation and curettage (D&C), in which the cervix is dilated and the contents of the uterus scarped with a curette. A D&C is relatively unpleasant to perform and included the risk of perforation of the uterus, hemorrhage, and infection. Vacuum aspiration, in which the contents of the uterus are sucked out by a vacuum aspiration machine, was not only quicker to perform than a traditional D&C, but also safer, more likely to result in the complete removal of all tissue, led to less blood loss and fewer major complications, and was more adaptable to local anesthesia.[8] Already in 1973, more than half of all abortion procedures were performed in outpatient clinics rather than hospitals. By 1980, 16.5 percent of all abortion facilities performed three-quarters of all abortions. As a result, abortion became more accessible throughout the decade. While 25 percent of all women who had obtained an abortion in 1973 reported that they had traveled outside their state of residency to obtain the service, by 1980 that number had fallen to 6 percent.[9]

The model of the freestanding abortion clinic appealed to physicians because it offered full control over policies and staffing rather than necessitating negotiations with hospital administrators and staff who might be unwilling to participate in abortion care. It equally appealed to feminists who sought an alternative to traditional medical care and valued the opportunity to open an abortion clinic and put their vision of woman-centered health care into practice. Inspired by the court victory and the growing self-help movement, for instance, a group of young women in Iowa City, Iowa, decided to form a feminist collective. On September 1, 1973, the Emma Goldman Clinic for Women (EGC) opened its doors to the public. The collective hired Dick Winter, a local physician, to perform abortions on Tuesdays and Thursdays and staffed the clinic with collective members, all lay health workers who received on-the-job training. During the first months of operation, Winter performed seventy-five vacuum aspirations. In addition to abortion, the clinic offered birth control counseling, psychotherapy, childbirth preparation classes, massage services, and legal advice.[10]

The EGC was part of a nationwide movement of women's health clinics. Many women saw access to affordable abortions as central to their self-determination and at the same time realized that abortion services provided clinics with a steady income, allowing them to support a range of other services not as easily reimbursable. Carol Downer, a California housewife turned women's health activist, established a group of clinics in that state, the Feminist Women's Health Centers (FWHC). Intrigued by Downer's vision, feminists in Michigan, New Hampshire, Florida, and Georgia opened clinics affiliated with FWHC. In Vermont and Massachusetts, feminists followed suit with clinics that were independent and, like the EGC, not affiliated with FWHC.[11]

Despite this momentum, the legalization of abortion did not produce a climate in which most hospital administrators and ob-gyn staff were willing to establish abortion services or perform the procedures. Nor was it easy to open freestanding abortion clinics. To be sure, some parts of the country, states such as New York, Florida, and California, for instance, saw the establishment of a range of outpatient abortion services in a very brief time period. But a New Jersey lawsuit in the mid-1970s illustrates the uneven implementation of the *Roe v. Wade* decision. Three out of four New Jersey residents had to leave the state to obtain an abortion. The Rutgers Women's Litigation Clinic and the American Civil Liberties Union finally filed a suit against three private South Jersey hospitals that forbid staff to perform abortions. In November 1976, the New Jersey Supreme Court agreed that the plaintiff, Jane Doe, had been illegally denied access to abortion.[12]

RESTRICTING FUNDING

If poverty prevented women from traveling to access legal abortion services, poor women were among the first to lose access to legal abortion. Following the 1973 *Roe* decision, the federal government routinely funded abortions through its Medicaid program, which provides health care to low-income Americans. One of the first priorities of antiabortion activists was to eliminate this federal funding. In 1976, Congress passed the Hyde Amendment, named for its original author Representative Henry Hyde (R-Ill), eliminating federal Medicaid funds for abortion for all cases except to save the life of the mother or when a pregnancy resulted from rape or incest.[13] Until the Supreme Court upheld the Hyde Amendment in its 1980 *Harris v. McRae* decision, the federal government had been paying for 300,000 abortions per year, at an annual cost of roughly $45 million. On the heels of *Harris v. McRae*, the number of Medicaid abortions fell from 295,000 in fiscal year 1977 to 194,000 in fiscal year 1978. As a result of the cutbacks, the financial burden of abortion shifted to the woman seeking the procedure, making access to abortion services difficult for many. In addition, in 1979 the Defense Department cut off funding for roughly 265,000 abortions a year for military personnel.[14] Had funding been available, one study found, between 18 and 23 percent of Medicaid-eligible women would have obtained abortions. After funding was eliminated, they carried their unwanted pregnancies to term.[15] While all women retained the right to choose an abortion, the implementation of this right had become the financial responsibility of the woman who sought the abortion.

The restrictions placed on Medicaid-funded abortions disproportionately affected nonwhite women, who are overrepresented among low-income Americans. In October 1977, two months after the ban went into effect, a twenty-seven-year-old single mother, Rosauro Jimenez, died of blood poisoning following an illegal abortion in a Mexican border town.[16] Issues of access and abortion safety took on a new level of urgency as abortion rights advocates considered Jimenez, who had sought the illegal abortion after Medicaid would not pay for a legal one, the first casualty of the Hyde Amendment. Even if poor women were able to come up with money for their abortions, they frequently took longer to collect the necessary funds, leading to a delay of their abortion procedures, which further risked an increased cost, since abortion costs rose with later gestational age.[17] Only a handful of states continued to offer some abortion funding for low-income women. In response to the virtual elimination of public monies for abortion, grassroots groups nationwide formed the National Network of Abortion Funds, which raised private donations for roughly 20,000 abortions per year, including cases of abortion that would have fallen under the Hyde Amendment's narrow exceptions. But the Hyde Amendment permanently transformed the economic landscape of abortion provision.

With the 1980 election of President Ronald Reagan to the White House, antiabortion activists gained critical access to important positions in the federal government.[18] Reagan appointed a number of antiabortion leaders to positions in his administration. C. Everett Koop, who coauthored the 1979 book and film series *Whatever Happened to the Human Race?*, which served as the intellectual foundation for many evangelicals in the antiabortion movement, became Reagan's surgeon general. Reagan appointed Robert Billings, a former executive director of the Christian right organization Moral Majority, to the Department of Education. Marjorie Mecklenburg, founder of Minnesota Citizens Concerned for Life and, with her husband Fred Mecklenburg, an early prominent leader in the antiabortion movement, was appointed to the Office of Adolescent Pregnancy Programs.[19] For the first time, antiabortion activists felt they had an ally in the White House. Newly invigorated by these developments, they approached the fight against legal abortion with a new sense of optimism and boldness.

Antiabortion activists had spent the previous decade fighting against abortion through political and legal channels in hopes of one day overturning the *Roe v. Wade* decision. Starting in 1973, legislators repeatedly introduced Human Life Amendments that would overturn *Roe* by defining life as beginning at the moment of conception. While these efforts were unsuccessful throughout the 1970s, antiabortion activists hoped the election of Ronald Reagan would finally bring success. And by 1985, passage of a Human Life Amendment had won the president's endorsement. But while most antiabortion restrictions in the early 1980s passed on the state level, the movement failed to gain significant support on the national level and legislators defeated several versions of the Human Life Amendment.[20]

Frustrated by these legislative failures, Reagan turned to executive orders. In the mid-1980s, he extended the bans on funding for abortion services by eliminating money for agencies that either advised women about abortions or referred them to abortion providers. The ban targeted a broad range of agencies receiving federal funding under the Title X Family Planning Program—from state and local health departments, tribal organizations, hospitals, university health centers, independent clinics, community health centers, and faith-based organizations to various public and private nonprofit entities. Enacted as part of the War on Poverty under President Richard Nixon, Title X funds paid for a wide range of health care services: family planning, screenings for breast and pelvic exams as well as screenings for and education about STIs and HIV, and referrals to other health care resources related to pregnancy testing and counseling. Throughout the 1970s, Title X was considered the flagship of programs providing individuals with comprehensive family planning and related preventive health services. Under Reagan, the Title X program was underfunded and stymied in Congress at every turn. In his first year in office, Reagan instructed the Department of Health and Human Services that Title X recipients would be allowed to offer only "non-directive" abortion counseling and refer a patient to an abortion provider only if the patient requested it. In 1984, Reagan banned international aid to overseas organizations that performed or advocated for legal abortion—the so-called global gag rule. And in 1987, he ordered the Department of Health and Human Services to ban Title X organizations from making any abortion referrals or even mentioning abortion as a possibility, extending the gag rule to domestic services.[21]

Reagan's executive orders meant that pregnant women seeking care at medical facilities that received Title X funds no longer obtained neutral and factually accurate information about all of their legal medical options. Health professionals could no longer counsel women about or refer them to abortion services even when women's medical circumstances warranted such referrals or women asked about abortions. Reagan's actions inaugurated reproductive policies via executive orders—as subsequent presidents rescinded, reinstated, and otherwise altered the gag rule according to their political preferences.[22] The gag rule also politicized reproductive health care information as state legislators began to dictate information about abortion that medical professionals should deliver to their patients and mandated often inaccurate counseling. Together with conscience clauses, passed in the mid-1970s, that allowed medical professionals to withhold abortion or sterilization services if health professionals felt such services violated their conscience, these restrictions on abortion care significantly compromised the quality of women's health care services.

REGULATING ABORTION CLINICS

Antiabortion activists quickly learned how to employ state regulatory systems in their favor and to fight the establishment of abortion clinics on the ground. In the mid-1970s, Susan Hill, then president of the National Women's Health Organization (NWHO), set out to open clinics in underserved areas of the country. She immediately met significant local opposition. "It became a confrontation all the way around," Hill remembered.[23] Between 1976 and 1980, Hill and the NWHO opened clinics in Wayne, New Jersey; Wilmington, Delaware; White Plains, New York; Fort Wayne, Indiana; Raleigh, North Carolina; and Fargo, North Dakota. In almost every case, local authorities met NWHO efforts with a range of procedural obstacles. In Wayne, a heavily Catholic area outside New York, the township's health officer argued that the clinic was an ambulatory care facility and thus needed a Certificate of Need to open. Certificates of Need (CON), issued by state health officials, regulated the construction of hospital facilities and were expensive and difficult to get. Hill objected that requiring a CON violated *Roe v. Wade*, which held that any restriction on abortion performed during the first trimester was illegal. State health officials relented only after the NWHO threatened to sue Wayne township.[24]

But the victory did not mean an end to the opposition. Instead, opposition leaders shifted their attention to a different arena of state power, the township itself. Led by councilman James Duggan, an Irish American, Catholic, conservative Republican, and member of the Knights of Columbus, demonstrators began to picket the clinic and the medical director's private home. In addition, Duggan, hoping to shut the clinic down, introduced a resolution to the Wayne Township Council asking that the county prosecutor's office investigate whether NJWHO was a clinic after all. If the office determined that NJWHO was a clinic, it would require not only a Certificate of Need, but also a zoning variance and a sprinkler system. While NJWHO remained open, the procedural challenges involved the clinic in a lengthy battle with local authorities.[25]

In other cities, too, state and local officials looked to regulations, building codes, and zoning laws to block the opening of abortion clinics. When Hill tried to open the Delaware Women's Health Organization in 1977, she found that Delaware had never repealed its criminal abortion law. Despite *Roe v. Wade*, abortion was still a crime in Delaware. The NWHO went to federal court to ask for a stipulation that Delaware's criminal abortion law was no longer valid.[26] In Fort Wayne, Indiana, the city blocked clinic renovations with building and zoning regulations and, once the building was ready, repeatedly sent unsympathetic inspectors who delayed the opening. Hill spent months arguing about the required permissions. The Fort Wayne Women's Health Organization (FWWHO) finally sued the City of Fort Wayne for damages of $1 million resulting from the endless delays. While city officials were eventually forced to permit the clinic to open, the opening was delayed by at least six months. And in Fargo, North Dakota, antiabortion activists attended a city commission meeting to challenge the issuing of a building permit for an abortion clinic in Fargo. City commissioners temporarily suspended the permit. But warnings from one commissioner that Fargo made itself liable to a lawsuit and Fargo mayor John Lindgren's support of the clinic meant the permit was reissued within twenty-four hours.[27]

Over the following months, as Hill prepared for the opening of the Fargo Women's Health Organization (FWHO), two antiabortion groups began to organize regular protest activities at the new clinic. Within a week of the clinic's opening, one of them, Partners in Vision, presented a petition to the Fargo City Commission rife with allegations about the clinic's disposal of fetal remains, asking for an injunction to close FWHO until the city could pass laws regulating abortion clinics. "The bodies of the aborted babies," the plaintiffs alleged, "are to be ground up and flushed into the Fargo sewer system without proper burials, and would be eventually dispersed into the Red River which could subject this City to lawsuits for contamination and pollution of the river by adjoining cities upstream [sic]."[28] Insinuating that employees of abortion clinics, like guards in Nazi concentration camps, treated bodies with a lack of respect and sought to commercialize as much of the business as possible, the petition further asked "if the human placenta will be sold commercially from the clients they operate on in performing abortions."[29] City commissioners declined the request for a public hearing on the issue and refused to issue an injunction against the clinic. While antiabortion activists in Fargo were unable to close FWHO, the publicity garnered by their appeal and prayer vigils educated Fargo residents to the tactics and arguments of antiabortion activists and attracted members to build an organizational framework. "The constant conflict with state or municipal officials exacts a daily toll on providers," abortion attorney Lynn Miller commented about such regulations. "Many times the experience takes on a distinct Kafkaesque air."[30]

Regulatory neglect could be as harmful to abortion clinics as overregulation. In November 1978, the *Chicago Sun-Times* ran a two-week-long exposé about four Chicago abortion clinics notorious for providing shoddy and unscrupulous services.[31] Over the course of several months, a group of investigative journalists and local civic investigators had infiltrated the clinics posing as patients or new employees. Reminiscent of journalistic coverage prior to *Roe*—and raising the impression that little had changed with legalization—the articles described abortions that six years after *Roe* were perfectly legal but not safe. Prioritizing profits over women's health and lives, medical staff cut corners, rushing women in and out of unsanitary procedure rooms. Physicians performed abortions in such haste that complications were common, and some women were still pregnant after the abortion procedure.

Staff in all four of the clinics investigated by the newspaper engaged in a range of fraudulent and dangerous practices jeopardizing women's health and making the abortion experience painful and unpleasant. They misinformed patients about the results of their pregnancy tests, sold abortions to women who were not pregnant, made up entries in patient charts, and failed to inspect the products of conception after an abortion to ensure that the abortion procedure had been complete.[32] Even when clinics sent specimens to a pathology lab, they frequently used laboratories that sent unreliable reports—and clinic staff regularly failed to share the results with patients.[33] The exposé described clinic owners who lacked interest in their staff's competency and professional demeanor. Some doctors were drunk while performing abortions; others had come to work at the clinics after losing their medical licenses elsewhere. The owners also employed residents who were not trained to provide abortions.[34]

State officials, in turn, did not enforce existing regulations governing the state's abortion clinics. Chicago health authorities failed to seek information that might alert them to poor abortion services, failed to force clinic compliance with inspections, and failed to enforce the closing of clinics that had lost their licenses. After Chicago public health officials revoked a clinic license, they neglected to inform the public about the revocation and failed to check whether the clinic had indeed closed its doors. As a result, at least two clinics continued to operate without valid licenses.[35] When a patient died at Water Tower Reproductive, the state attorney general failed to respond to repeated requests by a coroner to investigate the circumstances of the death.[36] Although enforcement of existing regulations could have prevented the existence of shoddy services, local authorities lacked interest in enforcing the rules and regulations governing abortion clinics. Feminists and members of the abortion provider community worried that the reports of medical abuses in abortion clinics would add fuel to antiabortion sentiments. And indeed, over the following decade, antiabortion activists incorporated the details about patients' experiences in the four discredited Chicago clinics, weaving these stories into often-repeated, if completely erroneous, warnings in which a handful of unscrupulous providers stood for the norm.[37] Indeed, stories of careless and unscrupulous abortion providers, who ran what sociologist Carole Joffe has termed "rogue clinics," became an integral part of antiabortion strategies to illustrate the dangers of abortion, and antiabortion activists relied on the testimony of disaffected clinic staff who would boast to antiabortion audiences about the illegal and unethical practices they had engaged in while working in abortion clinics to discredit the work of abortion providers.[38]

As these examples illustrate, abortion providers were caught between the twin evils of overregulation, on the one hand, and regulatory neglect, on the other. In many states and cities, antiabortion activists seized on a variety of regulatory mechanisms to prevent abortion clinics from opening, or to drive out and intimidate those that had managed to open. On the other hand, haphazard enforcement of health regulations, or outright regulatory neglect, made some local clinics unsafe or contributed to a public perception that they were.

PROTESTS AND HARASSMENT

In the course of the 1980s, antiabortion protestors escalated their aggressive strategies to intimidate patients and clinic staff. Activists sharpened their depiction of abortion as the murder of a child in both narrative and visual form and adopted a vocabulary that conveyed the violence of abortion in every term. They referred to "baby" rather than fetus, "deathscorts" rather than clinic escorts, "death culture" or "abortion culture" rather than American culture, "murder" or "child killing" for abortion, "abortuary," "killing center," or "child killing industry" for abortion clinics, and "killer" or "mass murderer" for abortion providers. Demonstrations became dramatic performances directed at abortion providers and women seeking abortions. Protestors accosted women entering abortion clinics, blocked their access, confronted them physically and verbally, and followed them home. They traced license plate numbers, called patients' homes, entered clinics and disrupted procedures, poured glue into front-door locks, picketed the homes of abortion providers and clinic personnel, sent threatening letters, and made threatening phone calls.[39] Many of the new tactics were developed by Joseph Scheidler, a prominent Chicago antiabortion activist who gained legitimacy as a leader in the movement when the National Right to Life Committee invited him to address its annual convention in 1983. When, in January 1984, President Ronald Reagan welcomed a handful of antiabortion leaders, including Joseph Scheidler, to meet in the White House, antiabortion leaders felt emboldened and legitimized by the political gesture. After getting arrested at a St. Louis picket, a protestor observed that the demonstrators "got a president and a justice department that supports everything we are doing here."[40] Clinic vandalism increased to such an extent that by the mid-1980s, security guards, bomb checks, and escorts for patients were considered essential at many abortion clinics. After the rise of a new antiabortion group Operation Rescue (OR), founded by Randall Terry in 1986 and focused on direct action tactics, picket lines in front of many abortion clinics grew into the hundreds. Unlike their largely peaceful predecessors, demonstrators of the 1980s, armed with posters, plastic fetuses, and specimens in jars, aggressively approached clinic staff and patients, frequently screaming at patients and family members as they systematically escalated antiabortion tactics.[41]

Clinic owners sought the help of the courts and police in order to curb this escalating harassment. In some cities, close collaboration with city officials and community support led to a productive relationship between clinic owners and the police. Claire Keyes, who ran the Alleghany Reproductive Health Center in Pittsburgh, for example, was careful to maintain cordial relations with members of the city council and the police chief. In turn, the local police precinct responded quickly when called and regularly assigned an officer to stand guard on procedure days. Terry Beresford, too, had positive experiences with the police in Washington, DC, where she directed the Preterm Clinic. But while some abortion clinics praised their local law enforcement officials, others were unable to get any help from the police. Up to a third of police officers ignored antiabortion activists who violated the law, and some even sided with the protestors. They offered antiabortion protestors coffee and told them to "keep up the good work." One officer showed Chicago antiabortion leader Joseph Scheidler where patients were sneaking into a clinic during a sit-in.[42]

On balance, police officers were more likely to do nothing than actively aid antiabortion protestors. In the majority of cases where law enforcement officials were uncooperative, officers failed to show up when called, failed to act on or lost complaints that clinics had filed, refused to search for explosive devices when called to a bomb threat, refused to enforce injunctions, and merely watched antiabortion activities from the sidelines, even when protestors violated the law. At other times, officers enforced the law so slowly that antiabortion activists still achieved their goals, arresting protestors who closed a clinic to prevent its opening, for instance, but acting so haltingly that the clinic was closed for the entire day. Police departments frequently excused their lack of action by claiming that they had to stay neutral. City officials and law enforcement in Yakima, Washington, failed to take the threats to the Yakima FWHC seriously until the clinic burned down in its third firebomb attack. Only then did Yakima's mayor finally speak out in support of the clinic, noting that "the severity of the situation requires that police provide the clinic security during non-office hours when it reopens."[43] By that time, clinic director Beverly Whipple dryly noted, there was no clinic to protect. The law, it was clear, was only as good as those who enforced it.

Even when antiabortion activists were arrested, they often escaped punishment. This made it difficult for clinics and their supporters to operate free of protest and required huge investments of their time and resources. Of 1,000 arrests at clinic sit-ins in St. Louis during an eight-year period spanning the late 1970s to the mid-1980s, only thirty people were convicted. Countless legal loopholes and court backlogs meant that activists could frequently postpone sentencing indefinitely. When in court, activists used their cases as a forum for their cause. "We are in the right legally, but I feel so helpless," noted Judith Widdicombe, who headed Reproductive Health Services in St. Louis. "The legal remedies aren't working."[44] Even when abortion clinics won their legal cases against antiabortion activists or against townships that sought to deny clinics the necessary permits, they did so at tremendous financial and emotional cost to clinic owners and staff. Susan Hill, who regularly went to court on behalf of NWHO's ten clinics, won almost all her cases against townships and antiabortion activists. But NWHO legal expenses for individual clinics could far exceed the clinic's annual profits.[45]

The lack of legal response meant the protection of abortion clinics and women's access to reproductive health care became privatized, the responsibility of clinic owners. Clinics were forced to shoulder the costs of clinic protection themselves. Many clinics hired security guards and installed alarm systems. These steps were often prohibitively expensive and turned clinics into fortresses.[46] The escalation of antiabortion violence had another costly effect: almost 80 percent of clinics lost their property and liability insurance, and some clinics lost their leases and were forced to close. New insurance policies were often ten times more expensive. The financial burden forced some clinics to cut employee salaries, eliminate extra programs, and raise the price of abortion. In this sense, clinic protests had a two-pronged effect on local abortion access: they created a formidable and intimidating environment for ordinary women seeking abortions, and they threatened the clinics themselves with financial ruin.[47]

Throughout the late 1980s, clinics and local law enforcement agencies developed counterstrategies and challenged the legality of clinic blockades. These efforts slowly bore fruit. By 1990, Operation Rescue's ability to amass hundreds of protestors had faded, owing in part to the resilience of the abortion provider community and to its success in raising the awareness of legislators and in reshaping the politics of police and FBI. Tragically, antiabortion extremism played a role as well. On March 10, 1993, barely two months after the inauguration of President Bill Clinton, antiabortion activist Michael Griffin shot abortion provider David Gunn outside Women's Medical Services in Pensacola, Florida. The killing of David Gunn led to an immediate escalation of harassment and violence against abortion providers. Within two weeks, Senator Edward Kennedy (D-Mass.) introduced the Freedom of Access to Clinic Entrances (FACE) Act. One week later, the Subcommittee on Crime and Criminal Justice, led by Representative Charles E. Schumer (D-NY), opened hearings on clinic violence. A long list of witnesses testified to their experiences with antiabortion activists. To illustrate that the federal government was finally listening, the hearings were broadcast on radio and TV. Abortion providers also increased their pleas to the White House to have the Justice Department investigate violence against abortion clinics.[48] Under Janet Reno, the Justice Department finally created a unit on antiabortion terrorism. And, in acknowledgment that local law enforcement agencies had proved inadequate in protecting clinics from destruction and sabotage, legislators passed and Bill Clinton signed into law the 1994 FACE Act, making it a federal crime to interfere with access to any facility providing reproductive health services.

While providers were relieved at the intervention of the federal government and the passage of FACE, the immediate relief that clinic owners hoped for did not materialize. Providers complained of being ignored by the agencies that should have enforced the new laws. Asked to investigate clinic fires, the Bureau of Alcohol, Tobacco, and Firearms was uncooperative. Worse, immediately after the shooting of David Gunn, abortion providers in Pensacola, Florida, and elsewhere became concerned about the behavior of Paul Hill. But attempts to have him arrested failed.[49] Less than three months later, Hill killed John Britton and James Barrett, a physician and a volunteer clinic escort, respectively, outside a Pensacola clinic. Other hotspots of aggressive antiabortion activism also failed to draw federal attention and shortly after became the sites of violence. Still, by late 1994, federal intervention showed some results. While the passage of FACE was only as effective as police authorities' willingness to enforce it, in many locations it was directly responsible for the declining number of violent outbursts and blockades at clinics, actions that had now become federal crimes.[50]

ERECTING BARRIERS TO ABORTION ACCESS

Over the course of the 1980s, antiabortion activists sought to follow the implementation of the Hyde Amendment and the gag rule with an attempt to invalidate the *Roe v. Wade* decision with a constitutional amendment. Failing that, they hoped to impose restrictions on the practice of abortion care. State legislatures passed a host of antiabortion regulations, from parental and spousal consent requirements to counseling provisions to bans of certain abortion procedures. Initially, as states began to draft laws that would restrict women's access to abortion, the US Supreme Court struck down attempts to limit access to abortion. In *Planned Parenthood of Central Missouri v. Danforth* (1976), the Supreme Court struck down a Missouri law requiring parental consent to a minor's abortion, a husband's written consent to his wife's abortion, a woman's written and informed consent, and a ban on second-trimester saline procedures. Seven years later, in *Akron v. Akron Center for Reproductive Health, Inc.* (1983), the court struck down a twenty-four-hour waiting period, a hospitalization requirement for abortions after the first trimester, parental consent to abortion for girls aged fifteen or younger, a doctor-only counseling provision, a requirement that women receive specific information during the counseling session, and strict instructions about the disposal of fetal waste. And in 1986, the court in *Thornburgh v. American College of Obstetricians and Gynecologists*—a case that challenged Pennsylvania's 1982 Abortion Control Act—rejected a state-mandated counseling script read by doctors to patients, a requirement that doctors attempt to save fetuses in post-viability abortions, a requirement that two doctors attend post-viability abortions, and a reporting requirement that allowed public access to abortion records.[51]

But, as the constellation of the Supreme Court changed with the retirement of six justices who had voted to decriminalize abortion and who were replaced by more conservative justices, activists on both sides of the abortion debate expected by the late 1980s that *Roe* might be overturned.[52] In 1993, the court considered Pennsylvania's 1989 Abortion Control Act in *Planned Parenthood of Southeastern Pennsylvania v. Casey*, which contained regulations requiring clinics to impose a twenty-four-hour waiting period, state-mandated counseling, parental consent for minors, and a reporting requirement. While antiabortion advocates regarded Casey as the long-awaited occasion for the court to overrule *Roe* outright, the justices felt bound by the earlier *Roe* decision and noted that legal abortion had become so established that its reversal was imprudent.[53]

The justices didn't overturn *Roe*, but they now felt comfortable imposing barriers to accessing abortion that previous Supreme Court decisions had struck down. Indeed, states wishing to impose abortion restrictions now simply had to demonstrate that the burden imposed on women's access to abortion was not "undue"—that is, placed no "substantial obstacles in the path of a woman seeking an abortion of a nonviable fetus."[54] This shift greatly undermined doctors' authority in abortion decisions, replacing the physician as gatekeeper to abortion with the state legislature, which could now set very precise terms under which abortions may take place. The court also began to treat women as a group that needed to be protected from their own choices. Upholding state-mandated counseling language suggested that women seeking abortions needed counseling, that physicians who counsel women before an abortion needed to be told how to counsel their patients, and that both parties were unreasonable and needed the state to step in.[55]

Empowered by *Casey*, states began to impose a host of abortion barriers that the Supreme Court upheld in subsequent decisions. Most common are state-imposed counseling, mandatory delay, and parental notification and consent laws. A majority of states now have all of these provisions. Counseling laws vary from state to state but tend to require physicians to read scripts to their patients that are biased against abortion and offer medical information that is not pertinent or is possibly misleading. In most states, mandatory delays after counseling mean that patients have to wait twenty-four to seventy-two hours between counseling and their abortion procedures, requiring several trips to the abortion clinic.[56] Most significant, in 2007, the US Supreme Court upheld the first ban on a particular abortion procedure—intact dilation and evacuation (D&E), the so-called partial-birth abortion procedure—in its *Gonzales v. Carhart* decision without granting an exception for a woman's health or life.

In addition, TRAP laws (Targeted Restrictions on Abortion Providers) impose restrictions on facilities that perform abortions, while hospitals-only and physician-only bills limit where abortions may be performed and by whom. Passed under the guise that such laws would make abortion services safer, none of these restrictions increased the safety of abortion procedures, which were already the safest outpatient procedures available.[57] All of them have made abortion services more difficult to access by placing obstacles in the way for women seeking abortion services or forcing abortion providers to raise their prices to meet burdensome and costly requirements.[58]

Recently, in the 2016 Texas case *Whole Woman's Health v. Hellerstedt*, the Supreme Court used the *Casey* standard to recognize certain kinds of limits on access to abortion as an "undue burden"—making abortion so hard to get that a woman's right to choose the procedure was unconstitutionally curtailed. Texas had required all abortion providers to have admitting privileges at a hospital not more than thirty miles from the abortion clinic. It also required all abortion clinics to be licensed as ambulatory surgical centers. Enforcement of these provisions would have reduced the number of abortion clinics in Texas from forty to around ten. The *Whole Woman's Health* decision (5–4) clearly signaled that there are constitutional limits to abortion regulations.[59] "In the face of no threat to women's health," the court stated,

> Texas seeks to force women to travel long distances to get abortions in crammed-to-capacity superfacilities. Patients seeking these services are less likely to get the kind of individualized attention, serious conversation, and emotional support that doctors at less taxed facilities may have offered. Health care facilities and medical professionals are not fungible commodities.[60]

In 2020, the court addressed the constitutionality of a law from Louisiana that virtually duplicated the invalidated Texas law, and affirmed its own previous decision (5–4), sustaining the "undue burden" standard. Chief Justice John Roberts, who had dissented from the majority opinion in *Whole Woman's Health*, now voted with the liberal majority to uphold the 2016 precedent—for the sake of precedent—but reiterated that he thought *Whole Woman's Health* wrongly decided. The court's recognition of some state limits as "undue" thus hangs by a thread; President Donald Trump's two appointees to the Supreme Court dissented, and would have allowed Louisiana to limit abortion access.

Even if *Roe v. Wade* should not be overturned, the practical impact of abortion restrictions has led to a return of the pre-*Roe* two-tier system of access in which women with means are able to obtain an abortion while women without resources are likely to have to carry their unwanted pregnancies to term. To poor, rural, young, and minority women, the right to choose abortion may hold no meaning.

Looking back over the past four and a half decades, state power played a much more significant role in circumscribing and restricting women's access to abortion than it did in protecting their access to abortion care. In the long run, the *Roe* decision did not offer women protections that could withstand challenges to abortion access. Instead, antiabortion activists' wide variety of tactics harnessed state power to their cause in a multitude of ways. Antiabortion activists did not passively wait for the US Supreme Court to acquire an antiabortion majority, however critical judicial appointments remained to the movement. They applied constant pressure at all levels of governance, from the three federal branches to state legislatures and down to local police power in municipalities. No leverage point was overlooked. Failing to acknowledge women as full human beings with moral decision-making capacities and the right to full autonomy, the *Roe* decision did not prevent this determined and creative marshaling of state power against women's reproductive rights.

NOTES

1. Susan Hill, interview with Johanna Schoen, May 2004, Raleigh, NC.

2. See, for instance, Frederick J. Taussig, *Abortion, Spontaneous and Induced: Medical and Social Aspects* (St. Louis, MO: C. V. Mosbach, 1936); Lawrence Lader, *Abortion* (Boston: Beacon Press, 1966); and Mary Streichen Calderone, ed., *Abortion in the United States: A Conference Sponsored by the Planned Parenthood Federation of America, Inc. at Arden House and the New York Academy of Medicine* (New York: Harper and Brothers, 1958).

3. Willard Cates Jr. and David A. Grimes, "Morbidity and Mortality of Abortion

in the United States," in *Abortion and Sterilization: Medical and Social Aspects*, ed. Jane E. Hodgson (New York: Grune and Stratton, 1981), 170.

4. Melody Rose, *Safe, Legal, and Unavailable? Abortion Politics in the United States* (Washington, DC: CQ Press, 2007), 110, 72; and David S. Cohen and Carole Joffe, *Obstacle Course: The Everyday Struggle to Get an Abortion in America* (Oakland: University of California Press, 2020).

5. Cates and Grimes, "Morbidity and Mortality," 170.

6. Chuck deProsse, interview with Johanna Schoen, May 31, 2011, Iowa City.

7. These statistics include abortion providers who performed more than five abortions per year. Guttmacher Institute, "Number of Providers, Abortions, and Abortions per Provider by Type of Provider and Metropolitan Status, 1977–82, 1984–85, and 1987–88"; and "Number of Abortion Providers by Provider Type and State, 1973–85 and 1987–88" (documents given to author by Guttmacher Institute).

8. Jane E. Hodgson, "Abortion by Vacuum Aspiration," in *Abortion and Sterilization: Medical and Social Aspects*, ed. Jane E. Hodgson (New York: Grune and Stratton, 1981), 229.

9. Christopher Tietze, F. S. Jaffe, E. Weinstock, and J. G. Dryfoos, *Provisional Estimates of Abortion Need and Services in the Year following the 1973 Supreme Court Decisions* (New York: Alan Guttmacher Institute, 1975). In 1980, 459 out of a total of 2,758 providers performed 1,000 abortions or more per year. See Alan Guttmacher Institute, Table 5, Number of Providers, Abortions, and Abortions per Provider.

10. Deborah Nathanson, n.d., folder Correspondence—Feminists Wanting to Start Clinics, box 64, Emma Goldman Clinic Collection [EGC], Iowa Women's Archive, University of Iowa, Iowa City.

11. Lynn Randall, phone interview with Johanna Schoen, October 22, 2012; Sandra Morgen, *Into Our Own Hands: The Women's Health Movement in the United States, 1969–1990* (New Brunswick, NJ: Rutgers University Press, 2002); D. Nathanson, n.d., and Paula Klein to Jackie Nowell, July 12, 1976, both in folder Correspondence—Feminists Wanting to Start Clinics, EGC; Anne Enke, *Finding the Movement: Sexuality, Contested Space, and Feminist Activism* (Durham, NC: Duke University Press, 2007); and Wendy Simonds, *Abortion at Work: Ideology and Practice in a Feminist Clinic* (New Brunswick, NJ: Rutgers University Press, 1996).

12. Lories Caratozzolo, "Abortion Ruling—For Some Too Late," *Patterson News*, November 28, 1976.

13. Since that time, the specific exceptions to the Medicaid ban have fluctuated. As a rule, since 1977 the federal government has not funded abortions in all but the most dire instances. The Center for American Progress data indicate that in 2001 only eighty-one women received federal funding under the Hyde Amendment. Rose, *Safe, Legal, and Unavailable?*, 110.

14. Rose, *Safe, Legal, and Unavailable?*, 72.

15. Stanley K. Henshaw, Jacqueline Darroch Forrest, Ellen Sullivan, and Christopher Tietze, "Abortion 1977–1979: Need and Services in the United States, Each State and Metropolitan Area" (report of the Alan Guttmacher Institute, New York, 1981), 62–65. Medicaid cuts would have been even more drastic, had fourteen states not continued to pay for abortions from Medicaid funds.

16. Roy Lucas and Lynn I. Miller, "Evolution of Abortion Law in North America," in *Abortion and Sterilization: Medical and Social Aspects*, ed. Jane E. Hodgson (New York: Grune and Stratton, 1981), 102–3; Cynthia Gorney, *Articles of Faith: A Frontline History of the Abortion Wars* (New York: Simon and Schuster, 1998), 280–81; Rose, *Safe, Legal, and Unavailable?*, 109–11; and Ellen Frankfort, with Frances Kissling, *Rosie: The Investigation of a Wrongful Death* (New York: Dial Press, 1979).

17. Stanley K. Henshaw, ed., *Abortion Services in the United States, Each State and Metropolitan Area, 1979–80* (Alan Guttmacher Institute, 1983).

18. For a careful analysis of this process, see Jennifer Donnally, "The Politics of Abortion and the Rise of the New Right" (PhD diss., University of North Carolina, 2013).

19. Victoria Johnson, "The Strategic Determinants of a Countermovement: The Emergence and Impact of Operation Rescue Blockades," in *Waves of Protest: Social Movements Since the Sixties*, ed. Jo Freeman and Victoria Johnson (Lanham, MD: Rowman and Littlefield, 1999), 241–66; and Diane diMauro and Carole Joffe, "The Religious Right and the Reshaping of Sexual Policy: An Examination of Reproductive Rights and Sexuality Education," *Sexuality Research and Social Policy* 4, no. 1 (March 2007): 67–92.

20. Jacqueline Darroch Forrest and Stanley K. Henshaw, "The Harassment of U.S Abortion Providers," *Family Planning Perspectives* 19, no. 1 (January/February 1987): 9–13; and Rose, *Safe, Legal, and Unavailable?*, 125–28.

21. The gag rule is also referred to as the Mexico City policy, since Reagan made his announcement while at the 1984 United Nations Population Conference in Mexico City. In addition, no private money could be spent for abortions on premises funded through the federal government.

22. Clinton rescinded the ban in 1993, but Bush reinstated it in 2001. Rose, *Safe, Legal, and Unavailable?*, 134–35.

23. Hill, interview, May 2004.

24. Susan Hill, interview with Johanna Schoen, February 3, 2008, Raleigh, NC.

25. Lorain Yoder and Joseph Kelly, "Wayne Target of Suit," *Patterson News*, September 10, 1976; Joseph Kelly, "Abortion Center OK Near," *Patterson News*, September 16, 1976; "Abortion Site Maligned," *Herald News*, November 4, 1976; James L Duggan, letter to the editor, *Wayne Today*, December 1, 1976; and Niles Lathem, "Abortion Foes Fail to Shut Down the Clinic," *Patterson Evening News*, February 15, 1980.

26. Susan Hill, Interview with Johanna Schoen, June 18, 2008, Raleigh, NC; see *Delaware Women's Health Organ., Inc. v. Wier*, 441 F. Supp. 497 (D. Del. 1977).

27. Ed Maixner, "Abortions Confirmed: Building Permit Suspended at New Clinic in Fargo," *Fargo-Morehead Forum*, September 4, 1981, 1–2; and Jim Neumann, "Lindgren Orders Clinic Permit Reissued," *Fargo-Morehead Forum*, September 5, 1981, 1–2.

28. Partners in Vision to the City Commissioners for the City of Fargo, ND, October 1981, file Fargo (3 of 3), box 5, Susan Hill Papers [SHP], Duke University Libraries, Sally Bingham Center [DUL-SBC], Durham, NC.

29. Partners in Vision to the City Commissioners for the City of Fargo.

30. Lynn Miller, Esq., "Clinic Licensing and Zoning Harassment," *NAF Quar-*

terly, Summer 1983, series Abortion, File NAF 1983, Takey Crist Papers [TCP], DUL-SBC.

31. Pamela Zekman and Pamela Warrick, "12 Dead after Abortion in State's Walk-in Clinics," *Chicago Sun-Times*, November 19, 1978, 1, 10, 44; and Pamela Zekman and Pamela Warrick, "Men Who Profit from Women's Pain," *Chicago Sun-Times*, November 13, 1978, 1.

32. Pamela Zekman and Pamela Warrick, "Nurse to Aid," *Chicago Sun-Times*, November 16, 1978, 4; Pamela Zekman and Pamela Warrick, "The Abortion Profiteers: Making a Killing in Michigan Av. Clinics," *Chicago Sun-Times*, November 12, 1978, 5.

33. Zekman and Warrick, "12 Dead after Abortion," 1, 10, 44; Pamela Zekman and Pamela Warrick, "Probe Michigan Av. Abortion Clinic Death," *Chicago Sun-Times*, November 17, 1978, 1, 4.

34. Pamela Zekman and Pamela Warrick, "The Abortion Lottery," *Chicago Sun-Times*, November 14, 1978, 1, 4–5.

35. Karen Koshner and Pamela Zekman, "Jury Subpoenas Records of Abortion Clinic," *Chicago Sun-Times*, November 12, 1978, 5, 52; Zekman and Warrick, "Abortion Profiteers," 1.

36. Zekman and Warrick, "Probe Michigan Av. Abortion Clinic Death," 1, 4.

37. Prominent antiabortion leader Joseph Scheidler took credit for the closing of several Chicago abortion clinics. See, for instance, Joseph M. Scheidler, *Closed: 99 Ways to Stop Abortion* (Rockford, IL: Tan Books and Publishers, 1985; rev. ed., 1993), 172–73.

38. Schoen, *Abortion After* Roe (Chapel Hill: University of North Carolina Press, 2015), 110–18, 139–40, 250. See also Carole Joffe, "Learning the Right Lessons from the Philadelphia Abortion Clinic Disaster," *Dissent* (January 31, 2011), https://www.dissentmagazine.org/blog/learning-the-right-lessons-from-the-philadelphia-abortion-clinic-disaster (accessed June 23, 2020).

39. Jeffrey Kaplan, "Absolute Rescue: Absolutism, Defensive Action and the Resort to Force," in *Millennialism and Violence*, ed. Michal Barkun (New York: Routledge, 1996), 129; and Alesha Doan, *Opposition and Intimidation: The Abortion Wars and Strategies of Political Harassment* (Ann Arbor: University of Michigan Press, 1997), 113.

40. Faye D. Ginsburg, *Contested Lives: The Abortion Debate in an American Community* (Berkeley: University of California Press, 1989), 51; and *Holy Terror*, 1987, Susan Hill Papers.

41. Ginsburg, *Contested Lives*, 51; and *National Organization for Women et al. v. Joseph M Scheidler et al.*, US District Court, Eastern Division, no. 86C788, Motion for Leave to File First Amendment Complaint, file Joseph Scheidler lawsuits, series Abortion, TCP.

42. Morris Turner, interview with Johanna Schoen, October 6, 2013, Pittsburgh, PA; Terry Beresford, interview with Johanna Schoen, September 30, 2012, Alexandria, VA; Rochelle Sharpe, "Clinics Get Little Support from Officials," *Abortion: The New Militancy*, Gannett News Service Special Report, December 1985, 11, file NWHO, General Reports, Rochelle Sharp, Police Response, Susan Hill Papers; and Sharpe, "Clinics Get Little Support," 11.

43. Sharpe, "Clinics Get Little Support," 12; Testimony of Beverly Whipple. FWHC, Yakima, WA, March 6, 1995, before the Subcommittee on Civil and Constitutional Rights of the Committee of the Judiciary House of Representatives, 99th Cong., 1st and 2nd sess. On Abortion Clinic Violence, March 6, 12, April 3, 1985, and December 17, 1986, serial no. 115.

44. Rochelle Sharpe, "Trials Make Winners Out of Those Arrested," *Abortion: The New Militancy*, Gannett News Service Special Report, December 1985, 13, file Joseph Scheidler, background series Abortion, TCP.

45. Sharpe, "Clinics Get Little Support from Officials," 12.

46. *FWWHO v. Nurses Concerned for Life*, Hearing on Diversity, September 5, 1979, SHP.

47. Testimony of Heather C. Green, Hillcrest Clinics, before the Subcommittee on Civil and Constitutional Rights, March 6, 1985, Abortion Clinic Violence: Oversight Hearings before the Subcommittee on Civil and Constitutional Rights of the Committee of the Judiciary House of Representatives, 99th Cong., 1st and 2nd sess. On Abortion Clinic Violence, March 6, 12, April 3, 1985, and December 17, 1986, serial no. 115; and Testimony of Beverly Whipple.

48. James Risen and Judy L. Tomas, *Wrath of Angels: the American Abortion War* (New York: Basic Books, 1998), chapter 8; Patricia Baird-Windle and Eleanor J. Bader, *Targets of Hatred: Anti-Abortion Terrorism* (New York: Palgrave, 2001), 210; and NCAP, October 6, 1993, file NCAP 1993, series Abortion, TCP.

49. NCAP, September 29, 1994, file NCAP 1994, series Abortion, TCP.

50. Rose, *Safe, Legal, and Unavailable?*, 96–97.

51. Rose *Safe, Legal, and Unavailable?*, 57–85.

52. Carol Sanger, *About Abortion: Terminating Pregnancy in 21st Century America* (Cambridge, MA: Harvard University Press, 2017), 30. None of the seven Supreme Court justices supporting the original *Roe v. Wade* remain on the court. More conservative justices have been appointed since then. With the recent replacement (during the Trump administration) of justices Anthony Kennedy and Ruth Bader Ginsburg with two conservatives (Brett M. Kavanaugh and Amy Coney Barrett), only three justices, Stephen Breyer, Sonia Sotomayor, and Elena Kagan, are seen as reliable votes in defense, raising the possibility that *Roe v. Wade* might be overturned.

53. Sanger, *About Abortion*, 31.

54. Rose, *Safe, Legal, and Unavailable*, 63–64.

55. Rose, *Safe, Legal, and Unavailable*, 57–85.

56. https://www.guttmacher.org/state-policy/explore/counseling-and-waiting-periods-abortion, accessed June 20, 2018.

57. Cates and Grimes, "Morbidity and Mortality," 170.

58. Reva B. Siegel, "The Right's Reasons: Constitutional Conflict and the Spread of Woman-Protective Antiabortion Argument," *Duke Law Journal* 57 (2008): 1641–92; Cohen and Joffe, *Obstacle Course*.

59. Sanger, *About Abortion*, 34–36.

60. *Whole Women's Health v. Hellerstedt*, 136 S. Ct. 2292, 2318 (2016).

14

The Work That Sex Does

PAISLEY CURRAH

Legal historian William Novak writes that "the idea that there is some kind of essence or structure . . . to this thing called 'the state' . . . is a source of constant confusion and misdirected, scholarly energy."[1] In fact, *the state* is not a singular entity, defined by structure or function, but a multitude of agencies, legislatures, and courts that rely on practices, laws, rules, and norms that operate—often at cross-purposes—at every level of government. Sex might be said to have a similar indeterminacy. The commonsense idea that sex has an essence, that female and male are easily distinguished from one another and mutually exclusive—what Harold Garfinkel called the "natural attitude" toward sex[2]—is belied by the lack of consensus on its definition.[3] On the matter of bodies and identifications and their histories, conceptual clarity is forced to give way to empirical messiness. There are several criteria governments can and do use for determining sex classification: for example, visible genitalia at birth, visible genitalia in the present, chromosomes, secondary sex characteristics, gender identity.

When the belief that *the state* is a thing, and a unitary one at that, converges with the cognate assumption that sex is defined by a singular agreed-upon property, the result is a mess of contradictions. Individuals who attempt to change how state entities classify their sex often find themselves in a paradoxical position, classified as M in one jurisdiction and F in another, as M by one agency and F by another. How is it that a judge in Illinois decides that a person who has an F on her driver's license is male? How is it that the California Department of Corrections places most transgender women in men's prisons even as that state allows women just like them to have an F on their driver's licenses? Whether or not an agency will change one's sex classification to M, F, or X is a matter of crucial importance to transgender and non-binary people. An examination of these policy differences also exposes how sex has been used, and is still used to some degree, as a technology of governing.

This chapter considers the recent past and potential futures of "intimate states" through the lens of sex reclassification. My examination of sex reclassification policies that regulated if and under what circumstances agencies and courts will allow an individual to change their sex classification revealed that these contradictory policies could not be adequately explained by the presence or absence of transphobia. That led me to three observations. First, until recently, the sex reclassification policies that harmed transgender people were a residual effect of the use of the categories of male and female to distribute rights and resources. Now that sex has been largely though not entirely decommissioned as a formal mechanism for this maldistribution—*Obergefell v. Hodges* might turn out to have been its death knell—the stakes in reclassification are much lower, and as a result obstacles to changing one's sex classification have abated in the last decades. This residual effect was not entrenched equally in different areas of governance: some areas were much more likely to yield to demands for reform than others. That led me to my second observation: the definition of sex in statutes, court decisions, regulations, and informally in agency practices—often made visible by sex *re*classification policies—has often depended on what work the definition has done (or continues to do) for particular state projects. Because different state actors do different things, sex has been called upon to do different kinds of work. Sometimes it has been a tool for nation-building, as in marriage law; sometimes it has been a tool for affirming identity and tracking individuals, as in identity documents. My final observation is that the structural privileges accorded to particular types of gendered people—male, heterosexual, cisgender ("heads" of households)—are slowly diminishing as market logics favor fungibility over status. Of course, the political right has tried, not entirely successfully, to enroll transgender people in the culture wars, and the barriers to sex reclassification that remain are now more likely to reflect red-state politics.

I use *sex* rather than *gender* to refer to the Ms and Fs on state-issued identity documents, in government records, and in judges' decisions. It's an understatement to say that sex and gender are both highly contested terms. Indeed, much of the battle between transgender people and conservative gender revanchists hinges precisely on the meanings of sex, of gender, or of both. Conservatives have generally held that one's classification as F or M should be based on one's genitalia at birth—or, in the view of the Republican National Committee, anatomy at birth *and* one's XX/XY chromosomal pattern.[4] Trans rights advocates argue that gender identity should be the sole determining factor. Many policymakers hold positions somewhere in between—requiring some sort of surgery, body modification, or verification by a medical expert. In my work, sex is simply whatever an entity whose decisions are backed by the force of law says it is. That makes it easier to keep the focus on what sex does, not on what sex *really* is or how it *should be* defined. Gender is used in discussions of shared, though often contested, norms, narratives, practices, and conventions that arrange bodies, identities, roles, and expressions in hierarchies of difference based on binary notions of male/female, man/woman, and masculinity/femininity.

Throughout the twentieth century and well into the twenty-first, some people in the United States had no certainty about whether they would be designated as M or F by the government. When some individuals walked into a government office to apply for benefits, to get a new driver's license, to sign up for selective service, to get married, or to get divorced, their sex classification often switched from male to female, or from female to male. Even within a single jurisdiction, almost every state agency—from federal to municipal—had and still has the authority to decide its own rules for sex reclassification. And, to complicate matters even more, both state and federal judges have found that one's sex classification for some social functions may not hold for others. The lack of a universal standard for classifying people as male or female still means that some state agencies will recognize the new sex of people who change it, while others will not. In New York City, a woman could be housed in a women's homeless shelter, sent to a men's prison upstate, and have an F on her driver's license. Before New York State made same-sex marriages legal in 2011, any marriage to a cisgender man could have been invalidated because of the sex assigned to her at birth. Were she to move to another state, all these questions would have been reopened.

From the vantage point of the transgender political movement, obstacles to gender recognition, including policies on sex reclassification, have been at worst symptoms of ill will toward trans people or at best unintentional neglect of the community's needs. If transphobia is the cause of unfair sex reclassification policies, so the assumption goes, arguments centering the humanity of trans people will bring about the solution. Thus, trans rights advocates work to dispel the apparently irrational animus toward people whose gender identity and/or expression does not comport with social expectations based on the sex assigned at birth. This is to be accomplished by invoking the commonsense mantras of transgender rights advocacy, which typically rely on medical accounts of the immutability of gender identity, invoke the liberalism of an embodied possessive individualism ("everyone has a gender identity"), describe forms of gender nonconformity as benign variations of ways of "doing gender," narrate nontraditional gender presentations and embodiments as forms of free expression, or deploy all or any combinations of these rationales.

The debunking transphobia approach has much to be said for it, not least that it has seen many successes in the last two decades. But I think it needs to be supplemented by an explanation that takes a longer historical view, one that would have us remember that until very recently the obstacles that trans people have faced with regard to sex classification were effects of gender-based oppression. In European and, later, American legal traditions, gender difference was codified in laws designed to limit the rights and resources available to white women (women of color were controlled by racial regimes). From marital property and inheritance laws to the inability to vote to exemptions for marital rape in the criminal sphere, the law's distinctions between men and women have illustrated how deeply patriarchal norms were incorporated into state structures. (In a few cases, such as divorce and child support laws requiring husbands or fathers to provide for ex-wives and children, or the different ages at which widowers and widows could begin drawing Social Security benefits, the distinction disadvantaged men, though for the purpose of protecting the public purse, not to redistribute wealth to women.) Over the course of the twentieth century, however, the machinery of state-sanctioned gender discrimination was slowly and unevenly dismantled in the United States. By the turn of this century, while much of that discrimination had been eliminated, states still distinguished between men and women in all forms of government-issued identification, in registration for selective service, in combat roles in the military (changed in 2015), in facilities traditionally segregated by gender, in restrictions on abortion rights, and in laws that limited marriage to heterosexual couples.[5]

The dismantling has been salutary, but it has not meant the end of gender subordination. Nor, for my purposes, has it freed sex classification from its legal entanglement in the long history of that subordination. It is too early to determine whether the Supreme Court's 2015 decision in *Obergefell v. Hodges* signifies a fundamental turning point. *Obergefell* held that the state institution perhaps most responsible for maintaining gender subordination, marriage, could no longer be limited to opposite-sex couples.[6] Although the stated rationale centered on the harms of excluding same-sex couples, the decision stands as a landmark of the disestablishment of gender. This article centers on the recent past, when contradictions between sex classification policies were at their most pronounced: before *Obergefell* yet after transgender rights claims had evolved from anomalies occasionally presented to policymakers into a larger and more purposeful movement, loosely from the late 1990s to 2015.

That there has never been a uniform policy governing who is male and who is female was not, in its origins, an effect of intentional hostility directed against people called transsexual in the twentieth century or transgender in the twenty-first. Nor is it merely an artifact of federalism. Instead, transgender people inhabit, and still continue to inhabit in many jurisdictions and for many agencies, what Susan Leigh Star and Geoffrey C. Bowker call residual categories: "that which is left over after a classification is built."[7] The borders of categories come into sharp relief in response to an unanticipated or abnormal situation not imagined in the first instance. Initially set out in the abstract, categories are defined fully *ex post facto*—though some almost immediately so—their interiors made visible only after a particular case troubles the assumptions and becomes its constitutive outside.

Like the proverbial ships passing in the night, investigations into sex definition by state bodies have not been in conversation with research on gender and distributive justice. Scholarship and advocacy about transgender rights has hewed closely to the language of recognition, focusing on the special case of sex misclassification. A little bit of tinkering with the rules, perhaps the adoption of a uniform standard for all jurisdictions and state functions or even the disestablishment of sex altogether, and the unfairness is reformed away. While it is essential for transgender rights advocates to seek short-term fixes to the problems of sex classification, in the longer term we need to advance a critical framework that identifies the historical formations that have produced it.

Feminist scholarship, by comparison, considers the ways in which gender has operated as a foundation for a host of other social arrangements— not just marriage, but the family, private property, the nation, race, and citizenship. But that scholarship takes the categories of M/F as a priori when examining how states use them to distribute rights and resources.[8] The situation faced by transgender people becomes, once again, an oddity, if it is mentioned at all. Rather than understand how the deviant case of the sexually misclassified might actually structure the normal situation, the issue devolves into the problem of sex misclassification suffered by a small band of gender nonconformers or "transsexual menaces."[9] What's more, the differing criteria for sex definition from agency to agency, from court to court, from jurisdiction to jurisdiction, from one social function to another, which should be recognized by scholars as a wellspring of data, have either been overlooked or examined as only illogical discrepancies in the classification of transgender people. Examining those differences in sex definition policies could do much to help us understand how gender works in particular contexts to distribute inequality. Such an understanding might also support, and occasionally challenge, theories of gender justice and histories of state-sponsored gender discrimination. Thus far, neither research on the ins and outs of sex classification policies nor work on gender as a distributive mechanism for states examines how these issues are not just connected but possibly mutually constitutive.

In this chapter, I take what is a heterodox approach for transgender studies, which, despite a collective anti-naturalism, is nevertheless an identity studies field and as such has consolidated around the category of transgender. First, I toggle the focus from those harmed to the institutions doing the harming. Second, I let go of the default assumption that transphobia is the cause of policies that harm trans people. Third, I do not assume that sex "misrecognition" constitutes a singular phenomenon. Instead, I examine the policies and decisions that constitute these injustices separately. The intellectual conceit of this approach is to start with apparently contradictory sex reclassification policies or decisions and then, instead of amalgamating them into a global explanation of transphobia, to separate the strands and push on them in a synchronic analysis to reveal the particular, and differing, governing rationalities at play. Instead of simply seeing an individual who has been classified as both male and female as representing a contradiction, a paradox, a bureaucratic mistake, and calling for that injustice to be rectified, I suggest that such a situation only seems paradoxical if one assumes that state decisions about F and M index something outside or before the decision itself, something that should be consistent regardless of the particular governing apparatus that decides. For the purposes of understanding these logics, it's necessary, at least provisionally, to let go of any notions about what M/F actually are, or how they *should* be defined. This is not to suggest that there aren't injustices in the here and now to be rectified. But it is to suggest that switching the conceptual apparatus can make visible the historical formations that factored into their production.

Underlying the assumption that contradictory sex classification policies indicate a mistake has been made is the idea that there is a knowable, universal, transparent relationship between the M or F inked on a document or the 01101101 or 01000110 pulses of electricity haunting government records and what it signifies. But this assumption might also stem from the belief that *the state* tends to express an underlying coherence, that *it* knows what it's doing. But there is no singular state. The ataxic disarray of state actors in the United States results not only from the federal structure but also from the uncountable number of institutions across all jurisdictions—from legislatures, courts, departments, and agencies to elected officials, political appointees, and civil servants and street-level bureaucrats to constitutions, laws, regulations, administrative rules, and informal norms and practices. What makes this hard to fathom, as Timothy Mitchell has suggested in an important critique of political science literature on the state, is that while in actuality states are messy, diffuse, and ambiguous, the "public imaginary of the state as an ideological construct is more coherent."[10]

Rather than assuming that states are, at any given moment, already defined by their function or form, it's more illuminating to first focus on what they do. In her work on the federal regulation of homosexuality in the twentieth century, Margot Canaday starts with the premise that "we can see the state through its practices; the state is 'what officials do.'"[11] Likewise, stories reproducing the idea that sex is simply "nature" render the disorder, the messiness, the actual indeterminacy of that category neat and clear by putting it spatially "outside" politics and temporally "before" the creation of political society. "Sex," however, is just as messy and diffuse a concept as "the state." And so, if the only thing we know for sure about sex is what a state actor says it is in any particular instance, and if "the state" is not unitary, coordinated, and hierarchically organized in an ultimately rational way, then it should come as no surprise that state definitions of sex are also plural.

Since at least the late 1960s, activists across the United States have pushed to make it possible for people to change the sex designation on their identity documents. Before this time, individuals had requested changes in their sex classification and some, on a case-by-case basis, got the result they wanted. But it wasn't until the 1960s that advocates for what we now call transgender people turned to reforming policies. Over time, these efforts were successful: most states changed their policies on birth certificates and driver's licenses. By 2002, all but Idaho, Ohio, and Tennessee would issue new or amended birth certificates.[12] The particular contours of those policies were far from ideal by today's standards, and many remain onerous. These policies required proof of surgery, and often a legal name change. Some states amended birth certificates to designate the original *and* the amended sex.[13] For example, the state of Arkansas required then, and still requires, "a certified copy of a court of competent jurisdiction indicating that the sex of an individual born in this state has been changed by surgical procedure and that such individual's name has been changed."[14] Since 2005, many jurisdictions have reformed these policies even more by dropping the requirement for proof of body modification—surgery and/or hormone therapy.[15]

Less constricted by statutes, driver's license policies during this period were often less stringent. For example, in the 1970s, New York State's Division of Motor Vehicles required a letter from the physician who had "performed the operation," but by 1987 that policy required only a letter from a physician attesting to the "true gender" of the individual based on "medical, psychological or psychiatric evaluations, with a medical determination that one gender predominates over the other."[16] Until 2011, however, for both New York State and the City—separate jurisdictions for the purposes of birth certificates—one had to provide proof of surgery to get a birth certificate that did not reveal the sex assigned at birth. For the purpose of the analysis here, however, what matters is not the difference between these identity document standards but the difference between decisions and policies that held that sex can change and those that held that it can't.

The case discussed below in relation to that difference, *In Re Heilig,* is not about birth certificates per se, but about the plea from a Maryland resident who, in the absence of a birth certificate from the state she was born in, requested a court order declaring her female. Reviewing the medical facts about the "new" phenomenon of transsexualism, the final court in *Heilig* determined that sex can change. It was not a groundbreaking decision, because many agencies and legislatures had and have policies and statutes on the books making it possible to change one's sex classification. But what's especially useful about this example of state action is that, unlike most policy changes for birth certificates and driver's licenses, as a judicial decision it rehearsed in great detail the thinking behind it. In other policy arenas, the rationales are often less accessible. And the reasoning in *Heilig* provides a good point of comparison to the explanations in decisions about sex classification for the purpose of marriage.

In March 2001, a woman living in Maryland but born in Pennsylvania petitioned a Maryland court to issue an order changing her name from a traditionally male name to Janet Heilig Wright and her sex classification from male to female. Wright had been born in Pennsylvania but was now a resident of Maryland. Maryland had a policy allowing the sex classification on birth certificates to be changed by submitting a court order indicating that an individual's sex "has been changed by surgical procedure."[17] While the Maryland Circuit Court granted Wright's petition for a name change, her request for a court order recognizing her as female was denied.

After a loss at the first appellate level, Wright appealed to the state's highest court, the Maryland Court of Appeals. Living in Maryland, what was she to do, asked her attorney, the longtime trans rights advocate Alyson Meiselman. Since the state legislature had a statute on the books that made it possible for one to change the M or F on a birth certificate issued in Maryland, the legislature had certainly recognized that sex can change. Why would the fact of her birth in Pennsylvania be the reason to deny her the opportunity afforded those born in Maryland? As a matter of fairness, the court should have applied that policy to residents of Maryland not born in the state. "Otherwise," the state justices suggested, two "similarly-situated post-operative, male-to-female transsexuals—one born in Maryland, and one not born in Maryland—while both citizens of Maryland would be regarded differently by Maryland law: one as male, one as female."[18] In addition, they argued, if a Maryland court can issue orders granting a name change—another situation in which there is no party contesting the change—why can't it issue a similar order about her sex? The Court of Appeals agreed. Writing for a unanimous panel of seven judges, Judge Alan J. Wilner found that the lower court could rule on the question and directed it to do so.

Because in earlier hearings of the case the Circuit Court and the mid-level appellate court addressed only the issue of jurisdiction, those decisions did not reach the issue of what standards Wright would have to meet to be declared a woman by a court order or whether she had provided evidence to meet those standards. However, much of the Court of Appeals opinion focused on the question of sex classification itself. In doing so, the judge was practicing the equity jurisdiction tradition that, in the words of an 1894 legal treatise quoted approvingly in the opinion, "recognizes new adjustments to new situations, not upon a dogmatic basis, but upon principles which address themselves to the conscience and intelligence, and therefore admit of a rational and progressive development."[19] Wilner produced an incredibly thorough review of the current medical literature on the topics of sex, gender, and transsexualism. A section in the opinion titled "Transsexualism: Medical Aspects" runs over 4,600 words and cites thirty sources, from John Money to Milton Diamond to the Harry Benjamin International Gender Dysphoria Association (since renamed as the World Professional Association for Transgender Health). The crux of the debate in legal arenas, the opinion observed, is whether gender, defined as a "psychosocial individuality or identity," or sex, which "denotes anatomical or biological" differences, is the "more relevant concept deserving of legal recognition."[20]

To understand "what gender is and whether, or how, it may be changed," Wilner listed seven factors that medical discourses contain under the rubric of gender: (1) internal morphological sex (seminal vesicles/prostrate or vagina/uterus/fallopian tubes); (2) external morphological sex (genitalia); (3) gonadal sex (testes or ovaries); (4) chromosomal sex (presence or absence of Y chromosome); (5) hormonal sex (predominance of androgens or estrogens); (6) phenotypic sex (secondary sex characteristics; e.g., facial hair, breasts, body type); and (7) personal sexual identity. After a lengthy review of the medical literature, Wilner concluded by enumerating the following "facts": (1) gender itself is a fact that may be established by medical and other evidence; (2) it may be, or possibly may become, other than what is recorded on the person's birth certificate; and (3) a person has a deep personal, social, and economic interest in having the official designation of his or her gender match what, in fact, it always was or possibly has become.[21]

For this court, sex can change. But which criteria should courts rely on to verify the change? The Court of Appeals left this question up to the District Court, though it offered guidance in the form of a review of the requirements that other courts and agencies have set. Most policies, the court opined, require transsexuals to show that their "gender has been changed 'by surgical procedure.'"[22] Although one's psychosocial gender identity may be more relevant than genitalia or other biological factors, surgery signifies that the change is "permanent and irreversible."[23] The case was remanded back to the District Court, which was instructed to give Wright the opportunity to present evidence of a permanent gender change. At this point, unfortunately, the litigation trail ends. It doesn't indicate whether Wright was able to provide the evidence the lower court would require to obtain the court order for which she had originally petitioned. But the ruling, and its rationale, remain.

What would be needed for such a court order? How is change of sex to be verified? Rules on the issue of criteria vary widely. At the time of the decision, the vast majority of the states that would amend the sex marker on a birth certificate required evidence that they had undergone some sort of surgery. In those policies, the visual factors, the parts of the body most associated with sex and open to surface inspection, mattered the most— one's external genitalia. There are some policy rationales that identify the psychological experience of gender identity as the primary factor, but still mandate that the fact be verified by "permanent" alterations to the body. Other agencies are moving toward a gender-identity-only standard. In the time since Wright first petitioned the Maryland court, legislatures in at least 15 US jurisdictions had enacted laws that allow individuals to change the sex designation on their birth certificate without having had any sort of gender-confirming surgery; other states have enacted such changes administratively. In 2011, the US Department of State issued a new policy requiring only a letter from a physician declaring that the individual is undergoing "appropriate clinical treatment for gender transition"—which is, effectively, a policy that requires no body modification. Many state agencies responsible for issuing driver's licenses are moving away from standards requiring permanent alterations to the body.

This positive decision, however, ends with one important qualification. If Wright were to get the court order that the Court of Appeals deemed possible, would she be female once and for all, everywhere, for all purposes? No. In discussing the effect of such a court order, Judge Wilner made this very clear: "[Marriage] is an issue that is not before us in this case and upon which we express no opinion." Like the M or F on a birth certificate, driver's license, or passport, the use of such a court order would be limited to situations in which this description of an individual's "legal identity" (the court's language) is *uncontested*. But that M or F appellation does not establish sex for all purposes. For those whose sex classification differs from the sex assigned to them at birth, the new classification will not necessarily stand when it is deployed in any area of the law or policy that relies on sex classifications to do its work. As the decision explained, "What effect a judgment has depends on the law governing what the judgment holder seeks to do, and that is true in this regard as well."[24] "What sex is" for identity purposes may not be what sex is deemed to be for other purposes. As the Maryland Court of Appeals said—it "depends."

Exactly as Judge Wilner suggested they might, the majority of the published appellate decisions before *Obergefell* regarding the validity of marriages involving one or more transgender parties have come to very different conclusions about whether or not one's sex assigned at birth can change for the purposes of marriage.[25] A brief word on how these cases fell under the scrutiny of state judges might be helpful here. While they may have been relatively rare in proportion to the general population, these cases were not necessarily—or even often—exceptional in any other way. That is, the people getting married did not construe their legal union as an intentional act of gender subversion. Instead, these marriages took place like everyone else's—the weddings were rushed or planned, the result of a long-term engagement or a short one, they took place at a courthouse, reception hall, or house of worship. And the bureaucratic part of this ritual was also no different. Couples applied for a marriage license, paid a fee, presented identification to an official, and made arrangements for an officiant. In the cases discussed below, it is unlikely that the clerks who processed the applications for a marriage were aware that one of the parties had a transgender history. Had they been, these marriage license applications might have been construed as attempts by people of the same sex to get married and, in the states that banned same-sex marriage at the time, the applications denied. While some individuals in the pre-*Obergefell* era might have been aware that case law on marriages involving a transgender person had not been settled,[26] most would have understandably assumed that the sex classification on their passport or driver's license or birth certificate established their sex for the purposes of marriage. They would not have realized that their sex classification could change depending on what it's being used for. It's when a relationship ends through disaffection or death that a court's attention would have been drawn to the issue of sex classification. In the case of the former, sometimes the non-transgender party wanted to have the marriage declared invalid, rather than obtain a divorce. This strategy, if successful, meant that any legal battles over child custody, alimony, or the disposition of property were made moot. In cases involving the death of the non-transgender person in the marriage, cases were brought by a third party with an interest in the estate.

Christie Lee Littleton, *née* Cavazos and born in Texas, married a man named Jonathan Mark Littleton in Kentucky in 1989. When he died in 1996, Littleton filed a medical malpractice suit against his physician, Mark Prange. Someone working for Prange's insurance company came up with a brilliant idea: if they could convince the court that Littleton, classified as male at birth, was still legally male, her marriage would be invalid. If she wasn't the surviving spouse, she would have no standing to sue. In the second case, J'Noel Gardiner, born in Wisconsin, had married Marshall Gardiner in Kansas in 1998; Marshall died intestate one year later. Gardiner, also assigned male at birth, had had her Wisconsin birth certificate changed to reflect her reassigned sex. Marshall Gardiner's son, Joe, argued that he was the sole heir to the estate, since Gardiner had been born male. J'Noel countered that she was legally female at the time of the marriage, and that, under the full faith and credit clause, the sex classification on her Wisconsin birth certificate should be recognized in Kansas. The third case involved the dissolution of the marriage between a transgender man, Michael Kantaras, and his wife, Linda Kantaras. Soon after they were married in 1989 in Florida, Michael adopted his wife's first child. During their marriage, Linda gave birth to a second child (with sperm from Michael's brother). When Michael filed for divorce and began proceedings to get custody of the children, Linda counter-petitioned. She argued that because Michael was a transsexual man, the marriage should be annulled and he had no parental rights. She threw in, for good measure, that his adoption of her first child was nullified by Florida's ban on homosexual adoption. While there is one clearly positive appellate decision from 1976, *J. T. v. M. T.*

(the marriage was valid because heterosexual intercourse was possible, a judge declared), most if not all of the other appellate cases found that sex is fixed at birth for the purposes of marriage.[27]

To decide that opposite-sex marriages involving a transgender person must be invalid, courts in each case made time the crux of the analysis. The Littleton judge asked, "*When* is a man a man, and *when* is a woman a woman?"[28] Waxing philosophical, he concluded, "The deeper philosophical (and now legal) question is: can a physician change the gender of a person with a scalpel, drugs, and counseling, or is a person's gender immutably fixed at birth?"[29] In all three cases, the short answer was—birth. Michael Kantaras was female at birth, and female at the time of marriage, according to the Florida appellate court: "Until the Florida legislature recognizes sex-reassignment procedures and amends the marriage statutes to clarify the marital rights of a postoperative transsexual person, we must adhere to the common meaning of the statutory terms and invalidate any marriage that is not between persons of the opposite sex determined by their biological sex at birth."[30] In reviewing the literature on sex assignment at birth, the Littleton, Gardiner, and Kantaras decisions relied on sex attribution made on the basis of a visual inspection of an infant's genitalia at birth. J'Noel Gardiner, the Kansas court declared, is "a male because she had been identified on the basis of her external genitalia at birth as a male."[31] But Gardiner and Littleton had changed their outward physical appearance, as both courts acknowledged. Both litigants had submitted to the courts detailed medical reports and surgical records. According to the Texas court, "Through the intervention of surgery and drugs, Christie appears to be a woman."[32] For J'Noel Gardiner, the Kansas court observed, her external sexual characteristics, "though all man-made," "resemble those of the opposite sex."[33] Still, in these cases, the sex assigned at birth trumped all else.

In laying out their rationales, the marriage decisions were careful to stick closely to the question before them: what is sex? However, given the range of criteria from which to choose, the lack of consensus on this question in so many other areas of law and policy, and the dissension in the medical establishment during this period over whether sex classification should be based on the present or the past, the relative uniformity of the outcomes in the marriage cases is suspicious. While the courts made a show of approaching it as a formal question of sex definition, the issue before them concerned an institution that is not simply a publicly sanctioned contract between two individuals. Marriage is and has long been an instrument of governing that turns individuals into families and nations. Defined in temporal terms ("til death do us part"), marriage plays a central role in binding the past to the present and the present to the future in building a nation.[34] It is, as we heard over and over again, in the rhetoric that justified same-sex marriage bans, in Justice Kennedy's opinion in *Obergefell* overturning these bans, and in the congressional findings prefacing welfare reform laws promoting "the foundation of a successful society."[35] Nancy F. Cott explains in her history of marriage in the United States that "the nation originally had few technologies of governance to monitor and control a people strewn unevenly over a huge expanse of land. Monogamous marriages that distinguished citizen-heads of households had enormous instrumental value for governance, because orderly families, able to accumulate and transmit private property and to sustain an American people, descended from them."[36]

Of course—and this is where the concepts of state and nation most obviously diverge—"the people" to be reproduced and sustained does not include everyone in the territory.[37] The "American people" refers to particular sorts of people, most centrally "white" people (in, for example, the words of the Immigration and Naturalization Act of 1790). In her work on miscegenation law and racial categories, historian Peggy Pascoe shows how marriage linked "white supremacy and the transmission of property." Among the many examples she describes, her account of Oklahoma's miscegenation laws stands out among them. Before statehood, Blacks and Indians had often married. After Oklahoma's constitution was put in place, "colored" and "negro" were defined as including "all persons of African descent," while the "white race" included "all other persons." (Indians still owned significant amounts of property when the territory became a state.) Pascoe explains that the effect of these laws was to "allow White men to marry and inherit property from Indian women while preventing Black men from doing the very same thing."[38] Miscegenation laws determined which racial groups could intermarry; rules and case-by-case decisions on an individual's racial classification dictated which group one belonged to. In these cases, sex classification was rarely in dispute, Pascoe points out, even though "laws against interracial marriage had depended on hierarchies of sex and gender as well as on hierarchies of race."[39]

The history of marriage law reveals its centrality as a distributive mechanism. From miscegenation laws to social welfare programs to immigration laws, marriage and laws of descent have been cornerstones of the biopolitics of nation-building efforts. Marriage channels individuals into a diachronically organized formation for social reproduction and inheritance—otherwise known as "the family." Still, why must sex be fixed at birth in these transgender marriage cases? In each of these cases, someone wanted to possess things generally conveyed by and indexed to the family form: children or property. Gardiner's stepson wanted his father's estate, Littleton's husband's physician's insurance company didn't want to pay out on the wrongful death lawsuit, and Kantaras's wife didn't want to share custody of their children. The work of securing (putatively) biological reproduction to a particular social formation (the family) is undone by the appearance of uninvited guests whose presence unmasks the naturalization of fatherhood through marriage.[40]

This may go a long way in explaining why sex reclassification policies concerning identity documents differed so starkly from those concerning marriage. Writing in 1992 about "the possibility" of a transgender man being inseminated after he had been reclassified as male by his government, a judge of the European Court of Human Rights exclaimed, "The whole of civil law and inheritance law could be thrown into confusion."[41] Policies that held that sex can change and those that hold that it can't reflected the differences between the state imperative to recognize and the state imperative to distribute. One thing that states do is keep track of who is who.[42] In large modern states, identity documents are one method for making an individual uniquely identifiable.[43] While most discussions of recognition now advance or criticize it as a method of affirming identity, recognition is also an instrument of surveillance, inventory, and control.[44] (When police officers pull my bearded, balding self over for speeding, it's not particularly helpful to them if my driver's license lists me as female.)

Certainly, the distinction I have drawn between recognition and distribution is more analytically pure than historically accurate in all cases. Not all policies and decisions on sex reclassification fell neatly onto the side of the equation that fits the argument here. As with the study of any empirical human phenomenon, there's a lot of messiness around the edges. Susan J. Pearson's chapter in this volume shows how instruments of recognition, such as birth certificates, were central components of state's efforts not only to surveil, but also to channel inheritance. I invoked this distinction, however, to argue that the injustices visited upon those whose gender identity is not traditionally associated with the sex assigned to them at birth are not simply matters of a "merely cultural" mis-recognition.[45] Before *Obergefell*, the discrepancy between state actors' positions that "sex *can* change" and "sex *can't* change" expose different governing rationalities. Unlike the *Heilig* case, which concerned recognition (who one is), the marriage decisions examined here centered on questions of distribution (what one gets). If the former reflected the state imperative to recognize, the latter was central in furthering biopolitical projects of national formation and distribution.[46] Before those who crossed the gender binary became widely legible under the banner of transgender identity, before transgender rights had coalesced into a political movement that policymakers took seriously, before the exponentially larger GLB rights organizations took on trans issues as their own, trans people were simply the dispersed occupants of a residual category, a problem to be adjudicated but not a constituency to be appeased. Without the protective carapace of identity politics, very different governing rationales could be laid bare by the seemingly contradictory outcomes in sex classification policies and cases. M and F were not immobile essences for these state actors, but malleable outputs in the service of different governing projects. While these differences were made visible by individuals who move from one gender to another, the significance is not limited to trans populations.

Importantly, the governing projects of recognition and redistribution are not always in conflict, nor is the distinction fixed in time. Recognition can be put in the service of distribution. Distribution itself can be expanded or shrunk, privatized or socialized. In the registers of recognition and judicial doctrine, ending the establishment of gender—and perhaps *Obergefell* was its last redoubt—resonates with the progress narrative of America, the slow but inevitable expansion of equality before the law. In the registers of distribution and political economy, however, the expansion of marriage to same-sex couples followed a fundamental shift in the family's role. It is no longer an incubator of citizens or the recipient of social support through policies such as those that made the breadwinner wage feasible. Instead, the family has become the provider of care as the "logic" of the markets have shredded the social safety net.[47] In our neoliberal economic order, the status accorded to particular types of people—male, heterosexual, white, for example—matters less and the fungibility of individuals matters more.

For the most part, then, the rationale for governments treating men and women differently is vanishing. Thus, the apparatuses that enforce gender distinctions—the systems for sex classification, which are revealed by decisions and rules for sex reclassification—have become much more elastic. Although states still classify people as M or F, or even gender non-binary, the consequences of sex classification now matter much less because an F designation can no longer be used to curtail civil and property rights, to deny equal access to education and the professions, or to enforce heteronormativity through bans on same-sex marriage. It is precisely because there is now so much less at stake in sex classification that policymakers and judges have less reason to reject proposals for reform and to deny reclassification requests. In the adjacent area of sex discrimination law, Justice Neil Gorsuch made that very clear in a jaw-dropping 2020 decision, *Bostock v. Clayton County*, which ruled that an employer who summarily fired a transgender woman when she announced her intent to transition had violated a statute banning sex discrimination.[48]

Of course, sex classification itself has not disappeared. It is a baked-in artifact of the days when gender did matter—and it still matters for identity and surveillance purposes. Moreover, the argument about the decline of state-sponsored sex discrimination does not mean that gender subordination is a thing of the past. It endures as an organizing principle of domestic life, the workplace, and cultural production. The persistence of gender subordination—in the realm of what political theorist Corey Robin calls "the private life of power"—outside the equalizing gaze of the state is something conservatives and all those who benefit from it are eager to maintain.[49] Indeed, one might see the assault on the very existence of transgender people carried out during the Trump administration—reversing the military's policy on allowing transgender people to serve, eliminating the Obama-era guidance on Title IX that advised educational institutions to allow trans students to use the bathroom appropriate to their gender identity, attempting to impose a singular definition of sex as defined at birth over all federal agencies[50]—as part of a revanchist backlash against "gender ideology," one that used state administrative apparatuses to re-prosecute a culture war that targets transgender people.

NOTES

I am deeply indebted to this volume's editors, Margot Canaday, Nancy F. Cott, and Robert O. Self, for their incisive comments on drafts of this chapter. I also wish to thank many of the contributors to this volume, who provided important feedback at a workshop.

1. William J. Novak, "The Concept of the State in American History," in *Boundaries of the State in US History*, ed. James T. Sparrow, William J. Novak, and Stephen W. Sawyer (Chicago: University of Chicago Press, 2015), 337.

2. Harold Garfinkel, "Passing and the Managed Achievement of Sex Status in an 'Intersexed' Person," in *The Transgender Studies Reader*, ed. Susan Stryker and Stephen Whittle, vol. 1 (New York: Routledge, 2006), 58–93.

3. Janet Shibley Hyde et al., "The Future of Sex and Gender in Psychology: Five Challenges to the Gender Binary," *American Psychologist* 74, no. 2 (July 19, 2018): 171–92.

4. The Republican Party would have sex set not at birth but at conception, and would base it not on a visible inspection of the genitals at birth and on chromosomes: "A person's sex is defined as the physical condition of being male or female, which is determined at conception, identified at birth by a person's anatomy, recorded on their official birth certificate, and can be confirmed by DNA testing." As is typical, such constructions of the F/M binary do not consider nonbinary and intersex people. Counsel's Office, Republican National Committee,

"Resolution Condemning Governmental Overreach Regarding Title IX Politics in Public Schools," February 25, 2016, https://prod-static-ngop-pbl.s3.amazonaws .com/media/documents/Resolution_Title_IX%20_Overreach.pdf.

5. Same-sex marriages were so inconceivable when most state marriage statutes were passed that in some cases the statute neglected to specify that this legal relation was available only to men marrying women. As the battle over same-sex marriages intensified in the 1990s, however, state laws and even constitutional amendments were written to make this exclusion clear. Outside trans advocate circles, however, little attention was paid to criteria for sex classification. Julie A. Greenberg, *Intersexuality and the Law* (New York: New York University Press, 2012).

6. 135 S. Ct. 2584 (2015).

7. Susan Leigh Star and Geoffrey C. Bowker, "Enacting Silence: Residual Categories as a Challenge for Ethics, Information Systems, and Communication," *Ethics and Information Technology* 9 (2007): 273–80; and Geoffrey C. Bowker and Susan Leigh Star, *Sorting Things Out: Classification and Its Consequences* (Cambridge, MA: MIT Press, 1999), 300–301.

8. See, e.g., Catherine A. MacKinnon, *Toward a Feminist Theory of the State* (Cambridge, MA: Harvard University Press, 1991); Linda Gordon, ed., *Women, The State, and Welfare* (Madison: University of Wisconsin Press, 1990); Gwendolyn M. Mink, "The Lady and the Tramp: Gender, Race, and the Origins of the American Welfare State," in *Women, the State, and Welfare*, ed. Linda Gordon (Madison: University of Wisconsin Press, 1990); Mike Savage and Anne Witz, eds., *Gender and Bureaucracy* (Cambridge, MA: Blackwell, 1992); Suzanne Mettler, *Dividing Citizens: Gender and Federalism in New Deal Public Policy* (Ithaca, NY: Cornell University Press, 1998); Wendy Brown, "Finding the Man in the State," *Feminist Studies* 18, no. 1 (Spring 1992): 7–34; Jacqueline Stevens, *Reproducing the State* (Princeton, NJ: Princeton University Press, 1999); Cathy Marie Johnson, Georgia Duerst-Lahti, and Noelle H. Norton, *Creating Gender: The Sexual Politics of Welfare Policy* (Boulder, CO: Lynne Rienner Publishers, 2007); and Carole Pateman and Charles Mills, *The Contract and Domination* (New York: Polity Press, 2007).

9. Janice Raymond, *The Transsexual Empire: The Making of a She-Male* (New York: Teachers College Press, 1994).

10. Timothy Mitchell, "Society, Economy, and the State Effect," in *State/Culture: State-Formation after the Cultural Turn*, ed. George Steinmetz (Ithaca, NY: Cornell University Press, 1999), 76. Karen M. Tani's research on welfare rights policy illustrates the dispersed nature of state projects: "The history of modern poor relief is not one of single-minded dominance of the poor, but of an ongoing contest between multiple powers, some great and others small, some rising and others in decline, with different relationships to the poor and varying agendas." Karen M. Tani, *States of Dependency: Welfare, Rights, and American Governments, 1935–1972* (New York: Cambridge University Press, 2016), 291.

11. Margot Canaday, *The Straight State: Sexuality and Citizenship in Twentieth Century America* (Princeton, NJ: Princeton University Press, 2011), 5.

12. See Lambda Legal, "Amending Birth Certificates to Reflect Your Correct Sex," November 12, 2002, https://web.archive.org/web/20021128233649/http://www .lambdalegal.org/cgi-bin/iowa/documents/record?record=1163.

13. Paisley Currah and Lisa Jean Moore, "'We Won't Know Who You Are': Contesting Sex Designations in New York City Birth Certificates," *Hypatia* 24, no. 3 (2009): 113–35.

14. Arkansas Code Annotated § 20-18-307(d).

15. Lambda Legal, "Changing Birth Certificate Sex Designations: State-By-State Guidelines," September 17, 2018, https://www.lambdalegal.org/know-your-rights/article/trans-changing-birth-certificate-sex-designations.

16. Patricia B. Adduci, Commissioner, Department of Motor Vehicles, State of New York, "Memo, Change in Required Documentation for Proof of Sex Change," April 29, 1987.

17. Md. Code Ann, § 4–214(b)(5) (2006).

18. *In the Matter of Robert Wright Heilig*, Brief of Appellant Janet Wright Heilig, Court of Appeals of Maryland, September term 2002.

19. C. Phelps, 1894 Monograph, cited in *In re Heilig*, 816 A.2d 68, 81 (Ct. App. Md. February 11, 2003).

20. *In re Heilig*, 73.

21. *In re Heilig*, 74.

22. *In re Heilig*, 77.

23. In contrast, courts and policymakers are reluctant to use hormonal therapy as a metric of sex reassignment. As the court in *In re Heilig* explains in a footnote, "Hormonal therapy alone, which usually can be terminated or perhaps even reversed, has not, to our knowledge, been recognized as effecting either a sufficient change or a permanent one." *In re Heilig*, 87.

24. *In re Heilig*, 87.

25. Major published appellate decisions on marriages or applications for marriage licenses involving a transgender person in the United States, 1976–2005, follow. Only the first case finds in favor of the transgender spouse. *M. T. v. J. T.* (1976), 140 NJ Super. 77, 355 A. 2d 204; *In re Ladrach*, 32 Ohio Misc. 2d 6, 513 N.E.2d 828 (Ohio Probate 1987); *Littleton v. Prange*, 9 S.W. 3d 223 (Tex. App. 1999); *In the Matter of the Estate of Marshall G. Gardiner*, 42 P3d 120 (Kan. 2002); *In Re Application for Marriage License for Nash*, 2003 Ohio 7221 (Court of Appeals of Ohio, Eleventh Appellate District, Trumbull County, 2003); *Kantaras v. Kantaras*, 884 So. 2d 155 (Court of Appeal of Florida, Second District, 2004); and *In Re Marriage of Sterling Simmons*, 355 Ill. App. 3d 942 (Appellate Court of Illinois, First District, Third Division, 2005).

26. During this time, the Social Security Administration field manual for employees advised them to contact a regional SSA lawyer to determine whether a marriage was legally valid for the purpose of Social Security disbursements.

27. *J. T. v. M. T.*, 140 N.J. 77, 355 A.2d 204, 205 (NJ Super. Ct. 1976) 77 (NJ Super. Ct. 1976); see also Ruthann Robson, "Reinscribing Normality? The Law and Politics of Transgender Marriage," in *Transgender Rights*, ed. Paisley Currah, Richard M. Juang, and Shannon Price Minter (Minneapolis: Minnesota University Press, 2006), 299–309.

28. *Littleton v. Prange*, ed. 9 S.W.3d 223, Court of Appeals of Texas, 1999), 3, 223; and Julie A. Greenberg, "When Is a Man a Man, and When Is a Woman a Woman," *Florida Law Review* 52, no. 4 (2000): 745–68.

29. *Littleton v. Prange,* 3, 224.

30. *Kantaras v. Kantaras,* 4 So. 2d 155, 161 (Court of Appeal of Florida, Second District, 2004).

31. *In Re Gardiner,* 20, 210. Citing, with approval, a lower court decision.

32. *Littleton v. Prange,* 6, 226.

33. *In Re Gardiner,* 8, 7.

34. As Tera Hunter points out, the marriage vows of enslaved people are better described as "Until Distance Do You Part." Tera W. Hunter, *Bound in Wedlock: Slave and Free Black Marriage in the Nineteenth Century* (Cambridge, MA: Harvard University Press, 2017), 23–60.

35. Gwendolyn Mink, "Ending Single Motherhood," in *The Promise of Welfare Reform,* ed. Keith M. Kilty and Elizabeth A. Segal (New York: Haworth Press, 2006); and Anna Marie Smith, *Welfare Reform and Sexual Regulation* (New York: Cambridge University Press, 2007). Justice Kennedy writes, "It demeans gays and lesbians for the State to lock them out of a central institution of the Nation's society." 576 U. S. 644, 17 (2015); and Melinda Cooper, *Family Values: Between Neoliberalism and the New Social Conservatism* (Brooklyn, NY: Zone Books, 2017), 107–9.

36. Nancy F. Cott, *Public Vows: A History of Marriage and Nation* (Cambridge, MA: Harvard University Press, 2000), 157.

37. Michel Foucault, *"Society Must Be Defended: Lectures at the Collège de France, 1975–76,* trans. David Macey (New York: Picador, 2003), 254–55.

38. Peggy Pascoe, *What Comes Naturally: Miscegenation Law and the Making of Race in America* (New York: Oxford University Press, 2009); Hunter, *Bound in Wedlock.* Adjacent to marriage, laws on descent have also been malleable in the service of white supremacy. For example, legislators in colonial Virginia reversed British common law that held that children inherited the status of their father. Instead, children born to African women would now inherit their mother's status. In one stroke, this made the rape of enslaved women less visible and increased slaveholders' wealth by enlarging their holdings in enslaved persons.

39. Pascoe, *What Comes Naturally,* 130. This is not to suggest that the relation between race and what I am calling sex in this chapter is analogical or even intersectional. Rather, as Riley Snorton and Kyla Schuller have shown, the relation between race and sex is not static, but depends on the processes and interests at play in a given historical moment. Schuller, for example, argues that "the rhetoric of distinct sexes of male and female consolidated as a *function* of race." Schuller, *The Biopolitics of Feeling: Race, Sex, and the Science of the Nineteenth Century* (Durham, NC: Duke University Press, 2018), 17. Snorton points out that "chattel persons gave rise to an understanding of gender as mutable and as an amendable form of being." C. Riley Snorton, *Black on Both Sides: A Racial History of Trans Identity* (Minneapolis: University of Minnesota Press, 2017), 57.

40. Paisley Currah, *Sex Is as Sex Does: Governing Transgender Identity* (New York: New York University Press, forthcoming).

41. *B v. France,* 232 Eur. Ct. H.R. (ser. A) 33, 66 (1992) (Pettiti J., dissenting).

42. As J. G. Fichte put it, "the chief principle of a well-regulated police state" is to ensure that "each citizen shall be at all times and places . . . recognized as this or that particular person." Cited in Jane Caplan, "'This or That Particular

Person': Protocols of Identification in Nineteenth-Century Europe," in *Documenting Individual Identity: The Development of State Practices in the Modern World*, ed. Jane Caplan and John Torpey (Princeton, NJ: Princeton University Press, 2001), 49. See also James Scott, *Seeing Like a State* (New Haven, CT: Yale University Press, 1998), 1–3.

43. James Rule, James B., Douglas McAdam, Linda Stearns, and David Uglow, "Documentary Identification and Mass Surveillance in the United States," *Social Problems* 31, no. 2 (December 1983): 222–34.

44. Scott, *Seeing Like a State*; Caplan and Torpey, eds., *Documenting Individual Identity*.

45. Nancy Fraser, "From Redistribution to Recognition? Dilemmas of Justice in a 'Post-Secular' Age," *New Left Review* 212 (1995): 68–93; and Nancy Fraser, *Fortunes of Feminism: From Women's Liberation to Identity Politics to Anti-Capitalism* (New York: Verso, 2013). Fraser discusses gender identity explicitly in Nancy Fraser, "How Feminism Became Capitalism's Handmaiden—and How to Reclaim It," *The Guardian*, October 14, 2015, sec. Opinion, http://www.theguardian.com/commentisfree/2013/oct/14/feminism-capitalist-handmaiden-neoliberal.

46. Nira Yuval-Davis, *Gender & Nation* (Los Angeles: Sage Publications, 1997).

47. Melinda Cooper, *Family Values: Between Neoliberalism and the New Social Conservatism* (Brooklyn, NY: Zone Books, 2017); and Robert O. Self, *All in the Family: The Realignment of American Democracy since the 1960s* (New York: Hill and Wang, 2012).

48. *Bostock v. Clayton County*, 140 S. Ct. 1731 (2020).

49. Corey Robin, *The Reactionary Mind* (New York: Oxford University Press, 2011), 15.

50. Erica L. Green, Katie Benner, and Robert Pear, "'Transgender' Could Be Defined Out of Existence Under Trump Administration," *New York Times*, October 21, 2018.

Frugal Governance, Family Values, and the Intimate Roots of Neoliberalism

BRENT CEBUL

At a moment when historians are developing powerful new modes of analysis by reaching across national borders, emphasizing sweeping flows of human beings, capital, and natural resources, this volume reminds us of equally powerful insights to be gained by taking up far more intimate scales—identity, marriage, household formation, sex and sexuality, infirmity, deviancy. Intimate governance, this volume's editors explain, is best grasped as traits and techniques most pronounced at the elusive borders between the public and private spheres, at the social margins, and in the decentralization of police powers across the federal system. Interrogating these sites of state action, they write, enables us to see how intimate governance has become so "absorbed into ordinary lives" that intimate state forces are "at times indistinguishable from society itself." The history rendered in these pages, then, urges scholars to ask "what state power in its various forms actually does," to understand what intimate governance has meant for citizen-subjects, and to trace its disparate but discernible cumulative socio-political effects over time.

This volume also underscores the value of capturing "traditional" political historical topics from more intimate angles of approach. Rather than view intimate statecraft as simply products of or exceptions to dominant ideologies or changing partisan "orders," intimate state practices have often defined and redefined the meanings and policy articulations of ideologies like liberalism, conservatism, or neoliberalism.[1] Indeed, intimate states' policing and sculpting of the body politic define zones of consensus that float beneath or cut across the usual ideological or historical breakpoints of American politics. And when challenges to those practices have emerged from the intimate margins, they have often held as much power to reorganize American politics as have more titanic clashes of parties, capital, or classes. An example: there was nothing inherent in mainstream political liberalism that guaranteed its eventual embrace of movements for LGBT rights. Rather, as several historians of sexuality have shown, bipartisan, Cold War intimate states so marginalized these citizens that they forged consciousness and solidarity, spurring later revolutions in the meanings of political liberalism—and conservatism.[2]

These dynamics played out from the 1960s through the 1980s as a range of insurgencies against intimate state practices triggered distinct but mutually reinforcing *neoliberal* reformulations of both liberalism and conservatism. Scholars have tended to approach neoliberalism from the largest scales, emphasizing disjunctive global economic forces or the alignment of neoliberal intellectuals with the interests of capital. The most recent accounts explain how democratic capitalist states were bent toward accelerating capital accumulation, discharging a range of public social welfare costs, and disciplining a broader citizenry to market logics. These interpretations make clear that the state did not go away under neoliberalism; it was reoriented. Despite offering significant insights, however, these accounts struggle to explain important contingencies, continuities, and cultural questions, particularly the ways in which neoliberal logics became embedded in the mainstream body politic or gained legitimacy through bipartisan projects of neoliberal intimate state building. Centering the longer history of intimate states, however, alerts us to the ways in which aspects of neoliberalism emerged *through* earlier intimate state practices.

To make this case, I build a brief genealogy of neoliberalism's intimate governance by illuminating a set of historical continuities woven through this volume, particularly around the fiscal and moral policing of social welfare policy. Though historical accounts of the politics of welfare often emphasize rhetorical debates about big versus small government or deserving versus undeserving poor, this volume reminds us that those debates played out within deeper consensuses concerning the maintenance of normative family forms and limiting public expenditures.[3] Indeed, state actors responded to and shaped these consensuses by frequently discharging to families the social costs of nonnormative persons or behavior. In doing so, they sought to privatize those costs—not because they existed outside the purview of the state, but because intimate state builders hoped to make families reliable adjuncts to state power. These twinned tendencies toward policing normativity and championing fiscal "frugality" were, for Foucault, defining characteristics of *liberal* states. As he argued, perhaps the fundamental tension at the heart of liberal state building was the "intensive and extensive development of governmental practice" alongside the "negative effects" of "invasive intrusions of a government" that "nevertheless claims to be and is supposed to be frugal." The "question of the frugality of government," he wrote, "is indeed the question of liberalism."[4] As we will see, the emerging liberal state's intimate policing of normative family forms and its commitments to fiscal frugality ultimately produced a series of tensions and rights claims that exploded in the 1970s. But these intimate state values and techniques did not go away. Instead, they were redeployed on behalf of much more frugal neoliberal intimate states.

It was during Reconstruction that the American state became more fully liberal—that is, committed to shaping individual rights in a nominally free market order.[5] State builders also sought to limit social expenditures, especially for African Americans. And so it was also during Reconstruction that the national state became directly invested in the institution of marriage. The Freedmen's Bureau sought to inculcate practices of marriage, largely because, as Richard White puts it, "the bureau's agents were fixated on black dependency": they hoped to discharge to families the costs of dependents.[6] Meanwhile, Southern states sought to leverage revenue or labor from freedpeople by creating exorbitant fees to ratify marriages, which enabled states to reclaim the labor of those who violated laws against unmarried cohabitation. Other statutes enabled the forced apprenticeship of young freedpeople. As Stephanie McCurry's chapter in this volume shows, freedwomen's pursuit of their rights to their children constituted profound claims to citizenship. Yet, as McCurry notes, those claims most often succeeded when agents' "moral sense aligned with their desire to get freedwomen and children off the welfare roll." African American rights in the emerging liberal state, then, were most likely to be secured when they aligned with the state's intimate and fiscal interests.

By the turn of the century, these interests created other forms of intimate interventions. As urbanization and industrialization sundered multi-generational families into which the social costs of infirmity or disability had traditionally been absorbed, individuals and families turned to government. While eugenicist ideas flourished in these decades, Molly Ladd-Taylor's chapter underscores how intimately linked were eugenicist practices and fiscal questions of incipient welfare states. Sterilization became a solution driven by "an assortment of factors, including the inadequacy of local welfare funding [and] concerns about overcrowding in the state institution." Minnesota's comparatively modest sterilization program, she writes, peaked in the late 1930s alongside Depression-era relief rolls. The persistence of coerced sterilization after the 1930s militates against simplistic renderings of "eugenics-inspired doctors and social workers," which obscures "the mundane sources of sterilization abuse." Fiscal insufficiencies structured them all: "poverty, the structures of Medicaid and hospital funding, and the limited contraceptive choices of poor women." Racism, ableism, and gender discrimination drove this history. But the emerging state's social frugality intersected with these values, placing fiscal constraints on a range of policy domains.

If the Gilded Age and Progressive Era was a period of pitched contestation over the boundaries of normative American identity and citizenship, the New Deal answered those debates by enshrining the white, heteronormative family as the moral, political, and fiscal center of the American project. And yet New Dealers' reading of American political culture as reflexively antistatist led them to emphasize frugality: the social wages paid to male breadwinners were most often buried in the tax code, framed as earned, or routed through market forces. These costs included the redistributional and racially bounded nature of Social Security and the GI Bill, support for collective bargaining by racially exclusive unions, and the creation of racially restrictive mortgage markets. Beyond well-known racial boundaries to the New Deal's intergenerational social wage, New Dealers' normative commitments clarify other orders of exclusion. As Clayton Howard has found, those deviating from heterosexual norms—those with "illegal connections," as the Federal Housing Administration's *Underwriting Manual* put it—were also excluded from the postwar suburban nest egg boom.[7] White, married men were understood to be better moral, financial, and fiscal bets.

Simultaneously, then, the New Deal not only disadvantaged nonwhite Americans but left sexually nonnormative Americans in a double bind. They, too, were less supported by the growing liberal state. And they groped against seen and unseen barriers to economic and social security. As Timothy Stewart-Winter reveals in this volume, this created economic, political, and cultural incentives for gay Americans like Walter Jenkins to form heteronormative families. As Jenkins's case shows, when those families failed to contain nonnormative sexual practices, behavioral correction through institutionalization was in order. Given that Jenkins was an elite, white male, his hospitalization operated on the somewhat less punitive end of the state's growing investments in institutions built to correct or penalize aberrant behavior. At the racial and gendered margins, however, as chapters by Tera Eva Agyepong, Anne Gray Fischer, and Regina Kunzel make clear, the growing medicalization of sexual psychopathy and clear biases in enforcement propelled increased carceral capacities that were much more disciplinary than rehabilitative. These constituted parts of a longer history of the entwined development of intimate and carceral capacities, in which the public fisc was not merely guarded but also enhanced: through forced labor in the Reconstruction South or, as William Novak's chapter reminds us, in the punitive fees, fines, and injunctions that continue to underwrite municipal budgets.

For a moment, however, Lyndon Johnson's War on Poverty attempted to expand the New Deal's social wage to include Black male breadwinners. But these efforts were channeled through more deeply held intimate and racial ideologies. Most infamously, in *The Negro Family: The Case for National Action*, Johnson staffer Daniel Patrick Moynihan argued for "a new . . . national goal: the establishment of a stable Negro family." He argued that a "tangle of pathology" led Black men to abandon mothers and children, destroying "the Negro family in the urban ghetto." Moynihan interlaced his moralism with concern for the public fisc, warning that "deviant" families were producing "a startling increase in welfare dependency."[8] Moynihan's concerns reflected Lyndon Johnson's views on the War on Poverty, which was never about creating durable or expansive forms of welfare provision. Rather, Johnson hoped to instill economic discipline, precluding the need for ongoing welfare support at all. In Johnson's more intimate moments, he often articulated this vision. On a call with a leading congressman, Johnson explained, "I'm going to take tax-eaters and make taxpayers out of them . . . I'm going to put 150,000 of them to work in ninety days' time on useful hardworking projects. Teach them some discipline and when to get up, and how to work all day."[9]

These fleeting efforts to bring Black families into the New Deal's social wage were undermined by a range of forces that defy easy partisan or ideological categorization and highlight how themes associated with intimate states—frugality, family values, and morality—have structured partisan or ideological changes rather than vice versa. As efforts to support Black male breadwinners collapsed, officials contemplated alternatives: meaningfully supporting single mothers or, perhaps, generating a universal individual wage. While political elites resisted such radical expansions of the social wage, the era's worsening fiscal crises led some officials to grant nonnormative family claims if they saved the public fisc. As Serena Mayeri's chapter reveals, prior to the 1960s, intimate states penalized nonmarital childbearing by excluding children from paternal inheritance and certain social welfare benefits in order to encourage marriage and avoid greater public welfare costs. As welfare rights activists and attorneys mounted assaults on such moralistic exclusions, officials pivoted to a "fiscal functionalism"—deemphasizing the importance of marital status if doing so ensured that the costs of child support remained private. The upshot was that officials were prioritizing fiscal frugality over normative family units. These changes were bolstered by a series of Supreme Court decisions that federalized rules governing welfare. These included decisions overturning residency laws, "man in the house" eligibility restrictions, and rulings against forcing welfare recipients to track down "absent fathers." These were remarkable rulings for a number of reasons, not least because they challenged moralistic policing of nonnormative families that forced recipients off welfare rolls.

These rulings were uneven, however, tending to fall on one side or the other of intimate states' moral and fiscal dimensions. That is, while courts invalidated certain practices policing welfare recipients' *morality*, they resisted expanding state or federal *fiscal* obligations to welfare recipients. When the Supreme Court declined to overturn regulations that put caps on welfare benefits, it effectively sanctioned states' frugality rather than establishing more positive intimate rights.[10] As the welfare rights movement succeeded in federalizing and liberalizing the terms of access to welfare, activists fought for smaller shares of resources. At the high tide of twentieth-century liberalism, as more and more rights claims were staked and granted, the ideology of frugality held firm.

In differing configurations based on locality and partisan affiliation, family values and frugality animated the emergence of neoliberal intimate states. Recent accounts of neoliberalism have particularly identified deeper continuities, emphasizing the ways in which the liberal state's institutional practices, class and racial orders, and policy agendas became rearticulated in neoliberal ways.[11] The erosion of welfare funding after the 1970s offers a case in point. While earlier works emphasized the seeming novelty of workfare over welfare, disciplining the poor to market logics, or the privatization of social risk, deeper intimate state commitments to normative family structures and fiscal frugality underscore just how durable these commitments have been. Which is not to say that nothing was new in the neoliberal era. Indeed, these values intersected with other forces and new contexts to authorize a much "stingier and less forgiving" state for a wider range of Americans than at any time since the onset of the Great Depression.[12]

Political liberalism and conservatism each underwent neoliberal transformations. And, while they followed different tracks, these transformations began as each ideology grappled with diverse and expanding sets of citizenship claims for state benefits and recognition in the 1960s and 1970s. Some of the most forceful claims were staked by single mothers, LGBT citizens, African Americans, and Latinx immigrants. These demands politicized distributional questions of governance, bringing them into the open at a moment of profound economic and fiscal instability. As the political parties reorganized and developed differing responses to these claims, each reproduced deep commitments to frugality and family formation, which formed sturdy conceptual boundaries to new articulations of liberalism and conservatism. Though neither path was determinative of neoliberalism, it was in their mutually reinforcing commitments to frugality and family values that liberals and conservatives created neoliberal intimate states.

Neoliberal conservatism might best be understood as a particularly bitter fruit of the New Deal's segregated and submerged family wage, which encouraged the belief that white families were independent of the state or that their benefits were earned rather than redistributed.[13] These politics were first articulated through ascendant Christian nationalism and racial populism that repositioned family values as the antidote to a decadent welfare state imagined to be captured by unworthy people of color. This was primarily a reaction against the citizenship claims made by a diverse range of individuals and on behalf of nonnormative family structures. Working- and middle-class conservatives' unthinking lack of regard for or comprehension of the New Deal's social wage alongside racist antipathy for welfare recipients harmonized with certain projects of state retrenchment. As Robert Self has written, "the conservative notion of family values . . . legitimated the transition to a neoliberal ethos in American life" because "heterosexual male breadwinners, as conservatives saw them, were not dependent on the state for either welfare or rights."[14] The idea that most white male breadwinners flourished independent of the state was a fundamental misunderstanding, however, and was the product not of conservative values per se but of the highly submerged, individuated, and fragmentary nature of the New Deal's frugally framed family wage. The culture wars of the 1980s and 1990s forged new iterations of conservative family values politics by burying these material realities beneath heaps of cultural and racial invective. All of this made for particularly punitive intimate policing of reproductive rights or access to welfare in Republican-dominated states.

Yet, it remained the case that the economic and social foundation of white male breadwinning *was* deeply contingent, and growing more so as globalization and stagnating wages necessitated women's work outside the home. The Reagan administration further undermined the economic security of the normative family by making Social Security subject to regressive taxation and through deregulatory measures that hollowed out middle-class work across years of banking failures, corporate mergers, and firm closures. This insecurity, however, was momentarily softened by a bipartisan deregulatory agenda that created vast markets of consumer debt. For millions of white working- and middle-class families, cheap debt fleetingly compensated for the ebbing New Deal social wage. As the political theorist Melinda Cooper puts it, "Fiscal austerity and credit abundance went hand in hand; the one could not exist without the other." Conservatives at once bolstered their family values bona fides by undermining the racialized welfare state and discharged to a broader range of families the mounting debts associated with austerity.[15] Household debt was thus "liberating and disciplining" to market logics, forming the neoliberal state's social wage.[16]

Liberals' path to neoliberalism began as they sought to somehow honor nonnormative citizenship claims but also worried they were fiscally unsustainable and politically untenable. Two policy commitments emerged: an emphasis on economic growth with which new tax revenues might restore the public fisc (and perhaps underwrite new forms of social spending); and, in growth's absence, the search for alternative, more frugal means of delivering social goods to those on the margins. The generation of New Democrats who took office in the 1970s, including Bill Clinton, began pursuing "entrepreneurial" growth policies with an eye toward downstream social redistribution. As California's governor Jerry Brown put it, the goal was to "build economic strength" but "in a context of social equity."[17]

Yet, the fiscal pressures, deficits, and federal austerity of the 1980s redoubled liberals' longstanding commitments to a frugal social state, which New Democrats began articulating in terms of their willingness to make "hard choices"—a deeply paternalistic framing that favored growth over redistribution and which increasingly dovetailed with conservative attacks on welfare. For liberals, "entrepreneurialism" as means and metaphor slipped easily from the realm of growth to the domain of poverty policy and welfare reform. New Democrats like Clinton became enthusiastic supporters of frugal, individualistic solutions for poverty such as entrepreneurial microfinance—small loans to poor women, especially, to start businesses. As Lily Geismer puts it, this approach "updated and extended . . . core tenets of post–New Deal liberalism" including "technocratic expertise" and emphasizing "growth over redistribution" all while promising to end the dole.[18] Crucially, however, microlending programs also enabled liberals like Clinton to champion their support for single, Black mothers in ways that plausibly distanced them from the cultures of poverty debates of the 1960s and 1980s. With entrepreneurship, liberals championed poor women's individual economic agency rather than dependency: they were at once their own "agents of change" and engines of national growth. As Geismer explains, this ideology fused the economic and the intimate: "self-employment, especially home-based businesses," New Democrats believed, "provided women a way to balance the demands of work and family."[19]

Liberals' fusion of entrepreneurial and intimate statecraft encouraged President Clinton to negotiate with conservatives over welfare reform. The Personal Responsibility and Work Opportunity Reconciliation Act (PRWORA) they forged set lifetime limits on welfare eligibility and instituted a range of mandatory work programs. But Democrats fought to include microenterprise as a work option that also allowed welfare recipients to maintain their benefits as they began businesses. Liberals' emphasis on "personal empowerment" and entrepreneurship thus created common ground with conservative anti-welfare politics, in terms of both constructing the frugal neoliberal anti-welfare state and recentering individualist rather than structural understandings of poverty.

But there were deeper intimacies between left and right neoliberalisms, particularly around the policing of sexuality and citizenship. At the very moment the parties hashed out their welfare reform agenda, they also crafted the Defense of Marriage Act (DOMA), which prevented federal recognition of same-sex marriages validated by any state, thus eliminating federal marital benefits for those couples. While DOMA erected stark sexual boundaries to rights delivered through marriage, PRWORA advanced its assaults on the rights of single mothers by invoking the sanctity of heteronormative marriage.[20] Indeed, PRWORA included titles that functioned rather like the Freedmen's Bureau, as Melinda Cooper writes, situating "welfare reform as a kind of demonstration project in family formation" and targeting "African Americans in particular."[21] PRWORA's preamble offered a striking recitation of such enduring intimate state commitments: "1) Marriage is the foundation of a successful society; 2) Marriage . . . promotes the interest of children; [and] 3) Promotion of responsible fatherhood and motherhood is integral to . . . the well-being of children." PRWORA also conditioned federal aid to state efforts to reduce illegitimate child births without increasing abortion rates—that is, by increasing marriage rates. The act funded marriage promotion initiatives, reflecting one Democratic think tank's search for solutions to "fatherless families."[22] While some critics of Clinton charged him with a cynical electoral politics of triangulation, the long history of liberals' emphases on heteronormative family formation, financial independence, and fiscal frugality troubles such interpretations. These intimate values cut across political eras and ideologies and have formed durable boundaries to the full rights of citizenship.

334 | BRENT CEBUL

In his chapter, Stephen Vider notes that the meaning of "family" has often been "defined less by the functions it fulfills for its members than the function it serves for the state." Through the legal construct of "functional families," Vider's households were recognized as legitimate, albeit for reasons of fiscal frugality that reverberate all the way back to Reconstruction-era freedwomen's efforts to secure their rights to their children. Though these particular histories have more than a century of state developments and much more besides separating them, they are intimately familiar. These were brittle sorts of rights designed to preclude further entitlements or support. While Vider notes that "the intimate state does not speak with one voice," in chorus, its voices do tell us much about the state as an "abstract and conceptual collective symbolic sphere—the state as a representation of the social body," as William Novak has put it.[23] As this volume suggests, such cold victories define many of the incremental expansions of intimate rights for those at the social margins. For those at the center of the twentieth century's social wage, meanwhile, the state's longstanding emphasis on frugality collapsed on them in a neoliberal age in which austerity trumped the state's maintenance of moral or normative family forms. The neoliberal social wage—paid in skyrocketing personal and family debt, mounting precarity, and intergenerational insecurity—might be understood as the New Deal's intimate state turned outside-in. That is, longstanding forms of intimate state policing, precarity, and extraction that once stalked the normative margins have come to define more and more Americans' experience of intimate statecraft and citizenship.

In their introduction, this volume's editors note that earlier periods of American statecraft "guarded the dominion of the patriarch over his family" and, in the twentieth century, "turned toward repair of social ruptures when that dominion weakened." The state, this volume shows, modernized through such intimate commitments. But the neoliberal age suggests that we may have entered a new phase of intimate governance, one in which household or family "repair" have lost traction in the face of austere frugality—the neoliberal state everywhere seeks to shed social costs. Paradoxically, however, the beginnings of a truly emancipatory set of intimate rights in which the state plays a positive rather than discharging role may be contained in just such amoral austerity. Indeed, the state's declining investment in family values—in which, as Serena Mayeri puts it, marriage was "the gateway to public and private benefits"—suggests the possibility that new rights might be forged on more universal or individual bases. To do so, however, the deeply rooted, ideological resistance to affirmatively funding positive rights—to child care, reproductive rights, a living wage—must be transcended in a new, more radical politics that surpasses the outmoded frugalities of liberalism and conservatism. Here, too, neoliberal intimate states may have planted seeds of their own demise. Though austerity has created greater burdens for a much broader range of Americans, these burdens might ultimately yield demands for more generous intimate states that positively nurture intimate liberties.

NOTES

1. On analytical problems associated with invoking political "orders," see Brent Cebul, Lily Geismer, and Mason B. Williams, "Beyond Red and Blue: Crisis and Continuity in Twentieth Century U.S. Political History," in *Shaped by the State: Toward a New Political History of the Twentieth Century* (Chicago: University of Chicago Press, 2019).

2. See, especially, John D'Emilio, *Sexual Politics, Sexual Communities: The Making of a Homosexual Minority in the United States* (Chicago: University of Chicago Press, 1983 and 1998); Allan Bérubé, *Coming Out Under Fire: The History of Gay Men and Women in World War II* (Chapel Hill: University of North Carolina Press, 2010, 20th anniversary ed.); David K. Johnson, *The Lavender Scare: The Cold War Persecution of Gays and Lesbians in the Federal Government* (Chicago: University of Chicago Press, 2006); and Margot Canaday, *The Straight State: Sexuality and Citizenship in Twentieth-Century America* (Princeton, NJ: Princeton University Press, 2009).

3. For a notable exception, see Marissa Chappel, *The War on Welfare: Family, Poverty, and Politics in Modern America* (Philadelphia: University of Pennsylvania Press, 2010).

4. Michel Foucault, *The Birth of Biopolitics: Lectures at the Collège de France, 1978–1979* (New York: Picador, 2008), 28–29.

5. Amy Dru Stanley, *From Bondage to Contract: Wage Labor, Marriage, and the Market in the Age of Slave Emancipation* (New York: Cambridge University Press, 1998).

6. Richard White, *The Republic for Which it Stands: The United States during Reconstruction and the Gilded Age, 1865–1896* (New York: Oxford University Press, 2017), 78–79; see Stanley, *From Bondage*; and Laura F. Edwards, *Gendered Strife and Confusion: The Political Culture of Reconstruction* (Urbana: University of Illinois Press, 1997).

7. Clayton Howard, "Building a 'Family-Friendly' Metropolis: Sexuality, the State, and Postwar Housing Policy," *Journal of Urban History* 39, no. 5 (2013): 938.

8. Robert O. Self, *All in the Family: The Realignment of American Democracy Since the 1960s* (New York: Hill and Wang, 2012), 26–28.

9. Lyndon Johnson, quoted in Guian McKee, "'This Government Is with Us': Lyndon Johnson and the Grassroots War on Poverty," in *The War on Poverty: A New Grassroots History*, ed. Annelise Orleck and Lisa Hazirjian (Athens: University of Georgia Press, 2011), 32.

10. On these decisions, see Karen M. Tani, *States of Dependency: Welfare, Rights, and American Governance, 1935–1972* (New York: Cambridge University Press, 2016), 260–69.

11. See, for example, Amy C. Offner, *Sorting Out the Mixed Economy: The Rise and Fall of Welfare and Developmental States in the Americas* (Princeton, NJ: Princeton University Press, 2019).

12. Self, *All in the Family*, 400.

13. On "submerged" social welfare policies, see Suzanne Mettler, *The Submerged State: How Invisible Government Policies Undermine American Democracy* (Chicago: University of Chicago Press, 2011).

14. Self, *All in the Family*, 399.

15. Melinda Cooper, *Family Values: Between Neoliberalism and the New Social Conservatism* (Brooklyn, NY: Zone Books, 2017), 246.

16. Stefan Eich, "Daniel Bell's Dilemma: Financialization, Family Values, and Their Discontents," *Capitalism: A Journal of History and Economics* 1, no. 1 (Fall 2019): 241–58, quotation at 254.

17. Brent Cebul, "Supply Side Liberalism: Fiscal Crisis, Post-Industrial Policy, and the Rise of the New Democrats," *Modern American History* 2, no. 2 (July 2019): 17.

18. Lily Geismer, "Agents of Change: Microenterprise, Welfare Reform, the Clintons, and Liberal Forms of Neoliberalism," *Journal of American History* 107, no. 1 (June 2020): 109.

19. Geismer, "Agents of Change," 113.

20. Anna Marie Smith, "The Politicization of Marriage in Contemporary American Public Policy: The Defense of Marriage Act and the Personal Responsibility Act," *Citizenship Studies* 5, no. 3 (2001): 303–20.

21. Cooper, *Family Values,* 102–3, quotation at 103.

22. Cooper, *Family Values*, 108–10.

23. William J. Novak, "The Concept of the State in American History," in *Boundaries of the State in U.S. History*, ed. James T. Sparrow, William J. Novak, and Stephen W. Sawyer (Chicago: University of Chicago Press, 2015), 344.

Acknowledgments

Over the several years between hatching the idea of this volume and bringing it to fruition, we editors have benefited from help from many scholars who are not directly represented between these covers. We feel very grateful to have been able to gain from the expertise and insights of scholars who took part in our 2016 workshop at the Radcliffe Institute for Advanced Study at Harvard University, including George Chauncey, Stephen Engel, Gary Gerstle, Linda Gordon, Kali Gross, Sarah Haley, Dagmar Herzog, Alice Kessler-Harris, Julilly Kohler-Hausmann, Sophia Lee, Eithne Luibheid, Joanne Meyerowitz, Michele Mitchell, Nayan Shah, and Karen Tani. We thank the Exploratory Seminar program of the Radcliffe Institute for hosting and funding that effort. Likewise, we are indebted to Brown University for hosting and funding a follow-up conference in 2018, where the discussion gained from the contributions of Andrew Wender Cohen, Crystal Feimster, Elizabeth L. MacDowell, Juliet Nebolon, and Meg Wesling, as well as from the participation of most of the contributors to *Intimate States*.

We appreciate the permission of the *Journal of American History* (*JAH*) to include here a revised version of Anne Gray Fischer's essay in volume 105 (March 2019), which began as a paper for our 2018 conference and subsequently won the Pelzer Prize (leading to publication in the *JAH*). Similarly, we are grateful to Duke University Press for permission to include here a revised version of Regina Kunzel's essay in *The War on Sex*, ed. David M. Halperin and Trevor Hoppe (2017). We are also indebted to the Department of History of Harvard University for the award of a publication subsidy.

Most of all we are grateful for the excellent ideas, hard work, and cooperation of our colleagues whose essays appear here, with special appreciation for Brent Cebul's ready fulfillment of our last-minute request for an afterword. Tim Mennel and Susannah Engstrom of the University of Chicago Press have helpfully smoothed the process of publication.

Contributors

TERA AGYEPONG is associate professor of legal history and African American history at DePaul University and research professor at the American Bar Foundation. She is the author of *The Criminalization of Black Children: Race, Gender, and Delinquency in Chicago's Juvenile Justice System, 1899–1945* (University of North Carolina Press, 2018). Her scholarship has appeared in *Gender and History*, *Journal of African American History*, and *Northwestern Journal of International Human Rights*.

MARGOT CANADAY is professor of history at Princeton University. She is the author of *The Straight State: Sexuality and Citizenship in Twentieth-Century America* (Princeton University Press, 2009) and is currently completing *Queer Career: Sexuality and Employment in Modern America*.

BRENT CEBUL is assistant professor of history at the University of Pennsylvania and the author of *Illusions of Progress: Business, Poverty, and Liberalism in the American Century* (University of Pennsylvania Press, forthcoming).

JEFFREY PATRICK COLGAN is a researcher at the Brooklyn Institute for Social Research. He is a frequent contributor to the CUNY Graduate Center's Gotham Center for New York City History blog and has worked with the Smithsonian Institution researching historical strategies for cultural heritage preservation in times of war and disaster.

NANCY F. COTT is the Jonathan Trumbull Research Professor of American History at Harvard University. Her most recent book is *Fighting Words: The Bold American Journalists Who Brought the World Home between the Wars* (Basic Books, 2020).

PAISLEY CURRAH is professor of political science and women's and gender studies at Brooklyn College and the Graduate Center of the City University of New York. His book *Sex Is as Sex Does: Governing Transgender Identity* is forthcoming with New York University Press.

GRACE PEÑA DELGADO is associate professor of history at the University of California, Santa Cruz. Delgado is the author of *Making the Chinese Mexican: Global Migration, Localism, and Exclusion in the US-Mexico Borderlands* (Stanford University Press, 2012). Delgado is also the author of the forthcoming work "Mexico's New Slavery: A Critique of Neo-Abolitionism to Combat Human Trafficking (*la trata de personas*)," in *Fighting Modern Slavery and Human Trafficking: History and Contemporary Policy,* ed. Genevieve LeBaron, Jessica Pliley, and David W. Blight (Cambridge University Press, 2020).

JEFFREY ESCOFFIER is a research associate at the Brooklyn Institute for Social Research. He is the author of *American Homo: Community and Perversity* (University of California Press, 1998) and the editor of *Sexual Revolution* (Running Press, 2003), a collection of the most important writing of the 1960s and 1970s on sex. His most recent book is *Sex, Society, and the Making of Pornography: The Pornographic Object of Knowledge* (Rutgers University Press, 2021).

ANNE GRAY FISCHER is assistant professor of history at the University of Texas at Dallas. Her work has appeared in the *Journal of American History* and the *Journal of Social History*. She is completing her first book, a history of women, police power, and the making of modern cities from segregation to gentrification.

REGINA KUNZEL is the Larned Professor of History and Gender and Sexuality Studies at Yale University. She is the author of *Criminal Intimacy: Prison and the Uneven History of Modern American Sexuality* (University of Chicago Press, 2008) and *Fallen Women, Problem Girls: Unmarried Mothers and the Professionalization of Social Work, 1890 to 1945* (Yale University Press, 1993).

MOLLY LADD-TAYLOR is professor of history at York University in Toronto, Canada. Her most recent book is *Fixing the Poor: Eugenic Sterilization and Child Welfare in the Twentieth Century* (Johns Hopkins University Press, 2020).

SERENA MAYERI is professor of law and history at the University of Pennsylvania Law School. She is the author of *Reasoning from Race: Feminism, Law, and the Civil Rights Revolution* (Harvard University Press, 2011) and is currently at work on a book that examines challenges to the legal primacy of marriage since 1960.

STEPHANIE MCCURRY is the R. Gordon Hoxie Professor of American History at Columbia University. She is the author of *Women's War: Fighting and Surviving the American Civil War* (Belknap Press of Harvard University Press, 2019) and *Confederate Reckoning: Power and Politics in the Civil War South* (Harvard University Press, 2010).

WILLIAM J. NOVAK is the Charles F. and Edith J. Clyne Professor at the University of Michigan Law School. He is the author of *The People's Welfare: Law and Regulation in Nineteenth-Century America* (University of North Carolina Press, 1996) and the coeditor with Naomi Lamoreaux of *The Corporation and American Democracy* (Harvard University Press, 2017).

SUSAN J. PEARSON is associate professor of history at Northwestern University. She is the author of *The Rights of the Defenseless: Protecting Animals and Children in Gilded Age America* (University of Chicago Press, 2011). Her current book project is *The Birth Certificate: An American History* (University of North Carolina Press, 2021)

JOHANNA SCHOEN is professor of history at Rutgers University. She is the author of *Choice & Coercion: Birth Control, Sterilization, and Abortion in Public Health and Welfare* (University of North Carolina Press, 2005) and *Abortion After Roe* (University of North Carolina Press, 2015).

ROBERT O. SELF is the Mary Ann Lippitt Professor of American History at Brown University. He is the author of *All in the Family: The Realignment of American Democracy Since the 1960s* (Hill and Wang, 2012) and *American Babylon: Race and the Struggle for Postwar Oakland* (Princeton University Press, 2003).

TIMOTHY STEWART-WINTER is associate professor of history at Rutgers University-Newark and the author of *Queer Clout: Chicago and the Rise of Gay Politics* (University of Pennsylvania Press, 2016). He is currently writing a book about Walter Jenkins, a longtime aide to Lyndon B. Johnson who resigned from the White House staff in 1964 after being arrested on a disorderly conduct charge.

WHITNEY STRUB is associate professor of history at Rutgers University-Newark and the author of *Perversion for Profit: The Politics of Pornography and the Rise of the New Right* (Columbia University Press, 2011). He also coedited *Porno Chic and the Sex Wars: American Sexual Representation in the 1970s* (University of Massachusetts Press, 2016).

STEPHEN VIDER is assistant professor of history and director of the Public History Initiative at Cornell University. His new book is *The Queerness of Home: Gender, Sexuality, and the Politics of Domesticity after World War II* (University of Chicago Press, 2021). His scholarship has previously appeared in *Gender & History*, *American Quarterly*, and *The Public Historian*.

Index